Designing Embedded Systems

Handbook + LAMP Project

(Applying Experience to Design)

By

Steve McClure

This book reviews the
Software Development and Engineering principles
involved in the design of Embedded Computer Systems.

I wrote this book from the aspect of
what I would do if I had my own company.

How would I treat other people.

What would be my goals.

As I review my thirty years plus in this industry
I have seen firsthand the style of many in leadership.
–
It would appear to do as little as possible
and to grab as much as you can.

This is the minimalist approach.

But that sounds like the declaration of a pirate!
I do not subscribe to such philosophy.

When people show intuitive and start a company
they are usually called entrepreneurs.

I'm sorry, but when I think of that word I get a bad taste in my mouth.
I immediately think of someone who is out to take advantage of others.

I certainly do not want to be considered as being such a person
or as being associated with such persons.

For a company is like a family and should achieve for everyone
that which a single person cannot achieve by themselves.

Welcome to my family…

Designing Embedded Systems

Handbook + LAMP Project

Copyright © 2014-2015 by Steve McClure
All rights reserved.

ISBN-13: 978-1483916231
ISBN-10: 1483916235

All rights in this book are reserved worldwide. No part of this book may be reproduced in any manner whatsoever without written permission of the author.

Printed in the United States of America

First Edition	April, 2014	Text Version 1-662
Second Edition	July, 2015	Text Version 2-2

Dedication

This book is dedicated to all those
who want to get back to the joy of engineering.

To the real reason we entered this field in the first place.

Which is, because we like to make stuff.

So, to the real engineers like Chris, Ken, Geoff, Carl,
Tom, Danis, Walid, Marc, Bill, Dan, Larry, …
and my Dad,
this book is for you.

Intended Audience

For everyone at all levels of engineering
who want to know how to design good
embedded software products
and
care for their development team…

To be a leader is to be a servant to others.
So what does it say when those in power steal from the group

Albert Einstein said that imagination is more important than knowledge.

When you build a team of people to create a product, what are the characteristic attributes you wish to add to the collective whole. For if you are simply searching for egotistical individuals then you are not building a family. Such 'team' members are only in it for their own glory (and reward) and if you haven't realized it by now, the reward is to be shared by all members of the family, not simply by a select few.

But what happens when these individuals are taken out of the picture?

You then have opportunity for the majority of the team to excel and they will excel, if you mentor them right. As a true leader you are to recognize the strengths and weaknesses of every member of your team. For as a true leader you become the father figure, for the true team is your family and as you well know, family will go the extra mile for their brethren.

So when you see someone who wants it all their own way then recognize that person as not being a leader but rather a dictator out simply to take advantage. For a true leader is first in every battle and last with every desperate retreat. They give their team the opportunity to excel. That means the leader provides his charges with the right work environment so they can prove themselves.

In a similar concept to great story writers who wrote books they wished they could have read when they were younger, I wrote this book to provide others with the concepts that would make an engineer a good and well respected engineer.

For this is the book I wish I had when I first started in this field...

Signed: *Steve McClure*

Table of Contents

Prolog

When I started in this industry I had no idea of what I wanted to do. Back when I was around thirteen or so I took a notion to electronics. This was in the early 1970's and the microprocessor was still someone else's dream.

But I was intrigued with physics and especially with the field of electronics.

I just wanted to know how things worked.

So I investigated and the first object to come under my scrutiny was the kitchen transistor radio. I supposed I should be happy (as should my parents) that it was a battery operated device otherwise I am not too sure of the harm that might have befallen me. As it was the radio never quite worked the same afterwards.

But it drew me further under its spell.

I found that there was a local shop in town and I encouraged my Dad to take me there. People were buying radio and television tubes (in the UK they called these 'valves') and I would see the shop assistant perform a test by placing them in a socket and seeing the heater element glow. I had taken my Dad there to buy a light dependent resistor and a relay. It was a long way to go to purchase only these two components but you could not find them anywhere locally and there were no such stores as Fry's or Radio Shack in Glasgow, Scotland when I was a youngster.

When I arrived home I took my soldering iron (I can't for the life of me remember where I got that) and soldered my purchases in such a way that I made a light beam sensor that would turn on an alarm bell (cannibalized from an old toy telephone) whenever my sister broke the beam upon entering my bedroom.

I don't believe I ever saw a circuit diagram for such a contraption yet I just knew how to build it. It worked and I was hooked.

The local newsagent had a number of magazines on display and one of them was called Practical Wireless. I bought it with my pocket money. I read that magazine cover to cover. I remember it used English words in ways that I was quite unfamiliar. I must have read that entire magazine at least twenty times (commercial adverts included). Now I noticed one such advert that described a medium wave / long wave radio kit (I guess I really am dating myself now). It came in a nice wooden box with a couple of knobs and switches. I obtained a postal order from the Post Office and sent off for the kit. It cost around five British Pounds and I had to mail my request to somewhere down in England.

It wasn't that I was unfamiliar in having technology around. I had grown up in a home that already had a television. My grandmother had bought one a few years before I was even born. So I was used to the concept of turning a knob and having a picture and sound miraculously appear out of thin air. That was normality to me. In fact I am told that I was more impressed with an old valve radio I once found when I was much younger.

Anyway, the radio kit arrived and I attacked it with much gusto and vigor. That and along with my 50 watt soldering iron. Nobody told me it should have been less than half that wattage. There were germanium diodes and transistors that fell under the attack. No one could doubt my enthusiasm. Needless to say, upon completing my work, not a chirp or voice was heard from the radio speaker.

My Dad took me and my efforts across the road to a neighbor who was an Electrical Engineer.

In my mind I can still see him with his spectacles perched on the tip of his nose as he looked over my work. To this day I have never forgotten his words.

"Stephen," he said. "Your soldering leaves much to be desired."

Yes, it was full of dry joints and most (if not all) of the active components had been damaged by the excessive heat. He took my efforts to his work where a kind lady fixed it up and when he brought it back to me the printed circuit board looked like new. It was quite a small printed circuit board with not that many parts on it but it still managed to pull voices and music out of the ether. It captivated my imagination.

From that point forward I have had a lot more practice and my soldering skills have greatly improved. But I still wanted to learn more. So I kept on getting the Practical Wireless magazine each month. Then I added more magazines such as Practical Electronics, followed by Everyday Electronics and Elektor.

When I finished school I then went on to attend University. My desire to learn electronics directed me to study Electrical Engineering. But I was somewhat disappointed. I found that the first two years of this course was a standard collection of basic engineering subjects more or less identical to that of Mechanical Engineering. There were no electronic courses for me to get my teeth into. Back then the course only provided a short introduction to electronics and this you only tackled in third year. [So you really only started to learn this topic when actively employed in the field.]

But there was one subject to which I took like a fish to water.

It was computer programming. We were now in the mid 1970's and I was exposed to the University computer. There were two IBM 370's and there were line printers and card punches and card readers. The video monitor was not around as yet but we did have golf ball typewriters. On this magical mechanical device we would type commands on its typewriter keyboard and the golf ball (a ball which contained the entire alphanumeric character set) would print out both our typed characters as well as the computer's response.

Now this I wanted to understand.

I wanted to know how it all worked.

So I talked to a friend of mine who was in second year Engineering. He had been working on a Fortran program. I obtained a printed copy of his incomplete source code, reverse engineered it and then made it function as a different program.

A program to solve the roots of a quadratic equation: $\mathbf{ax^2 + bx + c = 0}$

$$x = \frac{-b \pm \sqrt{b^2 - 4ac}}{2a}$$

You remember the equation. When you solve for x you then find the point(s) on the x-axis where the parabola curve would intersect.

Simply put, I had taught myself Fortran programming while the rest of the class were still learning about flowcharts.

I was now spending a lot of time in that computer room. I was getting top marks for computer science but my other subjects were beginning to suffer. I saw the writing on the wall. I changed faculties from Engineering to Science and decided to study for a Bachelor of Science Degree with a Computer Science major.

However, I still wanted to know the specifics of each computer component. I wanted to know how every part of the computer functioned. The rest of the Computer Science class were quite happy interfacing with the keyboard, screen and printer but I was wanting more. I was wanting to know what was under the hood. I wanted to know how the software and the hardware functioned as a combined entity.

I obtained my Bachelor of Science degree in Computer Science and started employment far from the régime of academia.

In my final year of study, one of my Computer Science projects had been to interface two computer languages so that they could communicate with each other. The languages were Cobol and Pascal. I graciously let my Lab partner Chris take the Cobol language part of the project while I did the Pascal. At that time I had vowed that I would never work in a Bank or use Cobol.

I was now in my first job. I was working in a Bank and I was using Cobol.

It was then when I learnt never to trust myself.

But at the bank they were also using some high level languages like BPL and TSL. Since no one there knew these languages I was assigned the task to modify an existing program and to make it work within the banking environment. This was to permit a stand-alone computer system to interact with the bank computer such that a customer could enter their account number / password and the computer would display and/or print out their bank statement. ATM's were just around the corner and had not as yet become common place.

I had to travel 50 miles from work to a nearby university. They had the Burroughs B6800 mainframe which would permit me to compile the TSL source code. I worked two weeks on that project and solved it. My work saved the company a lot of money. I later found out just how much. It was equivalent to my yearly salary. In other words I had paid for myself by two weeks work. At that point I became very quickly disillusioned with that working environment. I had a great desire to learn more. I felt that technology was moving forward and I was being left behind.

So I looked for a new job and that was when I entered the world of embedded programming. Straight away I was being exposed to microprocessors and various hardware peripherals. The code I wrote was being placed into EEPROMs and could run as a separate system in and of itself.

Now this was getting interesting.

When I didn't fully understand what I read in a specification, or in some technical literature or on a schematic diagram I would then go over to the electrical engineering group, introduce myself to one of the engineers and ask questions. I quickly found that engineers loved to talk about their subject. Twenty minutes later I would get back to my desk with my head buzzing with new information. Within a few weeks I knew everybody in all the engineering departments. This is still the same case today. If I am working on something that is not too clear, I will seek out the relevant engineer, introduce myself and find out the specifics.
I am always surprised to find that few others practice this method of learning. They generally struggle on in the dark waiting for the information to come to them.

So I have continued learning, changing companies and even changing countries. I have worked in large companies and also in small companies. Because of this experience I have seen the benefits and drawbacks of each type of company.

At the first embedded software company in which I was employed I was exposed to certain design methodologies.

Now that all sounds rather fancy.

Rather think of it along the lines of a method to do something.

This method was as follows:

> 'Before we start coding, let's try doing the design first.'

You see, at that time (and it still happens a lot today) when people started a computer project they immediately jumped in and began writing code. They would never consider working on the system design in order to first determine all the specific details.

So I was initially somewhat disgruntled. Why were they doing this to me? After all, coding was fun. Everyone else was just diving into writing their code when they started their projects.

I did not realize it at the time but I was being given some of the best training that I would ever receive.

Doesn't one create plans before building a house?

Why shouldn't one do the same when designing a computer system?

It still surprises me today when I see people simply dive in to writing code without doing a proper system design.

But what is the purpose of engineering?

The purpose of engineering development is to create a set of documentation that would show other people how to build and maintain the designed product.

The development engineer is one who creates a set of documents that others can use to manufacture the product. The documents would instruct others as to the functioning of the product, how the product may be enhanced and how the product might be maintained.

But if you say that the code is the documentation then you've missed the whole point of what it means to be an engineer.

General Concepts

What is an Embedded System?

Now some people might wonder as to what an embedded system might be. They know what a computer is, whether it be a desk top, lap top or tablet. But what exactly is an embedded system?

Well, an embedded system is any product that would have a computer system (hardware and software) 'embedded' within the device. This may provide a man-machine interface and/or might even permit the device to perform autonomous functions.

Examples of such may include the following products...

Microwave Oven	GPS Device for Car	UPS Power Supply
Electric Oven	Pulse Oximeter	Music Keyboard
Electric Range	Car Computer System	Video Game
Refrigerator	Pocket Pedometer	Copier
Washing Machine	Digital Power Supply	Ticket Kiosks
Tumble Dryer	Digital Multimeter	Cash Registers
HVAC Controller	Home Telephone System	Traffic Lights
HiFi Audio Amplifier	Home Weather Station	Blood Pressure kit
CD Player	Printer	Espresso Machine
DVD Player	Computer DVD Writer	Food Blender
Blu-Ray Player	Computer Blu-Ray Writer	Food Mixer
Television	Computer Scanner	Security Systems
Cable Set-top Box	Computer Mouse	Exercise Bikes
Satellite Set-top Box	Computer Monitor	Exercise Treadmill
Computer Tablets	Computer Hard drive	Fish Echo Sounder
Cell Phone	Computer router	Clock
Digital Camera	Computer Hubs/switches	Wrist Watch
Digital Oscilloscope	Many Medical Devices	etc. etc. ---

So you can see that embedded computer systems are everywhere hiding in many of the devices that we see around us. This book will now proceed to discuss the manner in which such devices can be developed.

Designing from Experience

But first, a few points to consider...

The Work Environment

Now this may depend upon your point of view. I have worked in various sized companies which used the open plan concept as well as offices. Some open plan spaces were contained in a small office whereas others utilized the entire floor space of the building.

The concept chosen all depends upon the level of work being performed.

If you are a department store in which the most complex of tasks is the taking of sales and the scanning in of sale prices then I see absolutely nothing wrong with the open plan concept.

However, if you are an engineering company and are performing tasks akin to rocket science then the money saved in implementing the open plan concept is simply thrown away as lost development time and the creation of error.

Libraries as places of study are quiet for a reason.

When someone speaks or makes a noise they are simply told to be quiet.

I do not believe that it should be that different when it comes to the work environment. Treat your people right and they will treat you right.

My experience has been this.

When you arrive at a new job you start off with great enthusiasm. When you find that you have been positioned in an open plan office that enthusiasm starts to be crushed. After a few weeks of head banging, attempting to understand and implement complex concepts with several independent groups of people having simultaneous conversations in your immediate vicinity, telephones ringing, sensing people walking past your 'office', you will find that a certain frustration develops for you yourself are quite aware that your work throughput has become blocked. There have even been certain establishments in which I have had the misfortune to be employed that utilized the intercom system on a regular basis. This was to obtain the location of certain people and the regularity of its use was in the order of at least once a minute. How much serious concentrated effort do you think can be obtained in a 50 second time interval?

Now as a young engineer I may not have been bothered that much by so many interruptions. One is new out of school and has limited experience. When applying yourself to thought tasks solutions quickly arise. There really is not that much to think about since your experience is somewhat limited.

However, as you get older, and hopefully more wiser, the engineer is now reviewing a greater wealth of project experience applied to the task at hand. Such people have been exposed to all manner of project design and are attempting to do their work well.

But they are constantly being hassled by interruptions.

So the perfect level of 100% concentration has been decreased down to periods of 20% or so. I'd like to see others try to do better when four independent intelligent conversations are taking place around them. I don't know about you but my mind will stay focused on its task if there is only white noise in the vicinity. But as soon as intelligent noise is heard, whether it is in the adjacent hallway or office or even more distant, my brain will lock onto the sound and attempt to decode it. I cannot switch this action off. It is part of who I am and in speaking with many others, it is also a part of who they are. It is simply in the design of man.

So how do we manage?

We go and purchase noise canceling headphones.

But they do not work too well and some 'intelligent' noise still gets through. Not to mention ear lobe pain after some hours of use.

So we go and purchase music systems and listen to music over headphones or earphones as we work. Sure, we do get a little more work done but it does not bring us back up to the level we know we can do if we had the peace and quiet required. We may have increased our productivity level from 20% up to 40-50% (if we are lucky).

Many now start to work late or to take work home with them in an attempt to complete that which should be finished at during the normal work day. This, all being the result of poor management planning.

Do not be confused into thinking that employees staying late is an act of dedication. It is simply a form of survival which is now eroding the person's family life.

It is one thing to perform the occasional extra effort in your own time at home but it is quite another when it becomes a regular basis solely as an attempt to keep productivity maintained.

Such actions can destroy the family unit.

This affects both the person's immediate family and the working family because if you have not noticed, the work life consists of being in the company of work associates for the order of eight hours a day, forty hours a week. That's a long time. If employees are getting frustrated in constantly working twice as hard to get the same work done then this toll will soon become apparent and the product will suffer.

People will get too busy and will not readily assist each other.

Then when they get too burned out they will leave. Management are often under the opinion that engineers are a dime a dozen but they really do not understand the time and effort it takes for such a person to adapt and learn the company's business. The more complex the product the greater the time required.

Management may also fool themselves into believing that everyone is working hard but the people are simply working at less than 50% efficiency and the project schedule indeed suffers. Time scales will slip and errors will creep in. I have seen it happen.

As I said earlier, libraries are quiet for a reason.

When you write exams at school it is also quiet for a reason.

Any form of intelligent thought requires peace and quiet.

Give your engineers such and you will see their productivity rise, realistic time scales will be met and people will help each other in getting the work done. In this you will have helped create the engineering family, a family of people which could be applied to successfully tackle any task put forward.

But if you are worried about the cost you *think* you are saving you will see it appear (multiplied) later in the project schedule as project overruns and many, many ECNs (Engineering Change Notices), all because the design was incomplete due to a noisy work environment.

On one project with a tight schedule I started to work at home. What I found was that one day, working in a quiet environment could be equated to three days at the company, in a noisy environment.

Management should consider such details.

After all, it's their money that's being wasted.

What's in a name?

When referring to other people call them by their given name or title. To simply say 'he' or 'she' is somewhat disrespectful and leads to a breakdown in team communication. Being respectful to others will gain you the advantage of future help. Being arrogant will destroy relationships both current and future.

Hardware versus Software

When developing embedded systems the hardware and software departments have to learn to work well together. Especially if the software interacts closely with hardware by driving peripheral interfaces and other such entities.

It has been my experience that since application engineers do not speak the same language as hardware engineers they tend not to mix. They may greet each other in the corridors however they will have little to do with each other technically.

This is a great pity for they are losing out on so much. A word here and there could save them endless debugging time.

Being an embedded engineer (as opposed to an applications engineer) means that I have always had close fellowship with those of the pure hardware discipline. I obtain and read their hardware schematics. I attend their hardware design reviews. I develop documentation and interfaces between the hardware components and the application code. I would know all the hardware fellows by name. The application developers would only know that they sit off somewhere in some specific corner of the building.

But there are times when the hardware people find out that this embedded guy can hold his own when it comes to schematic design and the understanding of both systems and software. For when I am in a quandary and have exhausted all the possibility for error in my code, I then start to perform a detailed search through the schematic as I look for any possible cause; and there have been times when I have found such. Ah, the first looks of contempt and ridicule that one receives from some engineers, when thoughts of 'What does a software guy know about electronics?' dust the air. Then such thoughts are replaced with 'My goodness, he is actually right.'

Such actions can be quite fun to watch. But it is much more than that for the embedded engineering developer can only do his work well if he understands both the hardware and software engineering principles.

One time I was called in from my home office. It took me around 45 minutes to commute. There was some issue with the code I had written. The IRIG Time Code generator I developed was creating some random irregular pulse width waveforms. I arrived at work and walked into the lab. There I found three senior hardware engineers pointing at the erroneous waveform on the digital oscilloscope. They would start the trace and then stop it. When they did this there would occasionally be an IRIG code bit of irregular width.

I quickly saw what had happened. They could not see it.
It was not my IRIG code generator that was at fault.
It was the operation of the digital oscilloscope.

When the trace stop button was pressed, the oscilloscope would immediately stopped drawing the new trace. This meant that the partially drawn trace was superimposed upon the incompletely erased old trace and where the two traces met there would at times be seen a strange irregular pulse width.

With a glint in my eye I repeatedly started and stopped the trace trigger until they understood and then I took the black marker that was lying adjacent to the whiteboard and wrote “Software Rules” whereupon I returned home to continue my work.

I only found out afterwards that I used a permanent marker.

To this day you can still see the writing.

Which is good, for the statement is still valid and true!

So, an embedded software engineer needs to understand technical equipment like digital oscilloscopes. That’s why I have one of my own.

But during this project I understood something very important.

I was not being bogged down with schedule details.

My manager was no doubt informing his superiors about such but we rarely (if at all) talked about it. He knew I was working at full speed. I would disappear from work for days at a time usually only coming back on Fridays during which I would keep the printer busy for several hours. When they saw me the standard joke was that it must be 'pay day' again. But they could see that I was generating tons and tons of design work and the same event was continued when the code was finally written.

Something interesting was happening.

I had been let free to do the design.

My immediate manager had worked with me at the previous company where I had been the guinea pig, where I had been the subject of the experiment in performing the design and then developing the code. What I didn't know was that current management were fretting. Here I was, half way through a six month project and not one line of code had been written. My boss kept higher management at bay. He refused them to even speak to me. He knew what would happen. If I were to become aware regarding their concerns I would immediately drop my design work and just jump into developing code. That is, to do the mistake that everyone else does by performing the design as they write the code. So I worked on the design in the quiet of my home study. Then I wrote the code to match the design. Again this was written in the peace and quiet of my home study, for developing code is the equivalent of playing six or more games of chess simultaneously (isn't it strange that chess games are also held in a quiet environment?). Suffice to say the project was completed ahead of schedule.

So when I see a company and the software developer offices (and/or labs) are in a noisy environment, I immediately know that the state of the development work will be sub-standard.

It only stands to reason.

You need peace and quiet in order to develop product!

Freedom of Expression

When you watch some science fiction or fantasy movie you are immediately impressed by the standard of work of those behind-the-scene geniuses who create the landmarks of middle-earth or of some far distant imagined planet.

Such wonders only result from people being provided a certain amount of liberty in order to express their art.

The same holds true with engineering and other disciplines for if you have not as yet already realized it, engineering (systems, software, hardware, etc.) is an art.

An art that is often bound by timescales.

If you make the schedule tight and closed then do not expect to see the work of a genius for you are subjecting your work force to the 70% rule.

If you are going to use a schedule plan as the only controlling factor in managing a project then you have sent the following message to your staff; do only what the schedule specifies and do it in the given time.

But a specific task as stated of the schedule does not identify everything known to the work involved and I assure you, the higher up the hierarchy you go the less they know of this detail. The person who does know the work is the one directly involved in its design and by giving them a time period in which to implement this work (along with rewards if they do so) you have now effectively curtailed their desire to use their high intellect to implement the unknown.

The engineer will not risk his bonus.

Actually that is not quite true. I should state that most engineers will not risk their bonus and advancement since there are a few engineers who are true to their chosen profession.

So if the schedule appears tight, upper management may not be getting quite what they expected.

It really is very simple.

If you train a person such that they will only get a reward if they meet the given schedule and you fail to give sufficient time for the work involved then the general result is that you may only get 70% of the work implemented.

Oh, don't get me wrong here.

The schedule task will be ticked off as fully completed.

The work would have been done.

But not all of it.

The results of this will not be immediately apparent.

But it will surface at the most inconvenient of times and this will occur when another person or project team attempts to use this 'completed' work. Their progress is now limited due either to the work being incomplete or not fully tested.

I know this is truth. I have seen it happen so many times.

And through this process creativity is stifled.

In order to get excellence people have to take risks. They have to have the freedom of expression that will allow them to try something new. Block this and you will get 'cookie-cutter' software.

On one project I worked I had the liberty to design all of the software. It was my domain. There was no one to tell me what to do quite simply because there was no one there to tell me what to do. For I was the only software engineer in the company. It was a case of make it or break it and it was all up to me.

I wondered to myself, "Where do I start?"

The thought came to mind, “Documentation.”

I had the ultimate in freedom of expression. I could implement the project as I saw fit in order to meet the overall requirements. But nobody had written any detailed requirements.

So I did.

I wrote Functional Specifications and Operator Manuals along with the required communication protocol documents. I spent three months designing the product and writing documents. I had freedom of expression and was going to make the best product I could for the given time.

But management was concerned.

Three months had gone by and there was no code to show for my effort.

There was only documentation.

I was kept totally oblivious to their concern for that was the work of my immediate supervisor. He shielded me from upper management and this, by the way, is the task of such a person.

For if I had known of their concern I would have become quite concerned myself and would have terminated my design work and dived right into the code.

My supervisor and I had worked at the same company some years earlier. At this company I had been a junior software engineer and had been tasked to work on a specific embedded project. At this company one manager had some unique ideas. He wanted me to do the design work before starting to code. This was not the norm for most people designed the project as they coded.

I had not really cared for this idea at the time. Every young engineer wants to dive into writing code for that is the fun part and here I was being directed into writing documents.

I did not realize it at the time but this was some of the best training I could ever have received. I remember that this manager also had some rather unusual concepts regarding schedules – the time periods identified were to be regarded as guesses and not cast in stone but periodically adjusted as more detailed information became available.

But here I was in my current project developing system documentation.

My superior handled the concerns of management. He told them that he had seen this process work at our prior company and he forbade any of them from discussing schedule with me.

My superior and I worked well together.

On joining this specific company I had been asked to take a hand-writing analysis test. This was a most unusual request and I had never done one before nor since. I was required to write out a few paragraphs to hand in for analysis. Since I knew what this was for I also wrote out my character set 'a'..'z', 'A'..'Z' and '0..9' (as a joke).

The results I received back were most astonishing and accurate.

The detail I remember that surprised me most was that it stated I was better at starting a project that at finishing one.

Now that was certainly true.

When I start a project I am finding out everything I can about the work and I find this the most enjoyable part of the design. But I am somewhat of a perfectionist and always want to make the design as perfect as possible. In this regard I am reluctant in letting go of the project since I keep trying to make it better.

What I found out about my superior was that his hand-writing analysis was the complete opposite to mine. He was better at finishing a project as compared to starting one.

But together we made one great team.

So he kept management off my back and he also kept schedules with their inherent inaccuracies far from me. For if you are constantly being reminded of how little time you have, you will not be prepared to try something new or to include some new feature that would make your product that one step above the competition.

After a little more than three months I was happy with the documentation and gave it out for review.

I obtained agreement with those concerned.

At that point I now had a fixed set of requirements and an accepted operators manual. I could now start on the code development.

So I used Structured English to identify the main parts of the program. It was an embedded application so there were microprocessors and interface hardware. There were serial ports and the usual digital and analog interfaces, a keypad and a two-line LCD display. No operating system was required. There was no need. The entire system was driven by state machines. That meant that when the device was eventually powered up it started operating immediately.

The Structured English constructs identified the main sections of the code and described some of the contained processes. Once completed, the titles of these sections became function names and the contained descriptions became comments. I now only had to fill in the code and it was done.

The entire project was completed one week ahead of schedule and was 100% finished. And I mean 100% completed.

But why did it work so well?

During its development I would often work at home instead of going to the company office. I found out that one day at home constituted three days at work. The effort of that one day in the quiet environment of my home resulted in three days of output. It was easy. I had no need of direction. I knew my bounds and what was expected of me. I would go in each Friday and spend the morning printing out documents. It was obvious to everyone that I was generating lots of output. The jokes did abound though. Comments like 'pay day already is it?'

The product was finished ahead of schedule. Management must have liked what I was doing for I quickly rose up in position and in salary.

But what I liked even more was the freedom with which I could design.

To counter this I have also worked in establishments in which the design was tightly held in the minds of others. I would find myself thwarted in trying to second guess what was required. I may had been earning more but the frustration was not enjoyable.

Now when I look back at the first design there was minimal discussion regarding schedule. I hardly ever saw any project plan. It was unnecessary. I knew what was to be done and went at it full speed. I told those who needed to know and they were happy with my progress.

I remember one morning when one director suggested a specific feature to be implemented. A couple of hours had passed and it was late morning. I was in the process of collecting my documents and code printouts when he came by to play with the test plate (this was a board that contained the entire product laid out for easy access). He started operating the device and was surprised to find that I had already implemented his suggested feature. Creating a clean design made it easy to do such things. Such examples always go over well with management.

So the project schedules were not apparent. My mind was not concerned with impossible time scales and milestones. For if you are thinking of such then your full powers of concentration will not be applied to the task at hand. They say, ignorance is bliss and at times that can be quite fortuitous. For even though the project required a lot of effort I still remember it as being one of the more enjoyable periods of my life.

Now this device also had the capability of recording time code signals.

The IRIG B and IRIG E time code standards were used and stored as one second frames with intervening sub-frames. I remember someone later asking if I had ever implemented state machines. At the time I could not remember if I had then I realized that the IRIG time codes were complex state machines. They were state machines within state machines implemented as nested case statements.

Now, if I was under the gun I would have stopped as soon as they were implemented and tested. As it stood I was not under the fear of schedule slip due to feature creep and the thought came to mind of a nice enhancement. The IRIG time code was being stored on an audio tape while the recording was being made. This meant that when the recording was being played back the IRIG time code could be extracted and the date and time of the recording displayed.

Traversing the tape in the forward direction permitted a specific time to be searched and found.

But what about the reverse direction?

Being oblivious to the wiles of the schedule gave me cause to ponder the possibility. I didn't think it would take too long to implement. It would be such a nice enhancement. If the audio tape was scanning in the reverse direction the IRIG time code would be extracted in the reverse order. I just needed to create a copy of the forward IRIG time Code state machine but flipped over in reverse order for the one second frame with each of the intervening sub-frames also independently flipped over in reverse order.

When I was finished I could now search the tape either in the forward or reverse direction for a specific date and time. It looked really neat. You entered the search criteria, the tape started playing and if the required time was still to come, the unit engaged fast search mode and scanned the code until the correct time event was found at which point the recorder entered play mode. If the search criteria was for an earlier time period then the fast reverse search mode was engaged until the required time period found. I could see the bits pass by in my head and also on the new digital oscilloscope we had just purchased. it was fun to watch. This is what is nice about embedded programming. You get to play with stuff to make it appear intelligent.

But I never would have implement these features had I been overly concerned regarding schedules.

So the schedule should be used by the person managing the project and almost kept hidden from the engineers implementing the work. For if they know that they have time on their hands they will slow up and if they know that there is not enough time then an incomplete task will result. It is best to monitor progress of a junior employee with no hint of schedule being identified. But this also means that the person doing the monitoring really knows and understands the task that is to be achieved.

Now I was an embedded software engineer that had come from the Computer Science world. A domain in which most of such people were quite ignorant of the internal components and operation of hardware. My fellow classmates were quite content with keyboards, printers and monitors whereas I was wanting to know how they all worked. So when I entered the domain of embedded systems I was now in an environment that consisted mostly of Electrical Engineers.

My classmates were nowhere to be found.

But I had always been interested in electronics and had done more than my fair share of research, reading hardware manuals and schematics. I could look at an embedded system in a way which was different to how the Electrical Engineer would look at such. For they tend to build the system using a bottom-up approach, starting with the lower components and building layer upon layer of complexity above them. There is only one problem with this approach. Ever heard of the leaning tower of Pisa?

Software people tend to design using the top-down approach which can provide a more stable approach. and in all this I learned to hold my own with the hardware folk.

Responsibility and Authority

All too often my working career has been along the lines that I have been made responsible for the authoritative decisions of others. In other words, I have responsibility for my work but I have no authority. I am sure that you quite understand what I mean for I know only too well that I am not the only one subject to such treatment.

Quite honestly this process does not work.

Under such a rule you will find yourself constantly at an impasse. It is not that you do not mind being responsible for your own work. No good engineer minds that. But to have no authority in which to change things; now that's the problem.

When progressing through a design, unable to make any authoritative decisions, it results in a feeling of frustration. The progress of the design is hindered. Quite often those with the authority do not have the detailed understanding of the project itself. Some companies hold peer reviews during which a design may be critiqued. This is the moment in which those with the authority now have to sign their approval and they are usually most reluctant to do so. This would infer that the process does not work. That, including the fact that it is most difficult to obtain a suitable time in which to gather all the necessary members and when you do get a time, half of them don't show up to the meeting (and it is quite obvious that the other half have not even bothered to read the work to be reviewed) you can readily determine why a project time scale can slip.

The solution is quite obvious.

The person doing the work is the most knowledgeable regarding the work to be performed. Once they have been given clear direction, they will then research the work and from such have the greatest understanding of all regarding what should and should not be done.

They have been given the responsibility to do this.

Why not also give them the authority to control their work.

Management generally do not know the work in detail and because of this want to have some semblance of control.

Why? Because if the engineer doing the work had the authority to control the work then it might appear that we would have no need for the manager. For what exactly does the manager bring to the table? Well, they do make nice pretty pictures for management meetings. Why? Because the higher up you go the less management understand the low-level project detail.

Now If the engineer had the authority to control his work, to make informed decisions based upon his own direct understanding as opposed to decisions made by management who only have a vague and incomplete understanding then the development of the project design would proceed at a much faster pace.

With the peer review process I found myself constantly waiting or looking for people to give me their approval to the design direction I proposed. So much time wasted in trying to get their approval. It wears the engineer down to such an extent that it is like trying to run with people holding onto your ankles. Larger companies are most at fault in this regard. They are top heavy with management. People who are more involved with financial aspects of the company than trying to make the technical decisions.

Leave the technical decisions with the person most suitable to make these decisions. That is, with the engineer who is most directly involved with that specific work.

In this the smaller company succeeds. In such a company, there are fewer staff and one person may hold a variety of roles. The engineer may interface directly with the customer and by such knows exactly what they want and how they can be pleased. The engineer is the systems person and can make immediate systems decisions since he is very familiar regarding the amount of software or firmware development work involved since he/she is the one who may also be implementing such work.

With this approach no design meeting and lengthy approval process is involved except the occasional chat with one's superior if such changes were to affect them in some manner. If the design change did not, then they need not be bothered. The engineer makes his decision and the task continues.

I have had direct experience with this process and it works. If you decide to make a major change that would affect a section of software based on a modification to the system under your control then you are at total liberty to do so. For you have the responsibility for such work and you also have the authority to make changes that directly affect your work. When operating in such an environment you are no longer second guessing what others may want. You just go and do it even if the system change might mean more software development.

As far as your work boundaries are concerned, you are the systems person and you are the software engineer so in a sense the peer review is really between you and yourself and under such conditions an agreed conclusion can be met quite readily. In this the project changes would be quickly implemented and the overall schedule might be unaffected or in some cases improved. Only in situations in which a change might increase schedule time would you involve those higher up. Otherwise they did not need to know. They do not have the in-depth knowledge of what is required and to spend hours getting them up to speed is but another delay to the project.

Status Reports

When providing a status report place it in a common spreadsheet that is accessibly by all the team members. Mention the issues you are currently being faced with. Other engineers might then see your difficulty and be able to lend assistance.

Code Reviews

Such reviews should be held at the completion of each task. They should be presented by the developer to give others a clear understanding of the work involved and the manner in which it may be used. If the task code is complicated then quite simply, it is not well designed.

The System Architect

In the workplace there are a number of different positions. These may range from the CEO (Chief Executive Officer, also called the Managing Director) all the way down to the office boy (or girl). In the case of an engineering company developing embedded software products the standard positions of directors down to managers may apply and are generally associated with people who manage the company, the top people being more concerned with finances whereas the middle managers are more concerned with schedules.

In most companies, especially those prior to recent decades, such senior leadership positions were generally held by engineers who understood both the financial and the engineering aspects of running the company. In many cases it was they themselves that started the company. However, in today's engineering companies we have the people in charge understanding the financial aspects of the company but sadly lacking when it comes to the engineering practices and disciplines. This was brought clearly to my understanding when some time back I found myself in the development lab brushing shoulders with one of these 'big guys'. Of the work we were developing he stated that he was most impressed. He stated that he didn't understand it or have a clue as how to make it but was 'most impressed'. Yet this unknowledgeable person are the type the engineer has permitted to climb the corporate ladder and hold him (and her) in submission. Don't you think it's time the engineers took the controls back again?

So the higher up the company one looks the people we see are less and less technical. Sure they can read a balance sheet and determine which numbers are bigger than the other (by the way, engineers can do that too). They are also loud spoken (ie. generally sales persons) and they thrive with confrontation (something which engineers generally avoid like the plague (ie. engineers are generally just too nice)).

So now we have the people running the show being the ones who are less technical savvy. Unfortunately these people usually have a lot to say regarding the cost of developing product. Remember, they are salesmen and saleswomen and they are just wanting to get a new product so they can rank up their bonuses. So again the wrong people are being rewarded for they wouldn't be able to sell product without the engineer, an engineer who, even if he did get a bonus, received one that was much more meager.

So the people who do not know are the ones who appear to have the most say in deciding how long something is going to take. They can't do the work themselves yet they magically have this ability of deciding timescales. It should be noted that the person at the top sets the tone for the company. If they are simply money driven then the people down the ladder will be similarly minded. This will attract a lower standard of person which will finally attract the lower standard of engineer. One who will adopt the 70% rule. This rule is one that the engineer follows when it is determined there is not enough time to complete the project properly. They know they will not get their bonus if they don't finish on schedule. But there is not enough time. So they perform 70% of the work, call it finished and throw it over the wall to the next fellow. Ever wonder why a product has so many ECO's (Engineering Change Orders (Also called ECNs (Engineering Change Notes))). These are issues that have been identified after the product is supposed to be finished and they cost an awful lot more to fix then than they would if the work was completed at the correct time.

So when schedule numbers are simply pulled out of thin air to satisfy upper management you are just postponing the inevitable crunch and creating lots of ECNs in the process.

What management is supposed to do is to provide an environment that is conducive in letting people do the work they are good at performing.

There should be a clear understanding in the company regarding mentoring and the manner in which an employee might develop and advance their career. For instance, a junior technical engineer wishes to progress towards a more senior role and a technical management path should exist to satisfy company and employee goals. Remember, a company is only as good as its employees so beware of companies that constantly retrench their employees. The company knowledge that is lost during such an event cannot be calculated. The bottom line for the stockholder might look good for the fourth quarter but the loss of company knowledge is off the scale and will affect all future quarters.

For many the goal of the company is just to make money.

The correct goal of a company is to perform an action which cannot be achieved by the individual acting by themselves.

With technical leadership a clearer understanding will be held by those in senior positions and we will see less of salesmen and accountants running engineering companies for such people neither appreciate nor understand the amount and type of effort that has to be performed to develop today's products.

Company Interns

A company should always be on the lookout for fresh talent. With this in mind the concept of internship should be encouraged.

Now this is not a new idea.

In times past it was standard practice for someone leaving school to join a company as a junior employee. This person would have the lowest rank. As such, the person would be watched and if signs of technical ability were noticed they would be sent for training to technical school for one or more days per week. If they progressed well they might then be apprenticed to an engineer or craftsman to learn the trade. This concept has worked very well for many decades and more but has become ignored in present day. There is a host of untapped talent out there. Not everyone has parents who are wealthy enough to put them through college or university. Look out for them. They could be currently working in the supermarket or in an electronic store. They are capable of so much more if they are just given a chance. Go to the local schools if they have a career day. By bringing in people on a junior level and training them you might find you retain your employees.

The company becomes more of a family.

In a movie about Edison there was a need for another engineer. Edison's reply was 'Can't we train the maintenance worker?' Now that's the correct attitude.

The Interview Test

I have only worked at one company in which they asked me to perform some interview tests. I know of people who have simply walked out the door at that point. After all, it really is an insult to your degree and your institution of learning.

Does the person's degree and work experience not qualify his abilities?

Consider this, is there anything in the interview test which could not be taught to an applicant in twenty minutes or less. If the answer is 'no' then the test is just the company's way of saying we do not believe in mentoring our employees. In other words, we will dump work on you and after that you are on your own. We expect them to be geniuses and know everything before they join the company.

Remember. If we are interviewing engineers who have some formal qualifications then they have already proved themselves by the fact they have a degree in their field of study. To subject them to a 'test' is degrading and basically states that the degree is worthless.

When I interview people I never give a test. I want to see where the person's interest lies. Do they have a desire to learn about the product being developed? Is this a person that will work well with the team? Will they be excited to work with us?

There was a learning video that I saw about thirty years ago (okay, I know that was some time back but the concept they presented was very good and is still true). In the video you saw young engineers being interviewed to work on a particular project. When shown the project some were excited, others showed no emotion whatsoever. Which ones would you choose?

Expert Guidance

If an expert is required then either bring them in or send an employee for training. Do not let them struggle to train themselves.

The Development Plan

Many years ago a contract engineer asked me a very specific question.

He said, "What does an engineer produce?"

I thought about it for a few seconds and then I gave my reply.

"Prototypes." I replied.

"No." he responded. "They produce documentation to provide the details that will allow other people to make the product."

His answer initially caught me off guard. But I immediately realized he was right.

The end result of the engineering effort is to provide a set of instructions that would allow someone to manufacture and maintain the product. If the documentation is not provided the product would be difficult to manufacture and certainly not easy to maintain. Remember, in this book we are talking about designing embedded systems. This is not some product like a house in which a plan might easily be created that would show the buildings foundations, the wooden structure (walls and roof) and the electrical and plumbing. In our case we are describing an embedded product in which each of the various components can be of high complexity. Documentation has to be provided and for good reason.

When I worked in the medical field I was introduced to the concept of creating a design history file. This was simply a directory on a hard drive that provided sub-directories for each department involved in the design of the product. These sub-directories stored the documentation, schematics, code, test results, etc. When the article was finished this design history file held everything that was required to produce and maintain the product. The file could then be given to some manufacturing company and they could independently build the product.

Well, that was the idea anyway. An idea that can be totally destroyed by a little word called 'schedule'.

I have found that when a restrictive time period is placed upon anyone then they are forced to cut corners. Their work, and in the case of an engineer, their design might not be as 'all inclusive' as one might hope. But what time you might think you are saving by using an 'aggressive schedule' applied to the initial design effort you will certainly pay for it later on. By forcing engineers into 'survival mode' they will in many cases meet your schedule but will only have completed at most 70% of the work. The finer details will not be considered and will be missing. Not to worry, they will come to light when you put all the parts together and you find the end product does not quite function as initially intended. This is when ECNs (Engineering Change Notices) will be generated for each and every missing detail and if you have not figured this out by now, ECNs are very expensive, they often involve multiple departments and they can result in additional verification and validation effort. I am sure you can understand that spending the time and effort up front to think through all the design issues is time and money well spent. But you do need to understand the design and have management that can appreciate the effort that is being applied.

On one occasion I had joined a company and was given opportunity to develop some design documentation. Now I should tell you that my documents tend to be quite detailed. I simply look at the design from the aspect of 'if I were to use this document, what detail would I need in order to do my work'. Does it provide all the detail that I would require. If it doesn't then the document is incomplete. Unfortunately, many project managers are ignorant of specific design details and just wish to tick completed tasks off the schedule. This marks many incomplete design documents as 'finished'. However, this 'time saving' will be lost later when someone has to use these documents.

So I created my document and entered in all the specific detail. It was a lot of work but it was not that hard to accomplish. After all, the details were already in my head and I just had to take the time and effort to write them down. As I started to produce my various documents I began to notice something unusual was happening regarding the people who were involved in reading and approving my documentation. These people were associated with various other departments. Individually they started to go behind my back and speak with my project manager. I must have counted about a dozen such individuals. Each spoke with my manager and basically stated that at last someone was writing down the detail. Now they didn't have to waste their time in reverse-engineering the design in order to obtain specific information particular to their work requirements. At this same establishment management had accepted a 28 paged design document from contractors responsible for a major component of the product. From my perspective, this document should have been 280 pages at least. Management really didn't understand the design and were now at the mercy of those contractors. Now creating design documentation really isn't rocket-science (unless, of course, you really are building a rocket). The engineer had to figure out the design in the first place. It is now in their head. They just have to take the effort to write the details down in a clear and logical manner. As an incentive, you just might need these details yourself six months down the line if the engineer has moved on to another company.

Success of projects

There are times when a good manager can create a great work environment for their subordinates and the development team can move on from strength to strength. I have seen this happen so I do know it does work. Unfortunately I have only seen this happen on the odd occasion. The general case is that a project does well not because of management but rather in spite of them. This is most unfortunate and should not be the way that things are done. Often management tend to thwart the process and slow things down simply because they do not understand the work involved. Again, if clear concise project documentation was being generated then everyone could read the details and come up to speed. If the detail is only in the code then there will be a problem. Upper management cannot read code and they now need to be informed and understand the engineering work. If this is the case then the engineer might be more appreciated for their efforts. For the rewards should be shared with the engineer and with the others who did the actual work. Actors and musicians get royalties for their work. Why should this not be the case for the engineer? Is the engineer not so deserving? The company does well because of all members of the organization. Profits should not be funneled away to the few at the top. Everyone should share in the rewards. The concept of 'minimal wage' is a crime when compared to a director making millions a year.

Software Coding

I started my career well over thirty years ago and I have seen all kinds of coding styles and not all of them are good. But what really constitutes a good coding style? Can code really be termed 'self-documenting'?

Everybody has a different opinion in this matter.

In my experience I have found that most programmers want to work on the new project yet they never want to maintain any existing project (not even their own). Why is that? It would appear that such work is beneath them.

But it is only when you attempt to maintain someone else's code that you find out how a program should have been coded. For is the code easy to read? Was the associated documentation existent and correct? Often this is not the case.

A long time ago in a country far, far away I had started a new job. At the time I was asking myself as to how one creates good code and here I was, newly employed in an engineering company, ready to commence work on their latest process control system. I was one of the younger engineers and there were a few older folk from whom I felt I could learn. It appeared to be a good project and I was looking forward to starting. Unfortunately, a couple of months after project commencement, management decided that they would rather have us maintain the existing process control system and so for the next 18 months I maintained code written by some other development team.

This resulted in a year and a half's experience of learning how <u>not</u> to write code.

I could not hope for better training but it was certainly not a pleasant experience.

The people who had developed the original system were mostly from the electrical engineering discipline. Now, Electrical Engineers have been trained in Electrical Engineering principles. The resultant work from these engineers gave the distinct impression they had been on a two week programming training course and had now been let loose to design a complex software system. Now don't get me wrong. Even though I am an embedded engineer I do know a lot of very highly capable electrical engineers but it takes a different mindset to write program code (especially program code that is to be maintained) and you do not develop this programming style of writing code from a two week training course.

My programming training was as an initial Bachelor of Science Computer Science Degree in which I was exposed to various languages from assemblers to Pascal, PL/1, Lisp and others. I also learnt the concepts of Operating Systems and theory of computing. My class-mates and I lived computers. We were immersed in computers. We even dreamt computers.

I will tell you what I mean. There was an occasion when I was learning about recursive programming. You know the kind, procedures that would call themselves and each time the procedure call was made it would use a slightly different parameter. Such code could be used to provide functions like the factorial operator or to even scan through linked lists. At the time I had not quite figured it out but one night I had a dream. In this dream I was looking at a terminal screen and lines of code were slowly being displayed. Each character of a specific line would appear one at a time and as each line completed it would scroll up and the next line would then be displayed. After a few such lines I realized that this was a recursive function, the answer to the tutorial problem I had been working on. I started to get excited. It was now making sense. I could see that the trick regarding recursion was to use the stack for the changing parameter. I lay there in bed and watched the program unfold on the terminal in my mind.

Now at that time video terminals were a new invention and the terminals we used at University could only display 24 lines of text. In a similar way this 'mind terminal' was no different. When the full screen content had been displayed the screen scrolled up one line and the top line was erased. There was nothing I could do. That first line of text was gone. It simply disappeared. There was no second page button that I could 'press' in order to restore the missing text.

And there was also no stopping the display.

The rest of the program I had been working on kept formulating and was being displayed in real-time. I could still see the text in my mind. I jumped out of bed, put the light on and was running everywhere looking for a pen and paper so I could write the program down.

Now that's what I call 'living computers'.

We ate computers and we drank computers.

You do not quite get this after a two week training course in programming.

But even a complete Bachelor of Science Degree in the subject of Computer Science is still not enough training for I saw my coding style change dramatically over the next few years when I worked in the 'real world' and by the fifth year I had developed a particular style.

It is true that you learn a lot while studying at university.

But in the same space of time in the non-academic world you learn about three times more. When I left university to start my first job one of my main concerns was what my employer expected of me. What did they think I knew. For I had no real experience. I knew a little about a lot of computer fields but not much of anything in particular. The 'real world' changed that, for now I started getting in-depth training about specifics.

I was now writing programs. Lots of them. Some time down the line I had to modify a program I had written six months earlier. When I did this I could have sworn that the code I was reading was not my own. But there was my name at the top of it and no one had changed it in the interim. It was definitely my code. But in my mind I had no knowledge of it. There was no spark of resemblance to anything I remembered. I had worked on so much other code during that six month period that my old code no longer matched my developing coding style so it looked as if it was someone else's code but with my name as the author. It took me a while but eventually I understood it again.

Now what are the chances of someone else being able to quickly comprehend their own or someone else's code?

How can the process be made easier?

Over the next few years my programming style kept on changing. I began to simplify my code and in the process discovered one of the biggest tricks to software programming.

You simply have to choose good function names, variable names and structure names. Names that are clear and unambiguous.

For the name states the exact process to be accomplished.

Or the name might identify the data that is being stored.

And you stay well clear of abbreviations if at all possible.

But when you start choosing the right names, a most wonderful thing happens.

The code starts becoming readable.

In the past we used emulators that required the user to type in the variable name in order to see its contents. A long name resulted in a lot of typing. This is no longer the case since you can simply place the cursor over the variable name and the content is immediately displayed. So there remains no excuse for not using a long descriptive name (unless you are aiming for job security).

Another thing is the use of the underscore as a word separator.

Eliminating the underscore and having all the words juxtaposed with the use of a capital applied to the starting letter of each word is simply ludicrous. Such a line of text becomes quite unreadable for all but the smallest of names.

Think of everyone else and simply use the underscore. A longer more readable name allows for less ambiguity and less error.

It's as simple as that.

Then there is the use of pseudo-code. This is a structured English construct that allows the reader to clearly understand the actions pertaining to a block of code.

Remember, the whole object is to make life easier for all and that includes yourself. When a function call has a clearly readable unambiguous name, there is then no reason to read the function definition in order to figure out what action the function performs. The function name tells it all. But if this is not the case then and the definition is just as vague, the reader then has to start reverse-engineering the code to determine what it really does and if this function can be safely used.

We should expect the unexpected. At times your code or operational steps may be quite valid but it is the hardware interface that is the issue.

In one such case I had written a communications driver to handle four RS232 serial interfaces. I had already written the code and verified it worked for a single channel. Now I was testing it for a multiple channel version. The asynchronous ports were linked to a priority interrupt controller and each serial channel had driver code assigned to different interrupt numbers and hence, different ISRs (Interrupt Service Routines).

For the next three weeks I struggled to get this code to work. I tried everything I could think of. It would work partially and then jump off into 'never-never-land' and crash the system. Eventually someone suggested I try the code without the emulator, to just let my code run by itself. I had never considered that since I was of the opinion that the toolset must be perfect. So I burnt an EEPROM with my code and placed it onto the PCBA hardware card. My code worked perfectly. It ran overnight perfectly. The code I had written was correct. It had always been correct. It was the hardware emulator that couldn't keep up with the interrupt load.

So part of the 'game' of designing embedded systems is to work with imperfect tool sets. You will find that just about every tool (software or hardware) has a bug in it and part of your job is to determine a work-around.

This is basically one of the principal reasons why it is difficult to determine accurate schedules when working with embedded designs. How do you know ahead of time which toolsets or hardware have bugs? So to circumnavigate this, a safety margin should be entered in the schedule for such possibilities.

Unit Test

Whether you operate as part of a software team or are a lone code developer the concept of Unit Test is an applicable one.

Simply put, when specific code has been written to implement an application or interface feature, additional code is developed in order to test this feature. This test code will become part of an entire test code suite that will be periodically executed in order to verify the operation of the system code already generated. Such code removes the effort of the programmer having to repeatedly test their code on a periodic basis after other code sections have been added.

It is one thing to develop and test a specific code module. The developer should not have to repetitively retest this code. This is where the Unit Test code comes into its own. So when a particular feature has been developed, it should be self-contained to the level that the API interface allows additional unit test functions to be created that will execute the test code and verify its operation. Once the developer has designed, coded and tested a functional unit, the unit test code is written to execute the function code and to verify its operation against expected results.

The code developer needs to be aware that such Unit Test code is required for this will have some affect on the function API design. It will enforce the design to be more self-contained for such designs are easier to test. If the application weaves its way through many other modules then the Unit Test will be such that all these modules will be tested as one making error analysis and the pin-pointing of any faults just that bit more difficult. The KISS principle of 'Keep It Simple Stupid' is an easy one to follow.

Years ago I heard the following statement...

'A good teacher is one that takes a complicated subject and makes it simple.'

All too often people tend to believe in the opposite philosophy. They take that which is simple and make it complicated. If the software appears unwieldy and difficult to understand then it has not been properly designed and errors will abound. Well designed software, no matter how complex, is easy to understand.

Risk Analysis

When designing a medical product there is a specific task which is identified by the name of Risk Analysis. This task attempts to determine the various risk factors associated with the operator when using the designed device and also the effect it will have on the patient themselves. This is a task that should be performed throughout each and every design and maintenance phase of the project. In fact, the task is applicable throughout every phase pertaining to the life of the device. So as the device is being designed right up to the point when the device is being retired and taken off the shelves, risk analysis should be performed in determining associated risk factors.

Risk Analysis is definitely applicable to medical products.

However, in my humble opinion, Risk Analysis is applicable to all products.

Each and every product should be analyses for risk.

The development engineers should be asking themselves how this product could harm a person, harm an animal or even harm the environment.

In the process of performing Risk Analysis, a list of possible adverse events is determined along with their associated seriousness. After such events are identified, possible mitigations are determined to either remove and eliminate the risk (or to at least lower the risk to a level that is as low as reasonably practical). For it is not always possible to completely eliminate risk (eg. a plane, even though carefully designed can still fall out of the sky when it flies through a wind shear or a flock of birds).

So Risk Analysis is performed at the start of the project, at every phase of the project and especially during the maintenance phase of a project (for this is a suitable entry point for risks to easily creep into the design). Risk Analysis should be performed by every member of the project team and should not be forgotten during code reviews.

Ignore Risk Analysis at you own peril for it will come back to haunt you.

Wizard Status

To those who work with computers, there are some who know all the angles, the keywords, the magic cookies and by such they may attain the status of Wizard.

But I know of no one who attempted it by this manner.

I had taken my punched computer cards (okay, I know I am showing my age but bear with me) and placed them in the card reader hopper. When this action is normally performed a card weight is then placed on top of the pile of cards. A couple of buttons are subsequently pressed (really neat buttons which light up when active) and then the cards are pulled individually into the machine at an incredible rate. Internal to the machine the cards are optically read, and are then ejected out to the left into a collection bin. As the cards are expelled from the reader they move so fast that they are seen simply as a blur as they fly through the air.

On this occasion, before I could start the card reader, another friend had arrived and placed his cards on top of mine so that both card batches could be read successively and thereby save time (except for the manual determination by the operator of having to later separate the two batches). Each card batch used JCL (Job Control Language) cards to identify to the computer mainframe the start and end of each batch of cards.

With both batches of cards now in the input hopper I pressed the buttons to start the process.

We talked a little and then I shot out my hand into the blur of ejected cards and took out a pile.

Now it just happened that my timing had been exact and I had taken only my cards from the machine. There had been no apparent delay between the reading of both batch of cards. The remaining card batch was still being read and being deposited into the output bin.

My friend's eyes went big.

"How did you do that?" he exclaimed.

Now if I had just shrugged my shoulders as if to state 'no problem' and casually sauntered away I would have achieved Wizard status as this feat would have spread through the University like wildfire. Those who would pass me by would then wonder as of what other miraculous feats I might be capable.

But unfortunately I blew it!

For my eyes also went big as I exclaimed, "I have no idea!"

So in an instant 'Wizard' status was gained and just as quickly lost.

It was both a very wonderful and yet a terribly sad day.

Card punch machine.

Card punch machines are boring. Especially when waiting for your buddy to finish punching some computer cards because he is your ride home. I'll call my friend 'Chris'.

The card punch machine provides the operator with the ability to punch codes into a paper card. These codes can represent letters or numbers or even mathematical symbols and the like. The machine in question had a hopper on the left that could hold a number of blank un-punched cards. As the operator typed on the alpha-numeric keyboard, blank cards were loaded from this hopper, punched and then placed in a receiving hopper. I was standing directly behind this receiving hopper as I waited for Chris to finish. Now each card Chris punched would be automatically placed in the receiving hopper and the card weight located on top of this pile of cards would rise slightly higher with each new added card. If the card pile were to reach the capacity of the machine a limit switch actuated by the card weight would block the operation of the card punch keyboard until some cards were removed. But this action was not immediately clear to the operator.

Now I was the guy who wanted to know how everything worked.

Chris was quite content in not looking under the hood if he didn't have to do so.

In just looking at the card punch I had immediately figured why the limit switch was there and how it could be put to another more interesting use. Chris still had to figure this out.

I let him type half a dozen cards and then, with the middle finger of my left hand gently resting upon the limit switch, I pressed it down. The slightest 'click' was heard and the card punch immediately jammed. The keyboard locked solid. No key could be pressed. The cards could not be punched. Tempers flared. No matter how hard the keys were pressed it was to no avail. I too looked concerned and asked what had happened. Eventually the half-punched card was ripped out of the machine.

I gently lifted up my middle finger.

Another barely audible 'click' was heard.

The keyboard unfroze and all seemed well once more with the world.

I let Chris get two more cards punched.

'Click'.

Again the keyboard locked and the card punch machine was subject to insult both physical and verbal. Shortly afterward another half-punched card was ripped from the machine.

'Click'

The card punch was working again.

It took great powers of concentration on my part not to smile or laugh and give it away and if you know me, my humor is not so easily stifled.

A few more cards were typed.

'Click'

Again more verbal and physical abuse. I really must complement the IBM engineers who had designed this product for it did hold up very well.

This time I kept the switch depressed for a long time and then I thought I would introduce software Chris to the wonders of hardware limit switches. I watched to see how long it would take for realization to occur.

'Click', 'Click', 'Click', 'Click', 'Click', 'Click'...

He eventually heard the noise and looked up.

It only took a moment for 'software' Chris to figure out what I had been doing.

I was really impressed.

Realization had not taken long at all.

And then the chase was afoot.

Know your Limitations

It is very important to know your limitations. To know the tasks which you can do well and to know the tasks of which you are not so good at accomplishing. This is the abilities resident within a good leader. Such a person does not try to tackle everything by themselves. For the leader is like the conductor of an orchestra.

Now most conductors can play one or two instruments really well but not every instrument. But they understand every instrument and know how they all fit into the symphony. So it is with the embedded engineer and as such, this person would make the ideal senior lead or manager. For they know systems, software, firmware and hardware whereas the software application engineer generally has little knowledge regarding firmware and hardware.

Now in my case I really hate inaccuracy so I do not do too well with the traditional project schedule charts.

Why?

Because these schedules are generally loaded with error.

The schedule detail is often vague.

For example, I have seen a project schedule which identified a software item which had been assigned a three month period simply because the project manager and hardware engineer did not know what was required nor how long it should take to complete. Something had to be placed on the schedule hence they identified a three month block by the title 'Software'. But the worst thing was that upper management were even more in the dark regarding the amount of software development work required (and you wonder why schedules are never met especially with regard to software?).

But do not think I am criticizing only one single company for this condition generally affects most companies since to many, software is still a black art (with embedded software being even more dark).

So to view a schedule that has the briefest and vaguest of software entries along with associated time scales that were literally just pulled out of the air is to throw the development engineer(s) a curved ball. I do not handle this well and if it bothers me then I am quite sure that I am not the only one affected in this manner.

Those who are not apparently affected usually fall into the category of being ignorant of the work involved and the time required.

But in considering my own strength and weaknesses I really must identify that even though I have enjoyed the task of writing code I have reached the stage that I would like to move on.

I am no longer simply a coder and when you are identified as a Software Engineer that is the work with which people most associate you. I am now more interested in the entire design process of which coding is really just a small part.

Unfortunately for many (and this even includes the younger software engineers) they think that coding is the design process and that the documentation is the code itself.

They could not be more wrong.

So if I am to work on a project I would desire to see that I will be involved in all aspects of the project – not just coding. In one company they simply wanted me to be a coder. Some enjoy such dedicated tasks but having coded for many years I have had enough of simply coding. I, for one, like to view the whole 'design' picture of which coding is only a rudimentary part.

But for some others coding is all they want to do. They just love to code. They are not interested in the design. They have an attitude of 'just tell me what you want and I will code it'. But such people become frustrated when they do not get clear and adequate instruction.

But acting like this they will not be growing as engineers and over time they may become even more frustrated. This will affect productivity and their general enjoyment of their profession.

Remember, people usually become an engineer (and this includes all types) because they like to make things.

That's why they are in this business.

So when mentoring others you must really know and understand their strengths and weaknesses in order to help them improve and make the project (and their life) a success.

Many years back another engineer helped me understand that with any agreement there has to be a win-win scenario. Both parties have to get something out of the association. The company obtains work of a high and increasing standard and the engineer obtains recompense and being mentored (ie. trained).

But if you have not noticed this by now, true engineers are not just in it for the money. They want to learn and they also want to feel appreciated.

I know this to be true for it also affects me in like manner.

If I feel that I am not learning and that technology is progressing and I am being left behind then I get the impression that I am falling down a slippery slope and it forces me to get out on the job market and do something about it.

I know that I am not alone in this.

So if you do not look after and train those in your employ your best people will be lost. An engineer takes a period of time in which to adapt to the ways of a company and to understanding the work at hand. That time is lost in training a new employee.

Clear Instruction

Many is the time that a superior will provide instruction to his/her charges by means of verbal instruction.

Now this is fraught with danger.

These days we often work with people of different races in which our common tongue of English may be their second language.

It is one thing to give instruction to someone of your own language group but it is quite another when it is given to someone from a different race.

Now this in no way implies that their capabilities fall short of yours. Their English may not be as elegantly presented as your own, however, you yourself may be totally inadequate in the use of their mother tongue.

So there will be translation issues and areas of misunderstanding.

Therefore, to stand there and give verbal instruction is to provide opportunity for the task to be misrepresented and by such, wrongly implemented. It is also the case that over the following days both parties will hear additional information from other sources such that their understandings will diverge. This generally results in the manager criticizing the engineer for not developing as to spec. This, of course, is why we are supposed to have a Software Systems Specification in order to eliminate such misunderstandings.

In this regard I am reminded of a story I heard regarding a specific discussion made between the allies during the second world war. Both parties involved used English as their mother tongue. They were at loggerheads with each other regarding some point and the issue took a week to resolve only for them to realize that they had both been stating the same identical plan. It was the choice of words used. The same word suggested a different implication to each respective party. Both parties used English as their mother tongue, however, since these countries were separate from each other, these words had developed slightly different meanings.

So if they didn't get it right what makes you think you will do any better?

When dealing with other engineers I generally break down the project into its constituent parts. When one person requires further detail in which to easily perform their work I create additional documentation.

In one case I had developed a communications protocol that transported all manner of system data. One developer needed to obtain a detailed understanding of a sub-section of this protocol in order to access specific information.

Now, the traditional approach of many would be that it was not their assigned task to figure such things out and would simply let the person suffer. My attitude is this. That developer could have been me. Would I have liked being in a situation such as that. No I wouldn't so I couldn't allow it to happen to another. By the way, that is supposedly the attitude that should be adopted by management. We work together to help the team, not just yourself and your own schedule. For you should have noticed by now that even though your schedule is flawless, if any other department schedule fails then the project as a whole fails.

Now even though management could not 'see' the need for the documentation I created I nevertheless, in my own time, went ahead and created such. I extracted the relevant sections of protocol and identified the parameters and data values that should be used. I spent time with the development engineer and greatly reduced the task time. But it was not just that. Because I knew the communication protocol intimately (since I had developed it) it also afforded me the opportunity to further verify and thereby ensure its accuracy. [After all, since it did carry sensor and control data for the entire system it was always a wise action to check and re-check it whenever possible.]

Such actions are often missed by management since they appear to have no intrinsic value. Remember, in most companies the rule is that the higher up the ladder you go the less specific detail the person understands [which is why they like pictures].

That is why each project requires a senior engineer who is the System Architect.

This role came into its own when I had to supervise three different contractors (and to make it even more interesting each of them spoke English as a second language). They each had University Engineering Degrees so they were all well qualified but it became quite apparent that the expression of what each task should accomplish would be an issue.

So I wrote down the tasks that they were to perform as work items. The tasks were clearly spelt out and each person knew what was required of them. The work progressed very quickly and proved to me that this was the way to manage. I only wished that I had received such instruction when I had been previously employed as a contractor.

Verbal instruction is open to misunderstanding and people on both sides can change their minds.

Clear and unambiguous written instruction is the only way to go.

Talking the Talk

It takes time to do things well. Especially things that you may not like. When I was in high school I had one year in which my class had three periods of English before first break. This was on a Friday morning to boot. It destroyed the week for me (and no doubt for many others as well). From Monday onwards you were dreading it. But immediately after Friday morning break you were on a high. During this English class the teacher always wanted some participation from the students and would look around to locate the next victim. It was usually during these times that I would find the inside of my case most interesting. For one must avoid eye contact at all costs otherwise all is lost.

This attitude of mine had continued throughout my schooling and culminated in the finals of my major computer science project. It was here that we learnt that each of us had to give a ten minute lecture. No more and no less. It had to be ten minutes exactly. A kitchen timer was there to ensure this as fact.

Now I loved computer science except for this part of the class requirement.

There was nothing to do to get around it.

It had to be done.

So I worked on the talk. I wrote it up and practiced it in an empty lecture room. I did it again and again. Twenty times or more. You can ask my buddy Chris for he heard the talk in its entirety each and every time.

With practice you quickly learned what not to do.

For instance, you don't hold a pen and point to some page on the overhead projector (that's an epidiascope for all those older than me - I used to sit behind one of these in physics class). For the projector does not just amplify the page it projects, it also amplifies any pen movement. This results in a blurred moving object with the rate of blur being proportional to the fear factor.

So as far as I was concerned, the overhead projector was out.

It was back to the blackboards.

So I practiced for several weeks until the great and eventful day arrived. Then it was my turn. I walked to the blackboard with my notes, then turned and looked at the audience. All thirty or so of my class mates were there as too were the lecturers from the Computer Science faculty department.

But I didn't see any of them. I knew that I was supposed to make eye contact with the audience so I moved my eyes as if I were looking at different people but in fact I was not focusing on anyone in particular. That way I would not see their facial expressions and be affected by their thoughts.

I started speaking and went through my talk. I wrote on the black boards. I drew drawings. There were two blackboards that could move up and down on rails. Once the first blackboard was filled I slid it up so as to draw on the lower secondary board. I did as I had practiced and then it was over. I went back to my seat totally drained.

My buddy Chris then leaned over and said, “You know, that was very good.”

I just looked back at him thinking he must be nuts. I was exhausted and glad it was over. On my way out one of my lecturers asked if I had ever considered lecturing.

She did not know what I had gone through to deliver that one lecture.

But I had done it too well.

A few weeks later some professors from Rhodes University in Grahamstown were to visit and a number from my class were asked to deliver our talks yet again; and I was one of them. But I did get a book certificate out of it and it was then when I bought my first paperback copy of “Lord of the Rings”.

So be careful, there are times when you can do some things too well.

The Company Afternoon Lecture

I had recently joined a company in which I found myself to be the only software person in a group of hardware engineers. I was something of an oddity. A little bit of an enigma. I was bringing something new and different to the table and they were interested in knowing more. So yet again I found myself being asked to talk about how you design a software project.

The time of the talk was a Friday afternoon and it was really just an excuse to meet together for a more social ending to the week. Which really is not too bad an idea for the Friday afternoon is not the most conducive of times in which to accomplish detailed work. [In this regard I once had a manager that would not allow us to code on a Friday afternoon because if you don’t get the code working during that period you will then spend the entire weekend at home mulling it over in your mind, trying to figure out why it did not work. Then on Monday you will arrive to work tired and spend that day and in all likelihood the next couple of days trying to fix the problem – the result being that half a week was wasted. So on a Friday afternoon he would have us write documentation or read technical magazines and the like. The other managers thought he was nuts. But he really was a genius, someone who really understood how people thought and acted, and of all people, the one who mentored me the most during my early years.]

Now with regard to the talk I was asked to give. I worked with another Electrical Engineer, a person of whom I knew from a previous company. He had been influential in bringing me into this new company and said that he would assist me if so desired. It had been a nice gesture on his part but he would have in all likelihood talked about all the important points and this would leave me with nothing to add. So I graciously refused and decided to do it all myself.

Again I practiced. I did not have as much warning so I did what I could in the time available. One of the main failings that people have when giving a lecture (myself included) is that they talk too fast. So I reminded myself to slow down.

When you speak slowly you often feel that you are going too slow but in reality you are giving yourself time to gather your thoughts for the next sentence and it really does work out well for it also gives the audience time to assimilate the words you speak.

I started the lecture and was talking for a few minutes at which point I became conscious of something I had never before experienced. This time as I spoke I was looking around and because we were in a small room I was now focusing on my audience. But they were not bored. They wanted to know more and were literally drinking in the words they heard.

They were holding on to my every word.

I had them in the palm of my hand.

I could take the lecture wherever I wished and they were with me. I was experiencing a delight and elation. I had heard of such things and this was the first time I had actually experienced it. With this realization I carefully continued with no break of concentration either on my part or theirs.

Usually these talks were a meager excuse to end the Friday work week. At the end of my talk everyone wanted to know more. There must have been an additional twenty minutes of questions. These were people more qualified than myself, mostly from other disciplines and of those some had doctorates in electrical engineering; and here they were interested in learning more from me. From this I found that everyone has unique experiences and views from which even the most educated can still learn.

Bamboozle Them

That was the request. The company was giving a presentation of our product to a large group of electrical and mechanical engineers and I had been asked to give a highly detailed presentation of the software in order to bamboozle them.

I felt that I couldn't do that.

So I made the talk as detailed and as clear as I could. In reviewing it I was beginning to feel that perhaps I had taken the level down too low for what I was presenting appeared to me as being very simple and child-like. I thought that I might have made it too simple and by such they would find it boring. I presented the talk and spoke for about twenty minutes. I had slides and pictures and talked in depth about how everything worked.

But the talk I had presented was from a software perspective. At the time I did not know that they were mostly electrical engineers and they sat in silence only because they did not have a clue about my lecture.

They were truly and absolutely bamboozled. My manager was delighted with my effort. Then the topic of discussion was changed and for the next thirty minutes they were all deeply involved in a highly active discussion regarding the color of the case of the manufactured device.

From this I learned what is meant by the phrase 'know your audience'.

JPL Open Day

If you ever have the opportunity to visit JPL (Jet Propulsion Labs) in Pasadena, California then I would encourage you to do so. You just never know who you are going to meet and what you might learn in the process.

The JPL Lady

I found out that JPL (Jet Propulsion Labs) in Pasadena, California was having an open day. How could I possibly refuse to visit? I took the day off work and with my Thompson Map Guide (no GPS back then) I planned my trip from Lake Forest in Orange County up through San Dimas to Pasadena and finally to JPL itself. Off to the left I could see Los Angeles and adjacent to that, Hollywood.

Immediately I was a kid again at the cinema back in Glasgow, Scotland. In my mind I could visualize the Universal Hollywood commercial at the end of the movie. In very large letters it said "When in Hollywood visit Universal Studios". This message was portrayed above the picture of the tour bus tram crossing a collapsing bridge in the studio back lot. Now that bridge must really be quite old as I was not even in my teens when I saw this commercial.

I remembered thinking, 'Yeah right, when am I ever going to be in Hollywood!"

I could see myself slouching in my chair with my feet resting on the seat in front of me. It was Saturday morning and I was at the ABC Minors. The movie house was full of kids and we were all there to watch Buck Rodgers and other such serial classics.

My thought had been "When am I ever going to be in Hollywood.".

But you should be careful what you think for you never know just what might happen in your future. I had never thought I would ever visit Universal Studios let alone be living in California, and here I was now driving up the freeway to Pasadena (and at the time, always reminding myself to stay on the right-hand side of the road).

I finally arrived at Pasadena and drove into the JPL car park. The place was like an entire University Campus dedicated solely to the science of space exploration. Having arrived I felt that I did not ever want to leave. [Ah, if I could only create a work environment like that with the pursuit of knowledge for the betterment of all.]

As I wandered from building to building, viewing all kinds of displays and exhibits, I found myself walking up a stairwell when I passed a lady who was traveling in the opposite direction. She asked me if I was visiting that day. I told her I was. She then asked as to my profession and I told her that I was an embedded software engineer. She then proceeded to tell me something of system design. She stated that when you design a product, make sure that you take the interface design right down to the lowest level of detail.

If you stop too high there is then ambiguity and the engineers that use the interface will assume specific details. When the product parts are finally brought together the interface will fail due to these invalid assumptions.

I do not know who this lady was but I have never forgotten her words.

Sometime later I worked on a project that included a major interface. A dozen or so engineered boards had to communicate over this interface. My superior had no idea as to how to build this system. I know this as fact because he told me. So I designed the interface and its operation as well as the message protocols. I remembered the JPL Lady's words and placed detail in my documents all the way down to the lowest bit level. I also specified what each bit state represented. There was no room for error for there was no ambiguity. As the hardware boards were updated I likewise updated my design and made sure it kept in sync.

Management did not understand the need for such detailed documentation. But I can tell you this. All the engineers that used the document did understand such need. My documents were used by Software, Firmware, Hardware, Verification and Validations, Production Test and Manufacturing departments. One engineer of the non-software persuasion even stated that if the software specification had been written to this same level of detail they would have had far fewer problems. It takes effort to bring a design down to its lowest component but it does pay off in the long run as far as the entire project is concerned.

The JPL ion engine

At the same visit to the Jet Propulsion Laboratories, I heard a fascinating talk about an ion engine that was under development. An engineer was standing under a canopy in the courtyard and he was preparing to present pictures and diagrams of this incredible device.

I saw that the talk was about to start so I quickly sat down.

There was still plenty of space. Some empty chairs here and there. As it turned out I think that most of these people had only been looking for a place to sit in the shade away from the heat of the sun for as the man started to speak about his subject his head turned less and less until it stopped, fixated in my direction.

When I realized this I almost laughed in surprise but I did not want to embarrass the speaker as I truly wanted to know everything that he wished to share about his subject.

It became a 'brain dump' as he poured out fact upon fact regarding the device yet he was talking to no one other than myself.

Even though there were people everywhere he was only looking at me since I was the only person giving any indication of understanding his words. For we were the only two who were on the same wavelength. I was greatly intrigued.

When you have a team you want people that understand each other and can learn from each other. An engineer is not in it just for the money. Now that in no way implies that you take advantage of them by payment in "thankyou's" for they will see through that very quickly. They are bright people and by such also wish to be stimulated by their work environment. If there is no stimulation, the intelligence that may be brought to the design will quickly die as the mundane becomes the norm.

Geography class

When I was attending University I took Geography as a filler class. I had heard interesting reports from other students about this department and since I was required to take an Arts course I decided that this would be it. The University deemed the arts course as being necessary since they felt that they were churning out too many scientists and engineers and not enough well-rounded people.

So I signed up for the geography class.

They handed me a green card.

I was to supply a photo of myself along with my name.

A week or two later I found out what this was for.

I was walking down a corridor and as I passed some geography lecturers they greeted me by name.

I was amazed.

No other faculty department would take the time to learn their first year student's names. For this class numbered well over a hundred individuals.

It was good to be called by your first name, especially by a senior lecturer.

You felt accepted.

It made you want to apply yourself with greater effort.

The head of the department was a man who certainly had a very special gift. He could lecture his class with no apparent effort. If he laughed, they laughed with him. If he was sad, they too felt his sadness. They were like putty in his hands.

There was one day when he arrived at university on crutches.

The class had started and his students were all waiting for him. They watched as he struggled through the twin lecture theatre doors. Then, after he was inside, he just stood there for a few seconds looking up at them. There was such a sense of pathos about his stature. All in all he looked quite pitiable.

It was then when the entire auditorium burst out laughing. Thirty seconds later they were still laughing. Slowly it subsided until he was able to speak. He simply smiled and said, "I just want to tell you, don't go skiing in the Majuba Mountains."

Once more the place was in pandemonium.

Then as the laughter drew to a close, the doors shuddered and a young student entered, also on crutches. Now the lecturer was much taller than she and as they stood there side by side; he looked down on her as she looked up at him.

The other students couldn't help themselves. For the third time the lecture theatre broke out in laughter. When it died down he smiled yet again and said to her, "I see you went skiing in the Majuba Mountains."

We all laughed so much that there was not a dry eye in the place.

Later on at the end of the course he gave his last lecture of the year. I had heard that this talk was not to be missed. We had been learning about the business district development and he had taken an apparently dry subject and made it fun to learn. In this final lecture there was a comparative study of three different shops, each belonging to a small shopping center of two quite different business districts. The shops were the butcher, the baker and the candlestick maker. His comparison between these stores had the students laughing in stitches. One set of shops were elegant and perfect but the other set were of the opposite extreme with comedic descriptions.

He had us all in the palm of his hand.

I too would like the gift of counsel.

The Planetarium

In my studies I took an astronomy course at university. I had always been fascinated regarding this subject and if it had been a complete course and not just a one year topic I would probably now be in a totally different line of work, living high up on a mountain in Hawaii or in some other such place.

It was an interesting course but the twin lectures held immediately after lunch on Tuesday afternoons were of particular importance. For this was the practical lab work and we did not have to wait until evening because the University had its own Planetarium. This building housed a Zeiss projector which could be used to project a starscape of the night sky from any point on the earth. And we had it all to ourselves. A nice air conditioned universe for two periods during hot summer afternoons. You couldn't wish for anything more.

During our course the famous British astronomer Patrick Moore came to visit the University Planetarium in order to present a number of lectures. I remember talking my Dad into attending one.

Now Patrick Moore might not be a recognized name in some places but having been born and grown up in the UK, we had heard and watched both his radio and television programs (The Sky at Night). Everyone in Britain who had a radio or a television knew this man. He was very popular and an instantly recognizable figure (perhaps it was the monocle he wore). We sat in the packed auditorium and listened to his booming voice resound. He had a microphone but there really was no need. He would talk without notes. He knew his subject intimately.

Later in my astronomy planetarium practical exam we were handed the presenters torch and given the opportunity to tell what we knew. It was initially strange to be standing in the room instead sitting looking up but you soon got used to it. We would point out different stars, rattle off right ascensions and positions on the earth. It was a subject that I enjoyed and because of such it was easy to learn. After completing and passing my course I remember the planetarium lecturing offering to train me to use the projector and to give lectures. What a fool I was. I said no. I had no experience in presenting lectures and felt somewhat introverted. It was a wonderful experience lost.

Physics Exposure
During my studies I tackled two years of physics. As the end of my second year I was allowed to mark physics papers. We were told to be very lenient, after all, they were medics, prospective medical doctors. I soon learned that a doctor sees the world differently from an engineer or a physicist.

During the vacation a list was posted identifying student vacation work. One of my lecturers was needing an assistant in the Electron Spin Resonance Lab so I applied. He gave me two weeks of training and then he left for his summer holidays.

Now before that time I had never seen a Varian Electron Spin Resonator.

It was a device that sent a beam of microwave energy down a waveguide into a metal cavity box that was suspended between the poles of a very large and powerful, water-cooled electric magnet. The control panel included a plotter and an oscilloscope display screen along with a myriad number of buttons, dials and switches.

I was not phased at all. I loved such environments

The object of the research was the study of diamonds.

It had been determined by certain individuals that a clear cheap diamond could be placed near a nuclear reactor and by such proximity the diamond's color centers could be changed. What this meant was that a diamond's color could be modified and since a colored diamond (eg. a blue diamond) was worth several times more than a clear diamond large amounts of money were now involved. This was of great interest to De Beers who was sponsoring this research.

With the diamond mounted on a quarts rod using non-paramagnetic glue (if memory serves) I was to take the diamond through a 90 degree transition while keeping the magnetic orientation such that specific waveforms on the oscilloscope were aligned. This was a lot to learn in only two weeks.

During my lecturer's absence I continued with the work and it turned out quite successful I might add. As time progressed I came to realize that they had not really been expecting too much from us students so the actual useful results I was providing came to them as an added bonus. They were simply wanting to provide us with more practical experience.

With the results obtained I then learned what Eigen values were all about as the resultant data I had collected was plugged into the Hamiltonian equation and out popped the electron energy levels.

Fascinating... as Spock would say.

One day a friend was visiting the lab. He had completed the second year Physics course and was wanting to proceed onto third year and asked me to consider doing the same. I told him that I had only completed the second year ancillary physics course since I had not contemplated doing physics as a major.

I told him that it would not be possible for me to proceed to the major course.

'Oh I don't know about that," said a voice from behind a piece of equipment. "I think I can arrange something."

Well, I guess the owner of this voice could do exactly that. It was the head of the Physics department. He had been quietly working on another electron spin resonator. I was not even aware that he was there.

All the same I decided against proceeding on to third year.

I felt that it might be too much work.

Now at this point in my life I wish I had taken it for there are concepts in Physics that I wish I understood more clearly and this would have been so if I had made that effort.

I also learned something important from this professor. He had performed months of research work and was wanting to make another check before publishing his results. The next day another scientist in Russia published his results based upon identical research.

All my professor's work was now to no avail. It had already been published.

Do not let fear hold you back from speaking your thoughts.

It was shortly after this that I saw a notice placed on the Physics Bulletin board. Research assistants were required to work for two months during the summer vacation at an arctic lab station.

I had two years of physics under my belt. I could have gone.

I now always wonder what experiences I might have gained had I applied.

So don't be scared to try something new.

Failure only comes in not trying.

To this date I have always wondered as to the spectacle of the 'Northern Lights'.

I missed out on an event in my life that would have provided that information.

Tales My Father Told Me

It would seem that the concerns of the hardware and software world are just the same as that in the mechanical engineering domain. My Father worked his life in mechanical engineering in the design of heavy mechanical devices that were used in power stations and in the mining world. These were such things as precipitators in coal power generation plants and refrigeration air flow fans for gold mines. Such devices were large in size and so were the resultant errors if any were made.

He did not have any form of engineering degree but worked from being an apprentice all the way up to holding the title of drawing office manager.

One of his mottos was, “Never hurry, never worry”

He said this because he found that if a person is concerned about a schedule they will worry. If a person is worried they will hurry, and if a person hurries they will indubitably make a mistake. Being “on time” with a major mistake on your hands does not help. As I said, drawing office mistakes result in blunders that can cost the company large amounts of money.

Another one of his mottos was, “After you finish the drawing, can you make it?”

For someone down on the shop floor was going to receive these plans and attempt to build it. So if you can’t make it, what are they going to do and when exactly will they determine the error. For it will generally occur at the most inopportune time while you are busy on the next project.

My Dad also had no desire to see any work after he had finished it. He wanted it perfect. He wanted it complete and he passed that design methodology onto me.

These stories are just as applicable to the embedded software field as they are to mechanical or electrical engineering fields. The same philosophy applies. Have you provided work of a sufficiently high standard and level of completion that when given to others it may be used as is. It is as simple as that.

Choosing Your Staff

When it comes time to choose the team that would work on the project you want people that have complementary abilities and are socially compatible. Getting a group of egotistical engineers that are all out for the sole betterment of themselves might not be the best choice.

You want a team that works well together.

You want a team that will listen to each other.

You want a team that respects each other.

You want a team that complements each other.

One day I entered the interview process in which I was now on the other side of the desk. I was looking for a new team member. The project work was growing and a new hardware engineer was required. We interviewed many people, both young and old. The engineering discipline is mostly a male oriented group but as time has progressed more women have become interested in this field. We were not biased. We interviewed both sexes.

But when interviewing one young lady both myself and another team member came to the same conclusion. She would not be suitable. It was not her qualifications. They were really very good. It was just that during the interview this young lady was very opinionated and did not appear to listen to us regarding the project requirements. Even though we found no objection to her qualifications she was not team oriented. She would have been most excellent if we had been looking for a person to head a team or to work on their own.

Another woman we interviewed was one that had been in my class at university so I knew exactly what she had been taught since I had received the same training. It was decided by the group that she had not been suitable. I met her later and she was upset with me. I think she believed that I had curtailed her chances. Actually I had suggested she would have been most suitable.

Then we interviewed a man who was many years our senior. Some might have thought he would be too old for the team but we all found him to be a most agreeable person. It was decided that an offer would be made and he accepted.

This man and I shared an office together.

I had created some software for a previous project and was now modifying it to suit the new task at hand. After spending around three full days of making code changes I decided to try it out and see what would happen.

His thought was that after making so many code changes, there would be no possibility that anything would work.

He was somewhat amazed when most of it did. We quickly developed a good rapport between the two of us. There was mutual respect. I used to say that we were the slowest pair to enter a building because we would always step back to let the other enter first.

So your team has to respect each other.

We would have gone the extra mile for the other at any time.

While working at this business we were shown a video that discussed methods used by some well-known companies when selecting staff members. One such corporation had prospective employees at an interview being presented with a mockup of the product they were going to develop. Some interviewees expressed their interest keenly whereas others had no such apparent desire – to them one programming job was the same as any other.

So who would you choose for your development team?

A person who just wants to get the job done or someone who is excited and cares for the end-product and desires it to work well for all possible reasons. Who do you think would put in the extra effort for the betterment of the entire team?

If you wish to create a team of arrogant engineers then provide them with a set of tests during the interview. You will obtain what you desire. A group that does not trust each other and is out for whatever they can get for themselves. The group mentality is not there. How can it be. For to ask for help is to identify your inadequacy and such people would not do such. They will provide work that does not interface well and although you will get product, it will, in all likelihood, not be quite what you were looking for.

When I am looking for an engineer I will review their work history and their qualifications. Having a degree in the requested field is not always the requirement. A person with many years expertise in the area of choice may be a better candidate due to their desire to learn. Even taking a junior person and apprenticing them may be most suitable for there is a wealth of talent out there and with university education costs being what they are, the apprentice model may just be making a comeback.

After reviewing their background I then spend time talking with them about themselves. What are they like. What do they do outside of work. Remember, you have never met the person before and you may be working in close proximity for the next few years. You want to know a little more about their character. What you are trying to determine is if this is someone that you can mutually work with. For in as much as this is your objective it is also their objective. It is certainly not in either party's interest if the interviewee and the interviewer have no rapport with each other.

There is a relationship that is to be developed by the work team. If this was not the case and all candidates were suitably qualified then the decision process would be that of throwing a dice.

Some companies with a desire to cut cost attempt to have one person perform two jobs. It may be to have a manager who will supervise a group of people yet at the same time work on part of the engineering development. The person involved might even perform this out of a desire to keep one's skill set current.

But quite simply, this does not work. I can talk directly from my experience. From what I have experienced in my own life and what I have seen by watching others.

When I myself was moved into the position of managing a group of embedded software projects there was one project in particular that I wished to keep on developing. Now when being transitioned into a managerial role it is hard to let go. You have been a development engineer for many years, you enjoy that type of work and now you are being coerced into watching others do that which you most love. It is very hard to remove yourself from such direct control.

In this I had been getting more involved with my own project and started to resent (in a small way) the disruptions that came when other engineers would come asking for my assistance. I have always believed in the 'open door' approach and wanted those I worked with to feel they could bother me at any time for any reason. In the past I had worked with managers who did not present that character trait. I knew that if you manage someone then you have to be available to them. Being gruff and unapproachable is simply a defense mechanism of those who do not have the answers and want to hide this fact from others. My attitude has always been 'if I don't know the answer then I will go and find out for you' for I would have the better chance of finding the correct answer and mentoring the person in the process. All too often the approach of those that 'managed' me was to dump vague requirements on my desk and quickly beat a hasty retreat before I could ask any questions.

I have always vowed to myself that I would never adopt that approach.

But here I was starting to resent being disturbed and beginning to keep my office door more closed than open. It was then that I realized that being a manager is all about being a people person. If you are not there for your people then you are not a good manager.

You are to be one step ahead of them. You are to be the one with the answers and the guidance, after all, you have the experience.

And I was not doing that. I immediately changed my approach when I realized that being a manager is all about those I managed and not about me. For you can be a great manager or a great developer but you can't be both. I found this out that time and I also repeated the experience when I was forced into a similar situation in a different company. You can manage or do the development work but you cannot effectively do both. Such an action just causes great frustration. Years later I had this ingrained into my psyche. I was working with the development of a video device and a laserdisc player was being used to generate a high quality source signal (okay, it was high quality for that time). The player was on auto repeat and the same disc was being played over and over again. It was about some musician and the section that stuck in my mind was that he saw himself as a father figure to the others in the production crew. It was his job to look out for their welfare. I have never forgotten that statement.

I have seen this character trait in a few managers who really cared for their employees. These managers were definitely not perfect by any means but they did hold true to this philosophy. They protected their charges from those above. This allowed the 'family members' to work in a safe environment in that they were permitted to act in an unhindered manner. If an employee is constantly living in fear of management and schedule then they will not be at liberty to give their best. This will result in inferior product.

Now if the CEO of companies could only learn what that musician taught and see themselves in like manner as the Father of their organization then it might be a different story. A functional family instead of a dysfunctional one. For the Father looks out for his children and allows no harm to come their way. When I worked on a different project there was a manager who understood a little of what the 'Father' concept involved and was protecting a member of his group. I knew this from a corridor conversation I overheard. There was an electrical hardware fault. Some electronic component was not acting as the product data sheet specified. So the younger engineer was being criticized for something outside of his control and his manager was protecting him (the actions of a good manager). In this I was greatly impressed.

However, this manager still wanted to do development work and although he and I had a good rapport he never had the time to do all the work that was required. He was fully loaded as a manager and did not have the time to develop. In this I saw that the issue was irrespective of discipline for he was hardware and I was embedded software. So you either manage or you develop. But you do not do both well.

Company Size

In my thirty plus years of experience I have been employed at over fifteen different companies. In some I have worked as a contractor and at others as a permanent employee. When looking at my resume many have stated that I have had a colorful career history.

Now this can infer that I do not stay too long at some companies and in a few cases that has certainly been the case. This could be understood that I have no company loyalty. But it should be noted, that the work contract in California states that you, or your employer, can terminate the work agreement at any moment's notice. Such conditions do not encourage long term associations. However, it has been my general ethic to leave only when a project has been completed.

But staying too long at a company can also identify inadequacies. Yes, the employee may be showing great loyalty however I have seen very large companies eliminate such people from their work force at a moment's notice. The company has no loyalty towards the employee. If they don't need you now they will remove you. It is all part of the bottom line in order to make the stock price look good. In actuality I have seen employers lay off much of their senior work force just to raise the stock price. Such loss of future company potential!

In the larger company you may be just one hundreds or thousands. You are employed to satisfy a very specific need. Once that need has been satisfied then you are dispensable. Often the senior employees of such large companies are either accountants or sales persons. They have no knowledge of current engineering practices or if they did they have defected to 'the dark side'. So to be employed in such a place is to have you tied into a narrow nitch with not much room for advancement. You must remember that most people in companies are looking out for themselves. There is the pecking order and the person at the top of the ladder sets the tone for the entire company. If this person is an accountant or simply a salesperson then money is the bottom line. They are not really interested in the design and development of engineering since to them it is a money pit.

At the start of a project they are not happy unless a large amount of money is being spent, for to them this identifies that the project is progressing. But later they are also not too happy when money continues to be spent. In many cases they are of the opinion that to reduce a project schedule you just have to throw more people at the project. But those with an engineering mind know intuitively that this action does not help and most often hinders. You need an engineering team that understands the project and such knowledge does not come quickly.

Now you are not going to advance to senior positions in such a company unless you have an accounting qualification. The person at the top generally want to have subordinates that they can understand and control. If this senior person is an accountant then they can understand the sales types but they have no room for engineers. For engineers speak a different language.

If the most senior person in the company is from the sales force then they will get on well with the accountants for they understand each other. Money is their common tongue. They too do not understand the engineer or the trials of the development process. I know this for a fact. One such person stood right beside me and stated his amazement at what we had created. In this statement he acknowledged that he had no understanding whatsoever regarding how the product worked. And this person was in authority? I was amazed.

Some forty years and more ago this was not the case.

A true engineering company had a board of directors mostly consisting of engineers who came from all disciplines. This was true the world over. I still remember hearing the tale of the CEO of an aircraft company who would periodically walk through his company's shop floor. This was the area where the aircraft would be assembled. This was his own company. He was the one that started it. During his walk he would stop and talk with various people along the way. If he spoke with a welder he spoke the same language as the welder. In fact, he could pick up one of these tools and perform the same act of welding as his employee. For he had done such all those years earlier. This man cared for his employees. He knew them and had concern for their welfare – but not just for them. He cared for their families as well.

In the avenue of science fiction we see this in the character of Pickard, the Captain of the Starship Enterprise – The Next Generation (TNG) television series. True, this is fiction but there was something in Pickard's character that we admired. But why? Perhaps it came to the surface when he and his number one were the only two left on board. In this scene Captain Pickard sits at the Conn and after stating that it has been some time, he cracks his fingers and proceeds to enter the controls that would fly the ship. He knew what was involved with the operation of every part of the ship. Why, he even knew when the ship's engines were out of alignment.

This principle came true to me in a unique way.

One company I worked at decided to have a week-end training session. During this there was an event scheduled for late Friday evening. I was really quite tired and had hoped for an early night.

My manager was trying to talk me into attending for it was supposed to be a 'fun' event in which you place some difficult task onto one of your workmates.

In reply I told him that I can't do that.

I said that I can't make someone do that which I was not prepared to do myself.

I did not know it at the time but this was the objective of the event.

It was to not ask of others that which you were not willing to do yourself.

It was the old adage – do unto others as you would have them do unto you.

And I had just passed this test with flying colors.

He then said that I did not have to attend and I had my early night.

It really is very simple but when attitudes change to those of purely financial then it becomes a case of being out there for as much as you can get without any concern for others and that appears to be the increasing attitude the more you step up the corporate ladder. So many just literally dump unpleasant tasks on others without any care for the person or for the person's family.

For it should be noted that a company is in itself also a family and should be looked after as such (a company that hires and fires at will is simply a self-centered dysfunctional family).

When various sized companies are compared, one often sees more loyalty with the smaller company. From my aspect there is also more 'fun' with smaller companies. For in such a company you are not just one of the crowd. You are more intimately known and you are not slotted into a narrow nitch with many others all vying for the same avenue of promotion. In a small company the engineer is tasked with not one but many disciplines. In the large company you might only be the embedded software programmer but in the small company you are that plus you may also be the Systems Engineer and interface directly with customers, obtaining first-hand information, you might also write the manuals and the specifications. You may even create test specs and test software and directly interface with the production department. You do it all. It is a lot more varied work and it is fun for you are always learning and advancing.

There was a time when I joined such a small company. We reviewed some training video about what made smaller companies excel. There were many examples given. One company was starting a new product line and were interviewing prospective employees. The employee would be shown the product and their response gauged. Some showed great enthusiasm whereas others were somewhat disinterested. Which persons would you hire?

Some companies were large and operations were slow. Some years later I had direct experience in this. I had a two week window to work on a small software project. A microcontroller. I placed a signed purchase request with accounting with the thought that in a day or so I would get the required compiler. After all, it was not that expensive and could be delivered overnight. I started project development, created the required state machine and started on the code. The existing compiler was old and was crashing every few minutes. Each day I persevered hoping that the new compiler would be delivered shortly. In the end my perseverance won and I eventually managed to complete the project only to find that my purchase request had not made it out of the person's in tray. I could have completed the project with less stress and in half the time if it had.

At one small company I joined it was a different story. The project I was initially assigned to work on had been placed on hold. An existing project was in difficulty. An engineer who had been working on this project had just left and there was no one to handle the work. They asked me to do so. The previous engineer had been using assembler language for the task.

He had been an Electrical Engineer and was not truly an embedded software engineer and so did not have a good understanding of software design. Assembler was not the way to go. A much higher processing language was required. The most suitable language for that time was Intel's PLM/51 for the 8051 microprocessor.

I was asked if I would prefer to execute the work in a different programming language. I suggested PLM/51 and I then went to lunch. That same afternoon when I arrived back, the PLM/51 compiler was sitting on my office chair. During lunch my manager had gone in his care and traveled the 90 miles to the supplier and back in order to obtain the compiler. He had placed it on his own credit card and later worked out the approvals and recompense. I can tell you, such actions made a very positive impression on me.

Every few months I also noticed that my salary was being increased. My work was being noticed and without any request on my part the company was showing that I was being appreciated.

Now it is all very well being given "thankyou's" for work performed. Unfortunately the local grocery store does not convert "thankyou's" into food items. In this I am reminded of the words of one of my first work associates who would say, 'Don't thank me. Buy me something!" So when the company attempts to encourage their employees to perform extra effort and they state that they will reward such, then this reward should be immediately forthcoming and not six months down the line for to do so the employee will become disillusioned.

Now it is the job of your manager to ensure that you have all the tools you need to do your work well. In this regard you should be sent on additional training courses in order to enhance your skill set. With this the employee is more inclined to go the extra mile and to do that which is required.

My experience has shown that the smaller company has illustrated greater encouragement and appreciation compared to that which I might have received from larger companies. As to myself I have also found larger companies very limiting and somewhat stagnant. One has to obtain so much peer approval prior to proceeding down any specific path and this makes you feel as if you are trying to run with people holding on to your ankles. This work ethic might attempt to ensure the employee only does what is required but it restricts their freedom of expression and also leaves them guessing with each subsequent decision. You cannot proceed while having to second guess every decision you are attempting to make.

Advancement from Within

All too often a senior position will be given to a new employee. When your staff see this they will fully understand that in order to progress one simply has to move to another company. In this you will lose many of your good employees who simply see no line of advancement for their career within the company.

Contract vs Full Employment

When a person is employed as a contractor they directly identify the hours they work against a given task. It is much on their mind as it is on that of their employer's. This keeps both parties more focused on the time spent on the tasks at hand.

When dealing with contractors specific instruction is required . The contractor requires explicit work details for the person generally does not know the project with any depth of detail and because of such requires detail instruction in order to proceed in a carefully managed direction.
Now, if only we were as caring with those who are full-time employed.

It should also be noted that employees distrust and reject contractors. Why should it be otherwise. An employee is on fixed pay whereas a contractor is paid by the hour (usually at a higher rate for the same work). This higher rate offsets the benefits the employee might obtain from the company. But when overtime is required the contractor wins outright. So why should the employee who is now on a fixed salary even concern themselves with helping the contractor? The overall result is that the project is adversely affected. Be fare. Pay your employees additional money when overtime is required. A 'free meal' is but an insult to your employees. Your employees have read the newspapers and seen the television news reports. They know the exorbitant salaries and bonuses received by higher management. The products come from the engineers who designed them. Such people are not a commodity. How about paying them what they are worth and giving them royalties with every sale of the product they made. It happens in the music and movie industries. Why should this not likewise be the case for the engineer?

Medical Software

When developing any embedded system, the company has a legal obligation to the customer. That is one of the reasons a company is formed, in order to protect the owners and employees of the company. It is one thing to design and develop a product for the betterment of mankind, however, it can be quite a task ensuring that no matter what, the product will not fail and possible permit damage to either person or property.

When developing a medical embedded system this task now has an additional legal obligation to a governing body called the FDA (US Food and Drug Administration). During the product engineering effort, the design will at some point come under review and the company must prove that it meets certain requirements.

Having worked for many years in the medical environment I have come to understand the basic philosophy.

It is simply this…

'Say what you are doing and do what you say.'

So if you, as a company, state that you always hold project meeting and design reviews and identify the points in the project plan during which such reviews are held then you must be able to prove such. For the FDA representative will ask for this proof. They simply want to know that you are following your own procedure and that the procedure is adequate.

The company now has to ensure that the staff are suitably trained and that this training has been registered. There are certain computer-based products on the market which are used for this purpose. In themselves these might be good products but one should, like all things, be careful in their use.

For the basic procedure should be simple to access and to understand.

In using such training products the employee is periodically presented with a specific document or procedure to review and after which, they are required to answer some questions and obtain a passing score. This task and its result becomes part of the employees record and the company can prove that such training was held.

All in all, so far a good thing.

But some companies, unfortunately, present the employee with an unending supply of documents and procedures to be reviewed. These documents and procedures are constantly changing and generally provide detail that far exceeds relevance to the employee's tasks. This implies that it is of minimal use to the employee who then feels totally unmotivated.

At the end of the presentation review the employee is presented with the test. This usually results in searching the document for the specific use of a word or phrase from the test question. In this the document search tool is put to good use. After the test is completed and the score is adequate the results are logged and the employee immediately forgets the document (and also the location in which the document might be found (the document is also simply numeric). There is generally no apparent easy way of finding the document if one were so motivated to do so. But that does not really matter because the reviewed details are usually forgotten quite quickly due to involvement in the current tasks at hand.

The documents may have been reviewed and the questions answered merely out of obligation but five minutes (or less) after completion the person has no idea where to find the source document, what it was called and remembers even less regarding what it was all about.

This is exacerbated when an 'aggressive schedule' is in effect.

So although the employee has spent time reading through and answering questions regarding the presented documentation such that the FDA requirement might be satisfied, the process has not aided the development of the product and now the work schedule is even further behind than before due to the time spent of this activity (sometimes several hours per week).

Within my company I would provide all documentation as an easy to read handbook in order to provide the basic company philosophy regarding the way things should get done. The details within this book you are reading is an attempt to do such. It provides all the necessary information for company standards with respect to designing embedded systems. It is an easy to read book and a quick read after which everyone in the company would then know what happens at each stage of project development.

The book is presented in physical form and would be on each person's desk.

The book would also be presented in eBook form.

Did I also tell you that each of my employees would also be given a full-sized tablet in order to access all latest project documentation?

Salaries and Paychecks

We have all seen it. The people at the top of large companies commanding exorbitant salaries while those at the bottom making minimum pay. But even consider an engineering company in which a well experienced engineer might be making $100,000.00 as an annual salary. It is common knowledge that those in charge of such companies are making in excess of twenty times that salary (and often, even much more than that!). But can it possibly be considered that such a person gaining that high salary is actually working twenty times as hard. They are not. So how can anyone be worth that much. In my humble experience I have seen that projects are developed not because of management decision but rather in spite of management decision. For such management (especially upper management) have little knowledge of the work involved. All they see is the bottom line and how much profit they can make. I know this for a fact. I have heard it from their very mouths. When it comes to engineering most upper management have no understanding of the work involved.

A psychologist friend of mine said that it was common knowledge in their profession that those at the top of companies were generally ruthless individuals who would bully and coerce their subordinates. Now remember, the person at the top sets the tone for the entire company. Their character traits are the traits that will be adopted by each successive layer of company individuals. These ruthless people have no problem in intimidating their subordinates and acting the oppressing tyrant. In fact, the psychologist sees them as psychopaths and if such people were to act like this outside of the company environment they would be taken into police custody and sentenced to a life in jail for harassment and fraud (ie. stealing other people's money). They are thieves and robbers and they are legitimately getting away with it.

Now can you consider a company in which everyone who worked on a product would get an equal share of the profits. For I assure you, even if I am the most gifted of embedded software engineers and my work is exemplary, the product would still not work without the other team members and likewise their efforts would be of no avail without me. That being the case, should we not all have an equal share?

I heard recently that there is a law in some countries that the top salary cannot be more that twelve times the lowest paid worker. Now isn't that a good idea? If the top person wants more money it can only result by giving the lowest paid worker a salary increase. What if this affected all companies? Well, there would be more money in the hands of the masses and they would spend their money on more products and the money would circulate instead on simply being hoarded by the few. Everyone would then benefit. Just a thought...

Product Knowledge

There have been many times in my life when I have developed a product for a single customer. Often this customer would want the device to operate in a very specific manner.

Now it should be known that there are Software Application Engineers and there are Software Embedded Engineers and they are not quite the same breed of person.

The Software Application Engineer is a person that is mostly interested in how the end-user might interface and operate the device. On the other hand, the Software Embedded Engineer has a greater knowledge and understanding of the product's internals for this person has a greater understanding of the lower level details.

Be that as it may, there have been products that I could have worked on in a more proficient manner had I been granted access to better training. If a specialist uses the device you are building then to ensure that you have built what is truly required and that it is working exactly as expected, you as an engineer should be fully trained as if you were the actual user.

As an example of this, consider a demonstration I saw that was presented of the Da Vinci Robotic Surgery tool. This incredible tool was on display in a shopping mall near Escondido in San Diego, California. This was certainly the strangest of places in which to come across such a device but they were wanting to increase public awareness. But I was most interested in this product for another reason.

A few months earlier my mother had just undergone a successfully robotic surgery and this was the very product that was used.

Now it is one thing to develop an embedded system from the inside, being totally familiar of all the internals of the device and its operating modes but it is quite another when viewed from the customer's perspective, which in this case would be the medical surgeon and the patient.

I spoke with the person demonstrating the device and was given the opportunity to sit down and operate the machine. I could not resist. My fingers were placed into specific hand controls that eliminated tremor and permitted me to move the various robotic limbs. I could turn my hands and see the limbs rotate as I watched them in a 3D stereoscopic viewing screen. When I opened and closed my fingers, the tool that was used for cutting and cauterizing also opened and closed in perfect synchrony. It was a wonderful device and within minutes I had successfully completed the test of moving several thin plastic rings from one conical shape onto another. Such control was highly intuitive and by spending some additional time with a surgeon in order to experience some minimal training it would allow me as an engineer to make a device that the customer would desire.

This would allow me to understand the required functionality and you would also gain the unwritten requirements that only come from someone trained in that field.

I have had the greatest of difficulty when I have been forced to rely on second-hand requirements. As an engineer I want to be directly involved such that I obtain first-hand information.

The Schedule

Now we come to the world of 'the Schedule'.

But a word to the wise...

Care and caution should be used when working out schedule development times.

The first thing that should be noticed is that these times are GUESSES.

When performing the engineering of a new product no one really knows how long it will take to perform the work. They may have some idea of the various tasks involved but there is no concrete understanding of the time required, especially for the time associated with tasks that occur later on in the project.

So when starting to develop a schedule only the major steps should be identified. You want to fully understand which tasks can be performed in parallel and which tasks are dependent upon the completion of other tasks. Only once this has been defined should some time guesses be assigned.

And remember, these assigned times are GUESSES.

Now the time periods assigned to the initial scheduled tasks can be determined with a fair degree of accuracy. However, as one reviews each subsequent task in the schedule the duration accuracy drops substantially. Attempting to guess at these times (and yes, they are indeed guesses) and to subsequently cast these guesses in stone, never to be changed, would be considered complete folly.

Yet this is often the accepted practice. Once upper management sees some fictitious end date they want to fix it. You can pull it in but they will be most upset if you with to extend it out.

Project schedule times must be adjusted as the project proceeds and as additional information comes to light. It is a dynamic process and should be treated as such.

The 'aggressive schedule' concept should never be used for it declares failure right from the get go.

Now when a development engineer reviews a schedule they have in their own mind some concept of the work involved and the time it should take. Some managers keep their engineers in the dark regarding the work complexity, hoping the engineer will accept a shorter time period. But if that is your philosophy then you are just fooling yourself, for if the schedule time is too short, management will be hit with the following problems.

Each engineer is different but my experience identifies that they generally fall into one of two groups. Now when I say the word 'engineer' I apply this term loosely to imply all engineers of all disciplines (hardware, software, firmware, mechanical, etc.)

Firstly, there is the true engineer. He or she delights is building something out of nothing. They want to excel and do good work. Their work is a reflection of their character (this is generally a case affecting all people) but in this situation these engineers are perfectionists and because of this they have to be 'encouraged' to finish their work since they are continually striving for excellence and when designing products that may be used in a medical environment, one could hope for none better.

But this type of engineer detests schedules. Why?

Because the schedule is always incorrect.

The schedule is usually vague, it does not provide enough detail and the supplied times are hopelessly short. These engineers strive for perfection and have to be managed in a specific manner for when their work is finished it will be perfect.

There will be no software or firmware or hardware bugs.

It is excellence personified.

But then there are other engineers. They know that reward is given for meeting schedule. They also know if the assigned work can be accomplished in the given time. These engineers can do excellent work (if they choose to do so and are monitored in that regard) but if they know such work cannot be achieved in the given time they will immediately adopt the 70% rule. They will implement 70% of the work and call it 'finished'.

After all, they want their reward and they are working within the boundaries that you yourself have established. So don't blame them for doing such.

In this regard, the person responsible for creating the schedule should have adequate project experience. The detail placed in a schedule is generally associated with the knowledge base of the one creating the schedule. Often such persons are ignorant of one or more development fields (usually software) thereby resulting in inadequate detail given to the scope of work involved and the associated time duration required. Such efforts are usually seen on the software plan as a nebulous solid block marked 'Software' tied to some inadequate time duration.

Then there is another term, the "aggressive schedule". This simply means that work has to be completed in a very short period of time and again no one has quite looked into it in detail for if they had, they would see quite clearly that this is an impossible task to achieve in the given time.

So for a schedule to be accurate, the person placing the time on the schedule should have had experience in performing similar work. If the task is one that has been repeated often (eg. fabricating printed circuit boards of a particular complexity has been completed tens or even hundreds of times) then a knowledge base of time versus complexity can be established and an accurate estimate determined.

But if this is the first occurrence of a work task which is to be performed then the estimate borders on guess work; and a guess means that it will be quite inaccurate and should be treated as such.

It should also be noted that providing a person insufficient detail and requesting their time estimate is simply a matter of manipulation and is neither to the benefit of the company, to management nor to the engineer.

An engineer is a member of humanity and like all human beings is programmed with the instinct for self survival.

When this person is faced with a schedule that provides inadequate time for a specific task they will then act in one of two ways:

1. They will either employ the 70% rule in which they will complete most of the work and call it finished, or
2. They will perform all of the work and be slightly late.

Although my experience has shown that most apply the first rule, myself and a few others employ the second. But to be fair, those that employ the 70% rule usually do so by company training. After all, reward is only given upon schedule completion. Management is simply providing poor 'potty' training.

Either way the project suffers.

My work ethic was recognized one time by a project manager who said that I took a little longer than other engineers to complete my work, but when I was finished, my project worked. Well, you know what that means don't you? It means that the other engineers against whom I was being compared were not really finished when they said they were.

Now the 70% approach created 'finished' products that would subsequently fail in time and bear several ECO's (Engineering Change Orders) placed against them over the coming months. Each ECO would cost the company many thousands of dollars and affect multiple departments (also inhibiting them from proceeding in their current tasks): so who saved company time and money in the long run?

But there are many occasions when uncompleted work simply gets past superiors because they themselves cannot tell the difference between an un-finished product and the finished article and this is very easy to do when faced with a task that is code based. The basic functionality may be there but the error scenarios have not been fully tested. For it is easy to create code that works in the lab, code that does not take care of error conditions and the need for retries.

So provide a time that it too short and be faced with either an on-schedule incomplete task (with many ECO's to follow); or obtain a working task with a smaller schedule overrun.

In this company the engineers who were working on these projects were also being subject to long hours. One specific project had to be finished and they were working 60 hour weeks.

But the following should be noted.

The best engineers are normally working at 95% efficiency. You can make them work longer hours for a week (or maybe two) and you will get a little additional work output but after that their efficiency will quickly drop and errors will abound.

They may be resident in the office for 60 hours or more but you will be lucky if you are getting 30 true hours of work delivered. They are getting tired, more errors are being created and the survival instincts start to kick in. This is also the time when you will start losing your best employees.

In one company I worked, my manager stated that I took a little longer than other engineers but when I was finished all of my code worked (that was another way of saying there were no subsequent ECNs tied to my work).

In this same company a higher-level manager could not understand why there were so many ECN (Engineering Change Notices) being generated.

Each ENC cost the company many thousands of dollars and involved different departments. A design change could even require a risk analysis consideration that can ripple through the company..

When I heard the manager ask about these ECNs I could not help but shake my head and laugh to myself.

The answer was so obvious.

Engineers are not fools. They were acting just as they had been trained.

The unrealistic schedules generated the observed response.

The engineers knew that reward was only given to meeting schedule. If you don't meet schedule then no reward. So these engineers, the ones that were happy to adopt the 70% rule, went ahead and did just that.

Their 'finished' tasks were never completely finished. Oh, they were called completed on the schedule and ticked off and as far as the schedule was concerned everything looked good. Management was pleased. The 'bad' engineer was rewarded.

Then sometime later, someone down the line had to use their work.

But it was incomplete and it did not work.

There were software, firmware and hardware bugs.

Sometimes work was simply 'thrown over the wall' to the next department with the thought that they will find the bugs for them. I have seen engineers that use that philosophy being well rewarded. Management were blind to the fact that such practices simply slow the project down. Would you want someone else's incomplete work to be applied to your development work and thereby slow down your observed capability? It does not do anything for the development speed of the overall project.

Now the engineer assigned to develop a task that is to be interfaced to the incomplete work now has to determine the fault so as to get their task to operate correctly. This ruins their schedule time line.

Now this 70% rule does not just affect the development engineer.

It traverses the system all the way up to senior management. As you progress up this ladder the rewards are greater (and so are the politics (which is just another name for greed)).

If you are going to reward a person simply for meeting schedule then the training you are providing, especially to those with lower morals, is that one meets schedule at all costs.

So they do.

But the project suffers.

There have been times when I have seen large holes in the project design. Parts are missing. Big parts. I could see managers and directors of the different groups standing there looking at this gaping hole. They act as if they can't see it. Perhaps they can't. Or perhaps it is a case that they do know what is missing and also are quite aware of the amount of work it constitutes. To take this as their own would subsequently compromise their ability to meet their current schedule (and their subsequent reward). So they play dumb waiting for some other conscientious person to do the work for them.

But you should remember one of the laws of the universe.

What goes around, comes around.

Conclusion

A company is totally dependent upon the person at the top,

If this person is non-technical and out for self gain then similarly endowed people will naturally gravitate towards them. The top person will want like minded people in his court. Such people have his concern and will do as required for they hold to the same values. Technical persons will not be welcome or accepted for they know too much. Such people will be held at bay. They speak a different language and can show up the ignorance of others.

Many such non-technical people have no concept of engineering practices.

They are sales people. They want to control others.

They buy companies just to get product to sell. They see design and development only as a money-pit. They are out to make money and lots of it (no matter the cost nor the manner in which it is achieved).

However, if the person at the top is technical, then similar technically minded people will gravitate towards them. You will then have a hierarchy of technically astute people who know the company product. They understand the design and development process and recognize what constitutes good work. They have come up through the company ranks and are familiar with each department.

This is the type of engineering company in which the true engineer desires.

Now how does a project get late?

It gets late one day at a time. Each time you lose a day that day is irretrievably lost. It is very difficult to 'pull-in' a schedule.

It will certainly pay to have a System Architect that knows the desired end result and the way to get there. To have someone who keeps the development person(s) focused and on track. This is the person who manages and guides the team. If the developer is being constantly harassed by schedules then their work will indeed suffer.

The developer should only be fully focused on the current task at hand. If they are worried about schedule then they are not focused on their development work.

So how do you manage the engineer?

The answer is quite novel.

The engineer should be told nothing about the overall duration of the schedule. Do you really think that an impending deadline is going to motivate the person? If they know of such then part of their mind is working on the task and the other part is thinking about the deadline. You will not get maximum work out of such a 'hassled' engineer. Remember the good engineer (and I assume you have obtained and mentored them to be such) works at 95% efficiency. They drive themselves hard. It is in their nature. They don't need someone behind them with a big stick.

What they do need is a clear idea of what is required. A clearly defined specification. At times management would comment on my designs as being too detailed. Yet I heard from those that used my documents that if the Software System Specification (and other documents) had been written to my standard then they would have had a lot fewer issues. As they say, the proof of the pudding is in the eating.

You have to remember that your work affects others in the company. If you 'save' time by doing an incomplete job then that 'saved' time turns up elsewhere as schedule over-runs which affect every person and group that uses your work (so there is a multiplication factor involved). Sure it is on someone else's schedule and they get affected but initially it really was your fault. Be careful. Life has the law of cause and effect. You have heard that what goes around comes around. Oh, it may take some time but it does happen.

So when managing a schedule, the System Architect should first work on the design to collate the required work instructions that are to be given to the engineer. These instructions should be detailed and complete. Failure to do so will cause the schedule to slip. An engineer should not be walking around the building trying to find the systems 'guy' so as to obtain missing detail. It is true that not all engineers would try to find out this information. Those who conform to the 70% rule will simply sit where they are and only implement what they see and go on to the next task and collect their reward for each and every incomplete task they 'finish'. They are only doing what you are training them to do. It is the higher level designer's fault if the project fails. It is also the System

Architect's job to ensure that the other departments have the details they need and implement the details that they have been given. They have to be monitored otherwise you will obtain an incomplete design. For just as some will provide an incomplete design, many people are minimalists (they will do the bare minimum, what they can get away with)

So when schedule times are severe and people have entered survival mode, they will only implement what they have to implement and the System design will not be fully developed.

Then you will see happen what you initially considered impossible. Because the design was improperly implemented (and monitored) they will go and change the System Design Specifications document to suit the imperfectly implemented work so that they match and now you have a design that is of a lower standard and the original specific details have not been implemented. Details which may also affect risk mitigation and now that document (and its implementation) has to be changed. So as a system architect, you have to monitor the entire system. The system design should have been finished prior to it being handed over to the other departments for implementation.

From a software perspective, the software architect (and yes you should have one) turns the system design into a set of work instructions for the programmer. The software architect gives sufficient work for the next few days so the engineer implementing the work is not overloaded. It should be known that this work instruction is to be finished during this time period and the software architect is always on hand to answer questions. The software architect is not off somewhere writing code; the software architect is writing the next set of work instructions and always checking produced output against the software specification.

Now I always find this quite ludicrous.

To have a senior software engineer sitting at a terminal writing code all day is the equivalent of having the designer of a skyscraper building out at the building site laying bricks. Sure, I grant you, he should know how to lay bricks but the person's talents should be put to better use. For they can see the bigger picture and should be telling others how to implement the design.

Don't waste the talent of your employees!

New Scheduling Method

There was a time when I worked as a contractor for a friend of mine. It was for a Point Of Sale application. Now this was a little outside my usual comfort zone for it was a PC Computer application that would execute in the Windows environment. I had created other Windows Applications so that was not the issue. It was just that this program was for the business world instead of that of engineering.

But the project did interface to scanners and printers and had a large number of networked computers. In fact it was designed to cater for 100 networked computers.

The common design of many Point Of Sale (POS) software packages is that one computer system is designated the 'Server' and the other computer systems act as POS Cash Registers used to taking customer sales. This normally works quite well unless some fault occurs with the network or with the Server computer system. When that happens the system is 'dead in the water' and the POS cash registers cannot function since they are prevented from retrieving product information from the Server.

The system I developed would overcome this limitation by using a distributed database. The Server database, when updated, would be distributed to all POS computer systems such that a Server or Network fault would not prevent the sales person from taking customer sales and entering quotes.

The sales and quote information would be reconciled after the Server and/or Network issues had been resolved.

So a friend and I worked together on this project. My friend knew more of the overall design and what was required. He acted as the System Architect. I acted as the developer. We would meet every three or four days on a regular basis although I could call for assistance at any time. The System Architect of any project (and each member of this team) should be immediately on-call for the project suffers if questions cannot be immediately answered.

So every three to four days we met and spent several hours together.

We would review the coming work task.

We knew the overall project plan and the final goal. There was no need to keep looking at project dates. To do so would not make the project go any faster. I was working full-time on the project. The project plan was in my friend's hands. He could include or remove sections as desired in order to make schedule.

It was not to be my worry.

My focus was strictly on the task at hand.

So I was given a task. It was clearly spelt out and each step identified. I knew exactly what was to be accomplished in the given time. In this I did not just know what was to be completed but I also knew how it was to be completed.

My friend was also there to guide me as I performed the work.

We made a great team, each being focused on our own task.

If at any time I did not understand something I could always ask. He was always on call to answer and to elaborate detail. He knew the requirements intimately.

He also knew a lot about software design and interfaces.

At one point I was implementing one of the main databases. This database stored all the sales information for the system. I had seen other applications that maintained this data as a single, variable sized record file. When the database was small the project sales report would traverse this file quite quickly.

But when the sales database was large involving several years worth of data, this report could take over an hour to complete. This was unacceptable.

I had been reviewing a different approach, one that split the sales database into a number of smaller databases, in fact quite a lot of smaller databases. There would be one for each day of each month, of each month of the year. This would allow for quick direct access to the required data when reports were to be generated. This also created a complex level of recursive functions that would access these files residing in the nested directories.

I started coding the functions and then I became concerned regarding the complexity. I was thinking of returning back to using the standard approach.

My friend encouraged me. He knew that the nested approach was better.

"The reports will be generated much faster," He told me.

He helped me by guiding me through the process and I persevered.

Within a day it all came together. The recursive functions could traverse the nested directory structure. It was now looking clean and elegant. I could see no error and felt convinced and sure of it working.

That was the beauty of working on shorter work loads.

They took three to four days to complete (this included the code generation, compilation and testing). Each week a section was completed and you had time to rest between each task. Knowing that these tasks were complete and fully functional also gave you a sense of achievement. You were building your design on a solid platform.

It then came time to test the sales report generation features. I made a request for the year sales report, a report that identified the sales totals for each month of a specific year. This was the report that took over an hour to complete when used with the large test dataset.

Using the nested database approach the report took six seconds. I thought something must be wrong. It could not be that fast. I ran the request again.

This time it took two seconds. (The dataset data was now all in memory).

I knew that there would be a speed improvement but I had not anticipated it as being of this nature. This would certainly make this product stand out against the rest. No matter how many years of data were stored in the system, this report generation operation would always be this quick. It would not slow down as more and more years of data were added to the database.

The design ensured this as fact.

It certainly paid to have a System Architect that knew the desired end result and the way to get there. To have someone who keeps the development person(s) focused and on track. This person manages and guide. If the developer is being constantly harassed by schedule times then their work will suffer.

The developer should be focused only on the task at hand.

Project Length and Burn Out

I have worked on small projects that might take the order of a few weeks and I have worked on larger projects that take the order of four years.

The project length can have a positive or a negative effect on the engineering team. Smaller projects tend to have dynamic change. The engineer feels that they are learning, growing as an engineer and that progress is being made. It also looks good on one's work experience.

Long projects can become lethargic. There is slow development. Some projects can feel as if they are going on forever. It should be the company's objective to ensure that the development team training remains consistent with the tasks at hand and that the team feels a sense of progress.

The Lab versus the Real World
Now there is a difference between the lab and the real world.

What you might find is that the product works great in the lab but when you place it out in the field it fails. What the developers have failed to take into consideration is the concept of error detection and correction.

When software is developed (especially under tight time constraints) the engineer will ignore the error conditions that may occur. After all, to properly handle all error conditions the code size will generally increase by a factor of three resulting in a likewise greater number of tests to be executed and verified.

For this is the difference between the laboratory and the real world. In the laboratory signals are clean and electrical noise is shielded. In the real world it is quite the opposite.

So how does the developed software handle such 'noisy' conditions.

In most cases it doesn't.

This infers that the right product has been designed for the wrong environment.

The system specification might identify the environment but if the system architect is not at the code design review to ensure that error conditions are handled correctly, poor code will be accepted which will then become part of the overall system thereby making it more difficult to change at a later stage.

The issue then becomes someone else's problem, that of the maintenance engineer. Yet in most cases management is ignorant of this and rewards the wrong people for their 'timely' effort and poor work ethic.

But as far as the company is concerned, reduced profits result in lower salaries so by bypassing correct system design you really are doing yourself out of your bonus.

What Constitutes a Leader

Now this is an interesting question. Often the people most inappropriate are placed into a position of leadership. Sometimes they are ignorant and keep you on their side by just telling you what you want to hear. Others use a different tactic. They become arrogant and loud. They make themselves unapproachable therefore many of their subordinates will not ask them detailed questions. They don't mind the questions from other senior staff for such people generally know less than them.

But the junior staff who are directly working on the issue, now their questions are avoided like the plague. so poor leaders are constantly telling other people what to do, they are the loud mouths of the conversation.

They leave no room for the others to talk.

But a true leader is quite the opposite. A leader steers the conversation. They say a word here and another there in an attempt to have everyone bring their thoughts to the table. If you have someone who controls and inhibits then those great ideas from quiet people will never be heard.

All too often the so-called leader is proposing some method and when someone is granted the opportunity to talk and suggests a better idea this 'leader' will quickly change their direction and make it sound that this was also their idea.

When I attend meetings I am usually the quiet one. In one company my review stated that my superior found this course of action intimidating. I found that quite unusual. People who know me see me as a most agreeable person. I had never thought of myself as being 'intimidating'.

The aspect of my character that my superior found somewhat daunting was that I would sit in meetings and barely open my mouth until the very end. It was only at that point that I stated a possible course of action with regard to the point being discussed.

In this my knowledge was sound and precise (and exact). It was this that he found intimidating. What he didn't know was that I usually only speak aloud in meetings when I am very sure of what I am about to say. If I am quiet then I am still formulating my decision. I have not as yet gained enough knowledge. So I only speak when I am 95+% sure. Then at the end of the meeting I might propose something different.

It was stated that my suggestions were invariably the correct approach and since I had been very quiet up to that point they may have felt that I had been judging them in some way. I assure you that was not the case. During the earlier part of the meeting I was quiet because I was still weighing the pro's and con's of the discussion and at that time had nothing accurate to present.

I hope that I am not the only person who acts this way, a person who thinks first and then speaks later. But in meetings, with one or more loud and dominant persons who are simply wanting to get their own way, the suggestions of the rest might not be heard and great ideas will be lost.

For the leader must respect all those present, especially those who are junior in experience. The leader is to be a father figure who looks out for and cares for the team.

You see, the leader is not necessary the person with all the ideas. For the leader knows the strengths and weaknesses of the team members. They must not control everything. They provide a framework for the others to work within. For many engineers who progress into team leads and management the most difficult aspect of their work is to let go and not try to develop themselves.

Often their fingers have to be pried loose so that they can delegate the work to others. It is true that in some cases they might be able to perform the work better and faster but this is where mentoring comes into the picture. The whole objective is to train so that the group can advance and the company can grow.

If the thought is just to have an engineer fill the current need and then discard them later you are not fulfilling your leadership role and the company itself will be sadly lacking and it will loses good talented persons as it remains static.

Mentoring and Training

I was watching a science fiction film the other day. Many of these movies are now available in formats that permit additional footage to be provided. Such extras often include short documentaries that provide more information regarding the film's production.

Now this specific film showed something that I have always known.

People perform well (or better) when they have been given all the required training. In this case, since it was a movie about being in space they sent the actors off to Space Camp where they could learn how to move about in zero gravity. The actors also had to pretend they were in the military so there was also some 'boot camp' training.

Through the process the actors understood more of what was expected of them.

Now there was one time I was working on an interface for a train numbering system. I had read up on all the documentation, I had seen train mimic panels in pictures and had heard my boss talk about the project. But it was only after spending a few minutes at the actual site and watching the engineers control the system that I really understood what was required. It didn't take much. I just had to be shown the product working environment along with the design and what was expected of me suddenly became a lot clearer.

Later I worked on medical products and although I was shown some aspects of how the final device was to be used there was no 'real' training as to what constituted valid and correct operation values. Sure, I knew how to place the product into different operational states but there was no 'feel' for how the product was to respond such that I would know immediately what constitutes a good result as opposed to a bad.

So no matter what you are designing, the developers should all have in-depth training to fully understand the product and to know its function. Just as in that movie, you will get a better response from your team if they fully understand what they are supposed to do. Just talking about it is not good enough.

The Design Environment

The current design environment is that which is known as 'the Company'. This entity has been developed primarily as a means of safety. To provide protection to those who wish to develop product and yet remain secure from the legal aspects that might be incurred from the sale of such product.

The company also has the distinct advantage of pulling the resources of the many in order to achieve that which was not possible by the one. A company may be created by one or more individuals. It may be funded by internal or external sources and it generally exists in order to make a profit and thereby survive. But the company should be for the benefit of all and not just a select few.

The manufactured product should also assist the customer or they would not purchase it. It is an item that will enhance their quality of life. It should be well designed and built to such a degree that it will reliably provide several years of faithful service with no (or minimal) risk to the user.

In all of this it should be noted that the creator of the company is inadequate in effecting all the resources required to manufacture the product. This person might have great knowledge but with the development time of many products often exceeding several man-years of effort and comprising of talent derived from multiple disciplines, it is nigh on impossible for even one single accomplished person to achieve their goal.

So in order for the company to live and grow, it then has to involve the talents of many. In the case of the development of products that utilize embedded computer systems, the involvement of various types of engineers are required. There would be those of the software engineering disciplines (both application and embedded) that would understand how to design and build the software required to drive such a product.

But such engineers, especially younger engineers with limited experience, often lack systems knowledge and do not fully comprehend the interaction of the product with the environment or with the other engineering disciplines.

Disciplines such as Electrical Engineering and Mechanical Engineering are directly involved and must always be considered. Engineers who are strictly software application orientated do not fully appreciate the work of the hardware engineer. The software application is executed on a hardware platform and providing access to the hardware interfaces is the domain of the embedded software engineer. [Application engineers neither have this knowledge nor generally wish to be concerned with these details.]

The embedded software engineer's experience covers system design, software application development, right down to hardware PCBA board bring-up. The embedded software engineer understands the overall concept of the software application but brings to the table the knowledge of how such an application will interface to the real world. This is the world of sensors, actuators and device drivers. To understand this environment, the embedded software engineer's experience covers many fields of study. As a rule, these principally include that of systems, software and hardware.

Unfortunately the embedded software engineer is often included along with the software development team and as such this person is poorly understood. For the Software team and the associated management generally have no desire to approach the hardware domain and only do so under duress. They want an environment that provides them just what they require in order to get their scheduled work completed. Such a hardware platform might include an LCD with a touch screen interface complete and audio front-end. This may come with an Application Program Interface (API) which they are content to use but don't ask them to develop or maintain this interface. For they have no desire to enter the world of the hardware engineer, board schematics, components, and associated test equipment. They simply want an interface that works. The applications engineer (and their managers) generally have no desire of entering this world for they really do not understand it.

So the embedded software engineer should be in their own department and directly interface with Systems, Software and Hardware for this type of engineer interacts with all three of these disciplines.

Project Design

When starting to design an embedded project it is necessary to create a System Design. Think of it from the standpoint of building a house. It would be foolhardy to simply lay a basic foundation when the height of the house is unknown. All too often people rush into the coding phase of the project. Management desires such because now they can see something they understand. The widget is now visible and it has some sort of functionality. But to rush into the coding phase is to rush headlong into disaster.

You first need to fully understand the product.

Given enough time and resources, an engineer could build absolutely anything.

Their intellect is vast and the world is their oyster.

The problem lies in knowing what people want.

This is where the System Design comes in.

Now many dislike this phase of the project because they feel there is too much writing involved. There is too much documentation to produce. But the real reason why people do not like the system design phase of a project is because it takes a lot of effort. The designer has to use their inherent talent along with their imagination in order to figure out what should be built.

As we all know, talk is cheap.

The world is full of talkers.

Most people find it easy to just open their mouth and speak about any subject under the sun and this includes talking about the system design.

But what you find is that the presented discussions are usually surface deep. There is little if any detail present. This fact is quickly determined when any attempt is made to use the provided information.

With this in mind I have made the following one of my own rules to which I abide.

You only truly understand something once you can write it down.

Now if the engineer resides within a small company it is likely that the developer will wear many hats. What I mean by this is that the engineer would not just design and develop the code, but he/she would also be responsible for performing the Systems Engineering tasks. This permits the engineer the right to proceed with this aspect of the design.

However, if the design is large and involves many other people from several different departments, then the embedded engineer might be dedicated solely to embedded development tasks. The Systems Engineer may be required to start the design long before other department involvement would be required.

There is also another proviso. If the design is such that the FDA or FAA are involved then there will be those who will review the design so be sure to apply the simple rule 'to say what you do and to do what you say'.

I have worked on a very large project in which the system design was started at (or very slightly before) other aspects of the project. The problem with this was that the other departments were calling out for the system documentation so that they could proceed. But there was no documentation. The system was still being determined.

Now there is an unusual phrase which states 'without a vision the people perish'.

Well, without a suitably detailed System Design the schedule very quickly goes to hell in a hand-basket. The result of this is that the development work will take longer and by such will cost much more than originally expected. Since the various departments are already under the starter's gun they simply begin by using the bits of the design that they can get their hands on and make meager attempts at understanding the final concept. All this means is that the design will go through many iterations and several changes (not always small changes) will be made with each iteration. When this affects code one may consider this as code re-factorization but if the changes are major then the re-factorization would also affect the software documentation process – if there is one. Again it should be noted: software code does not constitute (or take the place of) a software design document.

The proper approach regarding System Design of a large project is to start the system design prior to ramping up the staffing of the required development teams. This way the design will be created and finalized such that the other departments can be given a completed specification.

System Architect

Now every project should have a System Architect. This is the person who has experience in multiple disciplines. The embedded engineer lends themselves to this task more than any other engineer for the simple reason that such a person by the very nature of their work, interfaces with the following departments:

- Systems Department
- Software Department
- Firmware Department
- Hardware Department
- Production Department
- Manufacturing Department

In this regard the senior embedded engineer is a person who can bring the right qualities to the table. You might note that I am stating the word 'Senior' embedded engineer. By this I am not referring to a person with five years of experience or maybe even seven or eight years. In my 'humble' opinion such persons are still inexperienced and are still finding their way. I am talking about a person with fifteen to twenty (or more) years of experience.

It is like when you first started to learn a high level programming language. Sure you could write code quite quickly but it took the order of five or more years until you developed your own style. With this style you would find that others easily understood your work and could readily modify it if so required. Prior to that your code was simply thrown together. A hack (which is not a nice word).

So it is with the concept of the Senior Embedded Engineer for there is more to such a person than simply them being a coder. Compared to other engineers, the Senior Embedded Engineer makes a good System Architect because the nature of their work requires them to fully understand the system design. Linked to that is a complete understanding of the hardware and firmware (cPLDs, FPGAs) for with this knowledge they have to provide appropriate API interfaces for the Software Application Engineer. [The Software Application Engineer is generally a person who does not want to think below the level of the API interface. They don't want to see hardware other than a keyboard and a GUI screen and they certainly do not want to look at schematic diagrams.

Think of the System Architect as being the conductor in an orchestra. They will have had the experience of playing a number of different instruments and be particularly good at one or two (often the violin and the piano) but they understand the process and what is involved in playing each and every musical instrument. They need this knowledge if they are to have any hope of being able to lead the orchestra and have each member express themselves in the manner desired by the symphony composer.

But, as with an orchestra, the conductor will first study the piece of music and determine what he wants from the members of the orchestra long before the orchestra musicians sit before his baton.

This is much the same for the System Architect. There is much work to be achieved prior to incorporating the entire engineering team.

First a product concept has to be determined as to what is required. Is this an 'in-house' product or is the customer an external entity. Either way a Product Requirement Specification has to be developed. During this time the System Architect will sit down with the customer and determine the requirements. Now it should be noted that with regard to a medical product these requirements are what will be used by the validation engineer to validate the product. When this action is being performed the development company is validating (ie. ensuring) that the correct product has been built as per the customer's requirements.

The Product Requirements will then specify a number of individual statements. Each of these statements must be satisfied for the correct product to be built.

At this point the System Architect must put on his/her 'Validation Engineer's' hat and review each customer product requirement from the aspect of how it will be validated. What this implies is that later, once the final product has been built and is operational, a set of tests will be written to put the product through its paces. These tests will ensure that the product fulfills and meets the customer's requirements.

Since the System Architect was the person who developed the Product Requirements in the first place, he/she is the most qualified person to specify the tests that will be used to validate the requirement. To let the validation engineer figure the test out for themselves is to shirk your duty for the test should already be in your mind as you develop the requirement. At that moment you simply just have to write the test down on paper. This saves much Verification and Validation development time and will greatly reduce the amount of time required to implement the test phase.

Now the System Architect is one of the most important roles in any engineering company. For this is the person who truly understands what is required since they are intimately familiar with all aspects of the design and also have been granted the authority with which to ensure that the design is implemented as specified.

Remember that saying, 'without a vision the people perish.'

Truer words have never been spoken when applied to product development.

You see, the System Architect is designated the task of being the visionary. This person knows the form, fit and function of the final product and is able to express this design to others in the form of documents, pictures and discussion.

The System Architect (and their team if it is a large project) is used to create the System Specification. Such an architect should have experience in multiple engineering disciplines. In this regard my current experience has included software, hardware and firmware and such exposure has enabled me to understand that the System Architect should likewise have similar exposure.

The System Architect should work on a project long before the development group is assembled. This would provided the necessary time in which to develop the system documents.

Now in some companies a Systems Engineer might perform part of the System Architect task. However, if their understanding is limited in certain fields they will not provide the necessary detail that is required by each discipline.

The System Architect is the designer.

This task is not appropriate to just any development engineer.

For most development engineers (whether of the hardware, software or firmware disciplines) simply wish to be given direct information as to what is to be implemented. They do not wish nor have the desire to be burdened with the research and development of these specifications.

Their motto is 'just tell me what you want'.

However, in many companies the System Engineer would stop far short of this step. They would define a System Specification which was a set of requirements but would not provide the detail desired by the other departments.

This now is a dangerous point in the project.

For it opens up the door for the development engineer to start assuming detail and this is where the implemented design now starts to diverge from the intended design.

The System Architect also has to be involved in the design reviews of every department to ensure that the implemented design meets the original intent. To fail to attend these reviews is to allow error to work its way into the project. This is often the case when the system architect is overworked. For to miss these reviews is to allow divergence. The System Architect must also verify that the work is all being implemented as required.

As stated earlier, if the project schedule is rewarding incomplete work then the development team designs have the potential of using the 70% rule and detail will be omitted in order to obtain reward. In many cases I have observed this happen but without the necessary authority my observations were simply cast aside.

This simply resulted in the wrong product being designed and built.

It also resulted in potential errors creeping into the design.

Yet, with most project managers, even though they might have the authority to prevent such errors, they generally do not have the required kind of knowledge. Such a person is usually catering to management and schedule and cannot go into any depth regarding project design issues.

The project system architect should be authorized accordingly.

Validation

When a design is being validated, the completed work is being checked against the product requirements document. This is a case of 'Does the finished product do what was stated as per the Product Requirements?'.

As you can see, this is determining if the overall product actually met the customer requests and is a product that the customer wants.

Verification

When a section of a design is being verified, a section of the work is being checked against the system requirements. If software is being verified then this verification if subject to the software system requirements.

Technical Data Sheets

Each hardware interface is generally accompanied by a data sheet. These sheets are often provided as PDF files and these should be stored in the Hardware Design Directory for the relevant PCBAs. This will permit the entire team access to the same detailed information for each hardware interface.

In other words, they should not be obtaining their own documentation from whatever source otherwise different team members might be designing to different requirements.

The technical lead for the hardware PCBA design should also keep notes of any technical issues associated with each interface. Such knowledge will assist all other team members and reduce wasted parallel effort.

Memory Map and Interfaces

As the Embedded Software Engineer progresses their way through the design they will build up a picture of the various interfaces and the associated memory map. This information should be placed into a memory map table and made accessible to the entire development team.

The memory map will identify the various system components that may be accessed over the address and data busses. The addresses of the various component registers should be defined as well as their bus widths (8 bit, 16 bit, etc.).

Email

Company emails should close with the senders name and position plus any other suitable contact information.

For security reasons all emails should utilize the following termination clause:

> This e-mail and any attachments may be confidential in nature, contain propriety information or may have legal privileges.
>
> To review, use, distribute, disclose and/or copy the contents of this email is not permitted except by or on behalf of the intended recipient.
>
> If this email message was sent to you in error, or you are not the intended recipient, please delete and destroy the email message contents and associated attachments and notify the sender by a return of email.

The Design Methodology

The Waterfall Method

Now there are many different types of methods for developing an embedded system. The standard old tried and tested method is the 'Waterfall' approach in which one task leads to the next like water flowing down a waterfall.

Another approach of recent years is the 'Agile' method. Both have their plusses and minuses.

The 'Waterfall Method' is the standard design for developing a product. Like any design method it has its good points and its bad. Many people frown upon this design methodology yet I have seen it work, and very effectively at that.

The people (generally higher management) that do not like this methodology are so inclined because it takes some time before you start to see results. Results being something that looks like the end-product which includes some software application operating on a hardware printed circuit board.

As far as they are concerned paper documentation doesn't really count. However, it is in this documentation that the true design resides and when implemented correctly the final coding and implementing effort will be minimal.

So the waterfall method can be cheaper if implemented correctly, however, it does take time and efforts to do the job right.

Now as far as the size of the development team is concerned and the number of people involved, this may affect several engineering departments or it might be as few as only one or two persons.

All the same, the following documentation steps should be produced as the design is developed (and you do require people who can clearly express their thoughts on paper).

Product Requirement Document (PRD)

The person assigned to this task has to interface with the customer. Now the customer may be internal (from another department) or external (someone outside the company). It does not matter. The task is still the same. You are required to spend time with the customer in order to determine what is required.

In some cases the customer might have already developed a set of customer requirements. This document specifies what they believe they want. Unfortunately not all customers are engineers and their requirements will have been written in the language most familiar to the customer.

In this it would still be beneficial to take the customer requirements and use them as a starting point in the design of the Product Requirement Document (PRD). This PRD would identify the customer's requirements in more detail and would be written in the language appropriate to both the customer and the engineer.

The end-result of this task is the Product Requirement Document.

System Specification

The Product Requirement Document is then taken and written as an engineering document applicable to the relevant engineering departments. This System Specification becomes the top level document as far as the engineering development teams are concerned.

This document specifies each system requirement. It identifies each requirement by means of a statement that includes the word 'shall'.

For example: 'The product shall include a real time clock with backup battery.'

The System Specification is sub-divided into various sections, one for each engineering department (as required)

Systems and Controls Specification
This document identifies the functional aspects of the embedded product.

Application Software Documentation
This documentation package provides detail regarding how the software was developed, built and installed in the product.

Application Software High Level Design
Application software HLD documents provide the following specific details:

Software System Architecture
This document would identify the choice of Operating System (if an OS was required), identify the major system components and each of the interfaces. Dataflow diagrams would be used to indicate how data flows through the system. Any system timing constraints would be identified and the manner in which they should be satisfied are presented.

Application Software Low Level Design
These documents provide additional in-depth details. It simply takes the Application Software High Level Design and starts to add more 'meat' to the overall framework.

For example:

Interface Operation
This document would present each interface and discuss its operation. How is the interface controlled, what Application Program Interface (API) function calls would be required, etc.

Interface protocol definitions
Such a document identifies the structure of the various protocol messages and the manner in which they are used.

Embedded Software Documentation

It should be remembered that the embedded software engineer is a person who works in the software / hardware domain. Such a person deals with the software and hardware engineers and the embedded engineer's task is to provide the software application engineer with an interface to the hardware that is being controlled.

The embedded software engineer can read and understand schematic diagrams and is familiar with all the interface components and how they are controlled. This may include a RTC (Real Time Clock), temperature sensors, flow sensors, pressure sensors, flash memory, digital amplifiers, serial EEPROMs, stepper motors, etc. Such components may be driven directly by cPLD or FPGAs or might even be controlled by the processor itself via parallel or serial interfaces. Documentation specific to this section would incorporate the various detailed Application Program Interfaces (APIs) that were developed for the application code to interface with specific hardware.

For example, if a Flash memory API was created then it would describe a set of interface functions that would be developed to allow the application code to write to Flash memory sectors without being aware of the physical operations required to implement such an action.

Embedded Software High Level Design

The embedded software engineer would write high level design documents that would describe the various hardware components that can be controlled.

If such components are controlled over a software / hardware communications system that involves a protocol, this protocol would be developed and provided to both the software and hardware developers for implementation. This document would provide a frame of reference, defining the various protocol messages right down to the lowest bit value. Each message parameter would be clearly identified such that software and hardware engineers fully understand the implication of each of the possible set values. This removes any form of ambiguity thereby allowing ease of installation by both departments.

Embedded Software Low Level Design

If a protocol document was implemented as a software/hardware interface, a low level design document would also be created to identify each data component and any required transfer algorithms to convert raw hardware values into engineering units. Such documentation is useful not just for the software application engineer and the hardware engineer but also for the verification, production test and manufacturing departments. This documentation provides these engineers with the necessary details for them to develop test software for verification and validation purposes. Such details were initially determined for use by the software application engineers. By collating this information into a document numerous other departments now have the relevant detail they require to complete their tasks in a more timely manner. To limit the information depth of the documentation is to simply throw away design information. It carries little weight to say that the information is in the code, that a person 'simply' has to read the code and reverse-engineer the design. This should not be the task of the validation engineer who may not have access to the application code, or if they do, does not have the time to plough their way through realm and realms of source code to find the correct line. Remember, if someone has to reverse-engineer your design in order to find the details they require to perform their work then there is a system design document missing (or not enough detail presented in the current documentation due to the 70% rule).

Hardware Documentation

The hardware engineer is usually tasked with creating a Printed Circuit Board Assembly (PCBA). This part is comprised of a Printed Circuit Board (PCB) consisting of one or more physical layers. When such a PCB has been populated with various components is then called a PCBA (Printed Circuit Board Assembly).

Hardware High Level Design

In order to create a Printed Circuit Board Assembly, the engineer first defines the board functionality along with any interfaces. This information is placed in the Hardware High Level Design document and will be used to create the schematic diagram.

The schematic diagram (possibly captured using a software package like Orcad) identifies the various board components, their interconnections and any physical interfaces. Once complete, the schematic will be used by a routing program to create a Printed Circuit Board (PCB) which involves one or more copper layers.

At this stage the schematic diagram should be converted into a PDF file which is then placed on the server for use by each project departments.

Hardware Low Level Design

The low level design documentation would include a detailed operation of the PCBA including any relevant initialization and timing information. Many of today's components are programmed in some manner. Such details are often determined by the hardware engineer. These may include LCD display programming registers and dynamic memory options, and such are based upon the specific timing crystals used on the board. This documented information can then be passed directly to the embedded engineer for the hardware engineer has the greatest and most accurate understanding of these system details. It this information is left undocumented then the other team members are forced to reverse-engineer the design and may not get the correct information. This simply leaves room for error. So if specific details have been determined, write them down for the benefit of the project. Also, the reasoning behind why specific options were chosen should also be documented. But remember, if you are driving the project with an aggressive schedule these are the very details that will be lost. If that is the case, multiple other department engineers will be forced to spend many days reverse-engineering the design for the one day that would have been used to document the design. In other words, the overall project timeline will suffer.

Firmware

When developing firmware, the engineer is providing low level software that will be placed into cPLD and FPGA devices.

A cPLD (Complex Programmable Logic Device) is a hardware component which may be programmed to utilize a number of internal logic circuits in order to provide interface registers (digital input/output registers, interrupt registers, I2C interfaces, etc.) to hardware control lines and circuits. The cPLD is a device that contains its own programming. It can be erased and reprogrammed. When power is applied to the device it will immediately start functioning. High risk functions (eg. interrupt processing) should use cPLD devices where required. This safety may not be provided with cPLD devices that implement a lower layer Flash memory that loads its programming.

An FPGA (Field Programmable Gaye Array) can be considered to be a cPLD but of greater complexity. The FPGA contains far more internal components and has greater functionality. The FPGA is programmed via an attached EEPROM device. On power up the FPGA loads its programming from this external EEPROM and once this action has successfully completed the FPGA will initialize and start operating. This implies that it will not be functional immediately upon power up and this has the potential of being a point of failure in high risk systems such as with medical products.

Firmware High Level Design (HLD)

The firmware high level design would incorporate documentation that defines the overall operation of these cPLD and FPGA devices.

Firmware Low Level Design (LLD)

The firmware low level design would take the firmware HLD documents and provide additional detail regarding the method of their implementation. This would also incorporate the cPLD and FPGA coding statements in languages such as VHDL and System Verilog. Just as when coding with any programming language, these designs should be clear and well commented (be gracious to the person assigned to maintain your code). A design document should also be associated with each firmware code base and it should identify the concepts behind the code development. Code design reviews should be held prior to each 'formal' release. This will assist in good quality code being provided to other departments. In the medical world it is a given that such a design has to be verified. Since such verification tests have to be developed they should then be created with each release and this would ensure that the firmware code is operational and therefore usable by the other departments. You can understand that this would help minimize the philosophy of some engineers who hand over an incomplete design just to 'meet' their schedule with the thought that whoever uses the code would find the bugs for them. This 'style' of engineering happens regularly and simply eats up the development time of whichever group is required to use this code (and the original engineer still has to fix their work). But this passing on of incomplete work is not just an issue with the firmware group. It can happen with every department.

When incomplete (or bug ridden) designs are simply thrown over the wall to the next department, the engineers destined to use such designs will find that their tasks (eg. software) does not work. They then have to write test code to determine where the problem lies. Is it with their developed software code or has the firmware design failed. In other words, they are writing the verification code that the initial firmware designer should have developed to verify their own design. This passing of the problem onto other people is often a safety mechanism utilized by the initial designer, brought into effect because of some 'aggressive schedule'.

Production Test

The end result of an embedded design is a product with a number of hardware components that generally contain multiple interfaces to the outside world. When such a product is mass produced, a means must be set in place to verify the operation of each of the manufactured component boards. This usually involves the development of one or more sets of test fixtures. The final component boards are then placed in these test fixture and the fixture simulates the external environment. Under such conditions the board will then execute a number of tests to verify operation.

The production test group needs access to the detailed design documentation from all the other development groups. Inadequate (or inaccurate) detail provided in this documentation simply implies that the production test phase of the design will take longer. I know this as fact since I have worked in all aspects of project design from initial development right through to production test and manufacturing.

As an example there was one time, shortly after starting at a new company, I counted at least thirteen people who went behind my back to speak to my project manager. They seemed somewhat taken by the amount of detail I was placing in my design documentation. They basically told my manager that they were pleased with this approach since now they didn't have to spend all their time reverse-engineering the design in order to find out how it worked prior to starting their own task. This is not rocket-science. Simply place detail in your documentation that you know others will need if you were them. So a good embedded engineer would have spent time developing test system and would understand this reasoning.

But if your engineers just want to develop and have had no experience in maintenance and test they will not understand this need and the overall project will be adversely affected. It is just a simple philosophy of placing yourself in the other person's shoes.

Verification

This is generally a term that applies to the development of medical products and basically ensures that specific sub-sections of a product are operating as expected.

When various parts of a product have been designed they are then verified to ensure they are functional. In order to achieve this a verification test document is produced. This document would identify which equipment would be used and the steps which would be implemented to prove success.

As far as software is concerned, a specific aspect of the overall program might by verified by means of one or more unit tests. This is a set of code tests that are used to determine the operational status of part of the application. For example, if a database application was developed, the unit test might initialized the database, create a number of table entries, execute every API function and ensure that the expected results are returned. This might be part of a test suite that would be executed periodically to determine that subsequent changes to the overall system did not have any adverse effect.

It should be noted that the person who executes a specific test is not the same person who developed that test.

Validation
This is also a medical term which basically applies to the tests that would be applied to the final product. The determination is being made as to whether the final product provides the functionality as specified in the Product Requirement Document. A validation test will be created for each and every system specification and the test execution results are used to prove that the correct product was designed as per the customer's requirements. It should be noted that the person who executes a specific test is not the same person who developed that test.

The Agile Method

Today much is made of the 'Agile' method. Like every development method, it too has its good points and its bad. Its concept is still very much like the Waterfall Method for it should still provide the same design documentation.

That step is not bypassed.

In fact, it probably will provide much more documentation for each step of the Waterfall Method will be executed but on a smaller scale. Unfortunately for many there is the desire to bypass the documentation step and simply code. This code will be successively modified, albeit in iterative steps, until it starts to model the customer's requirements. But there is now an inherent danger for as soon as management sees anything that resembles the customer's requirements they will say, "ship it!".

But in all of this, the software engineer has simply performed numerous code iterations until it now meets the user's functional requirements. Another way of saying this is that the code is now a 'hack'. a kluge of code which has been stuck together to give some form of functionality. Now you could call these code changes by some fancy name like 're-factorization' if you like, but it is still a hack and many proponents of this methodology are hackers and they are generally not known for documenting their work [for if they were to do so then it would be seen for what it is and who wants to own up to a design that is simply thrown together.]

No one wants to maintain such work (which is why these developers are always so very keen on wanting to get on to the next new project) so when the next new engineer arrives in the company that poor person is given the 're-factored code' to maintain. There is generally no up-to-date documentation to illustrate the design process.

Management has been fooled into thinking that the Agile Method is a faster design process and true enough, they may have a working prototype in a shorter time frame but there is a great risk in the design documentation being far from complete.

Comparison of Methods

With the Waterfall method the developers should have completed each step of the design as they progress their way through the method. This means that the Product Requirements have to be fully understood and specified. In other words you have to know what you are building. You have to understand your customer as well as their needs. This takes time and effort, and this can make the Agile method quite appealing. For with the minimal amount of effort you can go off into the development phase and start creating hardware and software based on a rudimentary and incomplete design. Agile is based upon numerous changes. Well, that will include numerous iterations of hardware PCBAs and the firmware/software that runs on these PCBAs. This is an iterative cost. With each iteration the software application will be changed to suit the changing requirements. We have this marvelous word called 're-factorization'. I'm sorry, that is just a nice word for 'a hack'. For in a standard development environment in which management is breathing down the engineering department's back, they will be wanting something to ship ASAP. They want to see cash inflow.

So Agile provides numerous iterations in order to bring the design closer to the customer's requirements. Each of these iterations cost development money (cost of developing, building and testing new PCBAs, writing/modifying test code, writing/modifying application code, etc.) and these costs tend to be forgotten for the Agile approach is based on an unknown number of iterations. The first iteration may seem cheap but each successive iteration requires every step of the design process to be re-evaluated and the documentation to be updated accordingly (I find it really hard to believe that these steps are being performed in adequate detail). With many companies, I see the end result being a set of outdated, inaccurate documents and a set of hacked code. You should realize that something is wrong with the product when any engineer tells you that the software code is the documentation. That should be a major warning sign. You see, there are times when code is developed in a specific manner for an important reason. If this is not adequately documented then the next code developer will rewrite it to suit their understanding. This action can easily break the code in other places, and in the case of a medical product, even bringing in patient risk. The design has to be fully understood and documented otherwise you might see your profits disappearing with that first law suit.

The Engineering Team

The people that design and develop products are the engineering team.

They can consist of one or more of the following:

- Systems Engineers (or System Architect)
- Application Software Engineers
- Embedded Software Engineers
- Hardware Engineers
- Firmware Engineers
- Mechanical Engineers
- Production Test Engineers
- The Historian (Project recorder and verifier)

Seeing the bigger picture

When I see a need I act upon it. If I am at home and I see a dirty dish in the sink I will wash it, or if there is a washed dish on the draining board I will dry it.

At work it is the same thing. If you are an embedded engineer you are involved with a multitude of other people and disciplines ranging from systems design through to hardware (and firmware) and on to software and production test. For to be a good embedded software engineer you need to appreciate and understand the work involved in all these departments; and over the years you will find that you have gained experience in each and every one. The embedded software engineer will have written systems design documents, developed hardware schematics, used Orcad, created printed circuit boards, written VHDL and made test benches for production test. So when the embedded software engineer deals with these different departments there is an understanding and when they see a need they act upon it for the benefit of the project. But such is not necessary 'seen' by management. One time myself and other senior engineers were 'let go' from one company (in a belated effort to save money) the comments from the hardware department I cannot repeat here but the production test manager stated that I was the only one they cared about. Why? Because I gave them the missing details in the design. I could see the 'bigger picture' and knew what they needed even though the other managers in the project were quite unaware (or perhaps, did know but were quite unconcerned since it wasn't their 'job'). Actually, when it come to product development it is everyone's job. For a well-rounded and balanced engineer (and manager) knows that the development effort involves the entire design team and not just their own development group. As to care for only your own development team is to be short-sighted. For if any part of the development effort fails then the entire product fails.

Systems Architect (Systems Engineer)

System engineers design the overall system concept. They will directly interact with the customer and develop a set of product requirements. These customer based requirements will be further refined to become system requirements that will then be routed to the applicable engineering departments associated with the manufacture of that part of the product.

The initial Product Requirements is a document that identifies specific customer needs that the company now has an obligation to meet. This Product Requirements document may be for an external customer or for the company's product range. In both cases the document is written in terms that the customer understands. It also uses the language of 'the customer'. Later the product will be validated against this set of customer requirements to ensure that the correct product was indeed manufactured as requested.

The System Architect then uses the Product Requirements Document to develop the System Requirements Document. The System Requirements is a document that identifies the specific engineering work that has to be implemented. This document is written in terms that are familiar to the relevant engineering department. It uses the language of the engineer.

These system documents provide additional technical detail that was not evident in the Product Requirements. Such information might include specific software and/or hardware and also the applicable international standards that are to be used. A certain amount of freedom is given to the engineering teams but there are times when a specific direction has to be enforced.

Application Software Engineers

The application engineer is involved with the development of the application code. This would often include the User Interface (also called the man-machine interface). This interface may operate utilizing an LCD touch screen, associated graphics along with a sound system.

The System Requirements document provides the application software engineer with the detailed instructions they require. Such information will identify key features of the user interface and the product functionality. From that, the application engineer can develop the full user interface, the graphic buttons, user interaction and specific operation of the device. A user's manual would be developed to direct the result of this work. The application software engineer would develop high and low level software design documents that identify the software implementation. This design is finally translated into programming code which is usually written in a high-level language (eg. C, C++).

Embedded Software Engineers

The Embedded Software Engineer must have extensive experience for they have to cover a number of different engineering disciplines. For the Embedded Software Engineer's work overlaps that of the system, applications, hardware and firmware engineering groups. The Embedded Software Engineer is responsible for developing the application program interfaces (API's) for each hardware section and to write (and test) the Device Driver code used to implement these API function calls. In order to create such code, the embedded software engineer has to have intimate knowledge of the physical device(s) being interfaced along with an understanding of the schematic drawings pertaining to the Printed Circuit Board Assemblies (PCBAs) used to physically interface to the device(s). This awareness would be close to the understanding obtained by the hardware engineer themselves. The embedded engineer would also be required to fully comprehend the best manner in which the device interface would be utilized by the software applications engineer and all the time ensuring that the design implementation fits within the System Requirement constraints.

Embedded engineers may also create system interface documents that are used by the firmware engineers to develop CPLD and FPGA firmware code.

But beware the following. Just because an embedded software engineer has the word 'software' in their title they are often lumped in with all the other software application engineers and judged by their criteria.

This is simply wrong.

I will give you an example. When working on a protocol interface design that involved a critical communication interface (all system data traveled over this backplane), my software manager (and others above him) were of the opinion that design work would occur and once completed would be finished. No additional effort would be involved. But the system design was in a state of flux. This changed the operation and design of the ten (plus) hardware PCBAs and the FPGAs that controlled them. My manager did not see the necessity to allow me to be constantly on top of these design changes and to be attending all the system and hardware design reviews and to permit me to constantly interface with the ten or more engineers responsible. So in my own time I continued to work on the protocol design and kept it up to date with every design change that occurred. What was the result? Because I kept the design current and up-to-date when the hardware group developed their firmware and the software group developed their application there were no major issues during the integration of each code release. But my work was unseen and not understood by senior management. They did not appreciate the effort I went through to make this all work smoothly. In the words of others I was underappreciated.

My managers did not appreciate my efforts. But my fellow engineers did see their value. One even recognized that my work held the entire system together.

The hardware and systems engineers along with the production test and validation and verification engineers all used my documentation and it made their life easier. Why? Because now they did not have to reverse-engineer the system to find out how it worked prior to starting their own work.

So an embedded software engineer should NEVER be made part of the software group and directed by a 'software manager' because such a manager neither understands nor appreciates them. The embedded engineer should be in their own group held between systems, software and hardware for they interface with all three departments on an equal footing. They are not software application engineers and should never be treated as such.

Hardware Engineers

The Hardware Engineer takes a hardware concept and creates a schematic diagram that identifies all the electronic components and the manner in which they are interconnected. The Embedded Engineer should be included in such design reviews. This schematic diagram that is developed is then translated into a physical multi-layer Printed Circuit Board (PCB – the 'empty' board) upon which the electronic components will later be soldered. The final board which includes all the relevant soldered electronic components is known as the PCBA (Printed Circuit Board Assembly).

Once the hardware engineer has received the PCBA back from manufacturing, the board must then be tested. If the board contains any CPLD or FPGA devices then the firmware engineer supplies test code to ensure basic device operation. If the board contains one or more processor devices then the embedded engineer is tasked with board 'bring-up'. What this implies is that the embedded engineer is provided with a hardware tested PCBA board and the engineer develops test code that verifies the basic operation of the board interfaces (eg. memory, flash, gpio, etc.).

Firmware Engineers

The Firmware engineer develops code that executes on CPLD and FPGA devices. The CPLD device is a Complex Programmable Logic Device and is comprised of an internal structure of logic gates. The FPGA (Field Programmable Gate Array) is similar in nature but of higher size and complexity.

Both CPLD and FPGA devices are programmed using engineering descriptive languages (eg. VHDL, System Verilog). These languages allows the creation of clock signals, state machines, interface signals (eg. SPI and I^2C) and such to interact with the surrounding hardware. By using such devices, high frequency intensive operations can now be off-loaded from the processor or microcontroller. Having the CPLD and/or FPGA perform this work thereby allows the processor or microcontroller to have additional time in order to satisfy the needs of the application tasks without excessive undue interruptions for it is wasteful to have a processor driven Operating System being interrupted on a bit or byte basis.

Mechanical Engineers

The Mechanical Engineer is usually not considered as being part of the electronic development team. So much emphasis is placed upon the software and the hardware that it is often forgotten that the end result of their efforts has to be placed into some form of container, whether hand-held or free-standing. If the product utilizes an LCD display / touch panel then such a container must provide provision for such a device to be installed.

Production Test Engineers

The Production Test Engineer looks at the design from a different perspective. Their task is to ensure that the operation of a finished manufactured product can be verified. This is a task that is performed immediately after manufacture and before the product is sent out for delivery. This engineering task may be sub-divided down such that individual boards are verified for operation prior to the testing of the final product. To verify an individual board they will develop test hardware and associated test software in order to provide the PCBA board with its operational environment. This would allow the injection of test signals into the PCBA board and the obtaining of processed data such that board operation can be verified. Providing the test group with detailed documentation will allow them to more efficiently perform their tasks. The test hardware and software would be designed to allow the detection of failed product board components and possibly provide repair suggestions.

The Historian

Now this is a position that many people forget. In some cases they might even get the project manager to perform this task. To tell the truth, most of the project managers I have worked with have not had a good understanding of the product and really do not understand specific details. You can see this quite clearly when an engineer starts to describe some problem and the manager simply blocks the discussion. Most managers generally do not understand the issues and really do not want to know the details. They just want to know when it will be finished. Their position on product development is to design and develop product for the minimum of cost.

This reminds me of a scene I saw in a movie some years back. The space shuttle was ascending and one astronaut asked his fellow astronaut regarding how he felt about going into space on a vehicle that was built by the lowest bidder. Well, you know the saying. You only get what you pay for. So if you are going to be financially tight (which also corresponds to the amount of development time given to engineer the product) then the product might be delivered on time and at cost but it will be poorly designed and hard to maintain. It is a case of what you gain on the roundabouts you lose on the swings.

A good manager will realize that his job is to protect his team, understand their needs and clear the way for them to work as effectively as possible. That means he/she has to clearly understand their tasks and not simply put down a two months block on the schedule called 'software development' (a number which in most cases was simply pulled out of the air).

So back to the task of the historian.

The historian is a technical writer of the highest level. One might even state that the person is validating the entire design. The system architect is concerned with implementing the design of the product whereas the historian is validating that the design is true and properly documented. The Historian has a wide and detailed technical background and is a person who understands all aspects of the project development (eg. hardware, firmware, embedded and application software).

This person attends all the design review and ensures a correct final product by constantly reviewing the documented design as it holds against the system specification.

Any detected errors are immediately corrected.

The historian is like a watchdog.

The historian reviews everything in an attempt to look for discrepancies.

For example, If the hardware schematics use inconsistent control names as can occur when two different hardware engineers work on their own PCBAs, the historian requests the engineers to update the schematics and all relevant documentation. [These issues can be resolved earlier by the use of a Data Dictionary.] What normally happens is that the different name are retained and the potential for error has been increased.

The historian keeps up-to-date with the design of the product and periodically reviews all system, application software, embedded software, firmware, hardware documentation.

Any documentation errors are found and corrected.

It should be noted that as a project progresses the initial High and Low Level Design documents can quickly get out-of-date. The project timescale allocates time to develop such documentation but at the end of a product few consider the need to review and update these documents. Do not forget that the production test department and the manufacturing group are going to heavily depend on these documents. Any resultant errors will result in expensive maintenance and manufacturing costs so the money you might think you are 'saving' will quickly be lost.

The historian will help alleviate such problems.

Product Development

This section will discuss the Product Development process. This process will be represented by the product phase/task graphic and identifies the work that is to be performed during each phase of the project.

Product Development is implemented by the following phases:

- Design of the product
- Development of the product
- Testing of the finished design
- Mass production of the product

These four phases of product development will be represented graphically by the icons (Design, Develop, Test and Build). The three arrows that separate each icon identify the information to be transferred from one phase to the next.

Product Design

The Product Design phase identifies all the tasks associated with the design of the product (eg. Product Requirements).

Product Development

The Product Development phase identifies all the tasks to be performed during the development of the product (eg. low level documentation, code, etc.).

Product Test

The Product Test phase identifies all the tasks associated with the testing of the final product (eg Verification and Validation).

Product Build

The Product Build phase identifies tasks associated with the mass production of the product (with the completed design being placed in the Design History file).

Each Product Development phase has an associated action task type as shown:

- Systems
- Software
- Embedded
- Firmware
- Hardware

These action task types are displayed under the phase icon as shown below:

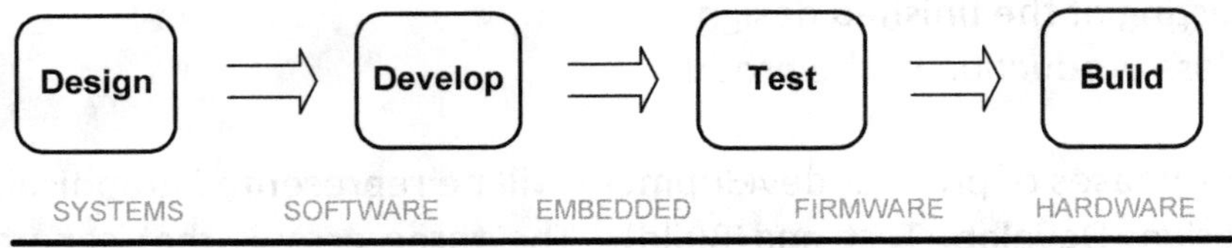

An action task type for a specific product development phase will be identified by the product phase being highlighted and the action task type shown in bold.

For instance, a Design phase Systems task is identified by the following graphic which would be located at the top of the relevant page:

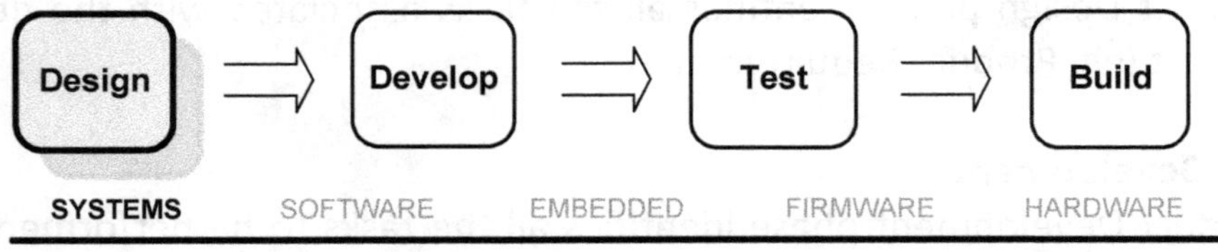

Likewise, a Test phase Software task would be identified by this graphic:

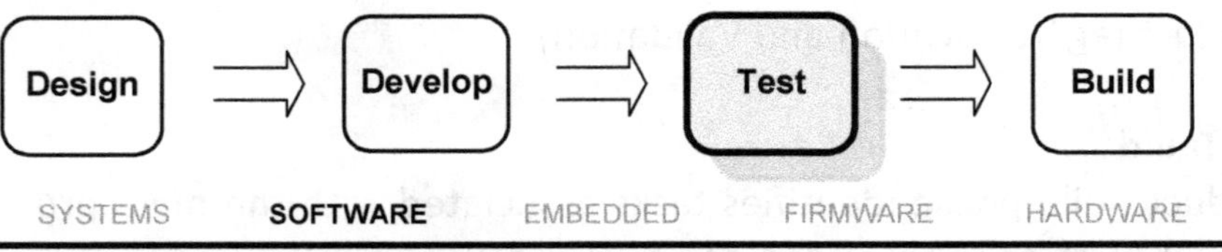

Systems Tasks
The Systems Task type identifies the work to be implemented by the Systems group; this work would include:

- Product Requirements, Systems Specifications
- Operator's Manual, Repair Manual

Software Tasks
The Software Task type identifies the work to be implemented by the Application Software group; this work would include:

- Software Design Specification
- Software Code Development & Test

Embedded Tasks
The Embedded Task type identifies the work to be implemented by the Embedded Software group (a group that acts as the interface between the Software and Hardware environments); this work would include:

- Review of Software Applications and Hardware Interfaces
- Interface Specifications (CPLD, FPGA, Protocols)
- Driver Code Development & Test

Firmware Tasks
The Firmware Task type identifies work to be implemented by the Firmware group; this work would include:

- Firmware Design Specifications
- CPLD and FPGA Code Development & Test

Hardware Tasks
The Hardware Task type identifies work to be implemented by the Hardware Engineers; this work would include:

- Hardware Design Specifications
- PCBA Design, Schematic Capture, PCBA Build and Test

Design Reviews

When it comes to design reviews the number of people attending such meetings should be carefully considered. It has been my experience that the people in the know are those who are directly involved with the development of the product. These people understand exactly what should be done and have a much better idea than most regarding how much time it should take to complete. The people higher up the chain of command are more alienated from the design and although might understand the generic concepts they do not necessary comprehend the specifics. Because of such, they are more difficult to get to agree on explicit details and as such are more hesitant in signing off on the review document.

That being the case, there should generally only be two or three people attending the review. This will also permit the review to proceed in a timely manner.

Everyone attending the design review should have done their homework. They should be familiar with the project and have thoroughly read the document. It should not be a case of going through every word of every paragraph of the document simply because a large fraction of those present are seeing the text for the first time.

This is also why the review audience is kept at a minimum.

The most important person who should be in attendance is the System Architect. It is this person who has the most complete understanding of the project and is the one who is guiding the team to the final destination. There are many ways to accomplish the project goals and much time can be wasted by those who want to have a say but are not directly involved in the actual development.

Meeting Reports

Your company philosophy should state that every meeting will be followed by a meeting report which will be distributed to all parties concerned. This can be in the form of an email which identifies those requested, those who attended, the main points discussed and the conclusions.

The reason for this might seem strange. It is to re-establish the points discussed and the agreements reached. Even though those in attendance might be in full agreement, it is amazing how different people will take different thoughts and notions away from such meetings.

People have their own unique outlook on the world. This is very much based upon their life experiences. Some of us come from different countries and for many of them English is a second language. However, it should be noted, that even if English is a first language, there are still nuances between words. The same word used by different people can imply different levels or conditions and because of such each meeting attendee will take from the meeting the aspects which they wanted. Whether it was agreed upon or not.

So, to save confusion and later disagreement, it is a most wise action to issue a meeting report that identifies the points discussed and the conclusions met.

The Meeting report format:

1. Meeting title
2. People requested
3. People attended
4. Main points discussed
5. Conclusions

In the case of medical product development it is necessary to store such meeting notes to prove to the FDA that the design was implemented correctly, however, this would be a good design philosophy for any company.

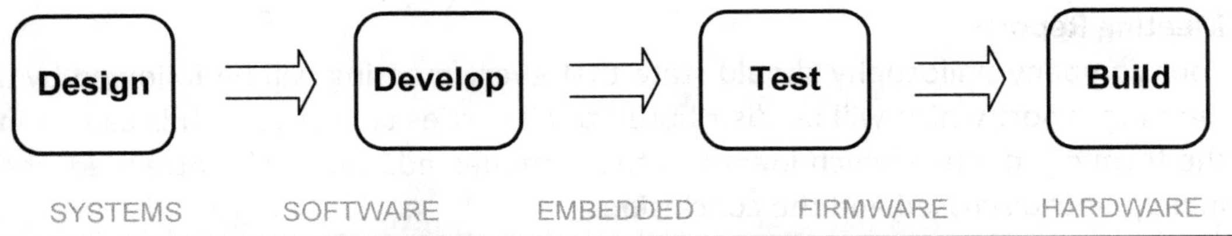

Project Initiation

Project Initiation occurs after:

- The customer requirements have been reviewed and a tender has been accepted; or
- An in-house development project has been reviewed and approved.

It is then when the project can proceed with the development of a schedule and a determination of the required staffing.

Schedule

It is very important to understand the true concept of a schedule. It is to identify a path to an achievable target. It must consist of realistic goals and objectives that can be strived for, but are not so far out of reach that are deemed unobtainable.

The System Architect will maintain two schedules.

The schedule presented to the development engineers will identify the tasks to be performed and the relationship of which tasks must be completed prior to the starting of dependant tasks. This schedule will identify milestones but will not identify due dates. [When engineers see due dates they can lose heart and work throughput drops. It is the task of the System Architect to keep the team focused and the schedule on track.]

The second schedule will include the due dates and this schedule will be used to monitor and manage the overall project progress.

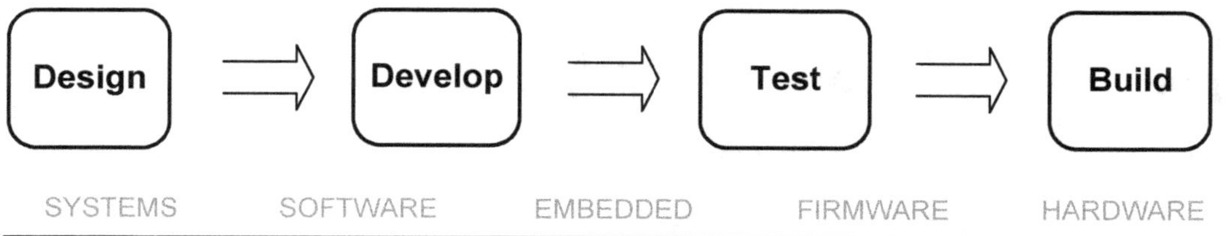

Staffing

Once a schedule has been created and some initial development times have been assigned, it may be used to provide a measure of understanding regarding the types of people (and the number) required to adequately staff the project.

It is understood that it takes several months to locate and select specific individuals for the development staff. By keeping the projects small the development staff can consist more of contractors than permanent employees.

If contractors are to be used, the following understanding should be noted:

The contract person does not require to understand the entire project but they do require specific and adequate work instructions. Providing a verbal 'statement of work' is totally unsatisfactory and will result in undetermined work being produced.

The development staff should only be assigned for the work at hand.

The initial staffing outlay would be for the systems design. This team is required to provide the completed understanding of the project prior to the developers being brought on board.

Once the system design nears completion, additional staff should be identified and brought in as the necessity arises. This is an ongoing, continual process and should also interact with the mentoring concept. When the need arises the procedure is to promote from within. This infers that such candidates should be recognized and be in training.

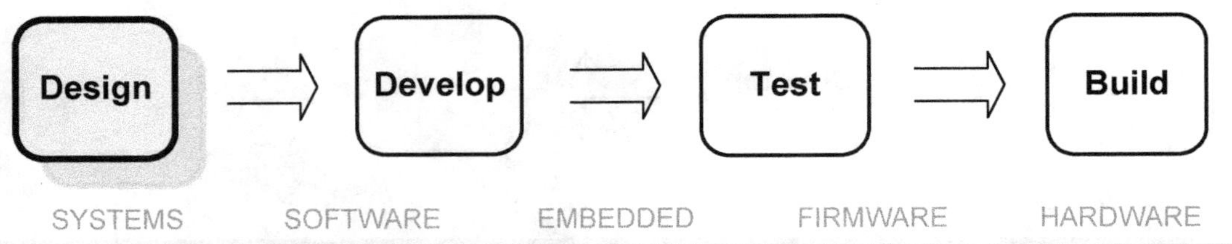

Design

The Design phase of the project affects all project team participants as the design effort flows from one group to another.

The work involved during the design stage is mostly paperwork.

The people who develop the product should have excellent writing skills. This skill set is not just for writing documentation for it should be noted that even in firmware VHDL and program code there are areas in which the documentation skill set is required.

If you have to read and maintain code that was written by another engineer and the descriptive text is poor (or non-existent) then you will fully realize the need for this skill. It is strange but many people who are expert in the field of talking do not always express themselves well with the written word. The opposite is also true. A person who has mastered the art of writing does not necessary speak well in front of others. This is just part of the deciding factors that must be determined when selecting the team. For it is poor judgment to utilize an expert coder whose resultant work can only be understood by a select few. This person's output will be difficult to maintain and even though you might get product quickly your maintenance costs (and the excess time others will spend in deciphering such work) will quickly eradicate your initial savings.

In this regard the System Architect must review the manner people from every department interface with each other (and because of such, should also be involved in the hiring process). To simply satisfy the need of one department can bring untold expense to all the others.

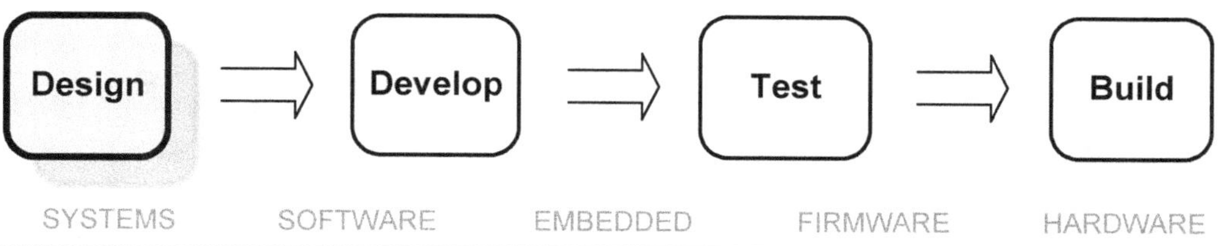

Project Directory Structure

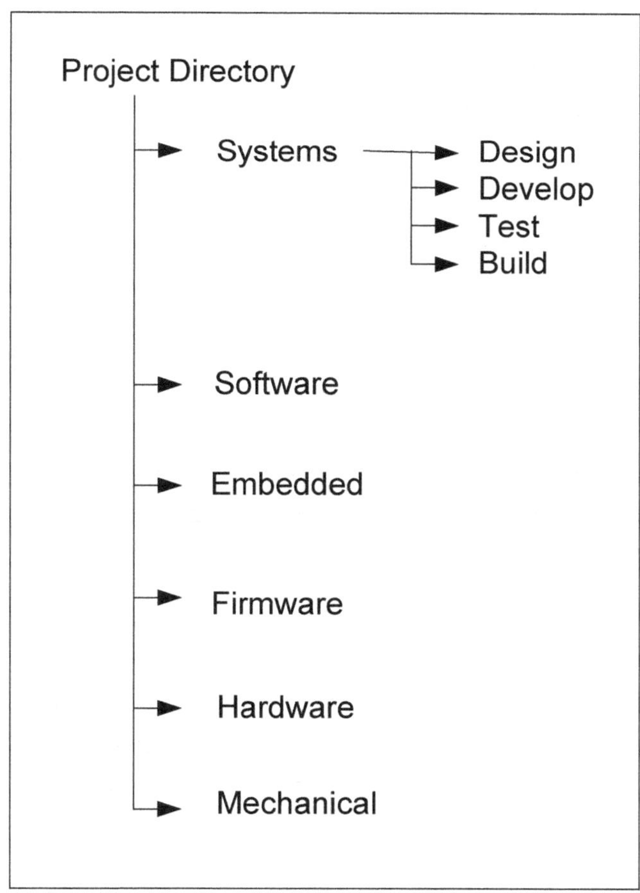

The above diagram is an example of a project directory. The Design, Develop, Test and Build sub-directories should also exist under the Software, Embedded, Firmware, Hardware and Mechanical directories.

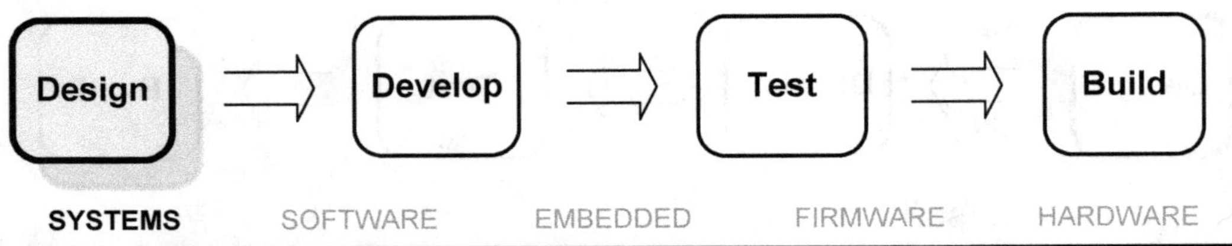

Systems

The Systems Design involves the following tasks:

- Writing the System Requirements, and then
- Developing the System Specifications

System Requirements

The act of generating System Requirements can be seen as being a very 'dry' task. But it really does not have to be such. For this is where the engineer can meet with the customer and find out knowledge of how the product is to interact with the real world. Determining such interaction can be interesting from the perspective of the involved physical interaction.

System Requirements are the instructions that state the purpose of the product. They identify what the product should do. They are statements that define each unique feature of the product, written in the language of the developer.

Initially, when starting a product, you might be given a document written by the customer themselves or by the marketing department of your company. This, of course, has been written in the language that the customer is most familiar and can be quite different to that of the developer. When working on smallish projects and having been faced with such documentation, the first task I would start would be to convert the customer's requirements into the developer's language because a single customer requirement could result in many interacting system requirements and by providing a System Requirements Document I was thereby ensuring that no customer requirement would be missed.

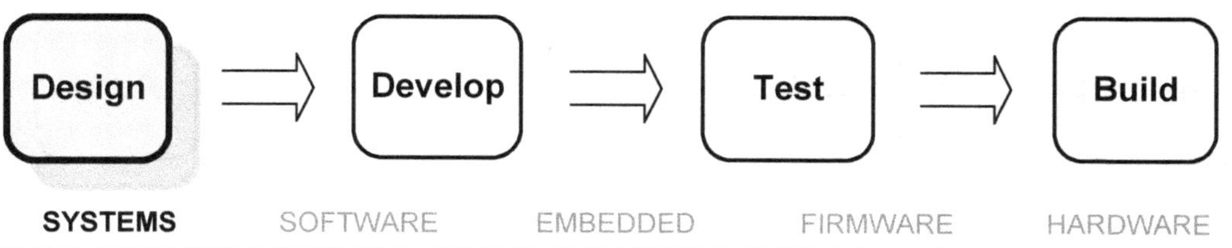

In companies that develop in-house projects in which they are their own customers, they can go straight to developing a System Requirement document. Having a marketing document and a systems requirement document that are somewhat identical simply wastes development time in maintaining two sets of very similar documentation.

When creating a set of system requirements the people involved should be very knowledgeable regarding the required product. They should spend time with the customer and know their requirements intimately for it is of no avail to create an incredible product if it does not meet customer requirements. It should also be noted with larger projects that may take several years to complete, that the customer requirements may vary with market trends of usage. In like manner system requirements may also change over time with some being dropped, others amended and a few new requirements being added.

This has to happen and should be expected.

Every system requirement is identified by a statement that uses the word 'shall' and is as shown in this following example.

> The product shall provide a calendar clock.

Having had experience in the Medical Industry I have been exposed to people who worked in the Verification and Validation department. In fact they sat in close proximity and I became very much aware of their abilities and of their requirements. Such people were tasked with verifying that specific lower level system specifications were correctly implemented and of validating that the overall design met the customer requirements. But I also realized that although they are technically astute, they were not necessary engineers.

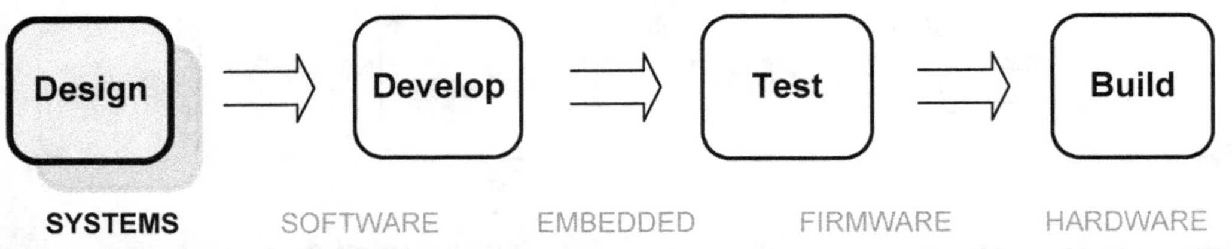

Now all developed projects in all industries go through the same types of tests even though there might not be a separate departments assigned to this task. For the final product must be what the customer requested and it must operate as per the system design.

The medical field does this check is a more formal manner for the output of each of these tests become a legal document which has to hold up under a court of law. A patient may be injured and the company taken to court.

So the System Requirement statement should be short and most importantly easy to validate or verify.

Although the above statement regarding the calendar clock looks clean it is not so easy to check for it brings up a number of questions, some of which are as follows:

1. Does the calendar clock use Days/Months/Years?
2. What is the exact clock format?
3. Does it use Julian Days?
4. Does it cater for leap years?
5. Are years 4 digits or 2 digits with a possible offset?
6. How accurate is the clock?
7. How is the clock initialized?
8. Is the clock maintained when the product is powered down?

So, when writing system specifications, although the author is attempting to leave flexibility with regard to implementation, attention should be paid as to how this requirement should be verified or validated. How would a person who may have less technical experience proceed to test this requirement.

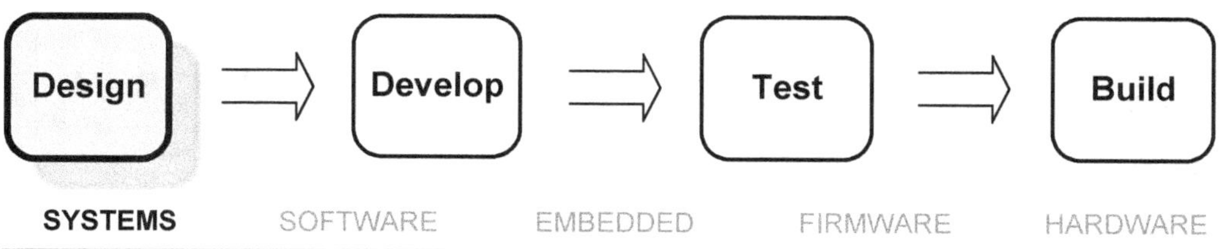

Always remember, as far as the medical profession is required, you verify a lower level system component of a design and you validate the overall design against customer expectation.

A component is verified against a lower level system requirement (eg. a hardware or software system requirement) and the finished product is validated against the overall Product Requirement Specification (or highest level System Specification). The verification of a system requirement might be achieved by means of a test or could even be by documentation, for example a code review.

When developing the requirement the statement should be short and to the point. The word "shall" (a word that is used to identify all requirements) should appear near to the start of the sentence. This makes the statement more readable with the subject being easily identifiable.

With regard to reviewing the above System Requirement for the calendar clock, a more suitable statement might be as follows.

A calendar clock shall be provided with the following features:

1. Provide a date using the dd/mm/yyyy numeric format (eg. 05/12/2013) and to cater for leap years.
2. Provide time using the hh:mm:ss numeric 24 hour format (eg. 17:56:04) .
3. Has the ability to maintain time during power down conditions.
4. Provide an accuracy of 1 second drift in a 30 day period.

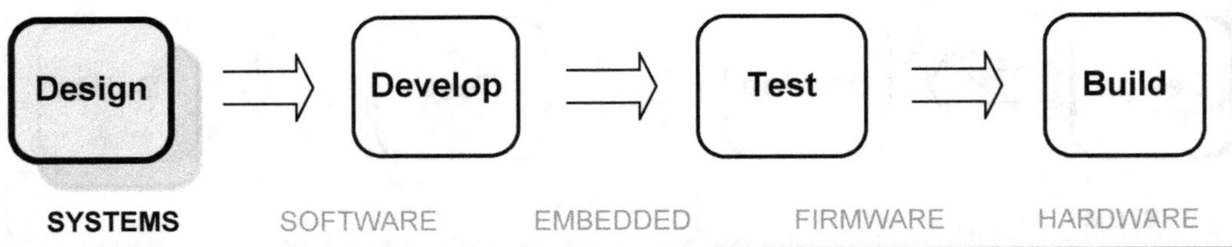

The people tasked with Verification and Validation may not necessary be engineers who have attained the standard associated with the developer who implemented the required feature. That, however, should not limit the person in testing if the feature has been correctly implemented.

In this regard, the person writing the System Specification, by having an intimate understanding of the product and being well knowledgeable of the various departments involved in developing the product, is also the most suitable person to define exactly how each System Specification requirement should be tested.

It really makes no sense to place this task on the verification and validation team for they do not have this level of in-depth knowledge. When such a task is placed upon V&V team members it simply wastes time for they are now tasked with attempting to determine how the requirement was implemented. They were not initially involved in this development process and are given the unenviable task of reverse-engineering the requirement.

The most suitable and easiest of solutions is to have the systems engineer who created the System Requirement identify how the statement is to be tested. This is the quickest and most accurate of solutions. The Verification and Validation engineer can then specify the complete test description to be used.

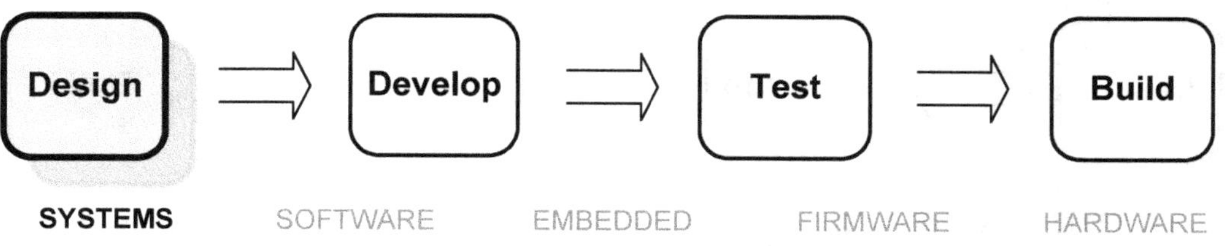

System Specification

The System Specification differs from the System Requirements in that further engineering details are provided for each of the relevant development teams (eg. software, hardware, etc.).

Fault Analysis

The Fault Analysis report identifies all the single-point failure conditions that might occur within the product are identified and the means whereby they can all be mitigated. It should be noted that compliance testing can be most severe. The authorized tester can perform actions such as the baring of a live wire and if such has enough freedom of movement the tester will short it across whatever component might be reached. This might seem like an absurd test but they have the full right to perform such for it lies fully in the realm of possibility that the wire insulation might have been manufactured with a deformity allowing such a electrical short condition to occur. So what happens under these conditions. Does the product go into meltdown and burn someone's house to the ground or has it been designed such that it recognizes such a fault condition and mitigates such an action by the blowing of a fuse. The same analysis should be implemented in software when regarding error conditions. Does the product attempt to retry and overcome such issues or does it just give up and crash. The development team must perform due diligence when it comes to product operation. In some cases lives may be at stake.

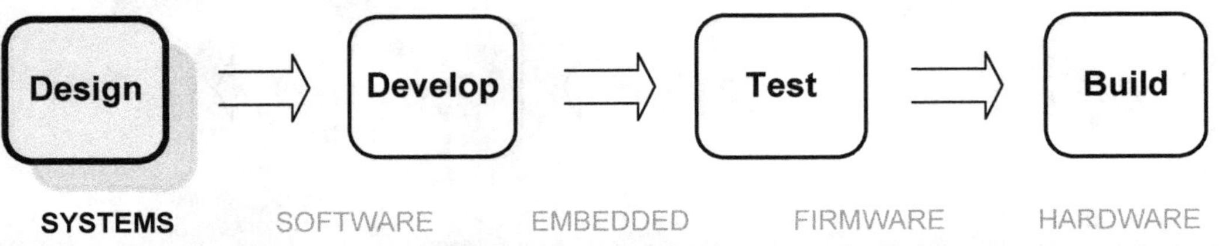

Data Dictionary

Now the concept of the data dictionary is not new. It has been around for many years. The purpose of the Data Dictionary is to document all the different system parameters (ie. sensors, controls, etc.). By providing these definitions there will then be consistency across all the various development teams since they will be utilizing the same name definitions and will have the same understanding.

For each parameter, the Data Dictionary will define as a minimum:

1. The full parameter name
2. An abbreviated parameter name
3. The parameter value type (eg. boolean, signed or unsigned integer and integer size (8 bit, 16 bit, 32 bit, etc.), floating point size (32 bit, 64 bit))
4. The parameter value range (eg. for integer16 [0..255])

When the concept of the Data Dictionary is ignored, each department tends to create their own non-consistent data names and this can provide much ambiguity when trying to tie a hardware schematic name with the software or system name. Such confusion can only lead to catastrophic error especially when associated with alarm signals or controls that are not validated and tested on a regular basic.

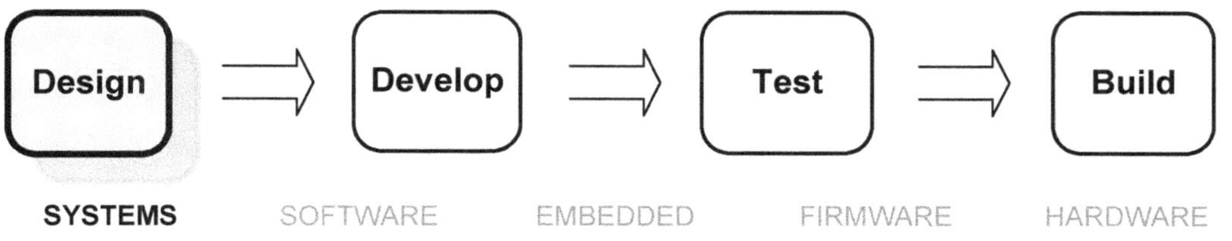

User's Manual

The User's Manual describes the operation of the product. This is an area of great concern for it is most visible to the customer and to the development team. People tend to forget this and only write this document towards the end of product development. This implies that the development team were designing without any true understanding of the final product. Just seeing what comes out of the design and writing the user's manual at that point is somewhat futile. The majority of the development team have been designing in the dark.

It is like the design of a motor vehicle. It may have the best engine in the world but if the external bodywork is not appealing then few will purchase the product. They want to know if it is easy to use. This is also the case with embedded software products.

I worked on one product in which I had limited development time. I could simply throw some code together to get something to work or I could design the product properly. The product provided the user with a keypad and a small LCD display. Nothing had been defined. So I defined the keypad buttons (symbols and text labels) and using that I created a user manual that defined each and every operation of these keys along with the information that would be displayed on the LCD screen. When this document was completed (it took a couple of months during which not one line of code was written) I then had it reviewed and now I had a complete specification regarding how the product would function. Sure there were some minor changes as we progressed into the implementation stage but the major details were all defined and when it came time to code the design it was a simple matter of translation. The operational definition was in the User's Manual. This was then translated into the required functional steps and the code was then written around these. It was not a case of trying to design while writing code.

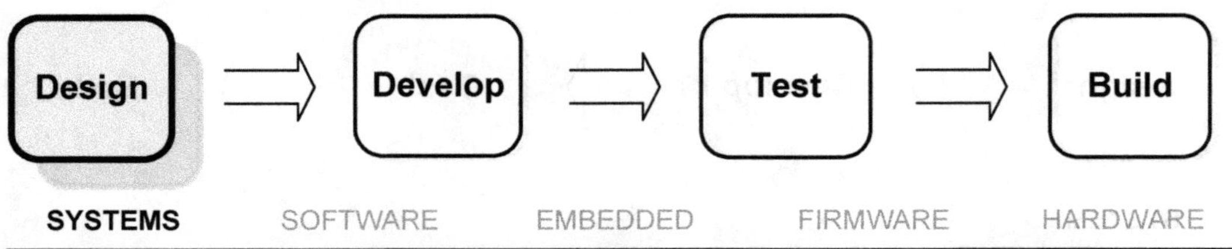

To design while writing code is to hack. It is an attempt to hit a moving target. This is one of the reasons why some cannot get the Waterfall method to work successfully. You simply cannot build a good product if you don't know what you are building.

So when you leave the design of the User Interface to the final stage of product development you are basically having each member of your engineering team attempt to develop the product in the dark. They will implement the design as each of them sees fit. This is why so many 'Waterfall' products fail to meet expectations.

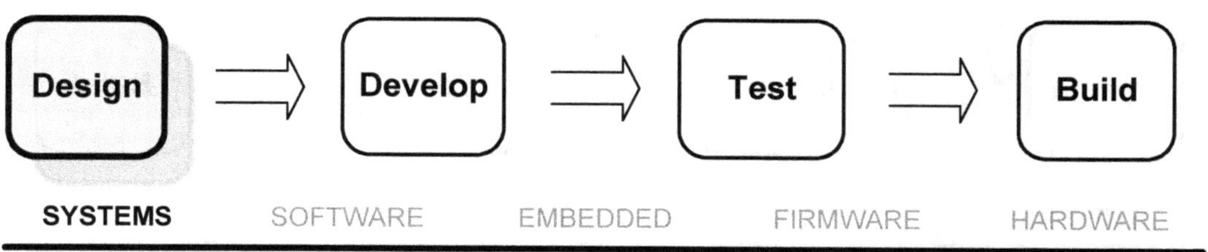

[This page intentionally left blank]

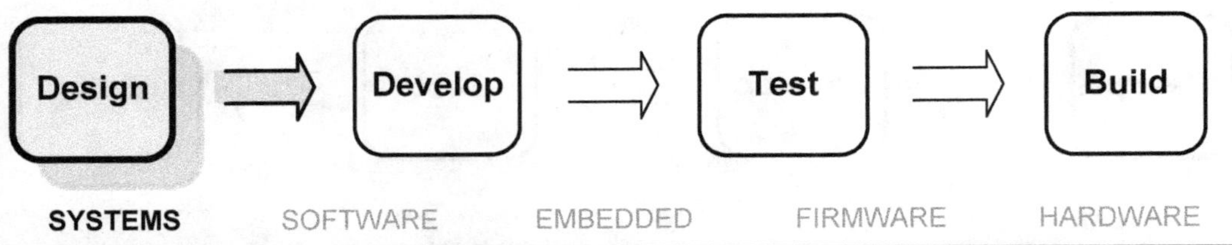

Design Systems Outputs

The Design System Outputs is the information that is required in order to permit the design process to effectively proceed to the other engineering fields. Failure to provide well defined, clear and unambiguous systems documentation will cause wasted engineering time that will result in budget over-runs.

The Design Systems Outputs include the following documents:

Product Requirements Document

Review:	Customer requirements identified. Each requirement has validation test.
Presenter:	System Architect
Reviewers:	Senior Software Application Engineer Senior Embedded Software Engineer Senior Hardware Engineer

System Requirements Document

Review:	Customer requirements in engineering terms. Each requirement has verification test.
Presenter:	System Architect
Reviewers:	Senior Software Application Engineer Senior Embedded Software Engineer Senior Hardware Engineer

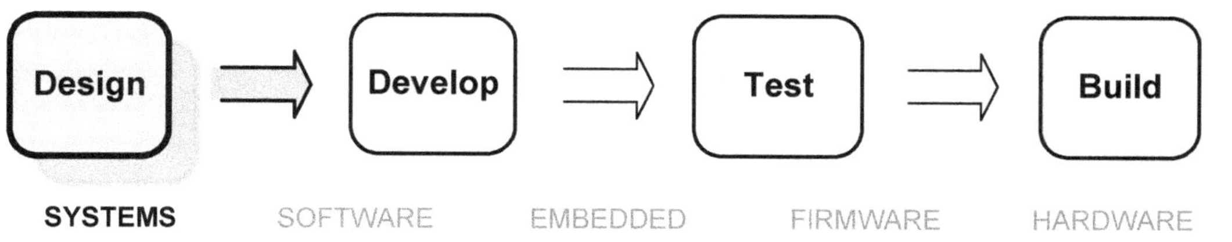

Operators Manual (Living Document)

Review: Define user product operation.

Presenter: System Architect

Reviewers: Senior Software Applications Engineer
Senior Hardware Engineer

Data Dictionary (Living Document)

Review: Identify control signals and their purpose.

Presenter: System Architect

Reviewers: Senior Embedded Software Engineer
Senior Hardware Engineer

Fault Analysis Document (Living Document)

Review: Identify single point failures.
Specify concern and mitigation.

Presenter: System Architect

Reviewers: Senior Software Application Engineer
Senior Embedded Software Engineer
Senior Hardware Engineer

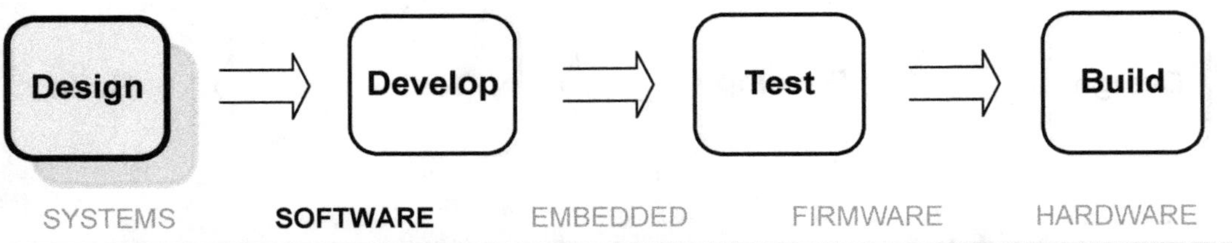

Software

Prior to starting the software design, the development engineers should fully understand all the relevant system design documents.

Since the software development team is generally responsible for implementing the user interface they should fully understand the intended operation of the product. If this device is an extension to the company's product range, the development team should be trained such that they fully comprehend the operation of these products and the intended enhancements. In the case of sophisticated medical products and the like, this training should be quite extensive, even to the point of gaining the level of understanding associated with the actual operators. This will allow the development engineers to identify erroneous and dangerous error conditions as the project design proceeds. It makes no sense to keep engineers ignorant of such matters.

Software System Requirements

The System requirements document contains information pertaining to the complete system. This involves detail for all engineering departments. The Software Systems Requirements document uses the System Document as its source. The relevant software systems requirements are then extracted and during this process more detail is added. This detail elaborates the actual requirement as well as proceeding to state the manner in which the requirement will be verified. In larger companies, (and generally with the development of larger projects), it is the task of the Verification and Validation department to develop tests to ensure that all the requirements have been fully implemented. Such team members do not have extensive software training and because of this will not have the background to develop such detailed and explicit tests.

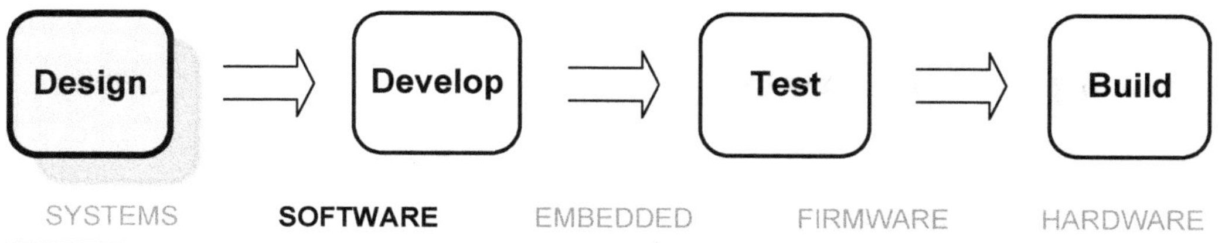

The senior software engineer who is creating the Software Requirements document does have this knowledge and should be the person who also describes these tests. By including both the requirement and the verification / validation tests, you are also ensuring that the departments that use the Software System Requirements document have all the information they need to perform their task. This will also ensure that any future requests for additional information from such departments will be minimal.

Software Architecture Document

This is a high level document and it takes the System Specification as its input and starts to lay out the top level software design plan. It should be noted that such detail is required prior to the involvement of the remaining groups. You cannot start developing hardware for a product if the software architecture is unknown.

The System Specification document would have provided instruction as to the products capabilities. From such requirements, the software architect will take these details and start to build the initial system concept. A good starting point is to lay out the various external interfaces (eg. user interface, communication interfaces (eg. RS232, Ethernet, USB, etc.)). From this it is then important to see how data flows through the system and a Data Flow Diagram would normally be created. Such diagrams are simplistic in nature (easy to understand) and involve three main elements (an external entity, a process and a data storage area). These elements are used to identify each interface, the process that accesses the interface and the location where the interface data is stored. This permits the architect to identify the external interfaces and the types of processes which are involved in processing the data as it is transferred throughout the system.

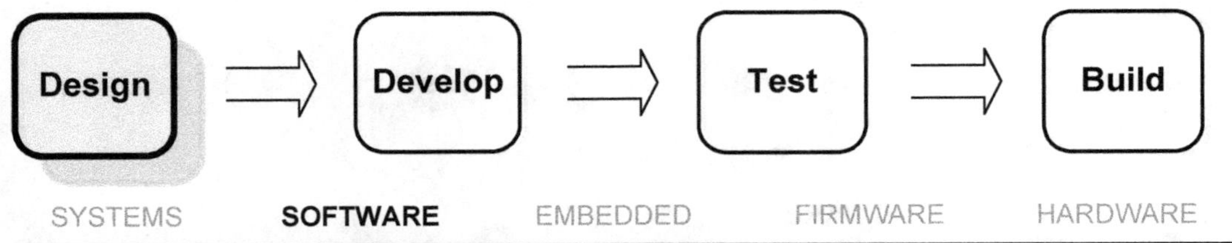

The following illustration is an example of a Data Flow Diagram:

Front Panel Keys
Data I/O Store
User Interface
LCD Display Panel LEDs
Data I/O Store
BIT Results
Mode
Background Diagnostics
Process A Task
Process B Task
Output Task
Sync1
Sync2
Data I/O Store (Including Front Panel Keys, LCD, LEDs), Analog I/O, Processed Results, Status Logs, etc.
Data I/O
Test Mode
Automatic Testing
LCD Display Panel LEDs
Digital I/O
Analog I/O
Stepper Motors
Test Data

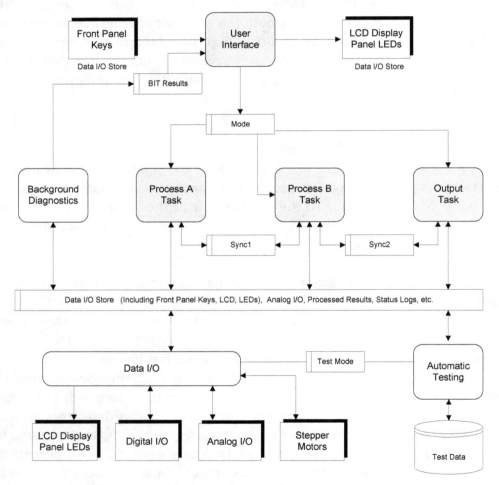

Process Control Instrument
Data Flow Diagram

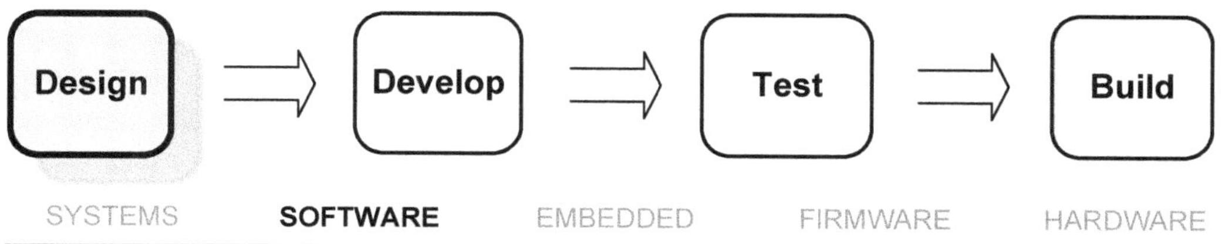

This DFD presents a number of different tasks (or processes). Tasks process data brought in from external entities (like a keyboard or serial interface). The processed data is then placed in some memory location (ie. a data store) for some other task to process. By this manner data can be clearly identified as it comes in from the outside world, is processed and finally leaves the system.

During this process the system complexity is being analyzed. If the complexity is low the design might be implemented with microcontrollers and state machines. This would keep costs down since no operating system need be included. On the other hand, if the user interface is extensive and there are a large number of concurrent processes in effect then an operating system would definitely be required. Under such conditions the type of product being developed would now direct your choice of operating system and processor hardware.

For instance, high risk products (such as medical devices in which the user and the patient may be harmed) might require an operating system which implements memory checking. In a multiple task environment the operating system should ensure that one task does not overwrite the memory address space pertaining to any of the other tasks. This means that a task will not cause data corruption of the program or data address space of any other task, a condition that can easily be caused by a run-away pointer variable.

Then there are operating systems that have been developed specially for the military and avionic environments. These operating systems have been validated for this purpose and this removes the necessity for the developer to perform this task. I foresee that it will not take long before the medical environment is forced to follow suit. One should keep this in mind if starting development on a new medical product.

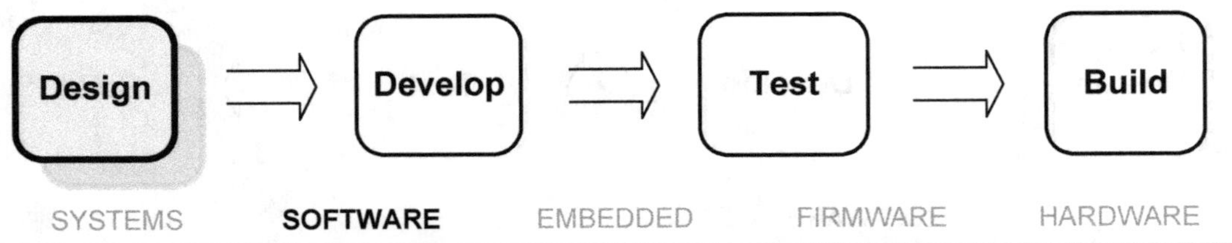

For with all COTS (Commercial off-the-shelf) products, there is the necessity that they have to be validated for medical use. This would also apply to any purchased operating system. Now it can be stated that if the application was validated and the application used a specific operating system then by the fact that the product was proved operational it then implies that the underlying operating system was likewise deemed operational. True, but what happens if a product fault was determined at some later time. Was it the product application that was at fault or was it the Operating System? Such blame or responsibility can be hard to prove.

Also consider the fact that embedded operating systems require a board support package. This is a set of software that is designed to permit the operating system to interface with specific physical hardware (processor / microcontroller, Ethernet PHY interface, etc.). With a validated operating system this board support package would be supplied by the provider of the operating system (OS) and would be associated with specific interface hardware. In order to maintain the Operating System validation the developer would also have to use the processor / microcontroller and associated hardware pertaining to the OS BSP. The validation would be violated if you yourself were to develop a different board support package. However, in less regulated environments you would be free to develop your own board support package.

Next the architecture design is broken down to the principal tasks. These tasks are sets of events that must occur on a continual basis. The specific details that must occur with each of these processes are identified and listed. Once each concurrent task and its set of functions have been identified and the various interfaces are known, a measure of the system's speed and capabilities has now been defined. The Software Architecture Document may then be reviewed and the hardware activities commenced. This will involve the selection of a suitable

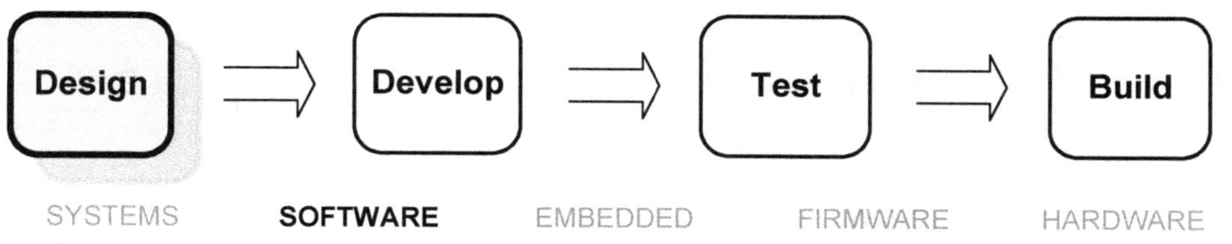

processor, along with its required memory and interfaces. The architect will hold discussions with the other group members such that suitable hardware is included in the design. If the company already has experience with a specific processor hardware (perhaps from a previous design) a modification of an existing product might be suitable for the new design.

Now there are times when a design might be ported. What this basically means is that a previous design which is operational on one product is being transferred across to a new physical platform. This process might also include the use of a new operating system. Such events often occur when a product is nearing the end of its life as far as its hardware implementation is concerned. This tends to happen when hardware manufacturers no longer sell one or more of the components required by the product's bill of materials. This means that the old software design now needs to function on top of new hardware.

Under such conditions it would be well worth the time to fully review the existing software. After all, it may be more than a decade old and if it has had multiple software patches a clean re-write may well provide a new base code that would be much easier to maintain. But in many cases, this does not happen for the simple reason that the original design is too difficult to understand. In this, a 'port' is implemented in which the code is transferred to the new system. This is not a wise decision for if the original code is poorly understood then the port is also carrying across any existing bugs as well.

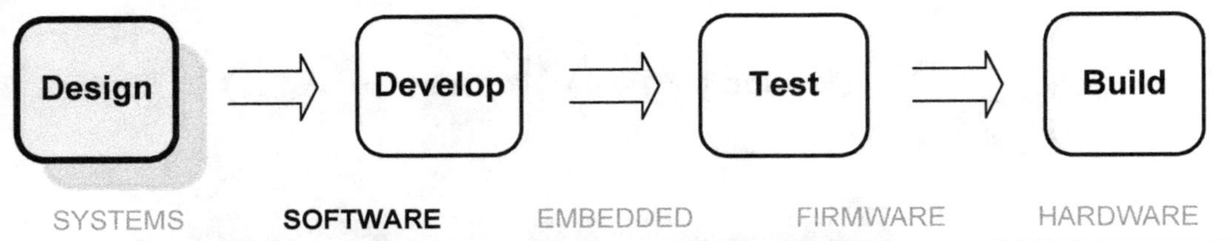

Software High Level Design Document

Dependent upon the level of product design complexity this may involve the creation of one or more documents. The Software HLD documentation is based on the Software Architecture document and proceeds to provide further explicit details. Simply put, this document is providing the detail required for the person who would be developing the low level design documents.

The Software HLD document would break the System Architecture document into its main components and provide detail as to their functionality. We are still talking about the feature overview (ie. the 'what') regarding the various tasks which are to be achieved. The implementation detail (the 'how') part comes in the low level design documents. With a smaller project this document might be part of the System Architecture.

Software Low Level Design Document

The Software LLD document is based upon the Software Architecture and Software HLD documents and it contains more detailed design specifics. For instance, if the design involved an Ethernet Interface with a message queue'ing system the Software LLD document would define the operations involved in this process (the types of queues used, protocol synchronization, etc.) .

In this part of the design task details and their associated interactions would also be defined (ie. the task initialization parameters, timers, semaphores, mutexes, memory pools, etc.). The low level steps that each task will accomplish will be identified using tools like Structured English (ie. pseudocode instructions). These instructions simply become the comments for the code that will be implemented later.

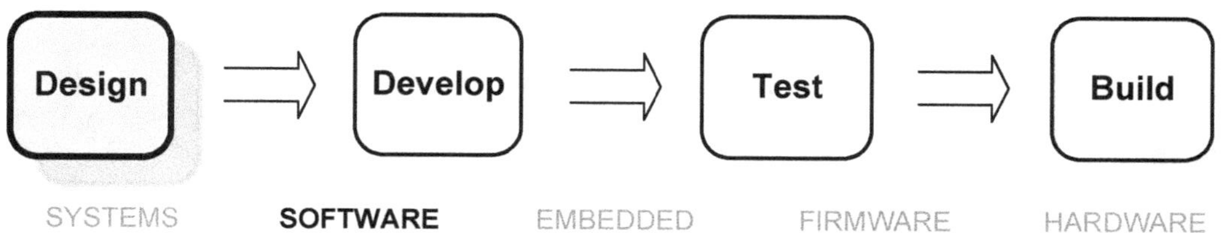

It is never justifiable to state that the code is the documentation.

The costs of product maintenance (bug fixes and enhancements) can be minimized by keeping good documentation. For in many cases it is often cheaper and quicker to re-write undocumented code than to spend ages trying to fully understand the original hacked (sorry, 're-factored') code. For the original designer might regard their code as being quite readable but in many cases that might not be so for the next person.

Protocol Documents

When the product is implemented through the use of multiple concurrent tasks which are being executed on top of an Operating System, tasks may communicate with each other or with the outside world.

Such communication is comprised of message structures. Protocol documents are created to provide the definition of these messages and will define the message types and the data being transferred. For example, a message might have a specific type identifier followed by a length field and data particular to this message type. All these parameters would be defined within the relevant protocol document for this physical interface.

Fault Analysis Document

When working in the medical field I was tasked with reviewing and summarizing the various international standards associated with risk analysis and how it pertains to software used by medical products. The documents were both close on fifty pages each but in reality they could easily be summarized as follows.

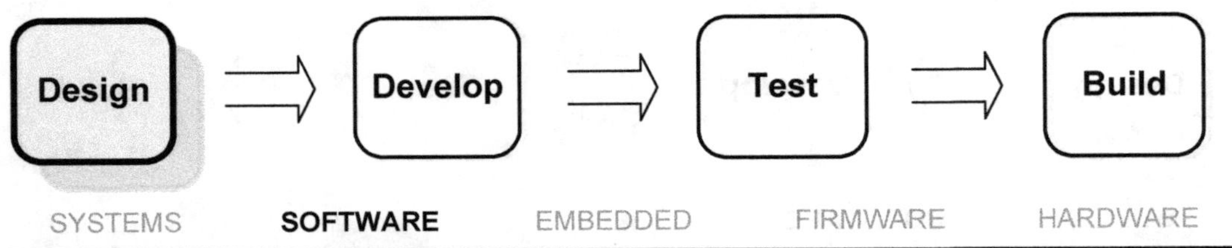

It is basically impossible to fully test a software product. Sure, you might fix most of the programming errors through Validation and Verification testing but that is really not the issue. The problem is associated with that elusive bug. The problem that might only occur once every two months, and when this problem does occur it can cause the most difficulty (or harm) to the patient. So how do you create test data for a problem you do not even understand. There is no trace data leading up to the event. It just happens and when it does your product fails. Sure, when you perform the old IT adage of 'have you tried switching the device off and on again' the problem seems to go away and everything is well once more. That is until some apparent random event occurs once more and again the product fails. This is the problem identified within these risk analysis standards. They are attempting to point the manufacturer of medical equipment in the right direction. They are saying that there is no amount of testing that will get all the system bugs (especially this type of bug).

So they desire that the Fault Analysis process be performed at every step of the design. The developer, whether they be hardware or software, has to be on the lookout for these elusive bugs. For they are not always software in nature. I have seen cases when hardware was at fault and was the responsible party in causing the software program to crash. It was a power supply issue. Computer hardware voltages are getting lower and lower and the differentiation in the voltages between what constitutes logic '0' from logic '1' is getting very fine. A poor supply earth was the issue.

However, there was one condition in my experience in which it was my own software that was at fault. It was a non-medical product and I was sitting quietly at my desk when a sudden realization took hold. I was reviewing a code fragment when a specific thought came to mind. If I were to have an interrupt at just this point in the process and a number of other events were in effect, there

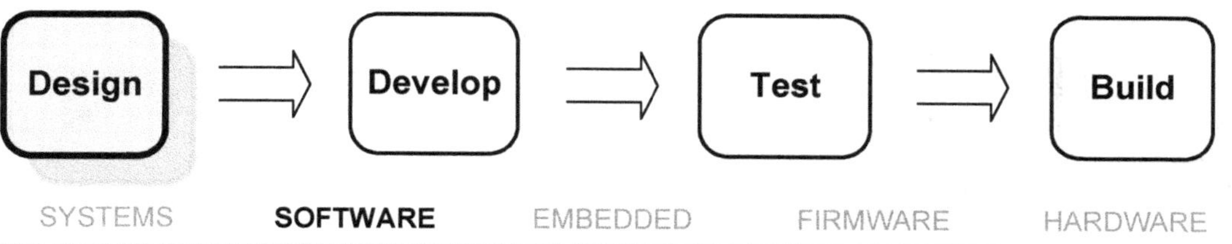

was a chance that the software would fail. Now the likelihood of these events all simultaneously happening was very slim but if they were to do so, the product would fail. This failure might only occur once every six months but in a product that was supposed to work on a continual basis the occurrence of these failures would start to mount and the product would get a bad name (ie. sales will go down).

I had written all the code for this product so I was totally aware of the entire system operation. Because of this I could 'see' the problem and immediately developed a fix. But would I have even been in a position to do this if I was under a demanding project manager and been forced to work as per the 70% rule, or would I have been able to think clearly if I was working in a noisy lab environment. Probably not. There have been times when I have seen between ten and twenty people all working is a cramped lab and sharing lab equipment.

It was a very noisy environment. Each time you tried to use some piece of equipment you were totally unaware of the state it was left in by the previous engineer. Was the hardware fully functional? Had one or more of the stored parameters been changed. When you next used the hardware to test your code and it did not work as before you were then forced to spend time trying to figure out why.

So when possible, give the development team their own consistent hardware, a quiet place to work and their designs will have less error. It only stands to reason and the result of this is that these elusive bugs will stand a much better chance of being found. For as stated in the international standards regarding risk analysis, no amount of testing will find these bugs for they are often design errors. They can only be found when the designer places themselves in the role of the computer and sees the design from its perspective.

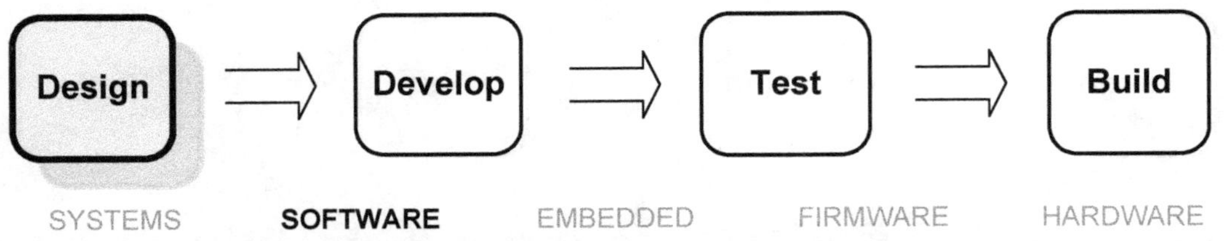

Operating System Features

When selecting an Operating System some specific features should be considered.

Task Profiler

When multiple tasks are battling against each other for system resources, it is always beneficial to have a task profiler. This feature permits the designer the ability to see which tasks are hogging the system. It will show up the tasks that require more time and hence should be allocated a higher priority.

Task Stack Monitor

When tasks are created there is no complete understanding of the function calling level and number of possible simultaneous interrupts that could occur. This being the case it generally forces the software engineer to simply allocate some block of memory for stack usage. If the program crashes this allocation is increased by some factor until the system appears to work. But just how much of the stack is being used and do we have a good-enough safety margin for these infrequent cases when the stack is heavily used. In this regard an OS with a task stack monitor is quite beneficial.

Code usage (Removal of dead code)

In many design environments there is a certain amount of code which is developed for testing. The use of such may be triggered by some variable or definition. The developer likes to keep the code around just in case it needs to be used. But in the medical world this constitutes as dead code and is required to be eliminated. Having an OS that can provide the developer with a trace of code which has been used gives them an understanding of what code is un-necessary and constitutes as being ‘dead code’.

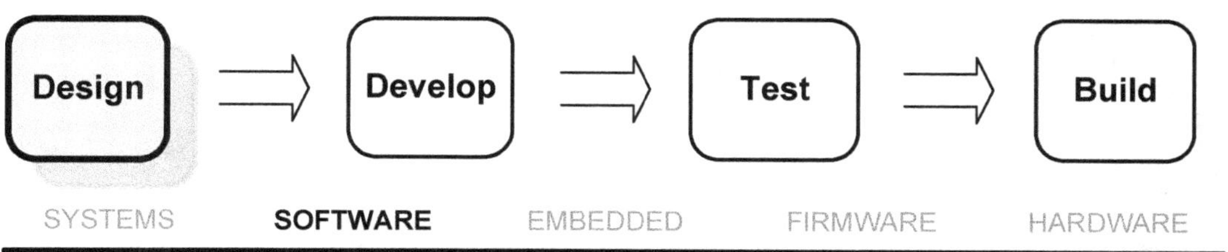

[This page intentionally left blank]

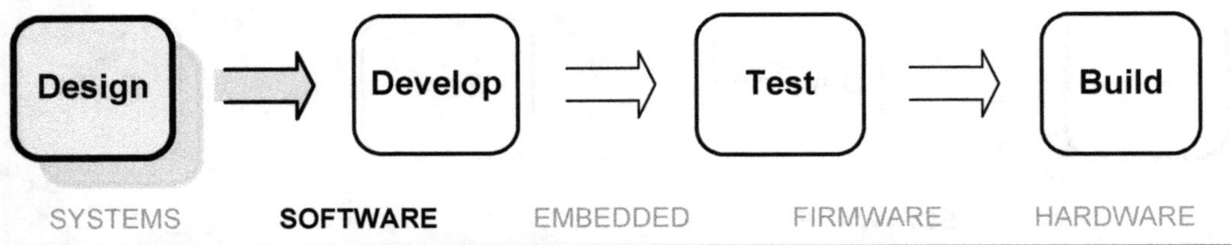

Design Software Outputs

The Design Software Outputs is the information that is required in order to permit the design process to effectively proceed to the other engineering fields. Failure to provide well defined, clear and unambiguous systems documentation will cause wasted engineering time that will result in budget over-runs.

The Design Software Outputs include the following documents:

Software System Requirements

<u>Purpose</u>: Define software System Requirements.

<u>Presenter</u>: System Architect

<u>Reviewers</u>: Senior Software Application Engineer
Senior Embedded Software Engineer

Software Architecture Document

<u>Purpose</u>: Provide a breakdown of System Components.
Provide feature lists.

<u>Presenter</u>: System Architect

<u>Reviewers</u>: Senior Software Application Engineer
Senior Embedded Software Engineer

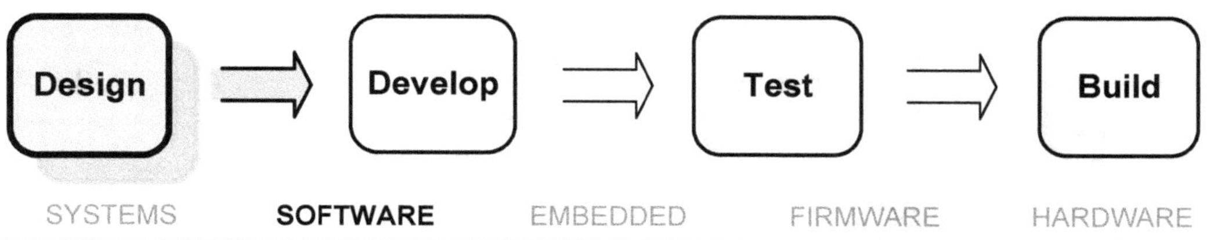

Software High Level Design Document

Purpose: Provide overall high level design details.

Presenter: System Architect

Reviewers: Senior Software Application Engineer
Senior Embedded Software Engineer

Software External Interface Document

Purpose: Provide interface control definitions.

Presenter: Senior Software Embedded Engineer

Reviewers: System Architect
Senior Software Application Engineer

Software Internal / External Protocol Document

Purpose: Provide protocol definitions.

Presenter: Senior Software Application Engineer

Reviewers: System Architect

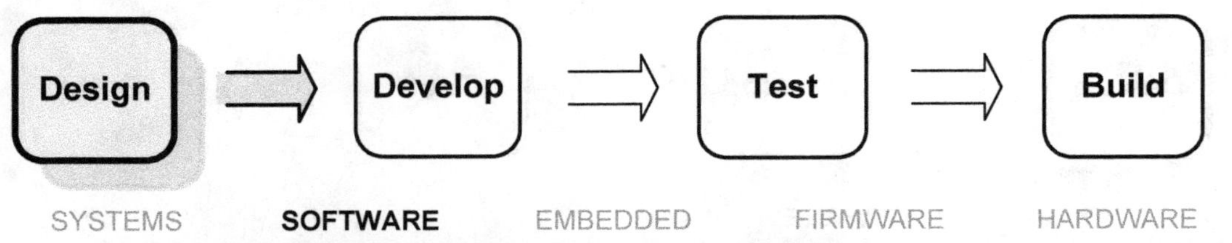

Fault Analysis Document

<u>Purpose</u>: Identify single point failures.
Specify concern and mitigation.

<u>Presenter</u>: System Architect

<u>Reviewers</u>: Senior Software Application Engineer
Senior Embedded Software Engineer
Senior Hardware Engineer

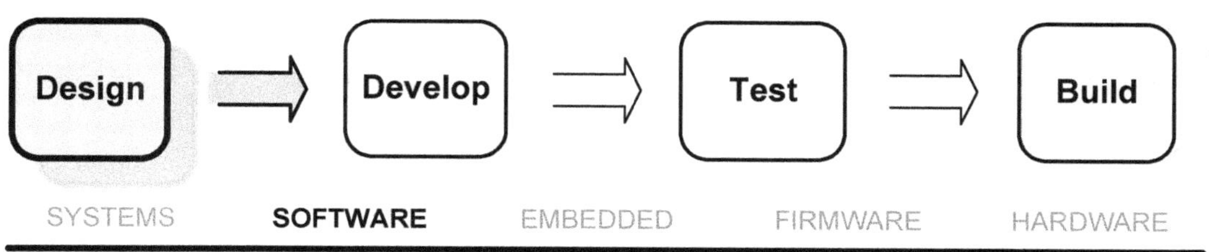

[This page intentionally left blank]

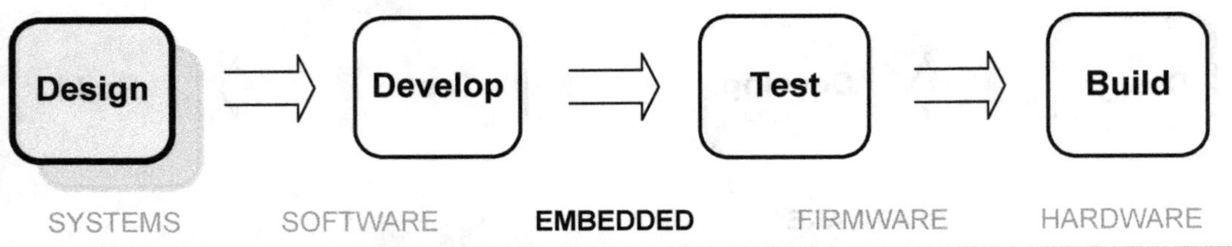

Embedded

The Embedded tasks include all aspects of the software design below the application yet above the physical hardware. This would include the system boot code, the board support package, the development of device drivers and the memory map.

System Boot Document

The system boot code is a set of code that is executed immediately after the processor is reset. This code might be quite straightforward as in the case of a microcontroller and be simply the positioning of some branch instructions at a specific flash memory location that directs the program counter to the main() function of the application.

On the other hand, this may be a more sophisticated set of instructions that first configures the processor and then copies a selected application from flash memory into RAM for subsequent faster execution.

In both cases a System Boot document is required to identify the specific details. All too often this description is ignored by those who believe that the code itself is the documentation. By being lazy (or rather, by being an incompetent engineer), specific design details can be ignored to the detriment of all. Is it really necessary for each subsequent person who works on the system boot code to have to go through a reverse-engineering process just to find the intent of the original designer.

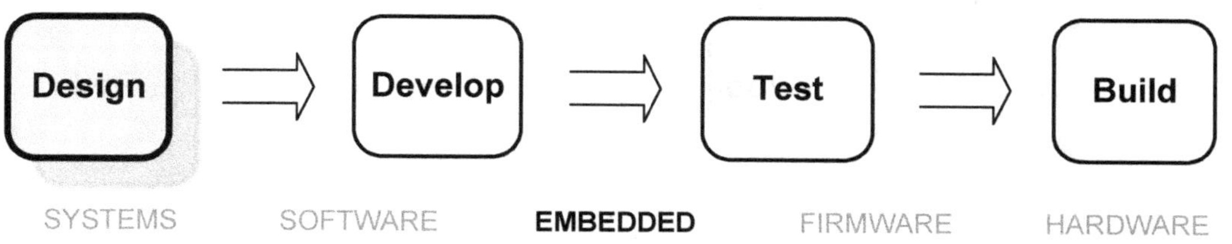

Board Support Package Documentation

The Board Support Package is a set of code that sits between the Operating System and the physical hardware. This code provides the final interface instructions so that the operating system can directly access the hardware. This may interface with a specific serial port, or might possibly provide the necessary Ethernet buffers and controls for the Ethernet PHY interface.

Each and every board support interface should be described, the relevant code identified and any specific enhancements identified. This will simplify time and effort if such changes have to be re-applied when transferring to a later revision of the operating system or even if tasked with moving to a new operating system. The board support documentation may also be referred as part of the verification procedure.

Device Driver Documentation

A software application engineer generally has a limited understanding of hardware. They really have no interest in such detail. So they will be most reluctant to even consider the thought of approaching a hardware engineer for they speak a different language and no one really wants to let on they are ignorant in such matters. But don't be too hard on the application engineer because they, in their own way, do bring specific expertise to the table.

Device drivers might include an API (Application Program Interface) to specific hardware like a calendar/clock, a Flash memory interface, cPLD and FPGA interface registers. These documented APIs provide the interface functions that allow the application software engineer the ability to control the device without having to understand the hardware specifics of the device.

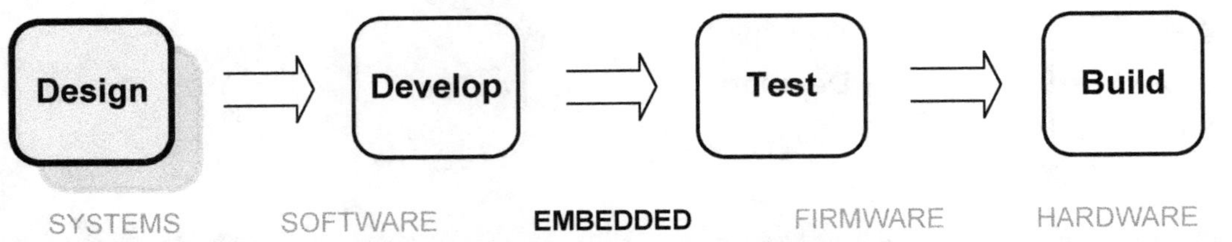

Memory Map

Although this is the initial design of the embedded system, the system architecture document will have described the various physical components that will be incorporated into the product. This implies that a start can be made to the Memory Map document for it should be clearly understood that such a document is a 'living document' and will be in a constant state of change as the product design proceeds.

This document will describe the various memory addresses, memory block size and memory bus widths for each physical component.

Such components may include the following:

- EEPROM memory
- Flash memory
- RAM Memory
- Serial Ports
- GPIO Ports
- etc.

The Memory Map should provide the following information for each physical component:

The component base address (eg. 0x8000 0000)
The component final address and size (eg. 0x8000 FFFF) Size 64KB
The component bus width (eg. 8-bit port width)

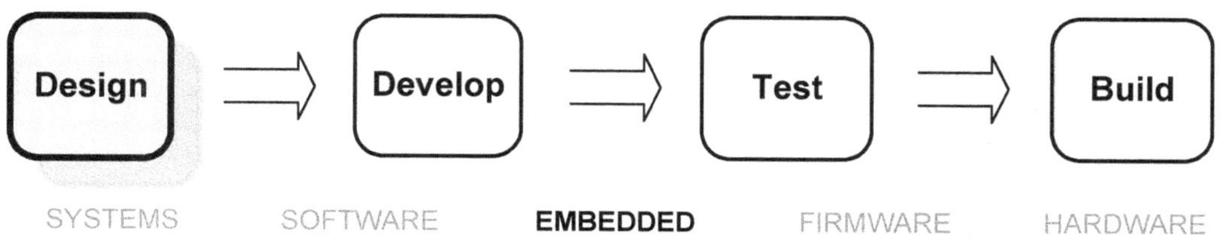

cPLD and FPGA Interfaces

Now some people might think that this is the wrong place to identify cPLD and FPGA design documents. They should be designed by the hardware engineers themselves. But some psychological analysis of the engineer is relevant at this point in time. The software application engineer generally sees everything from the perspective of the user. They are thinking about the various operator controls and how they will be implemented. This tends to make the software engineer think in a 'top down' approach, breaking the functionality into lower and lower levels of complexity.

But the hardware engineer does the opposite. He or she is thinking about each and every individual hardware item and how each of them are controlled. If there is an association or group usage amongst these items it is usually ignored and the resultant interface is difficult for the application engineer to use.

Now this is where the embedded engineer comes in. Such a person is caught between both these worlds and because of such understands each of them. But if the embedded engineer came from the hardware environment then they might be swayed by the 'bottom up' logic. I myself was initially trained in the software environment and so have the 'top down' concept in my mind and this is why I have seen the logic about why the embedded engineer should write such documents in order to aid the application engineer interface with hardware.

Now the hardware engineer does not mind having someone write design documentation for it should be noted that most engineers do not care for writing documents.

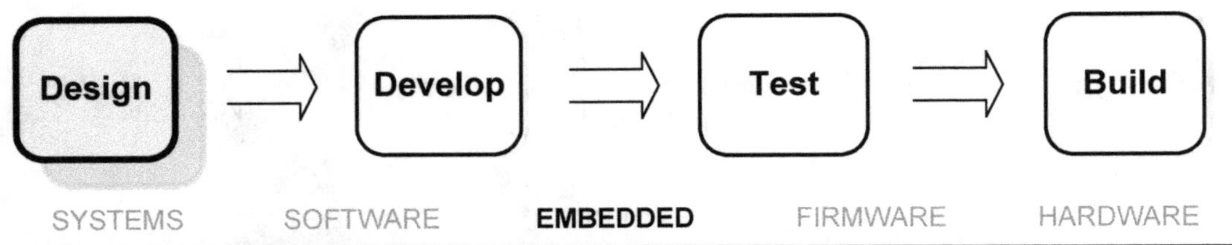

The modus operandi for most engineers is 'just tell me what you want and I will implement it'.

This criteria is associated with hardware firmware and software engineers.

But just as the System Architect is in a privileged position in which they understand the entire project from the viewpoint of multiple disciplines, so too is the embedded software engineer. The good embedded engineer has the systems knowledge and hence knows what hardware the application engineer needs to control. He/she also knows that the hardware engineer looks at the design from the 'bottom up' approach and does not appreciate the application engineer's perspective. So the embedded engineer is the correct person who should develop these design documents for once complete they would be understood and easily implemented by the hardware firmware engineer. The embedded engineer would created the API interface that would sit on top of these designs and this would be the interface used by the software application engineer, written in the language of the application engineer.

ISO 7-Layer Model

#7 Application Layer
#6 Presentation Layer (Present data to application, encrypt data to network)
#5 Session Layer (Controls connections between computers)
#4 Transport Layer (TCP built on top of IP protocol)
#3 Network Layer (IP protocol - transfer of datagrams)
#2 Data Link Layer
#1 Physical Layer (electrical connections)

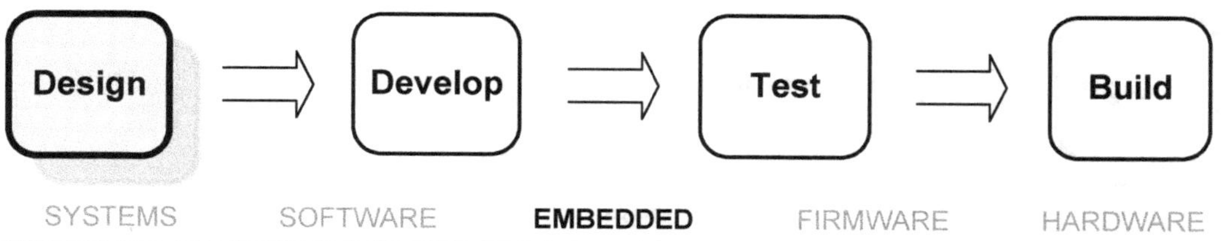

cPLD Interface Registers

This document identifies the various cPLD interface registers. Each register will be located at a different memory address and is generally accessed directly by the processor / microcontroller over a port of a specific width (8-bit, 16-bit, 32-bit, etc.). Each register bit is defined as well as it particular operational states. Sometimes multiple watchdogs are defined to protect from system latch up (especially in Medical software).

cPLD System Operation

This document describes the cPLD system operation and provides an understanding of how the part operates. The cPLD interface register and cPLD system operation documents provides the hardware firmware engineer with all the necessary information with which to engineer the cPLD firmware. The embedded software engineer has written these documents in a manner that lends itself to creating a cPLD API that will be readily understood by the application engineer.

cPLD Application Program Interface (API)

The embedded engineer utilizes the previously designed cPLD documents to create a set of functions to provide the applications software engineer access to the low level device. These functions provide the application engineer with the functions that control the device without them being aware of specific hardware details.

For example: A Flash interface would permit access to one or more Flash memory devices located at a specific memory address range and using a specific port width (8-bit, 16-bit, 32-bit, etc.). The application engineer would only specify the sector number and the data block being written.

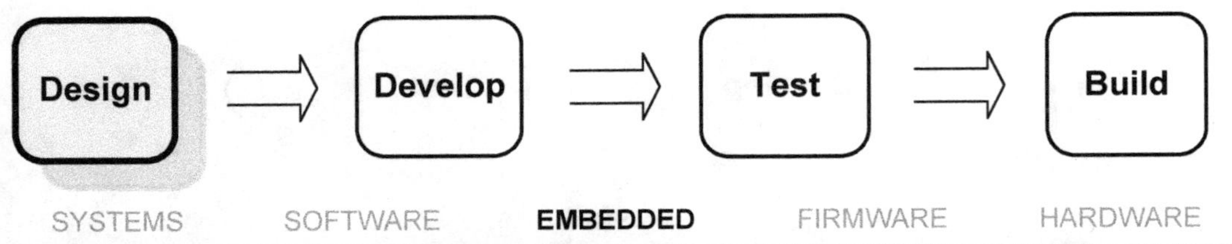

FPGA Interface Registers

This document identifies the various FPGA interface registers. Each register will be located at a different memory address and is generally accessed directly by the processor / microcontroller over a port of a specific width (8-bit, 16-bit, 32-bit, etc.). Each register bit is defined as well as it's particular operational states.

FPGA System Operation

This document describes the FPGA system operation and provides an understanding of how the part operates. The FPGA interface register and FPGA system operation documents provides the hardware firmware engineer with all the necessary information with which to engineer the FPGA firmware. The embedded software engineer has written these documents in a manner that lends itself to creating an FPGA API that will be readily understood by the application engineer.

FPGA Application Program Interface (API)

The embedded engineer utilizes the previously designed FPGA documents to create a set of functions to provide the applications software engineer access to the low level device. These functions provide the application engineer with the functions that control the device without them being aware of specific hardware details.

Interface Examples

Serial, GPIB, HDLC, I2C, I2S, SPI, SM, SDIO, NAND, LCD, USB, 802.11, MPEG

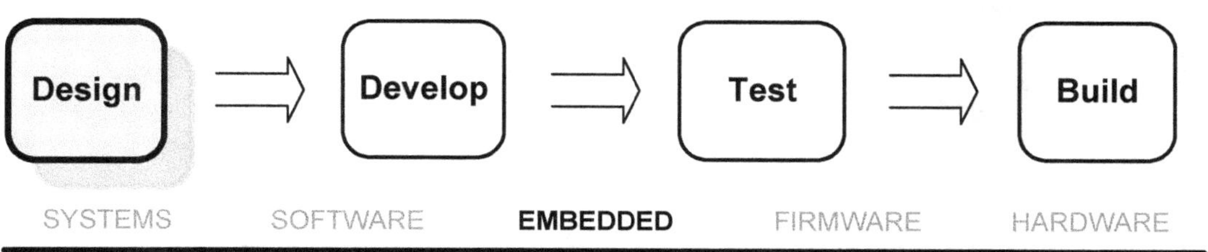

[This page intentionally left blank]

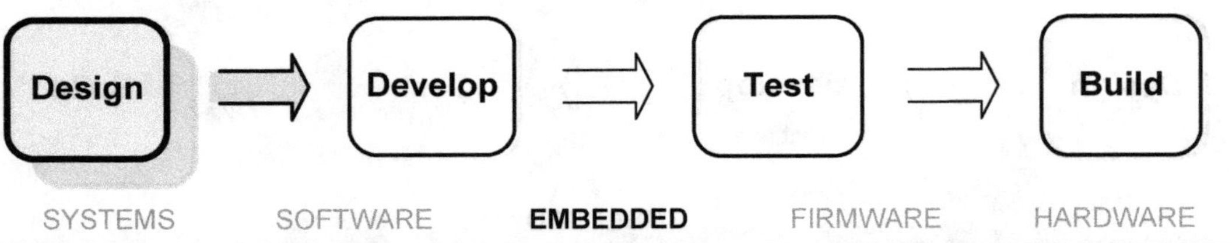

Design Embedded Outputs

The Design Embedded Outputs is the information that is required in order to permit the design process to effectively proceed to the other engineering fields. Failure to provide well defined, clear and unambiguous design documentation will cause wasted engineering time that will result in budget over-runs.

The Design Embedded Outputs include the following documents:

System Boot Document

Purpose:	Bootup procedure.
Presenter:	Senior Software Embedded Engineer
Reviewers:	System Architect Senior Hardware Engineer

Board Support Package Document

Purpose:	Describe Operating System interface overview
Presenter:	Senior Software Embedded Engineer
Reviewers:	System Architect Senior Hardware Engineer

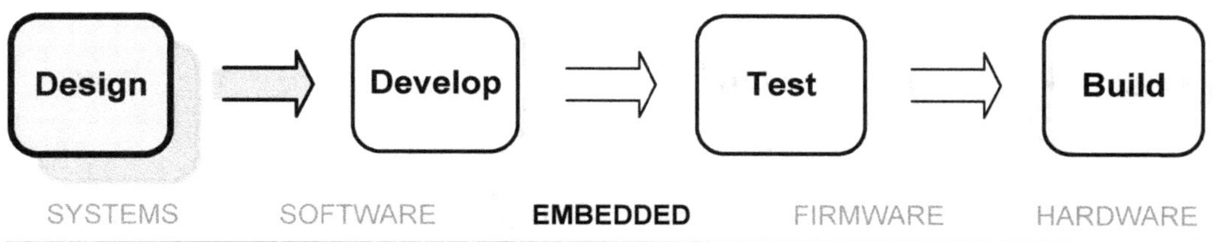

Device Driver High Level Design Document(s)

Purpose: Detail hardware interfaces

Presenter: Senior Software Embedded Engineer

Reviewers: System Architect
Senior Hardware Engineer

Memory Map Document [Living Document]

Purpose: Define memory map for all devices

Presenter: Senior Software Embedded Engineer

Reviewers: System Architect
Senior Hardware / Firmware Engineer

cPLD Interface Register Document(s)

Purpose: Define cPLD Interface Registers

Presenter: Senior Software Embedded Engineer

Reviewers: System Architect
Senior Hardware / Firmware Engineer

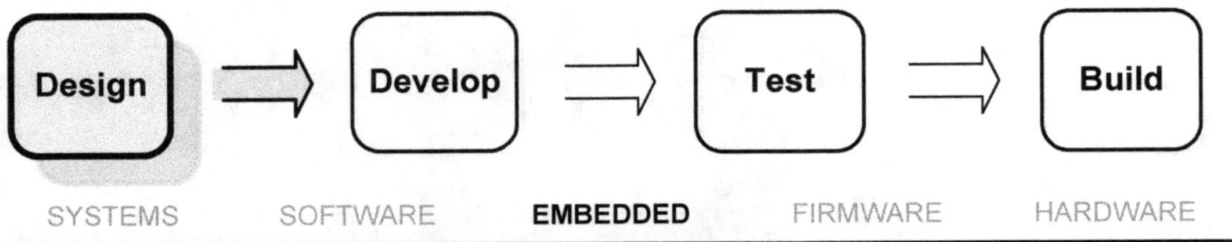

cPLD System Operation Document(s)

Purpose: Define cPLD system operation

Presenter: Senior Software Embedded Engineer

Reviewers: System Architect
Senior Hardware / Firmware Engineer

cPLD Application Program Interface Document(s)

Purpose: Define cPLD API functions

Presenter: Senior Software Embedded Engineer

Reviewers: System Architect
Senior Software Application Engineer

FPGA Interface Register Document(s)

Purpose: Define FPGA interface registers

Presenter: Senior Software Embedded Engineer

Reviewers: System Architect
Senior Hardware / Firmware Engineer

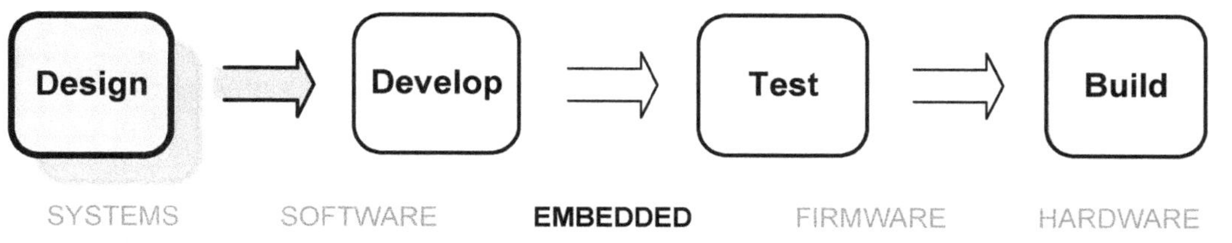

FPGA System Operation Document(s)

Purpose: Define FPGA system operation

Presenter: Senior Software Embedded Engineer

Reviewers: System Architect
Senior Hardware / Firmware Engineer

FPGA Application Program Interface Document(s)

Purpose: Define FPGA API functions

Presenter: Senior Software Embedded Engineer

Reviewers: System Architect
Senior Software Application Engineer

Fault Analysis Document

Purpose: Identify single point failures.
Specify concern and mitigation.

Presenter: System Architect

Reviewers: Senior Software Application Engineer
Senior Embedded Software Engineer
Senior Hardware / Firmware Engineer

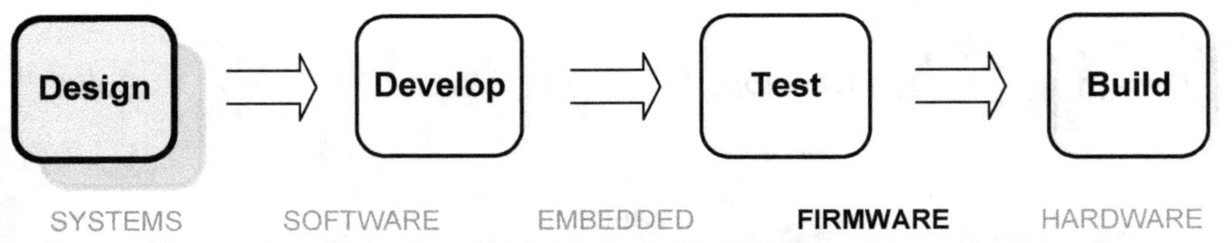

Firmware

The product firmware consists of VHDL or System Verilog code instructions that are used to program a cPLD or FPGA EEPROM. The firmware design documentation are the documents that would be produced to aid the development of the firmware to be installed into these devices.

The firmware design outputs would include the following three types of documents for every cPLD and FPGA part in the system:

cPLD/FPGA High Level Design Document

This document describes the hardware device functionality. For the most part it refers to the cPLD or FPGA Interface Registers and System Operation documents that were created during the Design Embedded process. Any additional hardware issues should be described in this section.

cPLD/FPGA Low Level Design Document

This document describes the cPLD and FPGA part with reference to its electrical interface and any specific internal register requirements to be implemented by the VHDL or System Verilog code.

cPLD/FPGA Verification Test Document

This document describes the verification tests that will be executed to ensure that the cPLD or FPGA is fully functional prior to being released to other departments.

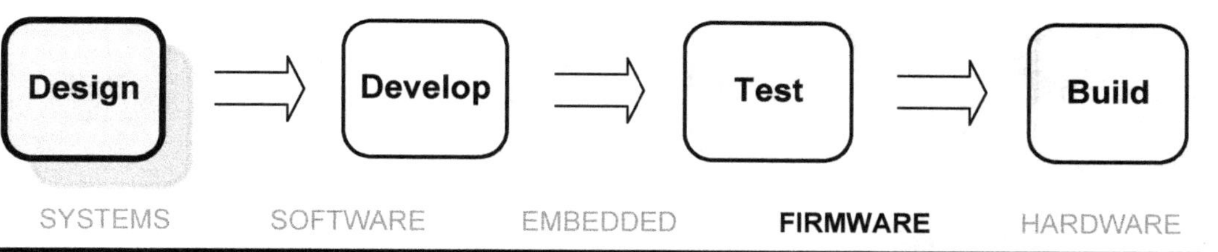

[This Page Intentionally Left Blank]

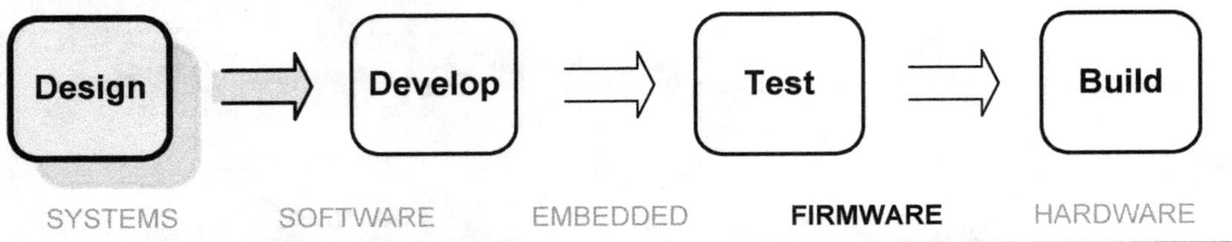

Design Firmware Outputs

The Design Firmware Outputs include the following documents and reviews:

cPLD High Level Design Document(s)

Purpose: cPLD top level design

Presenter: Senior Firmware Engineer

Reviewers: System Architect
Senior Software Embedded Engineer

FPGA High Level Design Document(s)

Purpose: FPGA top level design

Presenter: Senior Firmware Engineer

Reviewers: System Architect
Senior Software Embedded Engineer

Fault Analysis Document

Purpose: Identify single point failures.
Specify concern and mitigation.

Presenter: System Architect

Reviewers: Senior Software Application Engineer
Senior Embedded Software Engineer
Senior Hardware / Firmware Engineer

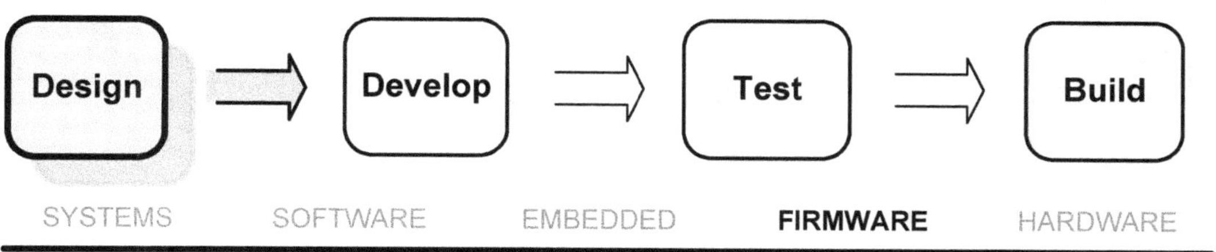

[This Page Intentionally Left Blank]

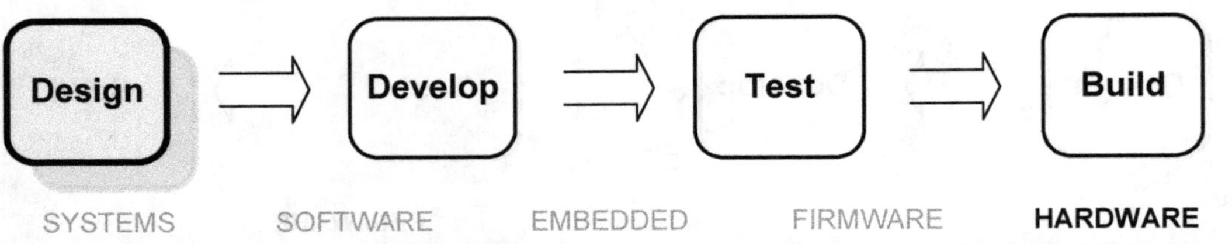

Hardware

The end result of the Design Hardware task is to provide the necessary information with which the hardware platform PCBA might be designed. This infers that the principal parts would have been selected and an initial memory map proposed.

Hardware Architecture Document

This document identifies the principle control hardware of the overall design. This may include one or more Printed Circuit Board Assemblies and the manner in which the various functions have been distributed over these boards and the manner in which they have been interconnected. For a smaller product it may only result in a single board. All the same, the various interfaces will be identified in block form.

Hardware High Level Design Document

This document applies more detail to the Hardware Architecture Document. Various interfaces are defined in more detail and the controlling devices defined.

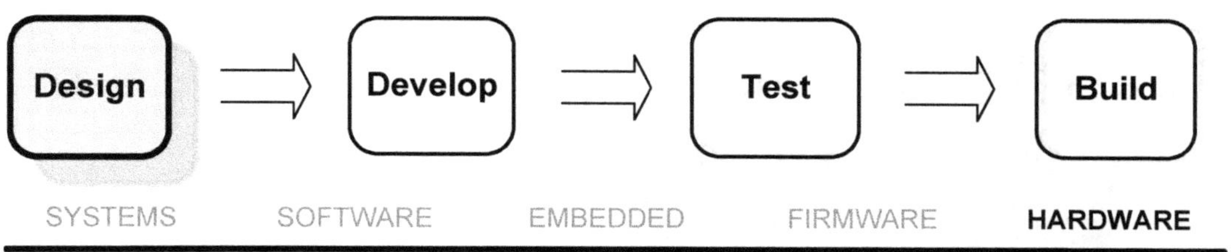

[This Page Intentionally Left Blank]

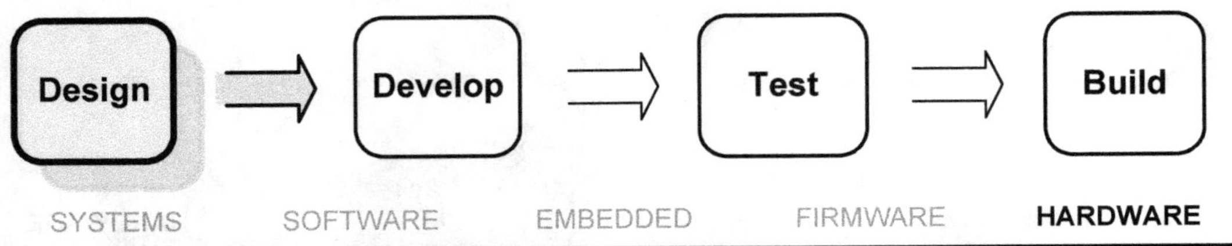

Design Hardware Outputs

The Design Hardware Outputs include the following reviewed documents:

Hardware Architecture Document

Purpose: Hardware architecture design
Breakdown into sub-components.

Presenter: Senior Hardware Engineer

Reviewers: System Architect
Senior Embedded Engineer
Senior Firmware Engineer

Hardware High Level Design Document

Purpose: High Level Design.

Presenter: Senior Hardware Engineer

Reviewers: System Architect
Senior Embedded Engineer
Senior Firmware Engineer

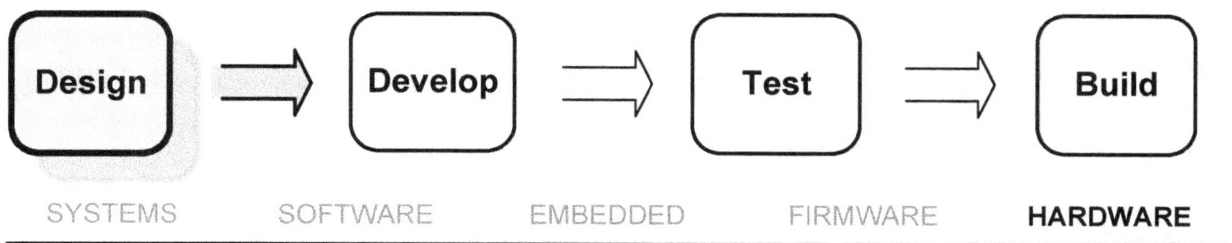

Fault Analysis Document

Purpose: Identify single point failures and mitigations.

Presenter: System Architect

Reviewers: Senior Embedded Software Engineer
Senior Hardware Engineer

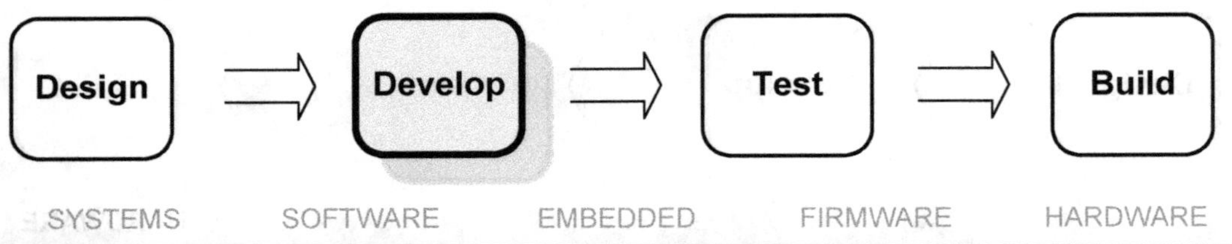

Development

The development phase of the engineering effort takes the design effort as input and the generated output is the PCBA, firmware and the coded application.

If the design has been documented in detail then it should be quite possible to pass the work onto a separate development team. This is where the concept of mentoring really comes into its own. The initial design was performed by the System Architect and senior members of staff. If the design effort is complete then all the information should now be available to the development team. All too often we see senior members of staff working on the low level aspects of the design. For example, a senior embedded engineer should be developing design documentation and mentoring junior staff. This senior engineer should not be writing code. Or to put it another way. Would you see the architect of a building laying bricks? Certainly not. It is a tremendous waste of their talent. But that is what we generally see throughout the industry. Highly qualified engineers performing low level work. Now I am sure that the building architect is very capable in laying bricks. I do not doubt that for a second as I am sure this person would regularly visit the building site and could tell at a glance good work from bad. But their time is spent in documenting the design and perhaps mentoring/training the junior building architects. They do not lay bricks.

This process is relevant even if the person has been fortunate in obtaining a university degree. But consider what such education brings to the table. An engineer, after enduring a three or four year computer science / engineering course will spend the next three to five years being trained in the first company in which they are employed.

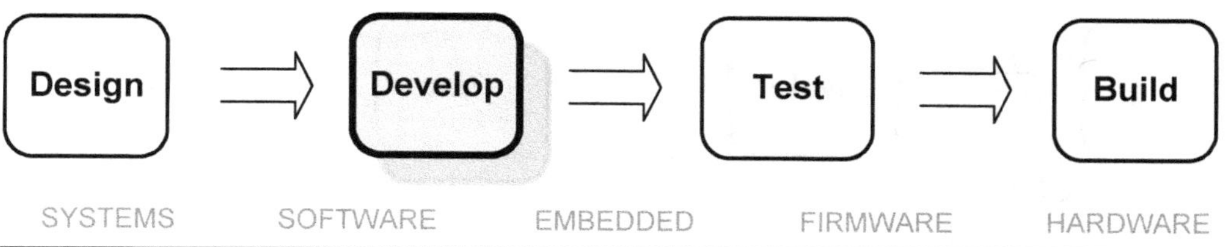

So what did they really bring with all that university training. Compiler theory might not be so relevant with most embedded projects. But if the company were to mentor these engineering interns then they would learn the relevant information at an accelerated rate. Think of all these potential engineering interns who are working at medial jobs simply because they do not have an engineering degree. All you need is a person who has a desire to learn. Give them a chance. You might be amazed at what you might find.

Also remember that software and firmware is an art form. When people are subjected to training by means of some engineering degree they are under a lot of pressure. This results in software and firmware code which is tackled at an accelerated rate. In my humble opinion it takes an engineer close on five years before they develop their 'style' of writing code. That is what happened to myself. During my early employment my coding style changed quite radically. One task that helped greatly in this area was being subject to tackling project maintenance, This task simply amounted to performing bug fixes and adding new features to code whose original designers were long gone. There was no design documentation of any worth. You had to reverse-engineer the design from reading the code. If memory serves there were two contract engineers employed at this company. They were quite pleased regarding the lack of documentation. They were setup for life since few understood the operation of the system. The company was most concerned with respect to ensuring they kept such engineers content and permanently in their employ (but if there is a proper design then such conditions do not occur).

So it was during this time that I learnt how not to write code.

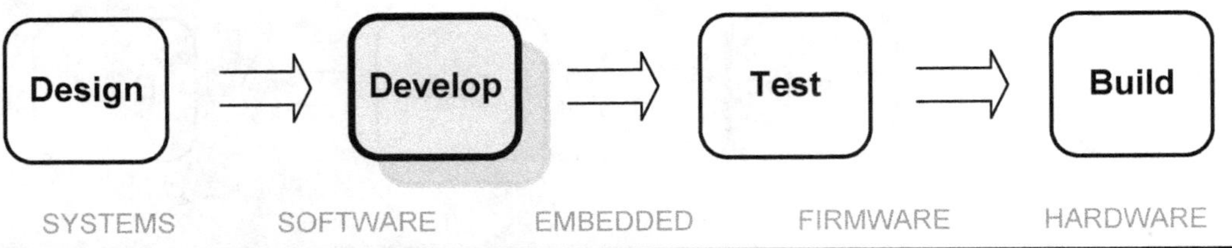

My personal coding style changed dramatically. My next employment had me working on a six month project. I spent close to four months writing design documentation (user specification, functional specification, operators manual, communications protocol), then I used program design language (Structured English) to describe the main steps used to implement the design. It was now the fourth month into the project and only now was I starting to write source code.

But there was something very interesting that was happening. When the source code was being written it was simply a translation of the structured English into code. No design effort was involved. In fact the documentation that I was using could easily have been given to some other software team to implement for all the detail was there..

The result of this is to state the following. If your project development team are designing as they write code then the result of their efforts will be a hack. A set of code that will not be easily maintainable. The up-front development cost may have been low but you should expect to spend a lot of money in maintaining your product and even more in salary, hoping you do not lose these development engineers.

The project I had worked on was completed approximately two weeks ahead of schedule and still managed to incorporate many additional features. Some years after I had moved overseas I heard from a friend of mine who spoke with the person assigned to maintain my code. The code used a dual processor configuration with each image based on many tens of thousands of lines of source code. This maintenance programmer was delighted. He found the code was easy to understand and it was well commented throughout.

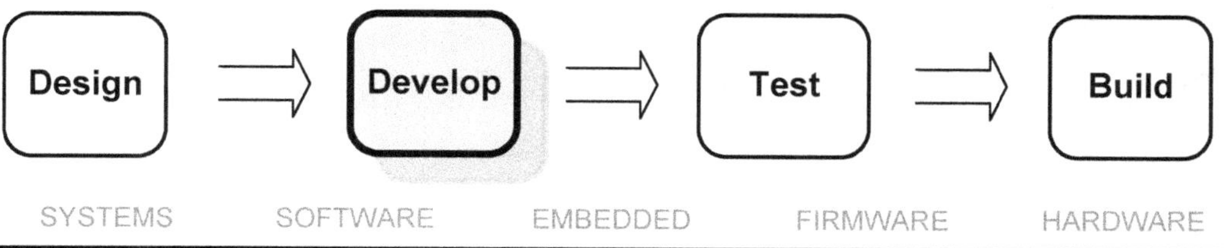

My coding design had made his life very easy. So consider these principles when you design a system and develop code. For one day, you might be the person doing maintenance.

The end result of the development phase is the creation of the working prototype.

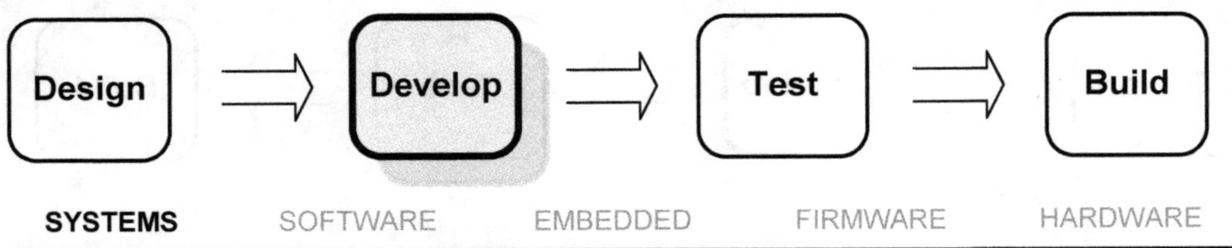

Systems

The system architect performed most of the product design work during the 'Design' phase. When the Development phase commences the system architect's involvement is to ensure that the remaining teams understand the project detail. The System Architect is the prime source of knowledge and is to hold training reviews in which appropriate sections of the system specification may be discussed in detail.

During this period of time additional information and possible design changes might occur. If this is the case, the system specification would be updated accordingly.

In this regard, the System Architect has the task of keeping all the other groups on tract and in sync.

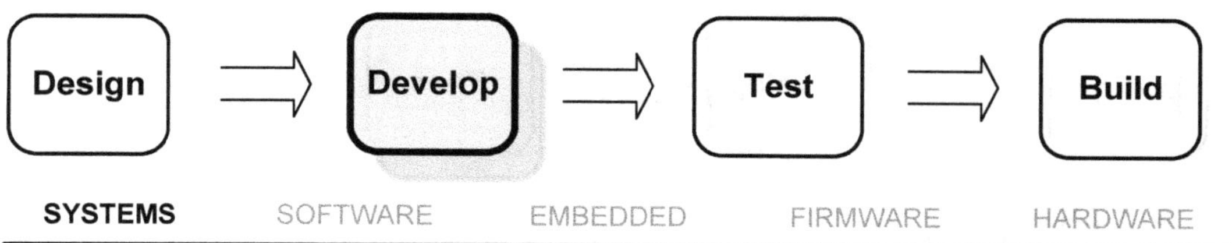

[This Page Intentionally Left Blank]

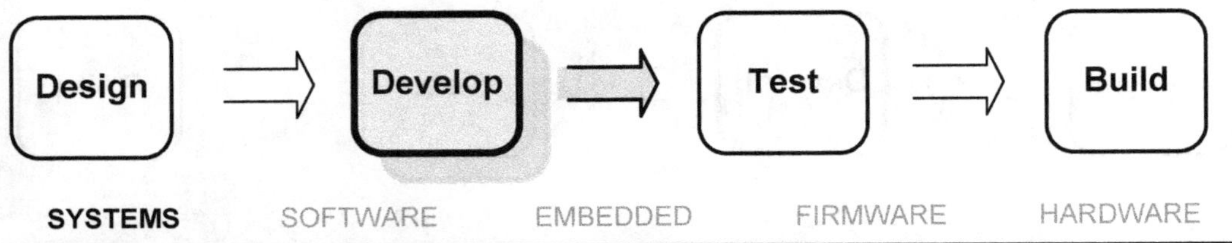

Develop Systems Outputs

The Develop Systems Outputs will include all necessary updates to the documents that were released during the Design Systems phase.

Please note that the risk analysis documents must be re-viewed periodically and updated in order to maintain low system risk. Such a methodology is appropriate for all types of design work (ie. not just the medical environment).

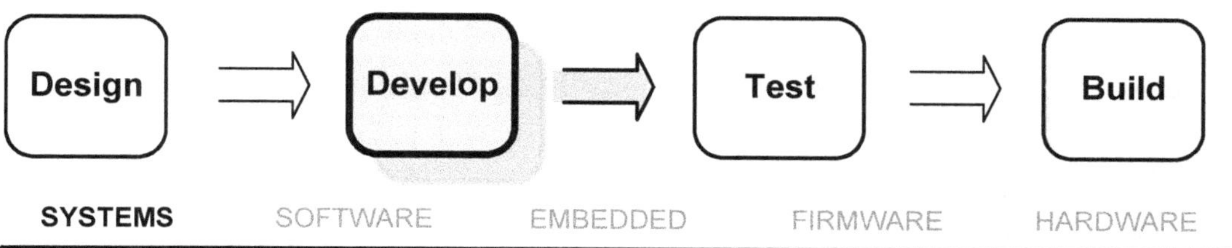

[This Page Intentionally Left Blank]

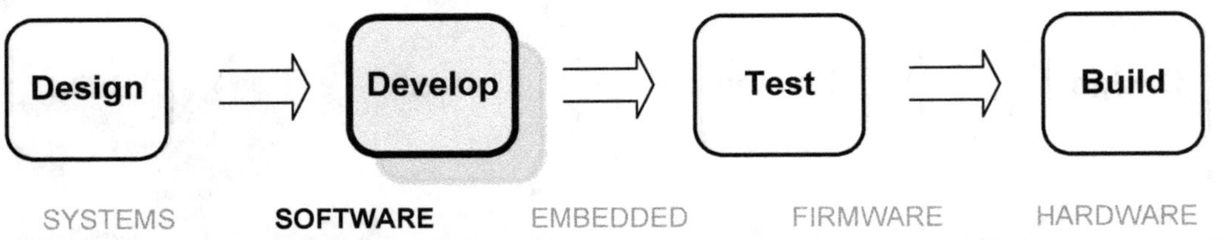

Software

During the software development phase the senior software application engineer will take the software design documentation and use it to create the Software Low Level Design documents. Work tasks (estimated 4 day duration) will be created for the junior software application engineer(s) to implement. The senior software application engineer is responsible for mentoring (training) the junior application engineers that have been assigned to the project.

Software Low Level Design Document

This document contains specific implementation details regarding how the system has been implemented. For example, a specific GUI user interface might be used and this document would describe how this was interfaced into the application software.

Software Toolset Document

When a software project is developed there are a number of code modules (C, C++, Assembler, etc.) that are created. Each of these code modules have to be written and then compiled (or assembled) and finally linked together to make executable code. The resultant executable object will then be placed on the embedded board (for example, in Flash memory).

The complete development toolset documentation will then provide the following information:

The Integrated Development Environment (IDE)
The Source Control utility
The Compiler toolset

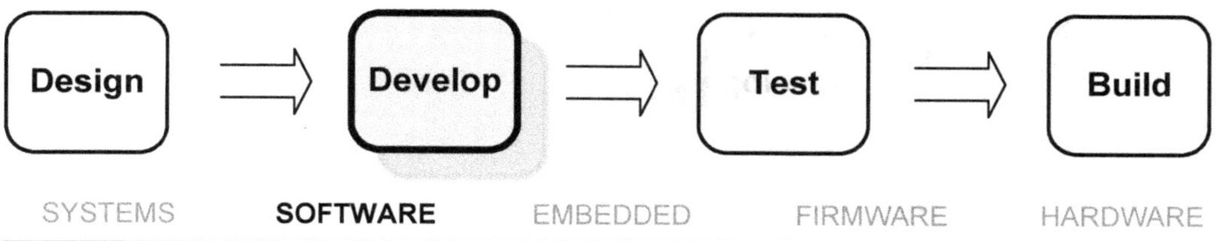

Integrated Development Environment

This section of the software toolset document will identify the Integrated Development Environment (IDE) that was used to develop the product source code.

Such IDE's provide a central development environment with access to the following tools:

project application version control
project application build tools
project application source level debugging

As a minimum, the following IDE Toolset information should be specified:

1. The IDE product identification
2. The IDE Manufacture's web site
3. The IDE version number
4. Additional IDE installed options
5. A copy of the IDE executable utility
6. The IDE installation instructions
7. The IDE requirements (ie. Windows OS, Linux, etc.)

These details are required in order to install the identical IDE environment on each development computer systems. This is not simply a current project requirement. There may also be a possible future need when embedded application bug fixes or enhancements need to be implemented and the original IDE environment is required to be re-established..

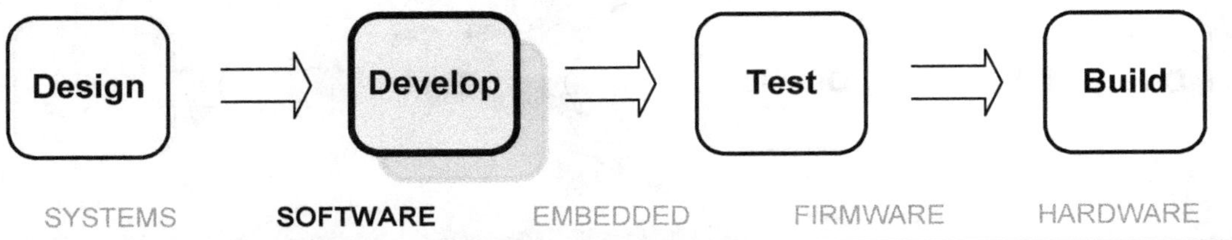

Project Application Version Control

This section of the software toolset document will identify the version control utility that was used when developing the project. Any unique installation features must be specified.

Version control is a utility that permits specific application files to be associated with a particular version of the final product software. The necessity of this feature applies to both small and large projects and ensures that a specific version of the application can be rebuilt – a feature required when attempting to determine specific programming bugs associated with a particular version of code.

The version control application is required for single person projects as well as large team projects. When a project team member edits a specific source file some version control utilities will lock that file such that no other team members might edit that file. This creates a safe environment such that edit changes performed by one engineer are not lost under conditions when two programmers work on the same file. However, this locking method does restrict the second programmer from continuing their work with editing that same specific file.

Other version control utilities will create separate copies of the source code file (separate branches) such that both programmers might perform their edits. This will permit them to continue development work but it does require an additional step to merge both sets of programmer edits back into the final version of the source file (a task that is usually delegated to the last person returning their file back to the version control system.

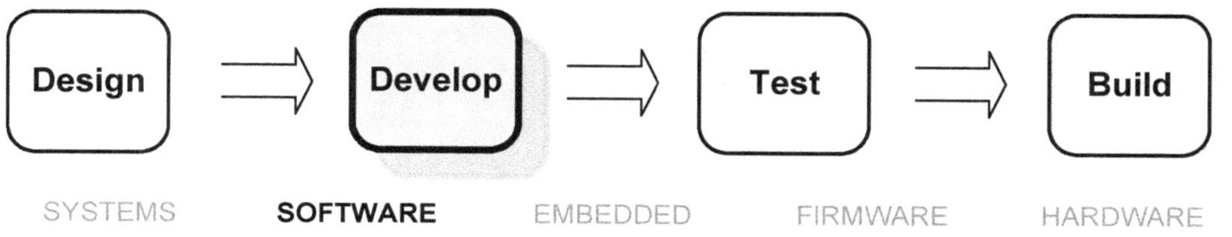

Project Application Build Tools

This section of the software toolset document identifies which programming compilers and assemblers were used to process the source code.

As a minimum, the following information should be specified:

1. The compiler / assembler product identification
2. The compiler and assembler version number
3. Any specific default options
4. A copy of the compiler / assembler executable code
5. The compiler / assembler installation instructions
6. The compiler / assembler requirements (ie. Windows OS, Linux, etc.)

It should be noted that bug fixes or product enhancements may be required at some point in the future. It may be necessary to re-install the compiler and assembler in order to achieve this goal. This implies that a mechanism must be in effect in which the exact same development compiler (and/or assembler) can be installed.

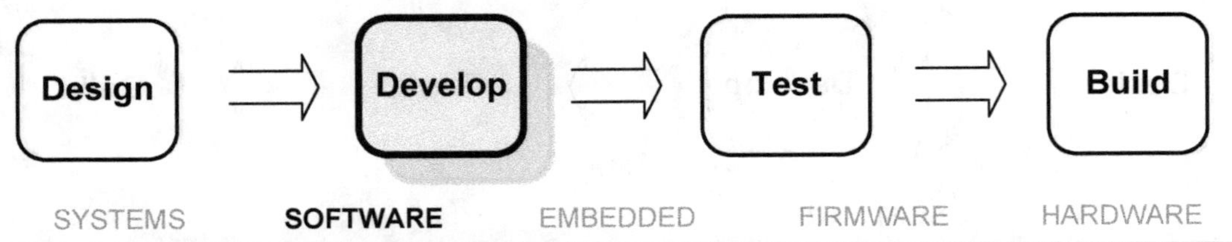

Linker

This section of the software toolset documentation identifies the linker used to process the compiled / assembled source code modules.

The Linker is a utility program that is used to link the compiled / assembled source code in order to generate a final executable image of the software application.

As a minimum, the following information should be specified:

1. The Linker product identification
2. The Linker version number
3. Any Linker installed options
4. A copy of the Linker executable code
5. The Linker installation instructions
6. The Linker requirements (ie. Windows OS, Linux, etc.)

It should be noted that bug fixes or product enhancements may be required at some point in the future. It may be necessary to re-install the linker executable in order to achieve this goal.

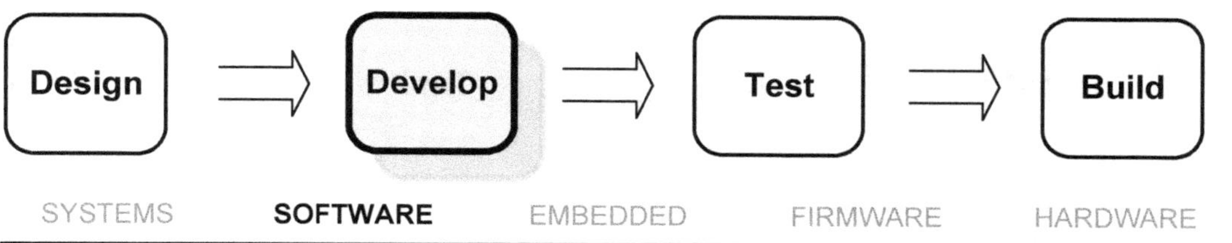

Make
This section of the software toolset document identifies which make utility was used to process the source code.

The Make file is used to specify the manner in which the source code modules are to be built. The make file specifies the module dependencies, include directories and object file names. The make file ensures that when a specific file has been modified, the make utility will rebuild only those modules which are dependent upon the file(s) that have been changed thereby reducing the time required to perform the project build process.

As a minimum, the following information should be specified:

1. The Make product identification
2. The Make version number
3. Any Make installed options
4. A copy of the Make utility
5. The Make installation instructions
6. The Make requirements (ie. Windows OS, Linux, etc.)

It should be noted that bug fixes or product enhancements may be required at some point in the future. It may be necessary to re-install the make utility in order to achieve this goal.

If the software make file is accessed by the IDE, the IDE configuration will also be identified in this document.

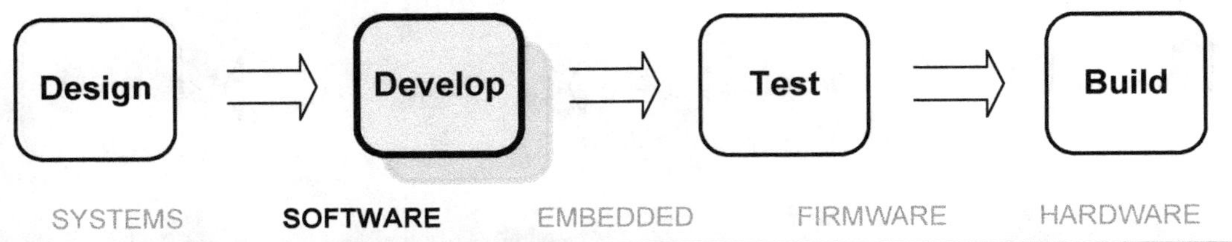

Software Build Process
This documentation describes the module directory structure identifying which specific file types are placed in which specific directories. It then specifies the instructions used to build the application executable image. The operation of the make file will also be described. It should be of sufficient detail to be understood by junior software engineers (a complex undocumented build process simply wastes productivity and is a source for error).

If the software build process has been incorporated into the IDE, the IDE configuration will be identified in this document.

Software Installation Process
This document specifies how the executable code image is loaded onto the embedded product. In many cases the application code resides in Flash memory. This documentation provides the installation steps that identify the process.

Software Upgrade Process
Once an embedded product has been created there are times when it is necessary to upgrade the product software. In times past this required the customer to send the product into a repair facility for this to be achieved. Current products may now be attached to the internet and the application update may be downloaded and installed by the customer themselves.

Whatever approach is used this document will define the process.

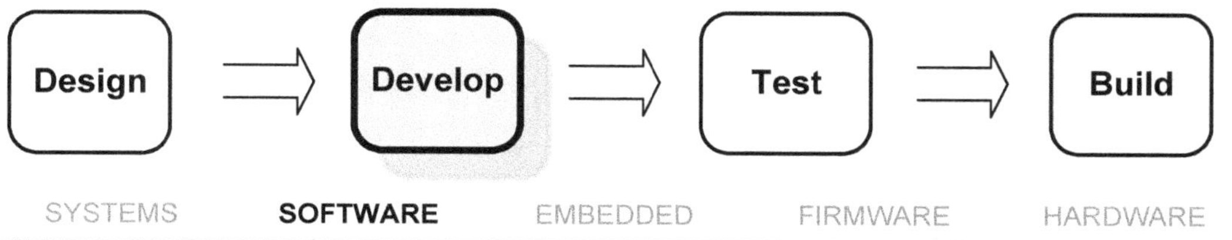

Software Program Design Language

Prior to developing software code it is often beneficial to determine a top-down approach by specifying the principal function and then breaking this function down into a number of steps. Each of these steps then becomes a sub-function in its own right and the process decomposes down lower and lower until we hit code.

In order to accomplish this program design language was developed. Now this is an old concept but it is still applicable for this reason. The top-down decomposition of the task into its inherent operations provides a breakdown into tasks and a sequence of events. Once determined, these higher level events consisting of an implied sequence of events become the function names while lower level events become actual code. This means that each level of pseudocode either represents a sub-function or it becomes a pseudocode comment for a block of code. This enables each block of code to be documented before coding actually commences. In this, the person performing the coding will keep in mind the events that are being processed and any subsequent person who has to perform product maintenance will have adequate documentation regarding the same.

Software Coding

When performing the actual coding process remember that the key to writing good code is the choice of the code variable name, function name or structure name. The use of the underscore is also encouraged as it makes the name more readable.

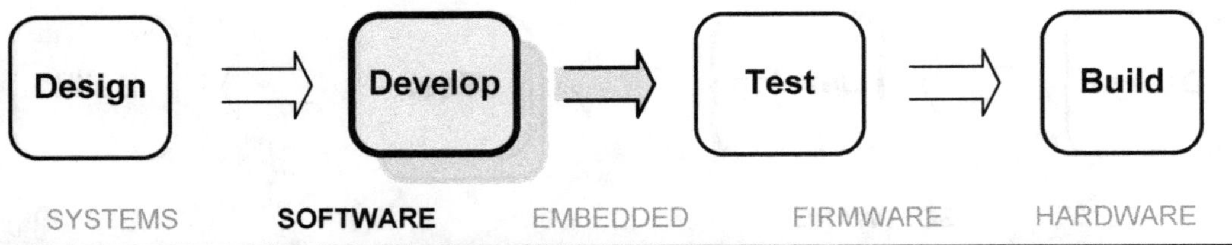

Develop Software Outputs

The Develop Software Outputs include the following:

Software Low Level Design Document

Purpose: Provide overall high level design details

Presenter: Senior Software Application Engineer

Reviewers: System Architect

Software Toolset Document

Purpose: Provide overall high level design details

Presenter: Senior Software Application Engineer

Reviewers: System Architect

Software Build Process

Purpose: Provide overall high level design details

Presenter: Senior Software Application Engineer

Reviewers: System Architect

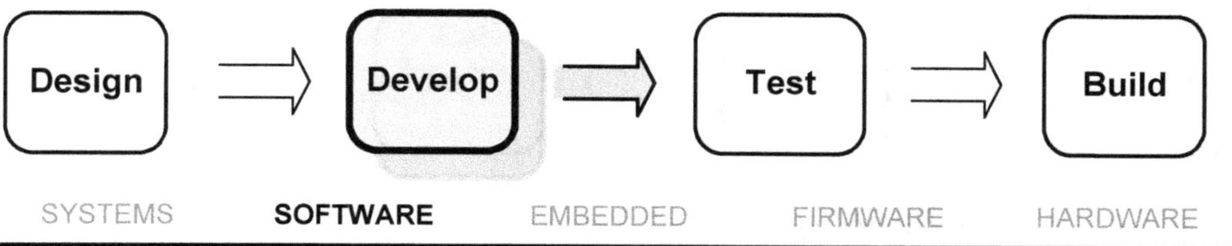

Software Installation Process

Purpose: Define software installation process

Presenter: Senior Software Application Engineer

Reviewers: System Architect
Senior Production Test Engineer

Software Upgrade Process

Purpose: Define software upgrade process

Presenter: Senior Software Application Engineer

Reviewers: System Architect
Senior Production Test Engineer

Software Code

Purpose: Define software code modules

Presenter: Senior Software Application Engineer

Reviewers: System Architect
Senior Production Test Engineer

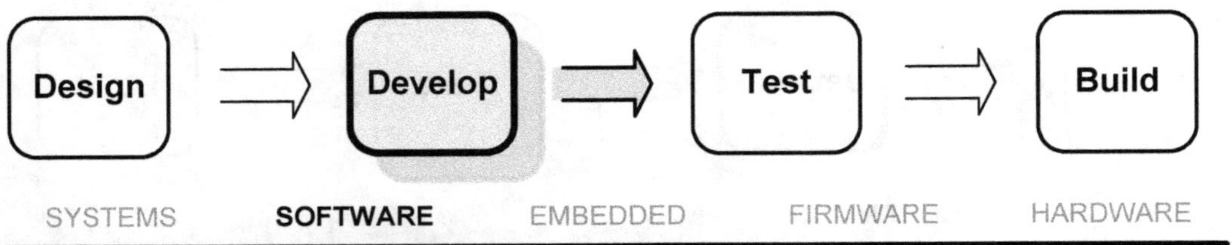

Update Risk Analysis Document

Purpose: Review overall risk analysis

Presenter: Senior Software Application Engineer

Reviewers: System Architect

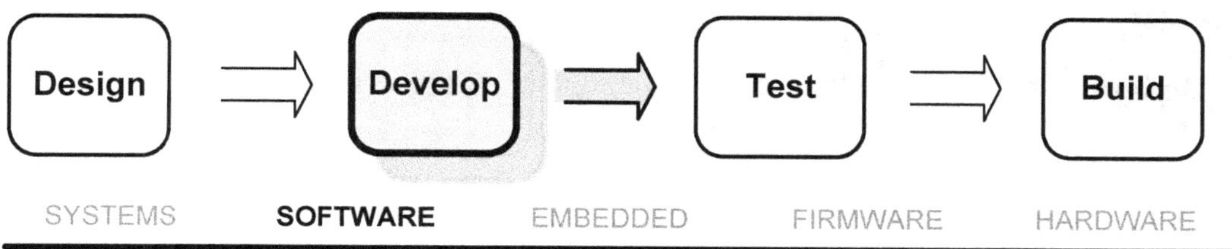

[This Page Intentionally Left Blank]

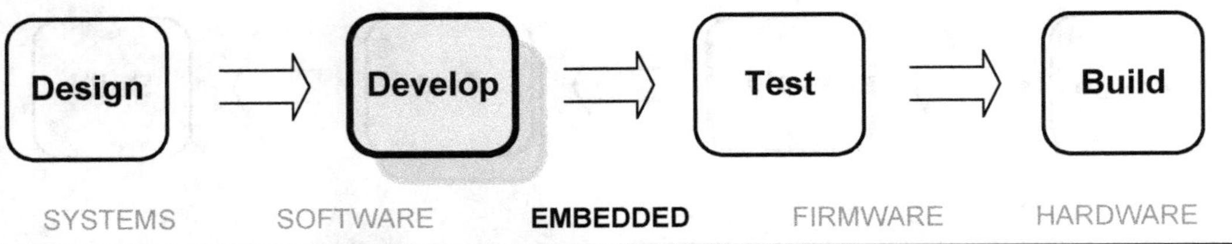

Embedded

The Embedded design features will now be implemented. This task involves developing the code for the following features:

1. Bootup Code
2. Board Support Package Interface
3. Hardware Drivers and API's
4. Additional detail to Memory Map.

Bootup Code.

The embedded design specified the manner in which the system would be started. This may be as simply as specifying a jump vector and placing a small piece of code (C or assembler) at a specific address location which will cause the processor to execute an instruction to jump to the main() function of the application.

In other systems it may be more complicated (involving assembler and C/C++ instructions) to copy the program from flash memory to ram and to transfer execution to the ram copy for faster execution. This may require some pre-existing bootup code to be modified or the generation of a new bootup utility.

Whichever method is required the code will be developed at this point in time. The low level design document will also be updated to describe the process in detail. To rely on 'documented' code to describe such is for the company to throw money away. Days can be wasted when a new developer has to reverse-engineer some ingenious 'trick' that was employed by the original developer in order to 'save time'. The System Boot document is also updated.

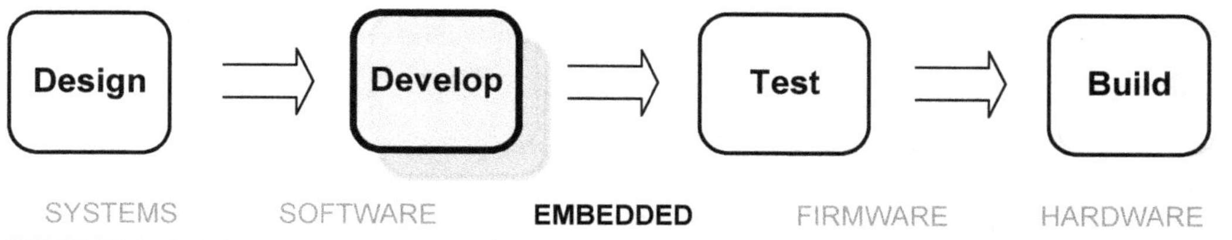

Board Support Package

The board support package interfaces are now developed. This includes writing code for each of the Operating Interfaces (eg. the clock tick, serial interfaces, Ethernet interfaces). The Board Support Package document is updated to fully describe the manner in which the implementation was effected.

Hardware Drivers and API's

Software driver code will be developed for each of the hardware interfaces. Most of these (if not all) will have associated Application Program Interface routines that also need to be developed. Low-level design documentation will be written to describe the implementation process. Unit test code will also be developed to verify the operation of these APIs.

Update Memory Map.

As the design develops additional detail will be determined as to the memory map. This might include application usage regarding the memory space (eg. common ram memory areas, or a breakdown of internal Flash memory usage). Such detail should be controlled by the senior embedded engineer such that this person alone is responsible for updating the memory map.

Update Risk Analysis Document

Risk can enter the system design at any stage of project development. On completion of embedded development the embedded tasks worked on during this phase will be checked against the risk analysis document in order to determine any new project risks or any adverse affect to current mitigations.

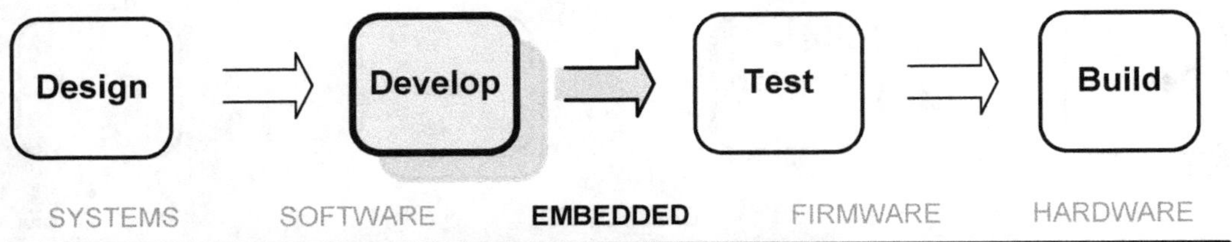

Develop Embedded Outputs

The Develop Embedded Outputs include the following:

Bootup Code Document

Purpose: Describe software boot implementation

Presenter: Embedded Software Engineer

Reviewers: System Architect
Senior Production Test Engineer

Board Support Package Interface Document

Purpose: Describe BSP interface implementation

Presenter: Embedded Software Engineer

Reviewers: Senior Embedded Software Engineer

Hardware Drivers and API Document

Purpose: Describe driver and API functions

Presenter: Embedded Software Engineer

Reviewers: Senior Embedded Software Engineer

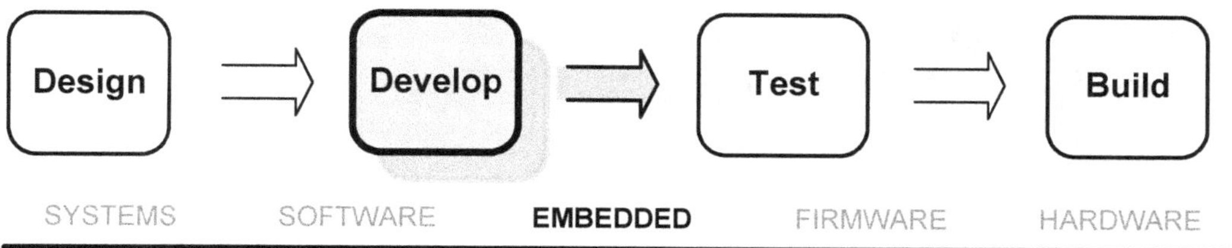

Software Code Design Reviews

Purpose: Check code against coding standards

Presenter: Embedded Software Engineer

Reviewers: Senior Embedded Software Engineer

Update Memory Map

Purpose: Review memory map updates

Presenter: Senior Embedded Software Engineer

Reviewers: Senior Hardware Software Engineer

Update Risk Analysis Document

Purpose: Review overall risk analysis

Presenter: Senior Embedded Software Engineer

Reviewers: System Architect
Embedded Software Engineer

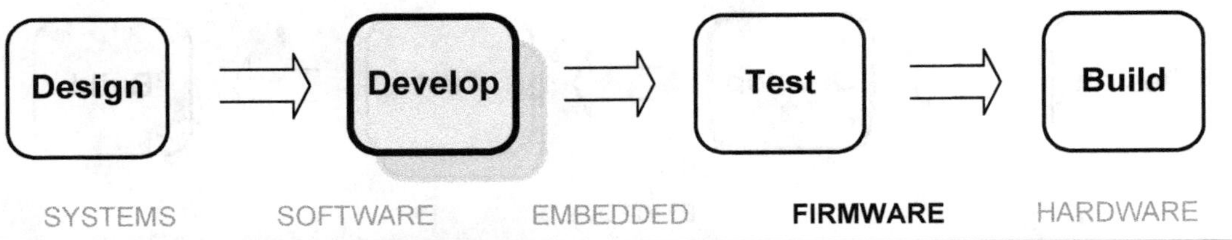

Firmware

The Firmware task involves...

1. Develop cPLD code
2. Develop cPLD Low-Level Design Documentation
3. Develop cPLD Verification Tests
4. Developing FPGA code
5. Developing FPGA Low-Level Design Documentation
6. Develop FPGA Verification Tests
7. Update Risk Analysis Document

With every project that involves firmware software development there should be at least two firmware engineers. This ensures that product knowledge will be maintained if the firmware engineer should leave the company. The junior firmware engineer should utilize the design documents and develop the cPLD code. The senior firmware engineer has the task of mentor towards the less experienced engineer. The senior engineer also has the task of developing the documentation. This approach should be used with all sizes of projects. The senior firmware engineer is training the junior engineer with the intent that the company foresees future growth. To have a senior engineer perform the tasks of a junior engineer is to have a company that is stagnant.

Develop cPLD code

If the hardware design includes cPLD components, the code for these devices is generated during this phase. Depending upon the complexity periodic code review should be held to ensure the design is well laid out and easy to maintain.

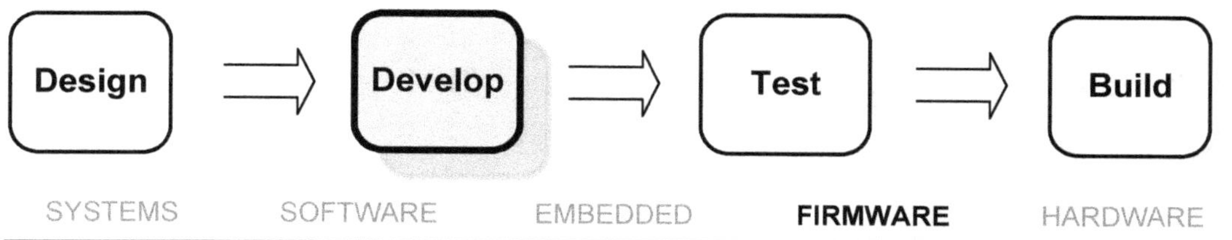

As with any software design, the code should be well documented and the choice of parameter names and control signals should match those stated in the data dictionary. This will ensure that schematic control signals match those defined within the software code.

Develop cPLD Low-Level Design Documentation

The cPLD low-level design document describes the low level implementation aspects of the cPLD design. This document provides additional detail to the descriptive text found in the cPLD source code. Source code documentation is usually brief in nature and insufficient when it comes to code maintenance issues hence the need for this document. This effort reduces production test, manufacturing and maintenance costs.

Develop cPLD Verification Tests

During the firmware design process appropriate cPLD verification tests were defined. This document is now updated to provide additional detail regarding the implementation of these tests.

Developing FPGA code

If the hardware design includes FPGA components, the code for these devices is generated during this phase. Depending upon the complexity periodic code review should be held to ensure the design is well laid out and easy to maintain.

As with the cPLD software design, this code should be well documented and the choice of parameter names and control signals should match those stated in the data dictionary.

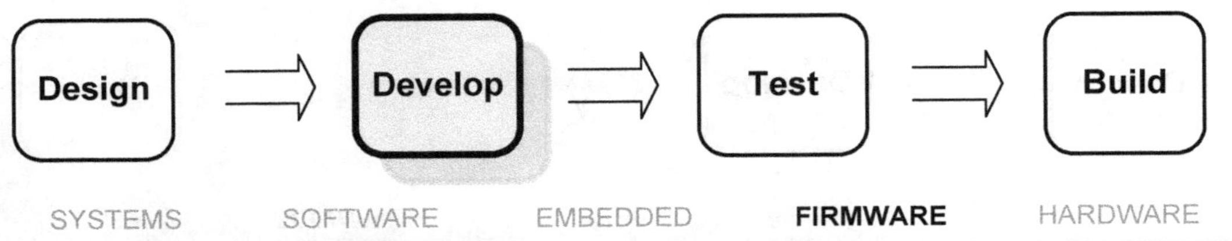

Developing FPGA Low-Level Design Documentation

The FPGA low-level design document describes the low level implementation aspects of the FPFA design. This document provides additional detail to the descriptive text found in the FPGA source code. Source code documentation is usually brief in nature and insufficient when it comes to code maintenance issues hence the need for this document. This effort reduces production test, manufacturing and maintenance costs.

Develop FPGA Verification Tests

During the firmware design process appropriate FPGA verification tests were defined. This document is now updated to provide additional detail regarding the implementation of these tests.

Update Risk Analysis Document

During this development process new information will be identified. This may affect the design implementation which may interact with the currently conceived system and either generate new risks or make certain risk mitigations ineffectual. To counteract this the risk analysis document should be reviewed and any adverse conditions identified and corrected.

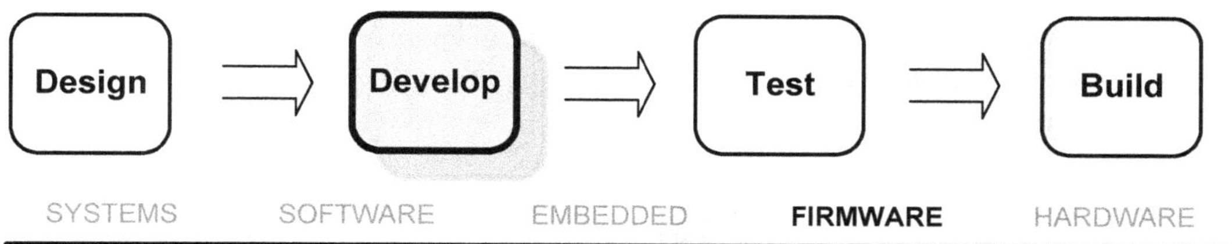

[This Page Intentionally Left Blank]

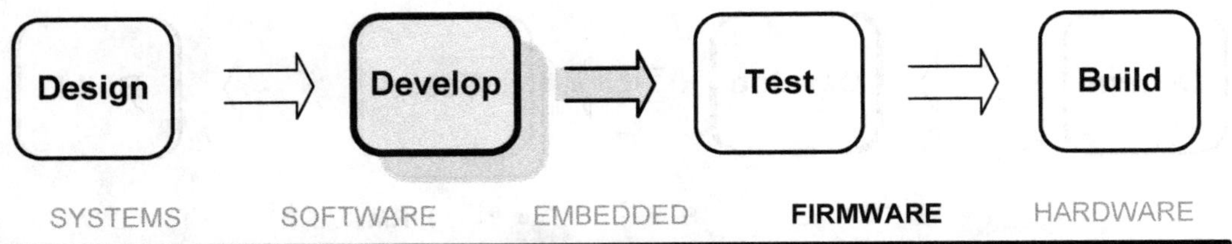

Develop Firmware Outputs

The Develop Firmware Outputs include the following:

cPLD Source Code

<u>Purpose</u>: Review cPLD source code

<u>Presenter</u>: Firmware Engineer

<u>Reviewers</u>: Senior Firmware Engineer

cPLD Low Level Design Document

<u>Purpose</u>: cPLD low-level detailed design

<u>Presenter</u>: Senior Firmware Engineer

<u>Reviewers</u>: System Architect
Senior Software Embedded Engineer

cPLD Verification Test Document(s)

<u>Purpose</u>: Review implementation of cPLD verification tests

<u>Presenter</u>: Firmware Engineer

<u>Reviewers</u>: System Architect
Senior Firmware Engineer
Senior Software Embedded Engineer

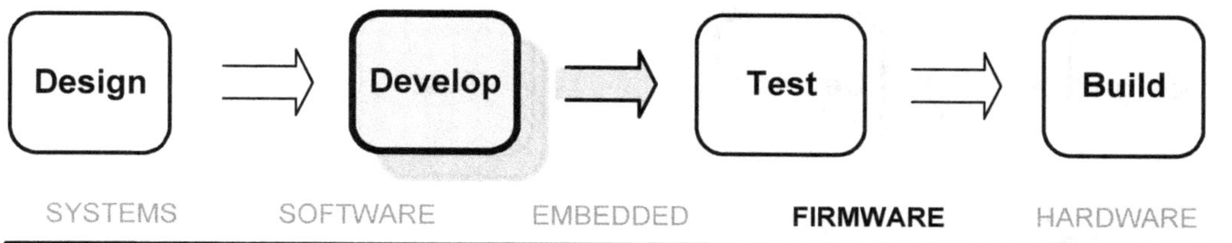

FPGA Source Code

Purpose: Review FPGA source code

Presenter: Firmware Engineer

Reviewers: Senior Firmware Engineer

FPGA Low Level Design Document

Purpose: FPGA low-level detailed design

Presenter: Senior Firmware Engineer

Reviewers: System Architect
Senior Software Embedded Engineer

FPGA Verification Test Document(s)

Purpose: Review implementation of FPGA verification tests

Presenter: Firmware Engineer

Reviewers: System Architect
Senior Firmware Engineer
Senior Software Embedded Engineer

Update Risk Analysis Document

Purpose: Review overall risk analysis

Presenter: Senior Firmware Engineer

Reviewers: System Architect
Embedded Software Engineer

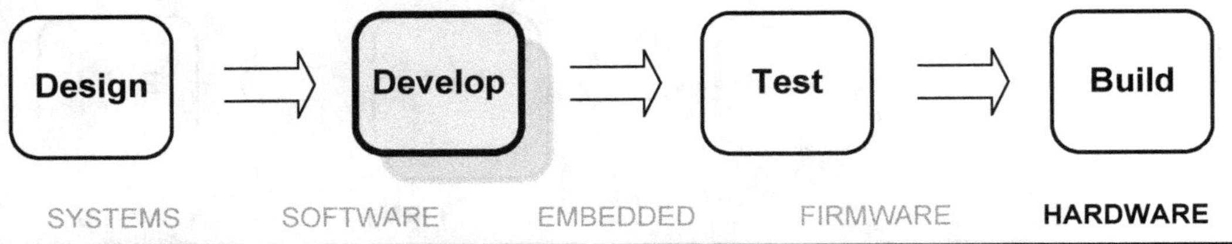

Hardware

The senior hardware engineer uses the hardware architecture and high level design documents in order to determine the number of PCBs in the system along with the relevant components and interface connections. As the design is broken down the senior engineer will mentor a junior engineer. Again, the aspect of company growth is to have senior engineers train the less experienced engineers. This allows product knowledge to be spread throughout the company.

For each PCBA in the product design, the engineering team will perform the following tasks:

1. Component datasheet Document
2. Generate a PCB schematic diagram
3. Generate PCB trace layout and drilling
4. Create a Bill-Of-Materials (BOM)

Component Datasheet Document

The junior hardware engineer will review the hardware architecture design documentation and search for suitable components. The hardware architecture and high-level documents will state the capabilities of the required parts. The engineer is faced with searching the Internet and various technical catalogs in order to find suitable components. These component data sheets will then be made available to all engineering departments such that the entire product development team is designing with the same information. A component datasheet document will be created that identifies why a specific part was selected and any differences between first and second source 'equivalents'.

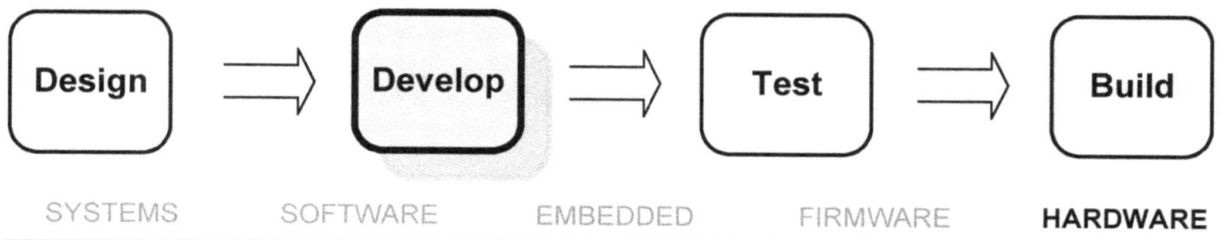

Generate a PCB schematic diagram
The senior hardware engineer will mentor the junior engineer as to the development of the schematic diagram. Company standards will be enforced. For example, control inputs should arrive on the left of the schematic page and exit on the right, positive edge clocking, no floating control signals, etc. The Data Dictionary has been created to identify all control signals. Some of these will have already been defined. These should be used on the schematic. Any new control signals should be added to the data dictionary as per the indicated format. The data dictionary also ensures the uniqueness of all signal names. If possible, and wherever space allows, certain states and address information should be displayed on the schematic diagram such that intent is clearly identified.

PCB Low-Level Design Document
The Senior Hardware Engineer is responsible for generating the PCB low-level design documentation. Each PCB schematic will only provide minimal detail. The low-level design document is used to provides additional detailed information (eg. why a specific part was used, timing analysis of various control signals, etc.).

Generate PCB trace layout and drilling
An engineer may be employed who has been trained in this field. This person understands the requirements which are specific to high-speed PCB design. Such knowledge would ensure that clock signals use traces of equal length since timing the edge of signals is now very important when high clock frequencies are being used and to be aware that analog and digital ground traces must be of sufficient current carrying capacity. For this engineer should also be verifying the electrical engineer's design in order to eliminate potential problems.

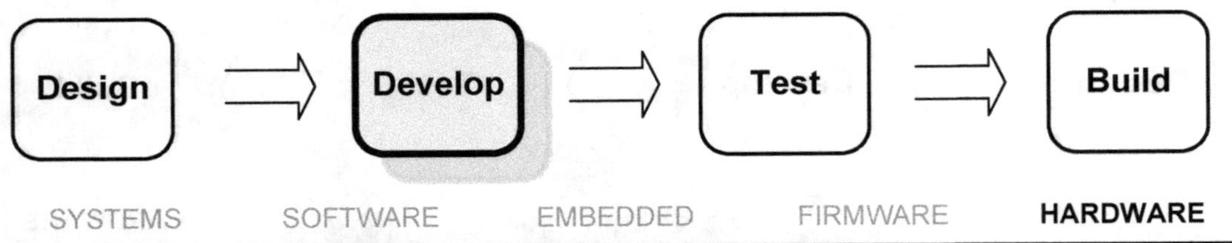

Create a Bill-Of-Materials (BOM)

Each Printed Circuit Board Assembly (PCBA) consists of a PCB and a number of components. The printed circuit board and the components soldered onto the board are each given a unique identification part number. This is the mechanism used by the company in order to identify each part or assembly which makes up the final product.

A database program is used to create these part numbers. Once the design is finalized, the hardware engineer enters the part information into the database along with primary and secondary suppliers.

The end result is that the final product will have a part number and a bill of materials. This list of materials will identify the major items that make up the product (eg. the product case, main circuit boards, wiring harness, etc.). Each level down will identify successive part numbers and they in turn may have a bill of materials (eg. the wiring harness might identify multiple end connectors and many wires of different colors and lengths; a PCBA part number will identify a PCB and the component part numbers that are soldered onto this PCB).

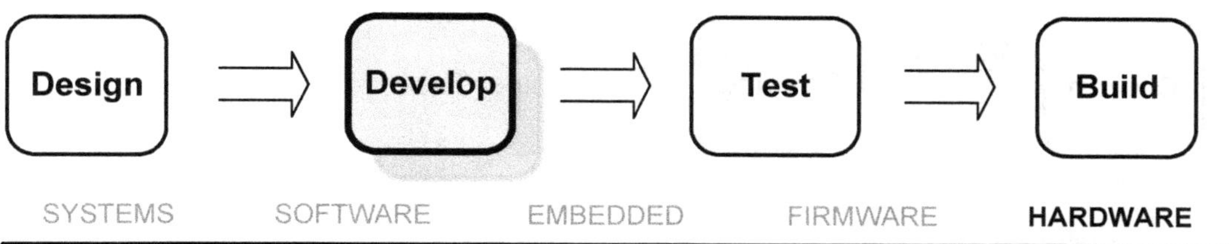

[This Page Intentionally Left Blank]

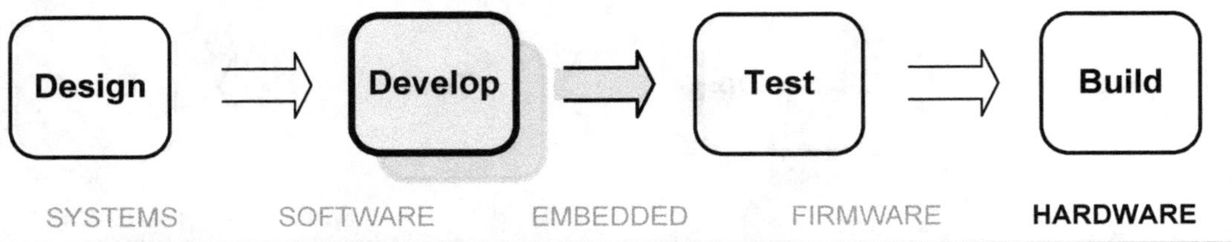

Develop Hardware Outputs

The Develop Hardware Outputs include the following:

PCBA Component Datasheet Document

Purpose: Identify why specific components were used
Differences between first and second 'equivalents'

Presenter: Junior Hardware Engineer

Reviewers: System Architect
Senior Hardware Engineer
Senior Embedded Engineer

PCBA Low Level Design Document

Purpose: PCBA Low Level Implementation.

Presenter: Senior Hardware Engineer

Reviewers: System Architect
Senior Embedded Engineer
Senior Firmware Engineer

PCB Schematics

Purpose: PCBA Schematic Capture.

Presenter: Senior Hardware Engineer

Reviewers: System Architect
Senior Hardware Engineer

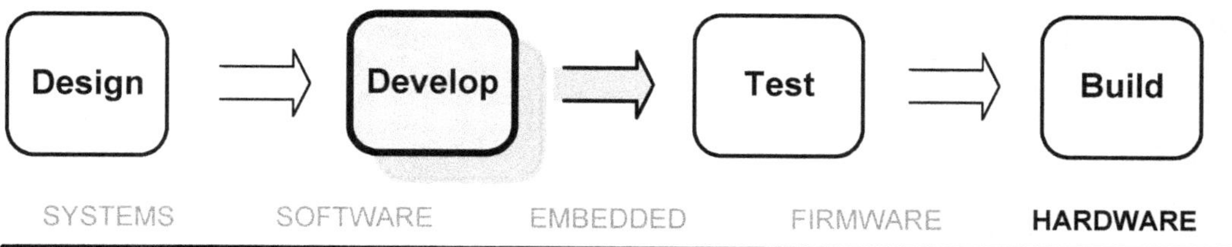

PCB Trace Layer Definitions

Purpose: PCB Trace Layer Design.

Presenter: PCB Hardware Engineer

Reviewers: System Architect
Senior Hardware Engineer

PCB Bill Of Materials

Purpose: BOM PCB Trace Layer Design.

Presenter: Senior Hardware Engineer

Reviewers: System Architect
Junior Hardware Engineer

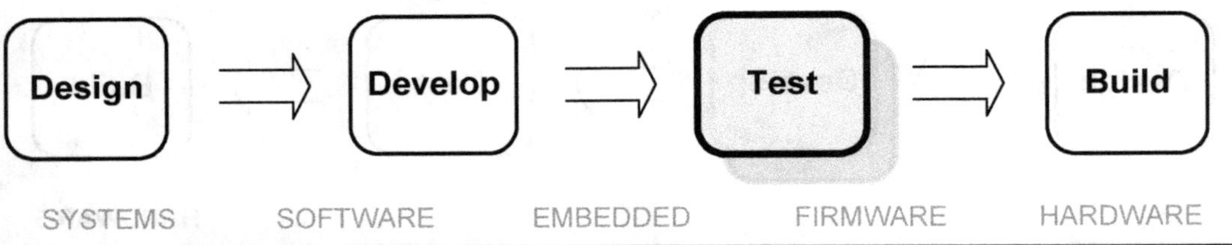

Test

The Test phase of the project affects all departments and for many it is a time for review. All too often the initial design effort drifts away from actuality as the design proceeds through development. This is now the time to review the created documentation and to ensure its accuracy. Many companies ignore this step in the process.

The philosophy of 'I'm alright jack' is used to give a false illusion of hope. There is a reason why many engineers will avoid project maintenance and production test like the plague. They avoid such tasks because they know the documentation is inadequate and in error. They know such detail intuitively because they have seen the first-hand efforts of their team members working under strict time schedules. They have seen the minimalist approach being worked out before their very eyes and in many cases they were the very ones at fault.

For if you only do what you believe is necessary for you alone to succeed then the entire team fails. When other junior (less experienced) engineers see the detail and size of my design documents they tend to laugh behind my back. That ridicule disappears when they need the information contained within. But that does not make them change their ways. Their documents are still the briefest of notes, usually a mere quarter or less of the size required.

But they get away with it because management wants to show progress on their aggressive schedule. So remember, a minimal timeline will generate minimalist work output. The design might proceed into prototype development but expect high maintenance costs later in the project lifecycle. The apparent cost savings during the design and development phase will be lost during project maintenance (the duration of which extends over the time that the product will

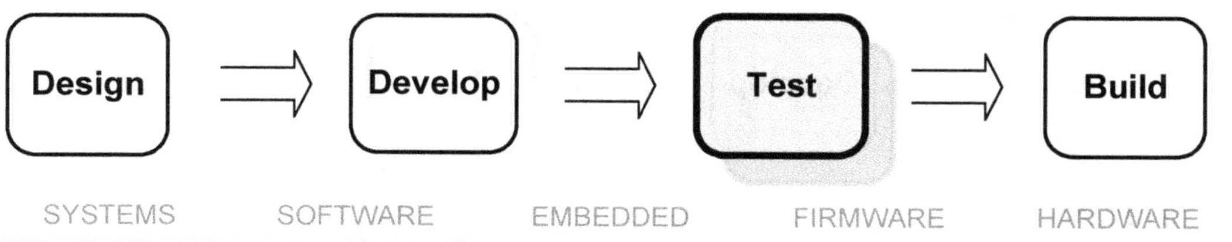

be sold) and if the design is poorly documented the project maintenance effort will be very expensive and reduce your profits extensively. Remember, when an engineer reads project documentation and sees error they then associate error with the entire document for now none of it can be trusted.

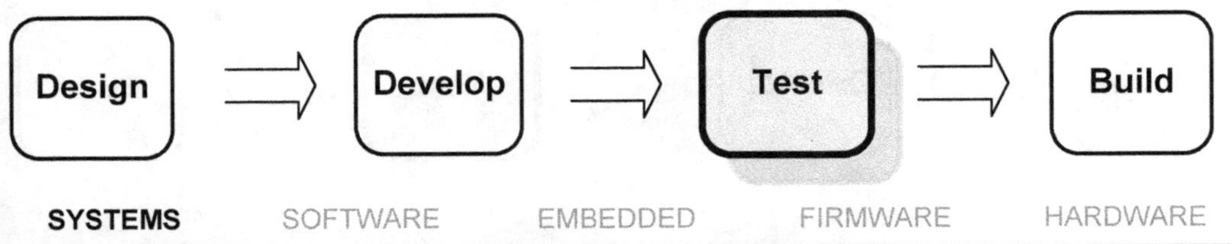

Systems

At this point in time all the documentation developed by the systems engineers should be reviewed. This task is not as daunting as it might first appear for as any changes to the design should have been reflected in the system documentation as such occurred. This would have been necessary to keep the other departments who read these design documents up to date. It should be noted that when (or if) such design changes occur, it is the duty of the Systems Architect to hold design reviews identifying such changes for this person is the one tasked with keeping the project 'on track'. The System Architect is the person who has the vision.

Please note the following.

If the documentation is allowed to becomes out of date it is then generally worthless for errors will abound. A time bounded engineer implementing the minimalist approach might not really understand who exactly reads their documents.

But the people concerned include the following:

Production Test Engineers
Validation and Verification Engineers
Maintenance Engineers
Manufacturing Engineers

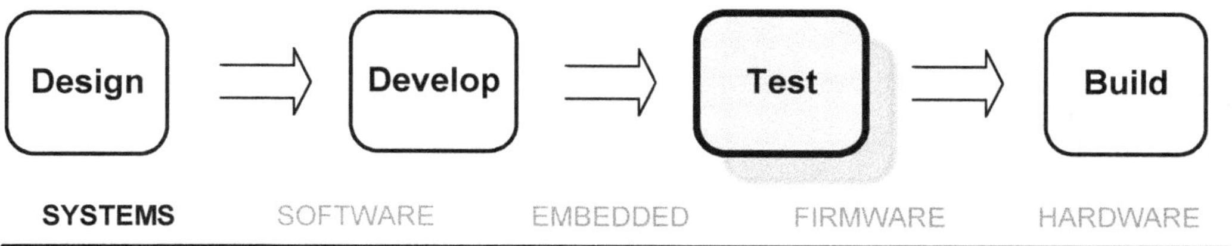

To 'save time and money' by developing inadequate documentation is to now force these engineering departments to reverse-engineer the design effort. If this is the case then say 'good bye' to all the company profits.

Do not become short-sighted.

For the minimalist approach is the company's downfall.

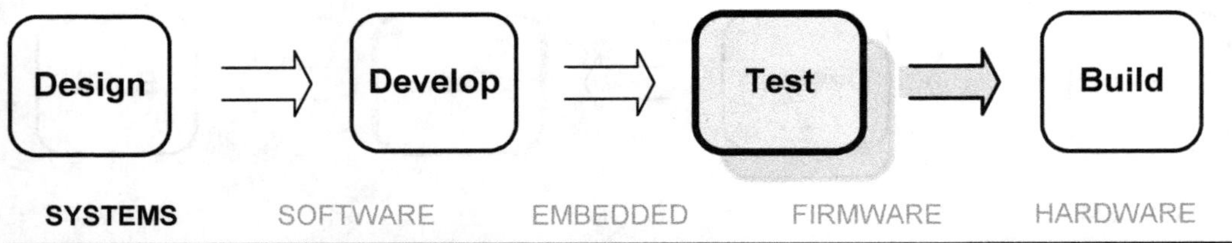

Test Systems Outputs

The Test Systems Outputs include the review and relevant updates to the following documentation:

Product Requirements Document

Purpose:	Customer requirements identified. Each requirement has validation test.
Presenter:	System Architect
Reviewers:	Senior Software Application Engineer Senior Embedded Software Engineer Senior Hardware Engineer

System Requirements Document

Purpose:	Customer requirements in engineering terms. Each requirement has verification test.
Presenter:	System Architect
Reviewers:	Senior Software Application Engineer Senior Embedded Software Engineer Senior Hardware Engineer

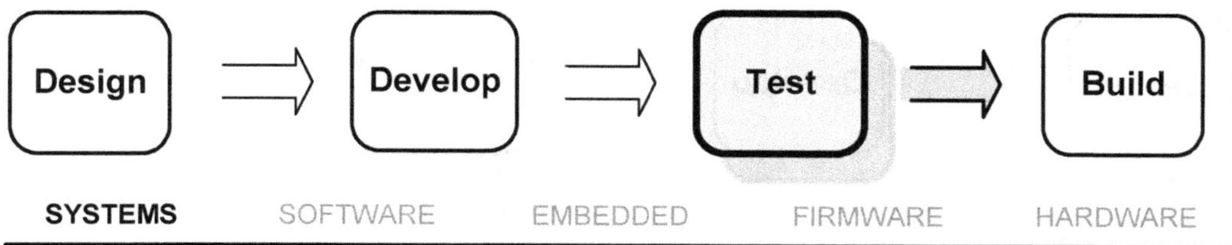

Operators Manual (Living Document)

Purpose: Define user product operation.

Presenter: System Architect

Reviewers: Senior Software Applications Engineer
Senior Hardware Engineer

Data Dictionary (Living Document)

Purpose: Identify control signals and their purpose.

Presenter: System Architect

Reviewers: Senior Embedded Software Engineer
Senior Hardware Engineer

Fault Analysis Document (Living Document)

Purpose: Identify single point failures.
Specify concern and mitigation.

Presenter: System Architect

Reviewers: Senior Software Application Engineer
Senior Embedded Software Engineer
Senior Hardware Engineer

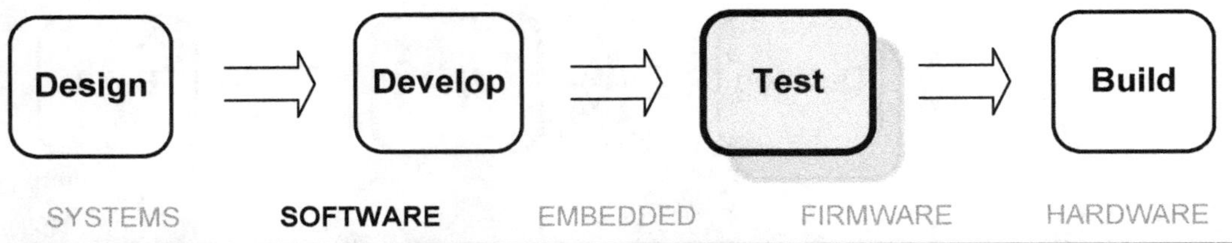

Software

When the software was being developed various tests were created in order to ensure that the product met the software system requirements. In a medical company test cases are developed by the Verification and Validation engineers. These engineers write test scenarios in which each system requirement is verified. In this the user would place the product into a particular mode of operation to allow a specific feature to be executed. But under many cases this feature is hidden. It may be a feature that affects one or more lower levels of the system and is not readily seen by the operator. The verification engineer does not usually have a computer software programming background and so is ill-suited in this effort. The software developer should then be the one tasked with this work since they are in actuality ensuring that the system requirement was met. This effort is often proved by software unit tests or even by a code review since the feature is hidden in the software and not readily apparent externally.

During this test phase the software engineer will write such verification test documents that prove the design has met the software requirements.

During this test phase the validation engineer will write the validation test documents that prove the design has met the product requirements. This in effect is proving that the correct product has been designed. In other words, the product the customer wanted has been built.

Any software (or design) errors that were detected would be corrected and the source code and documentation updated. Each time such occurs the entire product development team is informed of the changes.

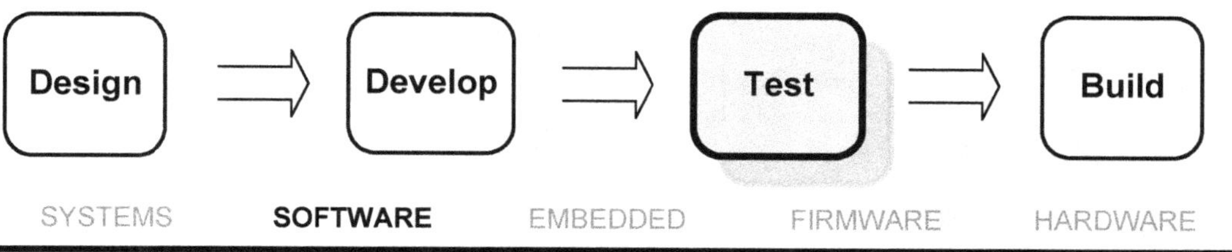

[This Page Intentionally Left Blank]

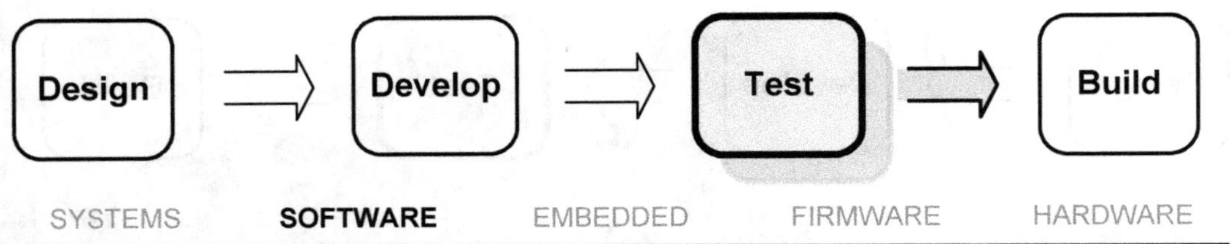

Test Software Outputs

The Test Systems Outputs include the review and relevant updates to the following documentation:

Software Unit Tests Document

Purpose:	Review each Unit Test Assign Unit Test against Software Requirement
Presenter:	Software Application Engineer
Reviewers:	System Architect Senior Embedded Software Engineer

Validation Tests Document

Purpose:	Review each Validation Test Assign Validation Test against Product Requirement
Presenter:	Validation Engineer
Reviewers:	System Architect Senior Software Engineer Senior Embedded Software Engineer

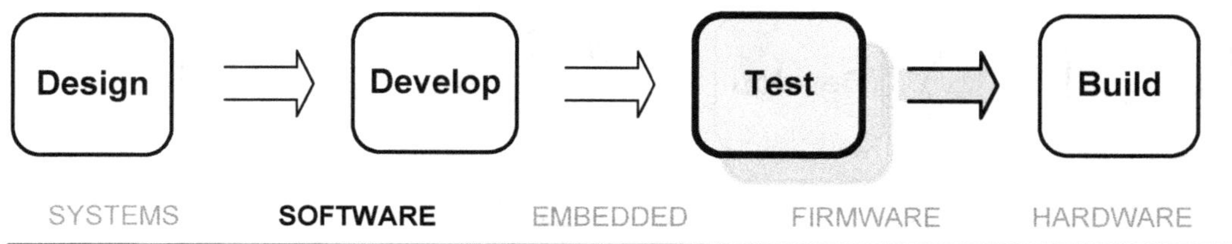

Fault Analysis Document (Living Document)

Purpose: Identify single point failures.
Specify concern and mitigation.

Presenter: System Architect

Reviewers: Senior Software Application Engineer
Senior Embedded Software Engineer
Senior Hardware Engineer

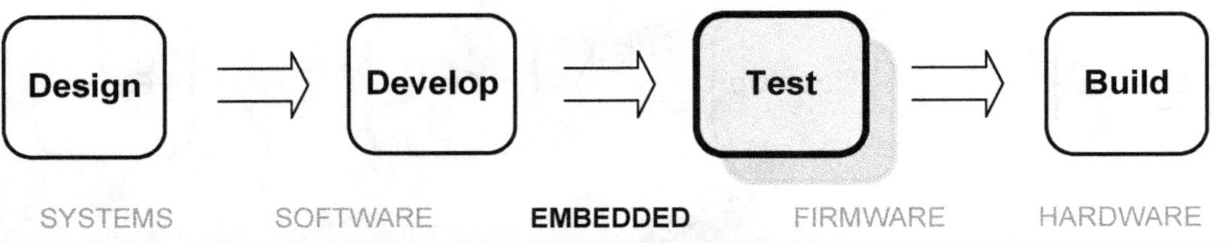

Embedded

The Embedded development work effort is generally hidden since it is a domain that resides below systems and software yet above hardware. Remember that when the product requirements were being specified the requirement was mostly with respect to how the product would function. This aspect of the requirement was carried over into the system specification. Although the system requirement provided more detail regarding the design, it attempted to still provide the engineer with a certain amount of freedom and expression. This implies that the aspect of the requirement still remained functional in nature resulting in few verification tests being required.

None the less, the unit tests that were developed for the various Application Program Interfaces would be formalized at this point.

Any software (or design) errors that were detected would be corrected and the source code and documentation updated. Each time such occurs the entire product development team is informed of the changes.

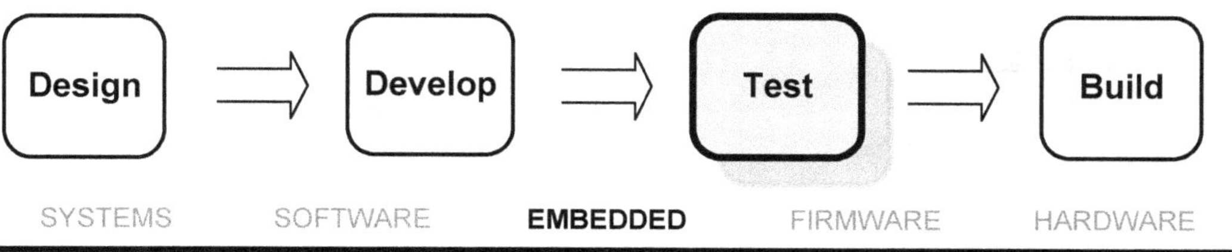

[This Page Intentionally Left Blank]

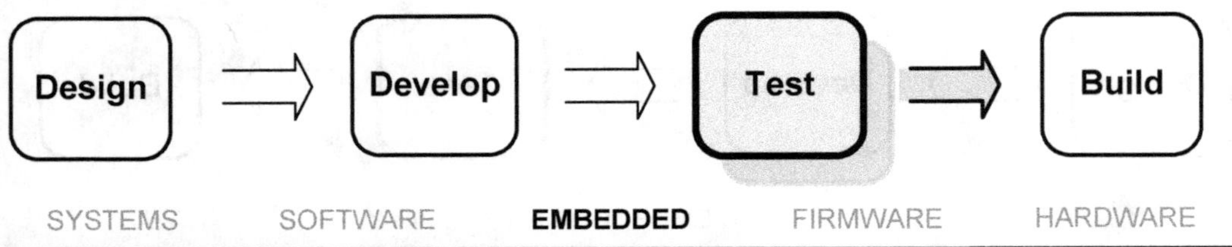

Test Embedded Outputs

The Test Embedded Outputs include the following:

Embedded Unit Tests Document

Purpose: Review each Unit Test
Assign Unit Test against Software Requirement

Presenter: Senior Embedded Software Engineer

Reviewers: System Architect

Verification Tests Document

Purpose: Review each Verification Test
Assign Verification Test against System Requirement

Presenter: Senior Embedded Software Engineer

Reviewers: System Architect

Fault Analysis Document (Living Document)

Purpose: Identify single point failures.
Specify concern and mitigation.

Presenter: System Architect

Reviewers: Senior Software Application Engineer
Senior Embedded Software Engineer
Senior Hardware Engineer

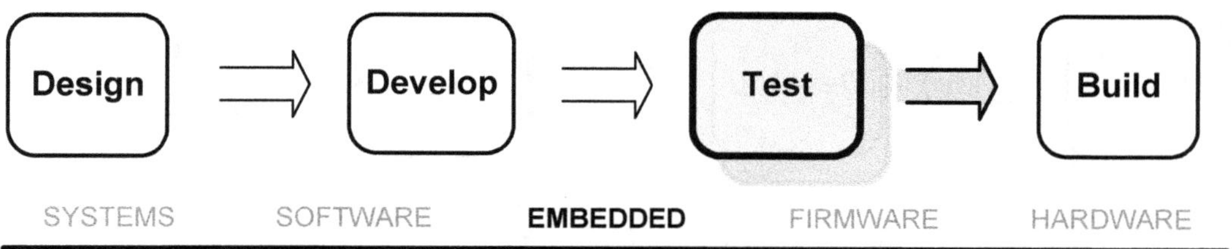

[This Page Intentionally Left Blank]

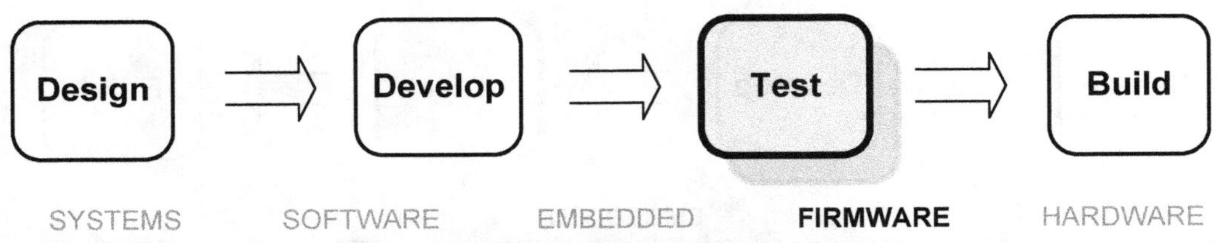

Firmware

The Firmware task involves the formalization of the verification tests. These tests are to verify that the firmware installed in cPLD and FPGA devices are fully functional.

The firmware verification tests were initially developed to test the cPLD and FPGA code releases prior to them being given for use by the other departments. These tests are now placed in their final form. Each test will specify all the necessary equipment along with its configuration. As with all validation tests, the test operator may not be the individual who developed the test.

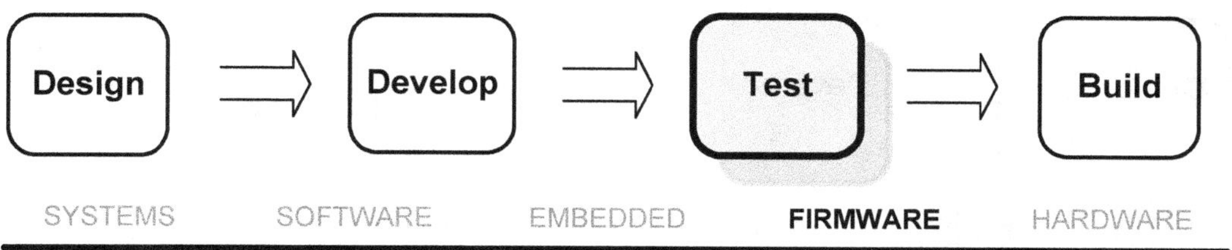

[This Page Intentionally Left Blank]

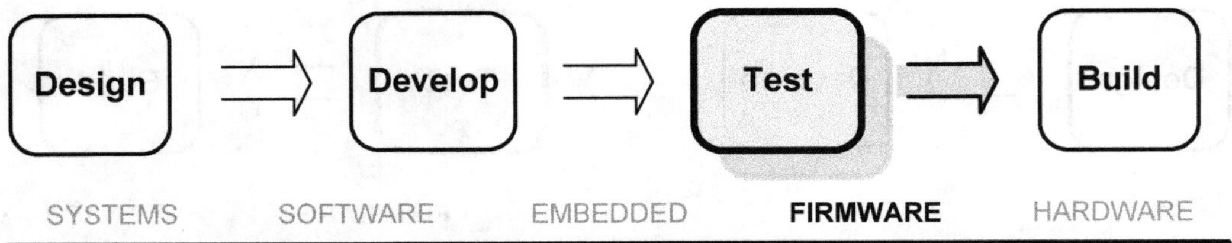

Test Firmware Outputs

The Test Firmware Outputs include the following documents:

Verification Tests Document

Purpose: Review each Verification Test
Assign Verification Test against System Requirement

Presenter: Senior Firmware Engineer

Reviewers: System Architect
Senior Embedded Engineer

Fault Analysis Document (Living Document)

Purpose: Identify single point failures.
Specify concern and mitigation.

Presenter: System Architect

Reviewers: Senior Firmware Engineer
Senior Embedded Software Engineer
Senior Hardware Engineer

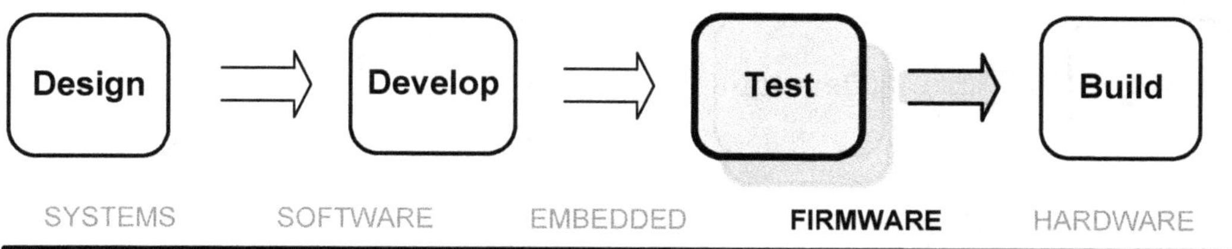

[This Page Intentionally Left Blank]

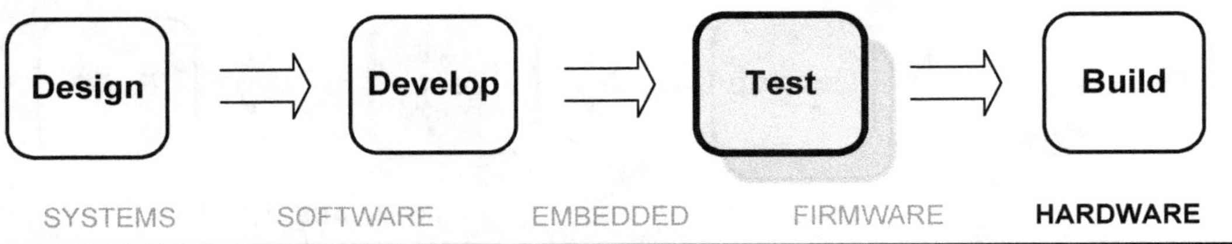

Hardware

The hardware task involves the formalization of the verification tests. These tests are to verify that the hardware PCBA is fully functional.

The hardware verification tests were initially developed to test the PCBA prior to it being given for use by the other departments. These tests are now placed in their final form. Each test will specify all the necessary equipment along with its configuration. As with all validation tests, the test operator may not be the individual who developed the test.

In order to test the device one or more test fixtures may have been created along with specific test hardware and/or firmware. This work may be implemented by the development engineer or may be performed by an entirely different group (eg. Production Test). If the company used its Production Test engineers then their work would also be performed along the lines stated by this document. They too would perform the Design, Develop, Test and Build phases with respect to systems, software, embedded, firmware and hardware that is built to test the product. In this regard this book and its design philosophy would be directly applicable.

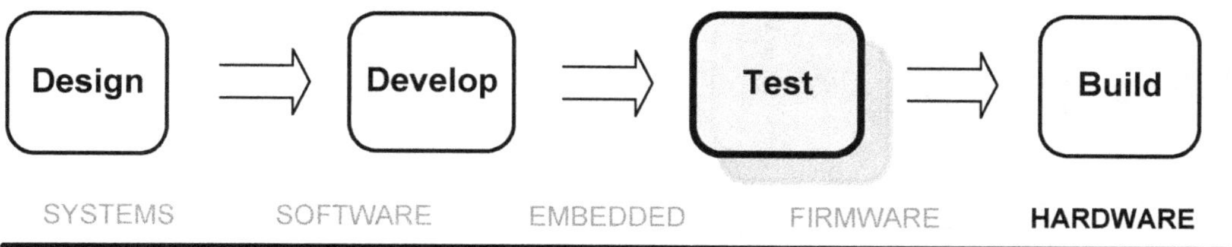

[This Page Intentionally Left Blank]

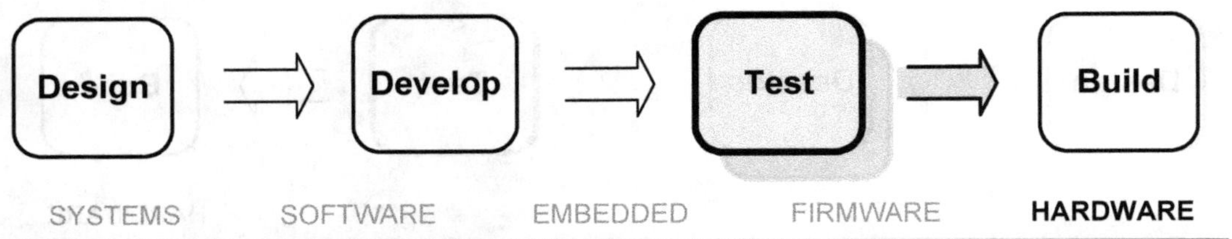

Test Hardware Outputs

The Test Hardware Outputs include the following:

Verification Tests Document

<u>Purpose</u>: Review each Verification Test
Assign Verification Test against System Requirement

<u>Presenter</u>: Senior Hardware Engineer

<u>Reviewers</u>: System Architect
Senior Firmware Engineer
Senior Embedded Engineer

Fault Analysis Document (Living Document)

<u>Purpose</u>: Identify single point failures.
Specify concern and mitigation.

<u>Presenter</u>: System Architect

<u>Reviewers</u>: Senior Hardware Engineer
Senior Firmware Engineer
Senior Embedded Software Engineer

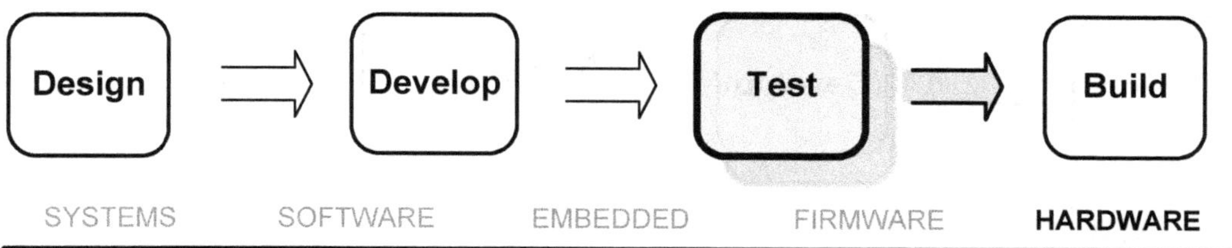

[This Page Intentionally Left Blank]

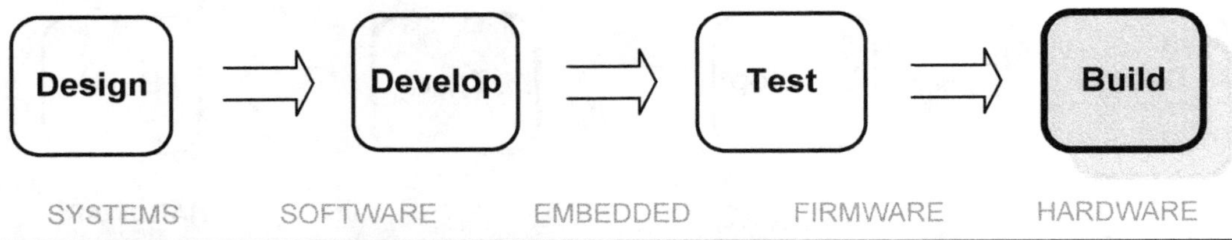

Build

This is the product manufacturing phase. It requires all the Design, Develop and Test phases to be completed and well documented. A number of product prototypes will have been built and tested and we are ready for manufacture.

All the design effort has been placed into the Design History File and this directory contains the device final build information for the first product run.

But the rest of the development effort is not finished.

The next task for the team is to determine how to improve on the product. There will always be others who will wish to take what you have and make something better and cheaper. So to prevent this from happening, your team must be the ones doing this first.

All too often the company throws away their lead and rests. They either eliminate their design team or place them on some other product. You should note that at this point your development team is full of ideas regarding how to make the product better. This is the time to work on these ideas while it is still fresh in their minds.

So while the manufacturing effort is in full swing the development team is now working on the next product release. A product that will be smaller, faster, cheaper. For I assure you, if you don't do it then someone else will.

So this is NOT the time to eliminate the design team.

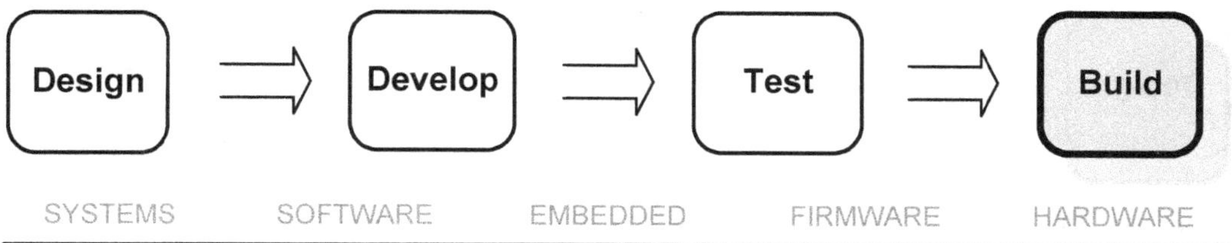

While the product is being manufactured the design team is there to assist with any bug fixes and they are starting on the next design for during the test phase the system architect and the senior lead engineers have been looking to the future. This is the reason why the development teams have senior and junior members. The senior members design effort is to document and mentor whereas the junior members are more 'hands on'. When you have your senior team members 'laying the bricks' you are throwing away their design effort capability and your company's future lead in the world market is being lost. For I don't know if you realize it but product life-cycles are getting faster and faster and new versions (with new features) are being delivered to the customer in record time.

In times past the product might have had a lead for several years and if the company was not pro-active in developing the next product they will soon be out of the market. The engineers that were part of the team in building the first product contain a wealth of experience and knowledge. To lose such team members is to throw money away. Most upper management think that engineers are a dime a dozen. If you lose one then you just hire another. That is folly on the grandest scale. A good engineer is worth his weight in gold (and more) and this experience should be held within the company and passed onto others through the act of mentorship.

Do not lose your product lead.

What you will also find is that there will now be project spin-offs. The designed product has brought forward the idea to develop something new. So break off a new development team. In this everyone moves up the promotion ladder. This is what the concept of mentoring is all about, and have fun in the process!

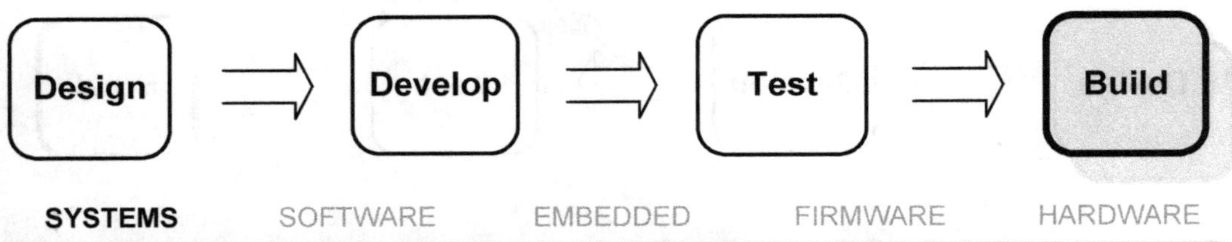

Systems

During the build process all manufactured product will be initially tested using the developed test fixtures (if such apply) prior to the final unit assemble. The completed device will then execute its internal built-in tests in order to verify operation. One or more manual operator tests may complete this process.

An error reporting database will be used to allow the manufacturing group to log any detected operational errors.

During the manufacture build process the system architect will be keeping watch for any such errors and will assign them to the relevant engineering group to be rectified. Any system design issues are corrected and the relevant design documents updated and the project team notified.

With regard to future design effort, through this product design work the system architect has been mentoring a junior engineer to fulfill this role. The junior system architect then takes a more authoritative role during the system build process while the senior systems architect moves onto the next project. This allows the trained junior systems architect to gain product maintenance experience as they will subsequently move into the role of Systems Architect at the completion of this task. [I have always found it interesting that many engineers (especially junior, inexperienced engineers) will shirk this aspect of product development. In this they continue to make the same mistakes. Their design effort is mostly undocumented and un-maintainable. Each engineer should spend some time in all aspects of product maintenance in order to determine what constitutes a good, well maintainable design otherwise they are doomed to repeat the process of generating a poor engineering effort.]

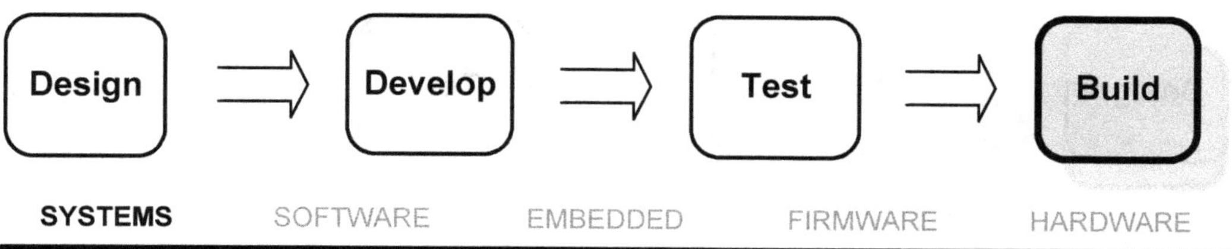

[This Page Intentionally Left Blank]

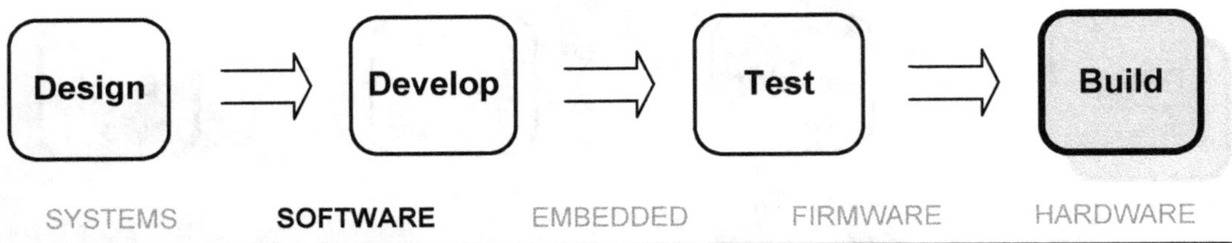

Software

During the manufacture build process the senior software engineer will be keeping watch for any reported build errors and will pass them onto the junior software engineer to be rectified. System design issues will be monitored and the relevant software design documents (including any code changes) updated and the rest of the project team notified.

With regard to future design effort, through this product design work the senior application software engineer has been mentoring a junior engineer to be his/her replacement. The junior engineer then takes a more authoritative role during the system build process while the senior engineer moves onto the next project. This allows the trained junior engineer to gain product maintenance experience as they will subsequently move into the role of the senior applications software engineer at the completion of this task. [Engineers need product maintenance experience if they are to become good engineers. The experience they gain while doing this type of work identifies the need for good documentation and well laid out and easily understood code. The engineer that shirks the task of product maintenance is an engineer who lacks this skill set. Such engineers will continue to make poorly designed products for the rest of their working life.]

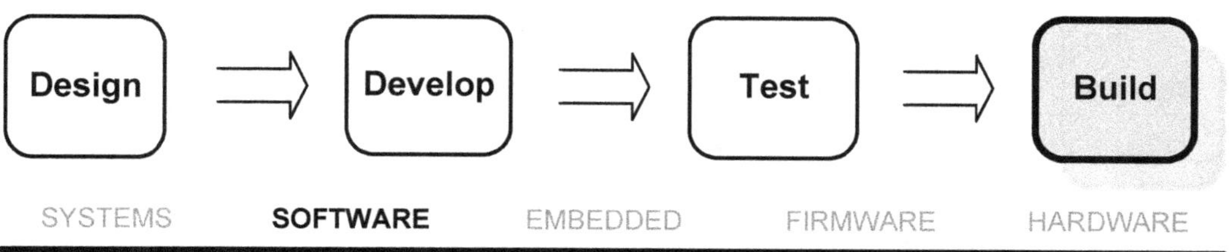

[This Page Intentionally Left Blank]

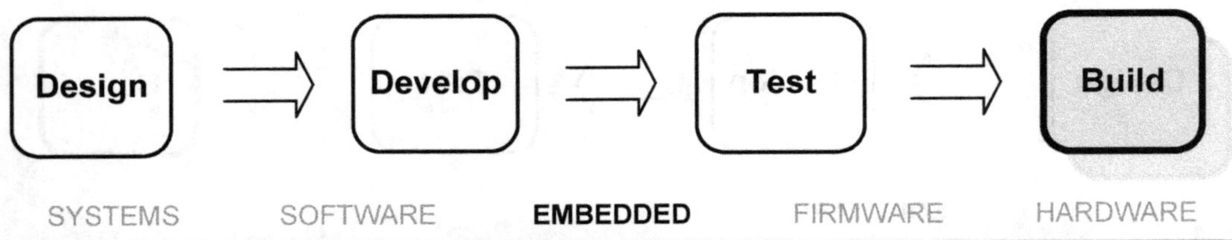

Embedded

During the manufacture build process the senior embedded software engineer will be keeping watch for any reported build errors and will pass them onto the junior embedded software engineer to be rectified. System design issues will be monitored and the relevant embedded software design documents (including any code changes) updated and the rest of the project team notified.

With regard to future design effort, through this product design work the senior embedded software engineer has been mentoring a junior engineer to be his/her replacement. The junior engineer then takes a more authoritative role during the system build process while the senior engineer moves onto the next project. This allows the trained junior engineer to gain product maintenance experience for they will subsequently move into the role of the senior embedded engineer at the completion of this task. [Engineers need product maintenance experience if they are to become good engineers. The experience they gain while doing this type of work identifies the need for good documentation and well laid out and easily understood code. The engineer that shirks the task of product maintenance is an engineer who lacks this skill set. Such engineers will continue to make poorly designed products for the rest of their working life.]

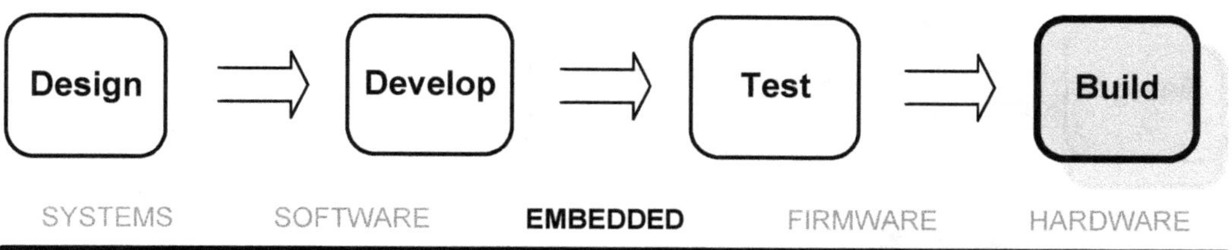

[This Page Intentionally Left Blank]

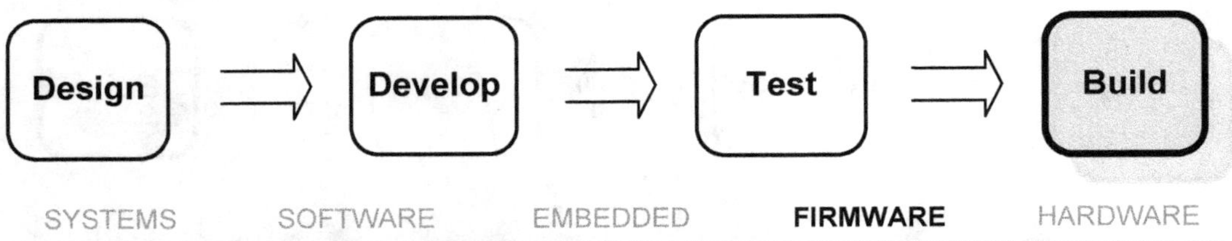

Firmware

During the manufacture build process the senior firmware engineer will be keeping watch for any reported build errors and will pass them onto the junior firmware engineer to be rectified. System design issues will be monitored and the relevant firmware design documents (including any code changes) updated and the rest of the project team notified.

With regard to future design effort, through this product design work the senior firmware engineer has been mentoring a junior engineer to be his/her replacement. The junior engineer now takes a more authoritative role during the system build process while the senior engineer moves onto the next project. This allows the trained junior engineer to gain product maintenance experience for they will subsequently move into the role of the senior firmware engineer at the completion of this task. [Engineers need product maintenance experience if they are to become good engineers. The experience they gain while doing this type of work identifies the need for good documentation and well laid out and easily understood code. The engineer that shirks the task of product maintenance is an engineer who lacks this skill set. Such engineers will continue to make poorly designed products for the rest of their working life.]

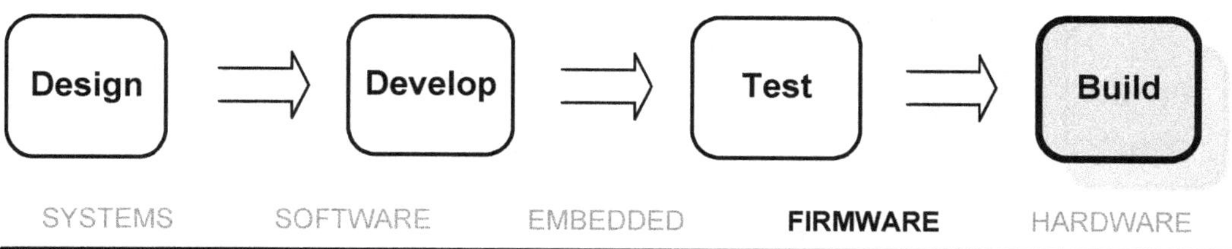

[This Page Intentionally Left Blank]

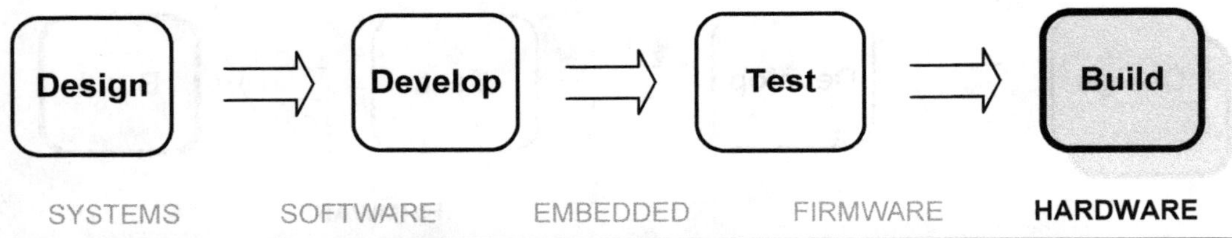

Hardware

During the manufacture build process the senior hardware engineer will be keeping watch for any reported build errors and will pass them onto the junior hardware engineer to be rectified. System design issues will be monitored and the relevant firmware design documents (including any PCBA board changes) updated and the rest of the project team notified.

With regard to future design effort, through this product design work the senior hardware engineer has been mentoring a junior engineer to be his/her replacement. The junior engineer now takes a more authoritative role during the system build process while the senior engineer moves onto the next project.

This allows the trained junior engineer to gain product maintenance experience for they will subsequently move into the role of the senior hardware engineer at the completion of this task. [Engineers need product maintenance experience if they are to become good engineers. The experience they gain while doing this type of work identifies the need for good documentation and well laid out and easily understood code. The engineer that shirks the task of product maintenance is an engineer who lacks this skill set. Such engineers will continue to make poorly designed products for the rest of their working life.]

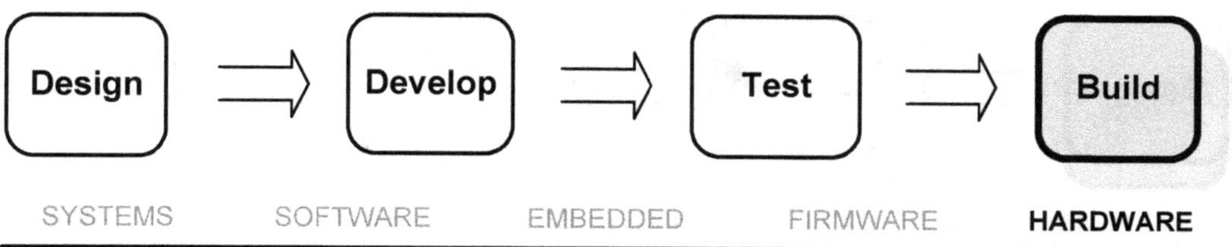

[This Page Intentionally Left Blank]

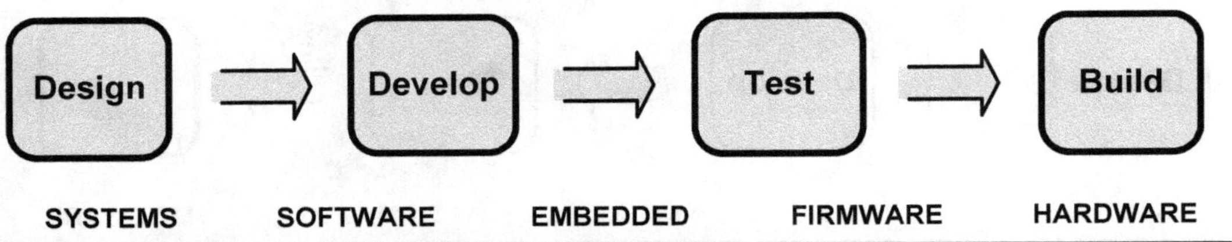

Project Finalization

All final project documentation (design, code, etc.) is stored in the Design History Directory.

The project is now complete.

Minor issue that result become the work load of the product development team tasked to create the next product iteration.

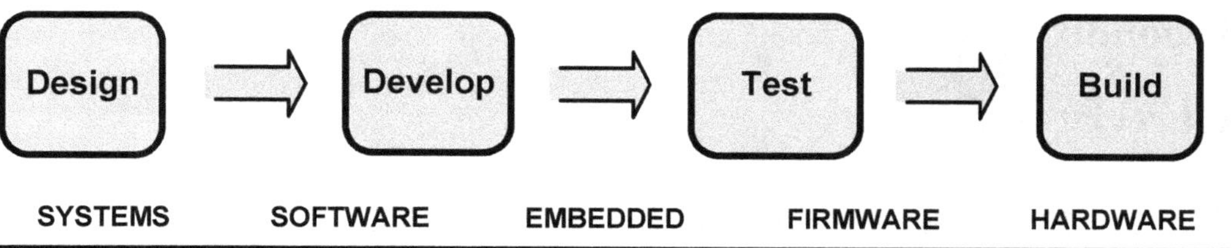

[This Page Intentionally Left Blank]

Appendix

Abbreviations

CPLD Complex Programmable Logic Devices
FAA Federal Aviation Administration
FDA US Food and Drug Administration
FPGA Field Programmable Gate Array

Development Team

The development team may consist of the following engineers:

- System Architect
- System engineers
- Application Software Engineers
- Embedded Software Engineers
- Firmware Engineers
- Hardware Engineers
- Mechanical Engineers

It should be noted that in smaller companies (or with smaller projects) there is a tendency to permit a single person to provide multiple roles.

Coding Standards

As is well known, every programmer has their own style of programming and when developing a product, or a group of products, a company might decide to implement a particular standard such that all code sets have a similar appearance.

Such a standard ensures compatibility and assists the development team in understanding other project programs.

One of the main requirements that should be apparent from the implemented programming style is the ability to clearly read code.

The biggest 'trick' in this is the choosing of a specific name that clearly and unambiguously identifies one item from another. If you can achieve this then you are half-way there.

This name is applicable to:

1. The module Name
2. The Class Name
3. The Function / Procedure / Method Name
4. The Structure Name
5. The Variable Name

So as you can see, such a choice of name is very important otherwise ambiguity abounds and where there is ambiguity there is room for error.

The use of white space is also important. Each section block should be clearly seen with structured English constructs (pseudo-code) identifying each major block. Always remember that code written today is anything but obvious when viewed six months down the road.

The following pages provide an example of a tested approach.

The Module
Every module should have a title block that identifies the following information.

- The Project Name
- The Module Name
- The Module Description
- The Date of creation
- The original author(s)
- Module Modifications (author(s), Date, Description)

The purpose of programming is to develop a set of instructions, which make logical sense to both a computer system used to execute the instructions and to a human being who has to develop and maintain these instructions.

With this regard, the use of logical clear concise unambiguous names for modules, structures, variables and functions cannot be overemphasized.

A program is built from the following types of files:

1. Header Files
2. Source Files

Header Files
In this methodology, the following types of header files are used:

1. The system constants header file
2. The system types header file
3. The system global variable header file
4. The module prototype header file

The advantage in this methodology is that it is a clean approach with specific definitions only existing in specific locations - a programmer immediately knows which file to edit for a given definition.

The disadvantage in this methodology is that a change to one of these files may result in the entire system having to be rebuilt. On current computer system this may result in having to wait an additional few seconds longer for the entire system build to complete - this additional time delay is hardly an issue in regard to the conceptual gain in code layout clarity.

As stated earlier, this methodology is for small development projects since the time to build an extensive code base could become a factor.

Variable names should use underscores between each name.

The use of the Camel Case method of variable naming is discouraged due to the resultant 'unreadability' of the word.

For instance:

Compare the variable name: **maximize_local_neural_network_weights**

and the variable name: **MaximizeLocalNeuralNetworkWeights**

and judge which version is more readable.

It becomes very tiring reading screen upon screen of CamelCaseVariableNames WhichIsWhyITendToDiscourageItsUseAndIHopeByThisYouUnderstandMyReason.

The object of code is that it is not simply machine readable.

It must be human readable and by that, I mean readable by a number of different human beings of varying qualities of eye strength. Spending time debugging a program just because you cannot detect an additional character in a Camel Case name is a waste of a person's time and a tremendous source for error.

For these reasons I would discourage the use of Camel Case names.

Module Title Block
Each header file contains a descriptive title block, which identifies:

1. The module name
2. The customer's copyright information
3. The project name
4. The original author
5. The module creation date
6. A brief description of the module
7. The module version history information

System Constants
A project system constants header file is identified by the name "literals.h".

This file is included in every source module.

Integer Definitions
A common programming problem exists with the manner in which a specific compiler defines the integer variable type. For instance, one compiler may identify an '**int**' as a 32-bit quantity whereas another compiler identifies it as a 16-bit quantity.

This confusion can easily develop into programming errors.

To bypass this problem the **uint** and **sint** literal definitions have been created as shown below:

```
/* Variable Integer definitions */
#define  uint8    unsigned char
#define  uint16   unsigned int
#define  uint32   unsigned long

#define  sint8    signed char
#define  sint16   signed int
#define  sint32   signed long
```

These literal definitions are located in the system definition header file.

Compiler Defaults

Compilers usually have specific default settings - for example, when defining a char variable, one compiler may default this to an unsigned char. However, another compiler may default to a signed char. It is also possible to further complicate the situation by overriding the compiler defaults at compile time.

To remove this confusion the integer definitions are used as discussed above.

Example

The following extract is an example of a system constants definition header file:

```
//**************************************************************************
//  Author: Stephen W. McClure
//    Date: March 2014
// Project: Designing Embedded Systems [Book]
// *************************************************************************
// This program is proprietary to Company Name LLC. and belongs
// exclusively to Company Name Inc.
//
// It is distributed under a license agreement allowing operation on a
// specified computer system.  Reproduction, disclosure, or use, in whole or
// in part, other than as specified in the license are not to be undertaken
// except with prior written authorization from Company Name LLC.
//
// (C)  Copyright 2014 by Company Name llc.  All rights reserved.
//
//**************************************************************************
// Purpose:
//
// This program provides a home control application.
//
//**************************************************************************
//
// File Name: hc_literals.c
//
// This file includes all the common literal definitions.
// *************************************************************************
// Version History:
//
// Version: 1.00       Date: 02/10/2014       Author: Steve McClure
//  Reason: Initial release.
// *************************************************************************
// Version: 1.01       Date: 02/12/2014       Author: Steve McClure
//  Reason: Added matrix changes.
// *************************************************************************

#ifndef HC_LITERALS
#define HC_LITERALS

// Serial Interface
//#define BAUDRATE B9600
#define  SERIAL_PORT_0    "/dev/ttyS0"
```

```
#define  SERIAL_PORT_1     "/dev/ttyS1"
#define  _POSIX_SOURCE     1 /* POSIX compliant source */

#define  BAUDRATE     B4800


// Literal Definitions
#define  Uint8   unsigned char
#define  Uint16  unsigned int

#define  INVALID      0
#define  VALID        1

#define  FAILURE      0
#define  SUCCESS      1

#define  X10_OFF      0
#define  X10_ON       1


// Day Name Literals
#define  SUNDAY       0
#define  MONDAY       1
#define  TUESDAY      2
#define  WEDNESDAY    3
#define  THURSDAY     4
#define  FRIDAY       5
#define  SATURDAY     6


// Calender Month Literals
#define  JANUARY      1
#define  FEBRUARY     2
#define  MARCH        3
#define  APRIL        4
#define  MAY          5
#define  JUNE         6
#define  JULY         7
#define  AUGUST       8
#define  SEPTEMBER    9
#define  OCTOBER     10
#define  NOVEMBER    11
#define  DECEMBER    12


// Days in year
#define  DAYS_IN_STANDARD_YEAR        365
#define   DAYS_IN_LEAP_YEAR           366


// Sensor/Device Literals
#define  SENSOR       0
#define  DEVICE       1

#define  OFF          0
#define  ON           1
```

```
// Main Loop Execution Periodic Sleep
#define   EXECUTION_SLEEP_MS       333    // Execute loop delay in milliseconds


#define   HS_NORMAL_MODE                0
#define   HS_NORMAL_MODE_TRIGGER        1
#define   HS_TV_MODE                    2
#define   HS_TV_MODE_TRIGGER            3

#define   HS_SECURITY                   0
#define   HS_SECURITY_DELAY             1
#define   HS_SLEEP                      2
#define   HS_SLEEP_DELAY                3
#define   HS_FAMILY_LIGHTS              4
#define   HS_STEVE_LIGHTS               5
#define   HS_GO_TO_BED                  6
#define   HS_MASTER_WATCH_TV            7

#define   HCE_HOUSE                     0
#define   HCE_UNIT                      1
#define   HCE_TYPE                      2
#define   HCE_STATE                     3
#define   HCE_TIMESTAMP                 4
#define   HCE_TIMEOUT                   5
#define   HCE_DESCRIPTION               6
```

Discussion

1. The use of the definitions #ifndef HC_LITERALS, #define HC_LITERALS and at the end of the file #endif ensure that the include file will not generate a compiler error if it is included multiple times.

2. When defining various common device states, use the device as the first part of the state name - this keeps the various device states distinct from each other.

3. Column alignment aids in readability and reduces the likelihood of mistakes.

System Types

A project system types header file is identified by the name “typesdefs.h”.

This file is included in every source module.

Example

The following extract is an example of a system types header file:

```
//*****************************************************************************
//  Author: Stephen W. McClure
//    Date: March 2014
// Project: Designing Embedded Systems [Book]
//
//*****************************************************************************
// Purpose:
//
// This program provides a home control application.
//
//*****************************************************************************
//
// File Name: hc_typedefs.c
//
// This file includes all the common typedef definitions.
//*****************************************************************************
// Version History:
//
// Version: 1.00       Date: 04/03/2014       Author: Steve McClure
//  Reason: Initial release.
//*****************************************************************************
// Version: 1.01       Date: 04/03/2014       Author: Steve McClure
//  Reason: Added changes.
//*****************************************************************************

#ifndef HC_TYPEDEFS
#define HC_TYPEDEFS

typedef struct
{
   Uint16  hour;
   Uint16  minute;
}
TIME_OF_DAY;

typedef struct
{
   char    name[255];
   Uint16  index;
}
   HOUSE_STATE_PARAMETER;


typedef struct
{
   Uint8  house_code;
   Uint8  unit_code;
}
   X10_CODE;

#endif
```

Please note the following:

1. The use of the definitions #ifndef HC_TYPEDEFS, #define HC_TYPEDEFS and at the end of the file #endif ensure that the include file will not generate a compiler error if it is included multiple times.

2. The typedef construct is used to permit a variable to be defined simply by using the typedef name, for example:

   ```
   SETUP_DATA_MSG    setup_data;
   ```

3. In order to help reduce the number of different variable names, the typedef is written using capital letters and the variable of that type uses the same name but in lowercase letters.

4. When the typedef is defined, the typedef name with an underscore, for example SETUP_DATA_MSG_ follows the struct reserved word. This permits the compiler to recognize pointer variables, which point to the same structure as that which is being defined.

5. Column alignment aids in readability and reduces the likelihood of mistakes.

System Global Variables

A project system global variables header file may be identified by the name "publics.h".

The public variables are defined by including the system global variables header file in the main source code module.

If the project is large and requires an external variable header file then each public variable definitions may use the extern prefix. By using the following construct the program may use a single header file to define the public variables and the same file to define the external variables. This permits no variable declaration differences to exist between public and external header files if two separate header files were to be implemented:

```
#define  extern
#include "sysvars.h"
```

The external variables are defined by including the system global variables header file in all other source code modules as follows:

```
#include "sysvars.h"
```

Note:

The utilization of a single variable file, (as opposed to defining variables as public or external in the various modules as and when required), has the following benefits:

1. All global variables are defined in a common area.

2. There is no longer any possibility of mis-matched definitions due to a variable being defined public as an `int` (say), and elsewhere being externally referenced as a `long` - not all linkers catch these mis-matches!

Example

The following extract is an example of a system global variables header file:

```
//****************************************************************************
//  Author: Stephen W. McClure
//    Date: March 2014
// Project: Designing Embedded Systems [Book]
//
//****************************************************************************
// Purpose:
//
// This program provides a home control application.
//
//
//****************************************************************************
//
// File Name: hc_publics.h
//
// This file includes all the common variable definitions.
//****************************************************************************
// Note:  1. Variables may be defined using the "extern" construct.
//        2. In the main program, the "#define extern" construct is
//           used prior to including this file.  This effectively
//           removes the "extern" from the following definitions
//           thereby permitting the variables to be defined as
//           public.
//        3. In all other programs, this file is included as it
//           stands thereby permitting the variables to be defined as
//           externals.
//
//  THIS IS THE GENERAL CASE AND HAS NOT BEEN IMPLEMENTED IN THIS EXAMPLE.
//
// ***************************************************************************
// Version History:
//
// Version: 1.00       Date: 04/03/2014       Author: Steve McClure
//  Reason: Initial release.
// ***************************************************************************
// Version: 1.01       Date: 04/03/2014       Author: Steve McClure
//  Reason: Added matrix changes.
// ***************************************************************************

#ifndef HC_PUBLICS
#define HC_PUBLICS


// InterruptControl exit flag
static int exit_flag = 0;

// Device reset startup condition
Uint8   device_reset = FALSE;

// MySQL Database Variables
MYSQL  *conn1;
MYSQL  *conn2;
```

```
// Global variables
int fd; /* File descriptor for the port */


// Setup serial interface
struct termios new_options;
struct termios old_options;


// House State Table Parameter Names
HOUSE_STATE_PARAMETER  house_state_parameter [ ] =
        { { "security",              0 },
          { "security_delay",        1 },
          { "sleep",                 2 },
          { "sleep_delay",           3 },
          { "family_lights",         4 },
          { "steve_lights",          5 },
          { "go_to_bed",             6 },
          { "master_watch_tv",       7 } };


// Sunrise/Sunset Times
TIME_OF_DAY  sunrise;
TIME_OF_DAY  sunset;


// Common Timeout variables
long int    sunrise_timeout   = 0;
long int    sunset_timeout    = 0;
long int    midday_timeout    = 0;
long int    midnight_timeout = 0;
long int    dusk_timeout      = 0;
long int    dawn_timeout      = 0;


// Time flags
Uint8  daytime   = FALSE;
Uint8  midday    = FALSE;
Uint8  nightime = FALSE;

Uint8  between_dawn_and_dusk  = FALSE;
Uint8  between_dusk_and_dawn  = FALSE;

Uint8  small_hours_of_the_morning = FALSE;

#endif
```

Discussion

1. The use of the definitions #ifndef HC_PUBLICS, #define HC_PUBLICS and at the end of the file #endif ensure that the include file will not generate a compiler error if it is included multiple times.

2. Note the use of descriptive typedef and variable names. Unambiguous names greatly add to the readability of program code and the myth of self-documented code could actually become a reality. The time saving in program maintenance is enormous.

3. Column alignment aids in readability and reduces the likelihood of mistakes.

Module Prototypes

Each source code module (ie. ".c" file) which contains function definitions will have an associated prototype header file. The name of the file will be identical to the source code module except it will utilize the ".h" suffix.

For example:

digital.c - The digital source code functions definitions.
digital.h - The digital source code function prototype definitions.

Example

The following extract is an example of a module prototype header file:

```
// ***************************************************************************
// Module name: control.h
// ***************************************************************************
// This program is proprietary to Company Name LLC. and belongs
// exclusively to Company Name LLC.
//
// It is distributed under a license agreement allowing operation on a
// specified computer system.  Reproduction, disclosure, or use, in whole or
// in part, other than as specified in the license are not to be undertaken
// except with prior written authorization from Company Name LLC.
//
// (C)  Copyright 2014 by Company Name LLC.  All rights reserved.
// ***************************************************************************
// Project: Home Control / Security
//  Author: Steve McClure
// Created: 04/03/2014
// ***************************************************************************
// Description:
//
// This header file contains all the prototype definitions.
// ***************************************************************************
// Version History:
//
// Version: 1.00       Date: 04/03/2014       Author: Steve McClure
// Reason: Initial release.
// ***************************************************************************
// Version: 1.01       Date: 04/03/2014       Author: Steve McClure
//  Reason: Added matrix changes.
// ***************************************************************************

#ifndef ControlH
#define ControlH

/* External Prototypes */

int  system_initialization (void);
int  system_reset (void);
int  configure_digital_ports (void);
int  configure_analog_ports (void);
int  determine_system_voltages (void);
int  determine_system_current (void);
int  determine_time_of_day (void);

#endif
```

Please note the following:

The use of the definitions `#ifndef ControlH`, `#define ControlH` and at the end of the file `#endif` ensure that the include file will not generate a compiler error if it is included multiple times.

Source Files

The source module is comprised of the following sections:

1. Module Title Block
2. Function Title Block
3. Function Parameters
4. Function Code Layout
5. Comments

Module Title Block

Each source module contains a descriptive title block, which identifies:

1. The module name
2. The customer's copyright information
3. The project name
4. The original author
5. The module creation date
6. A brief description of the module
7. The module version history information

Function Title Block

Each function is proceeded by a descriptive title block, which identifies:

1. The function name
2. A brief description
3. The passed parameters
4. The returned parameter

The following style should be used:

```
//***********************************************************************
// Get Decimal Number
//
// This function permits the user to enter a single key value.
//
// Return:  FAILURE - [ESC] key or invalid character was pressed.
//          SUCCESS - Valid number entered.
//***********************************************************************

uint8  get_key (uint8  key_size, uint32 * count_ptr)

{
  uint8   key;

  ...  code ...
}
```

The Return description should be used to describe the returned parameters only if the concept is not straightforward and obvious. The selection of clear and unambiguous names would help in this matter.

Function Parameters
Each function may utilize the following types of parameter:

1. Passed Parameters
2. Returned Parameters

Passed Parameters
The following style is used to define the function name and associated parameters:

```
int  status_display (char * status_string, int  timeout)

{
   uint8   key1;
   uint8   key2;

   ...  code ...
   ...  code ...
}
```

If there are too many parameters to list on one line, the following style is used:

```
int  status_display (char * error,
                     char * test_message,
                     int    count)

{
   uint8   key1;
   uint8   key2;

   ...  code ...
   ...  code ...
}
```

Return Parameter
The return parameter is to be used for returning the function status.

The function status is either:

1. SUCCESS
2. FAILURE

These literal constants are defined in the "systypes.h" file as follows:

```
#define  SUCCESS     1
#define  FAILURE     0
```

Function Code Layout

The function code layout style for the following constructs will now be discussed:

1. The For Construct
2. The While Construct
3. The Do... While Construct
4. The IF Construct
5. The Switch Construct

For Construct

The code layout style of the FOR construct is as follows:

```
for (index = 0; index < COUNT; index++)
{
   key = getch();
   ...
   ...
}
```

While Construct

The code layout style of the WHILE construct is as follows:

```
index = 0;

while (index < COUNT)
{
   key = getch();
   ...
   ...
   index++;
}
```

Do While Construct
The code layout style of the Do .. WHILE construct is as follows:

```
index = 0;

do
{
   key = getch();
   ...
   ...
   index++;
}
   while (index < COUNT);
```

Note: This construct is rarely used.

If Construct
The code layout style of the various IF constructs are as follows:

```
if (index < COUNT)
{
   function1();
}

if (index < COUNT
{
   function1();
}
else
{
   function2();
}

if (index < COUNT)
{
   function1();
}
else if (index == COUNT)
{
   function2();
}
else
{
   function3();
}
```

```
if (index < MAX_ITERATIONS)
{
   function1();
   function2();
}
else if (index == MAX_ITERATIONS)
{
   if (test == ACTIVE)
   {
      test_function3();
      test_function4();
   }
}
else
{
   function_3();
}
```

Switch Construct

The code layout style of the switch construct is as follows:

```
switch (digit)
{
   case TEST_INVALID:
          return (FAILURE);
   case TEST_ONCE:
          perform_memory_test_once();
          break;
   case TEST_CONTINUOUSLY:
          perform_memory_test_continuously();
          break;
   default:
          return (FAILURE);
}
```

Error Detection

There are many ways to handle error situations, which are detected within a function.

The manner, which will be utilized, is to exit from the function as soon as the error has been detected. This permits a clear concise logic flow exiting the function.

```
...
/* Test if error occurred */
if (error = = DETECTED)
   return (FAILURE);
...
```

The method whereby the error condition is delegated to the distant else part of an IF condition is discouraged since such code becomes difficult to read when the function is of a significant size.

Pseudocode

Pseudocode (also known as structured English) should be used to provide a description of the function of the subsequent lines of code, as shown below:

```
/* Do Forever */
while (1)
{
   /* Wait for a key press */
   key = getch();

   /* If [BRK] key pressed - exit */
   if (key == BREAK_KEY)
   {
      return (FAILURE);
   }

   /* If [ENTER] key pressed - return number */
   if (key = = ENTER_KEY)
   {
      *number = result;
      return (SUCCESS);
   }
}
```

Comments

Comments should only be used where it is necessary to explain in detail the actions of a code fragment. The comments should be well to the right of the code such that the code and the comments are clearly delineated.

Both `/* comment */` and `// Comment` styles are permitted:

```
/* Capture interrupt triggered on positive edge */
TCR.BIT.IEDG = SET;

// Prevent fan from working
disable_fan_fault();
```

Example

The following example illustrates the overall code layout style:

```
// ***************************************************************************
// Module name: main.c
// ***************************************************************************
// This program is proprietary to COMPANY NAME and belongs
// exclusively to said company.
//
//
// It is distributed under a license agreement allowing operation on a
// specified computer system.  Reproduction, disclosure, or use, in whole or
// in part, other than as specified in the license are not to be undertaken
// except with prior written authorization from COMPANY NAME.
//
// (C)  Copyright 2014 by COMPANY NAME.  All rights reserved.
// ***************************************************************************
// Project:
//  Author: Steve McClure
// Created: 04/03/2014
// ***************************************************************************
// Description:
//
// This module monitors the system current usage.
//
// Note: The system must be operational for at least twenty minutes prior to
//       executing this test.
// ***************************************************************************
// Version History:
// Version: 1.00       Date: 04/03/2013       Author: Steve McClure
// Reason: Initial release.
// ***************************************************************************
// Version: 1.01       Date: 04/03/2013       Author: Steve McClure
// Reason: Added general changes.
// ***************************************************************************

/* Header Files */
#include "hc_defs.h"
#include "hc_types.h"

#define  extern
#include "hc_vars.h"          // Public declaration of global variables.
#include "sensors.h"

/* External Prototypes */
#include  "service1.h"
#include  "service2.h"
```

```
//*****************************************************************************
// Process ON Events
//
// This function places required events into the house_code_events table
//
//*****************************************************************************

void process_on_events (void)
{
    int  house_state_security;
    int  house_state_sleep;

    // Determine home security state
    if (get_house_state_security (&house_state_security) == SUCCESS)
    {
        // Has the house security mode been engaged?
        if (house_state_security == SECURITY_MODE_ACTIVE)
        {
            // Yes - Security mode status engaged
            security_mode = TRUE;
        }
        else
        {
            // No - Home mode status engaged
            security_mode = FALSE;

            // Reset the security detection flags
            reset_security_detection_flags();
        }
    }

    // Determine sleep state
    if (get_house_state_sleep (&house_state_sleep) == SUCCESS)
    {
        // Has the house active mode been engaged?
        if (house_state_sleep == SLEEP_MODE_INACTIVE)
        {
            // Yes - Active mode status engaged
            sleep_mode = FALSE;
        }

        // Has the house sleep mode been activated?
        else if (house_state_sleep == SLEEP_MODE_INITIATED)
        {
            // Yes - Sleep mode status pending

        }
        else if (house_state_sleep == SLEEP_MODE_DELAY)
        {
            // Yes - Sleep mode status pending

        }
        else if (house_state_sleep == SLEEP_MODE_ACTIVE)
        {
            // Sleep mode status fully engaged
            sleep_mode  = TRUE;
        }
    }
```

```
    // Is the HOME SECURITY mode engaged?
    if (security_mode)
    {
        // Yes - Keep a watchfull eye on things...
        process_front_porch_light();
        process_barking_doggy();

        // Check to see if there is an intruder
        process_intruder_check();
    }
    else
    {
        // No - Home Security is deactivated
        // Let the user control the house lights
        process_laundry_light();
        process_pantry_light();
        process_main_hallway_light();
        process_front_porch_light();
        process_inside_entrance_light();
        process_kitchen_light();
        process_kitchen_nook_light();
        process_steve_bedroom_wall_light();
        process_common_bathroom_light();
        process_common_washroom_light();
        process_study_ceiling_light();
        process_familyroom_light();
        process_lounge_light();
        process_master_bedroom_light();
        process_master_bedroom_closet_light();

        // Determine if fast transition occured which might
        // allow the system to turn off lights quicker.
        determine_fast_transition_events();
    }

}
```

Code Editor

Tabs versus Spaces

The code editor each programmer uses must be configured such that it replaces the TAB character with the equivalent number of space characters. This will permit a file, which has been modified by different programmers/editors to be displayed and/or printed with the correct indentation.

Note: It should be noted that the Make file makes use of the TAB character.

Point Of Sale Business Application (POSBA)

POSBA was a project I worked on for over a year. It was my own personal project. I developed it under my own company name. During this process I learned a lot about of what to do and what not to do.

This was a PC application that would overcome many of the limitations of business point of sale software packages. I did plenty of research into the current issues. POS applications generally run on multiple computer systems over a network. The usual concept is that one of these computer systems acts as the server and holds the point of sale customer and product inventory databases which is made available to the client POS computer systems that are used to take sales from the customers.

An establishment might then have one server, a LAN network and a number of POS terminals complete with cash register drawers and printers. When all is well and operational such a system is quite effective. But when something goes wrong with the server PC computer system or with the LAN network, every single POS terminal is now inoperative. Even if one or more of the POS computers are functional they can no longer obtain customer or product information from the server. When this occurs the shop is now forced to implement a manual method of taking hand-written sales receipts often using previously printed inventory price books. The shop loses money. Producing manual sales receipts is time consuming so the number of sales per hour slows down. The inventory price books might only be printed every quarter and therefore the pricing information might be out-of-date. Then, after the system has been repaired, the manual price receipts have to be re-entered into the accounting system. This is a tremendous waste of time and a great inconvenience for the shop owner. This problem is also exacerbated when the application software is buggy and database corruption occurs.

So there were the issues faced by client. I really felt that I could do better. I had previously used C++ Builder to develop another Windows application and was using the same tool set for this product. It was so 'easy' to start to create the GUI screens and I was 'pulled' in that direction. I should have stopped there and then to first create all the documentation and determine a basic schedule. But it didn't seem that complicated. That is the problem for all engineers. They can develop and build absolutely anything they put their mind to. They do not foresee issues for every problem can be surmounted. So that was my big mistake. I simply dived into developing code for I wanted to show the customer progress as soon as possible. In all this I totally underestimated the work involved. Looking back I would now estimate the work as a six man-year project. I was working on the system by myself and had finished half the work in close to 18 months (so you can see that I was putting a lot of effort into the development of the product).

I had seen the pitfalls of the older software systems that many stores were using. So I worked on developing a better system, a system that would still function even if the server or the network went down.

This then required a distributed data base.

So I worked on developing one.

The final outcome still had the server computer holding the customer and inventory databases. All updates to these databases were effected on this computer. But when a Point-Of-Sale (POS) computer was brought online, it would access the network and periodically check the server database versions. If the POS system determined that its own database was out-of-date it would then proceed to download the latest database from the server and then install it on its local system. This action was applicable with every relevant database. So within a few minutes of system startup, each and every POS PC terminal would have the latest system databases on their local systems. This would also occur within a minute after any server database changes (like the entry of a new customer, inventory item or product price change); these changes being effected with the next customer sale. Now, if either the server or the LAN network (or even both) were to fail, the POS PC system could still continue to make sales since they each had all the relevant database data locally and on-hand. When the network and server was restored, the local sales receipts could be posted to the server and the server databases updated. This operation also allowed the POS PC terminals to take and issue customer quotes. So as you can see it was quite a complex system and to my knowledge it worked perfectly. Remember I fall under the category of the 'perfectionist' and would fix every bug detected during testing before proceeding to implement the next feature. I was always building the next feature on a bug-free platform code base.

Many of these accounting systems would log their sales information in a continuous data file using variable sized records. This was an attempt to minimize the size of this data file. The only problem with that approach is that these systems become very slow as successive years of business transactions are added. So it was with my customer's existing system. When they started using the system it was certainly fast. Then as the years progressed it would get slower and slower. This was noticed when printing out the yearly reports. The first year 's data was near to the start of the file and would be accessed quickly but this was not the case for the data close to the file's end. In this the entire file had to be scanned (remember the data entries were of variable size). With five or more years of data in the file, the accounting report generation process for the latest year would take hours to complete. There was a mechanism that could be used to eliminate the earlier years of data from the database file but this utility did not come without risk. It was an operation that could corrupt the data file and under such conditions require a restore of the original database. There was also a problem if the posting of the sales records from the POS terminal PCs to the Server sales database were to fail. If you tried to execute the process you now obtained duplicate entries. Database corruption and recovery were fraught with issues.

I felt that there must be a better way.

I had used some file access routines that permitted directory traversal. There was a notion that made me feel that these could be put to good use. The final sales database resulted in a directory structure based upon year and month. Within these directories were accounting sales files for each individual POS terminal. It was now easy (and quick) to access the records of individual POS terminals and to search/modify just their records without affecting the entire sales database. Now I could re-post POS sales entries and duplicate entries would be ignored. Database repair was now simple and effective. Then the surprise came when I generated the first sales tax report for the final year. To test the system I loaded in the customer's previous five years of sales data and had converted it to this new format. The customer's previous software package took hours to generate this report. My system took the order of 6 seconds. In truth, I initially thought there was an error on my part. I ran the report again. This time it took 2 seconds. The data files were already in system memory so the process had run faster.

So you can see, with every computer system there is always room for improvement and given enough time even an embedded software engineer can develop a GUI software application. This specific application consisted of over 3.5 million lines of code, included user documentation and interfaced to till slip printers and could also print bar code labels).

To view and download the demo application, documentation or to purchase the source code, please access the following web site:

www.quantumbluetechnology.com

Linux Installation (32-bit)

This section describes the Linux installation and the LAMP Home Control Program that interfaces to an X-10 system.

Purpose: To create a Linux Installation.

Program: Linux Mint 13 MATE 32-Bit Version (or later revision)

Obtained: http://linuxmint.com

Access the Download screen
Select Linux Mint 13 MATE 32-bit version (or later revision)
Take note of the MD5 value:
eg. 43ca0be4501b9d1a46fea25ec2cd556e

Select the 'mirrorcatalogs.com' site and download and save the .iso file.

Once downloaded, verify the MD5 checksum number for accuracy

Equipment: Windows or Linux Computer System
DVD-Writer to create Linux Disk

Procedure: Use DVD Burning utility to burn disk with .iso file.

Insert Linux Disk into computer system for Linux Installation
Power on computer system (Boot from Linux DVD-ROM)
Start the Linux installation (overwrite any existing system)

Select timezone and English language options

Your name: orion
Your computer's name: orion-itx
Pick a user name: orion
Choose a password: rootpass

Select option: log in automatically

Do not check [ ] Encrypt home folder

Click [Restart Now] to exit and restart the system.
The DVD-ROM is ejected – Remove and store the disk.

Power down the computer system
Power up the computer system

ORION-ITX System D2500CC
The Orion ITX system used in this example has the following components:

1. Two core Intel Atom CPU D2500 @ 1.86GHz
2. 4GB DDR3 Memory (6.4GB/Sec)
3. 64 bit instruction set
4. 8 USB Ports
5. 2 SATA Ports

ORION-ITX Linux Mint Components
Installed 32-bit version of Linux Maya

Start the Update Manager (Shield Symbol on bottom line at the right hand side).
1. Enter password
2. Updates are downloaded
3. Select 'Install Updates' (and accept further updates) as many times as are necessary to update the system
4. Replace any configuration files (as required)
5. Restart the system when completed updates (just to be safe)

   However, the MySQL interface did not load in the correct 64-bit MySQL.h header files and the MySQL code would not compile (so resorted back to the 32-bit OS).
   Image Backup – Completed

The following Linux components are now manually installed:
LAMP (Linux, Apache2, MySQL, PHP5)

<u>**Install apache2**</u>
Use the Terminal: **sudo apt-get install apache2**

Test installation by accessing the following web page: http://localhost/
(Displays "It Works!" message)

<u>**Install PHP**</u>
Use the Terminal: sudo apt-get install php5 libapache2-mod-php5
Use the Terminal: sudo /etc/init.d/apache2 restart

Test installation by creating the following 'php' web page...
Use the Terminal: sudo gedit /var/www/testphp.php
Place the following code in this file...
<?php phpinfo(); ?>

Save and close the file...

Test installation by accessing the following web page:

http://localhost/testphp.php
(Displays PHP information screen)

Install MySQL

Use the Terminal: sudo apt-get install mysql-server

Enter your 'root' password: datapass

Now change the bind address.

Use the Terminal:
sudo gedit /etc/mysql/my.cnf

Change the line:
bind-address = 127.0.0.1 to use your ip address (eg. 192.168.1.176)

Install phpMyAdmin

Use the Terminal:
sudo apt-get install libapache2-mod-auth-mysql php5-mysql phpmyadmin

Select webserver to reconfigure automatically: apache2

Configure database for phpmyadmin with dbconfig-common? <Yes>

Password of databases's administrative user: datapass
MySQL application password for phpmyadmin: datapass
Confirm: datapass

Edit php.ini file...
Use the Terminal: **gksudo gedit /etc/php5/apache2/php.ini**

Remove the ';' from the start of line: ' ; extension = mysql.so '

Restart apache2
Use the Terminal: sudo /etc/init.d/apache2 restart

Edit apache2.conf file…
Use the Terminal: sudo gedit /etc/apache2/apache2.conf

Add the following line to the bottom of the file…
Include /etc/phpmyadmin/apache.conf

Restart apache2
Use the Terminal: sudo /etc/init.d/apache2 restart

MySQL Administration

Using a Web Brouser:
Access the PHP MySQL Administration page: http://localhost/phpmyadmin

Sign in as 'root' using password 'rootpass'.

Navigate to Privileges.
Add new user 'steve', password 'william' (grant all privileges on wildcard name).

The following database was only used for test purposes:

Navigate to Database / Create New Database (use 'collation')
Created database: home_control with table 'state' User 'steve', password 'datapass'.
Created database: test with no tables.
Delete this database when finished testing.

Note: The home system database is created using the Linux program: hc_main.c

Keyring
When asked regarding the "Keyring", specify the password: 'keypass'.

Linux Image Backup

Purpose: To create an image of the Linux Hard Drive.

Program: qt4-fsarchiver

Obtained: sourceforge.net

Equipment: qt4-fsarchiver DVD-ROM (Live DVD)
Linux Computer System
Removable CD-ROM drive (USB Interface)
Removable Hard Drive (USB Interface)

Procedure: Attach the removable CD-ROM to the Linux computer system.
Attach the removable Hard Drive to the Linux computer system.
Insert the qt4-fsarchiver disk into the CD-ROM drive
Do not remove the CD-ROM until the backup is completed.

Power up the Linux Computer System (Boot from the DVD-ROM)
Ubuntu OS will automatically install.

Select the qt-fsarchiver icon located at the top left.
Enter password: ubuntu

Using the Ubuntu file manager:
Create a folder in the removable Hard Drive

Using qt-fsarchiver:
Enter the backup filename: eg. orion_121201_1950
Select 'Partition Save'
Select 'Notes to the backup'
Select 'Available backup overwrite'

Select the relevant sda (ext4) drive to be backed up

Store in backup directory 'media \ Vantec1N \ Steve123'
Select the number of processor cores (orion_itx has 2 cores)
Select 'gzip standard' compression setting
Select [Save Partition]
Enter notes in 'Description of the backup'
Select [Back partition]

Backup process now starts.

When completed a 'success' dialog box is displayed.
Accept the dialog box and shut down the system.

Linux Image Restore

Purpose: To restore an image to the Linux Hard Drive.

Program: qt4-fsarchiver

Obtained: sourceforge.net

Equipment: qt4-fsarchiver DVD-ROM (Live DVD)
Linux Computer System
Removable CD-ROM drive (USB Interface)
Removable Hard Drive (USB Interface)

Procedure: Attach the removable CD-ROM to the Linux computer system.
Attach the removable Hard Drive to the Linux computer system.
Insert the qt4-fsarchiver disk into the CD-ROM drive
Do not remove the CD-ROM until the restore is completed.

Power up the Linux Computer System (Boot from the DVD-ROM)
Ubuntu OS will automatically install.

Select the qt-fsarchiver icon located at the top left.
Enter password: ubuntu

Using qt-fsarchiver:
Enter the backup filename: eg. orion_121201_1950
Select 'Restore Partition'
Select the relevant sda (ext4) partition to be restored
Select backup file from 'media \ Vantec1N \ Steve123'
Select the number of processor cores (orion_itx has 2 cores)
Select [Partition Restore]

Partition restoration process now starts.
When completed a 'success' dialog box is displayed.

Linux Home Control Programs

There are two Linux Home Control programs:

1. hc_main
2. hc_ti103

hc_main

This program creates the MySQL **'system_control'** Database (if it is required). The program also creates the following tables (if so required):

house_state [name, value]
house_code_events [house, unit, state, timestamp, description]
house_code_states [house, unit, state, timestamp, description]

If the tables are created, the 'states' table is populated with the currently utilized X-10 sevices (this includes their house and unit codes along with their descriptions).

The program then connects to the 'system_control' database as a user.

The program subsequently opens a serial port (4800,8,N,1) to the W800RF32A (RF X-10 Receiver).

All received X-10 commands are input via comms port '/dev/ttyS0' (Orion-ITX top RS232 Serial Port) as character strings which are then converted into their 'house / unit / state' codes.

The serial port receiver is configured to wait either for 4 characters or until an inter-character timeout of 100ms has expired.

A forever loop is then executed:

a) The serial port receiver waits for either 4 characters or the inter-character timeout to expire.
b) The 4 byte data is then converted into the true house / unit / state values. If this is a true valid code, the code parameters (house, unit and state) are displayed on the console.
c) A timestamp is then computed .
d) The 'house_code_states' table is then updated for the received X-10 house/ unit / state.

This program is built using the command line:

```
gcc hc_main.c -o hc_main `mysql_config --cflags --libs`
```

Sign in as SuperUser and issue the following commands:

```
chmod a+rw /dev/ttyS0
chmod a+rw /dev/ttyS1
```

This program is executed in a terminal window using the command:
./hc_main & (Use '&' if you want the task to execute in the background)

hc_ti103
This program connects to the MySQL 'system_control' database as a user.

The program subsequently opens a serial port (4800,8,N,1) to the TI103 (X-10 Line Interface).
All transmitted/received X-10 commands are via comms port '/dev/ttyS1' (Orion-ITX bottom RS232 Serial Port) as ASCII character strings.

The Web page utilizes PHP to build dynamic web pages. These pages include the ability to let the user press specific buttons to turn X-10 devices on or off. The PHP code executing on the web server detect the button presses and enter the device state changes into the MySQL 'house_code_events' table.

The hc_ti103 code connects to the 'system_control' database and monitors the 'house_code_events' table.

A forever loop is then executed:

a) When a MySQL table entry is detected it then uses the entry's house / unit / state information in order to build a TI103 command string.
b) The string if output over the comm port to the TI103 Line Interface when sends the command over the household wiring to the physical X-10 device.
c) The MySQL entry is then deleted from the 'house_code_events' table.

The transmit process is fully operational.

The receive process has still to be implemented.

This program is built using the command line:

```
gcc hc_ti103.c -o hc_ti103 `mysql_config --cflags --libs`
```

Sign in as SuperUser and issue the following commands:

```
chmod a+rw /dev/ttyS0
chmod a+rw /dev/ttyS1
```

This program is executed in a terminal window using the command:

./hc_ti103 & (Use '&' if you want the task to execute in the background)
(Use '>' to re-direct the task output to a separate file for storage)

Web Pages

The Web pages utilize the following tools:

a) JavaScript
b) PHP
c) SQL

The following web site provides various examples: http://www.w3schools.com/

JavaScript
JavaScript is used to provide code that executes on the browser itself (on the PC or iPAD).

This code provides the real-time display of the system calendar/time. The code is started when the page is loaded and is set to repeatedly execute every 500ms.

PHP
PHP (PHP: Hypertext Preprocessor) is a server-side scripting language and supports access to MySQL).

PHP is used to perform the following operations:

a) Connect to the MySQL Database Environment
b) Access the 'system_control' database
c) POST button states to the server to insert entries into the database tables

A 'form' is created in which various 'buttons' are created. This includes the button variable's name and value if it is pressed along with any associated display label. When this button is pressed, the data value associated with the button is 'posted' to the web page (ie. action="web_page_name.php" method="post"). The 'php' file is accessed on the web server and the php code executed.

Each time this php code is executed it accesses the MySQL database and updates the tables accordingly.

SQL
MySQL provides the Database Tables used by the Home Control system.
PHP interfaces via MySQL commands.

Serial Comms Port
The serial communications port is used to transfer data serially as per the RS232 standard.

Project Example (Home Control)

This project example identifies the applied concepts that were provided in the previous section.

The Home Control project is an application that would be familiar to all engineers. They all live in homes and they all have appliances that are controlled.

This project will be implemented using the following tools:

1. PHP Dynamic Web Page Interface Controls
2. MySQL Database
3. Java Script
4. Linux Operating System
5. C Programming

which will be interfaced to Infrared Sensors and X10 lamp control devices in order to provide an automated lighting system for the home.

Note:
The code example provided in this book is provided "as is" with no indication as to suitability of purpose.

It should also be noted that the code examples are in the C programming language. This code could easily be written in C++ but the decision to keep it in C was to allow for understanding by a wider audience.

The Home Control / Security system is best discussed by means of the various web pages that have been developed. Each page presents a picture of your home below which is identified the navigation screen name.

These screens are as follows:

1. Security
2. Master
3. Lounge
4. Kitchen
5. Family
6. Steve
7. State
8. Events

These screen names are displayed and the user may transition to the relevant screen by simply pressing the relevant button name. The idea was to have these web pages be displayed on an iPAD such that the user could then use the system to control the house lighting and security system.

There is one additional screen (the Systems screen) which we will discuss layer.

The next line on the web page is a text description that informs the user as to the use of the displayed screen. Below that is the user interface. In the case of the Security screen it is a plan layout of the home and location of family members. For other screens it may be a number of push buttons that can either control house lights (or other devices), or can select a specific operating mode (a sequence to switch off various lights for watching television).

The Security Web Page

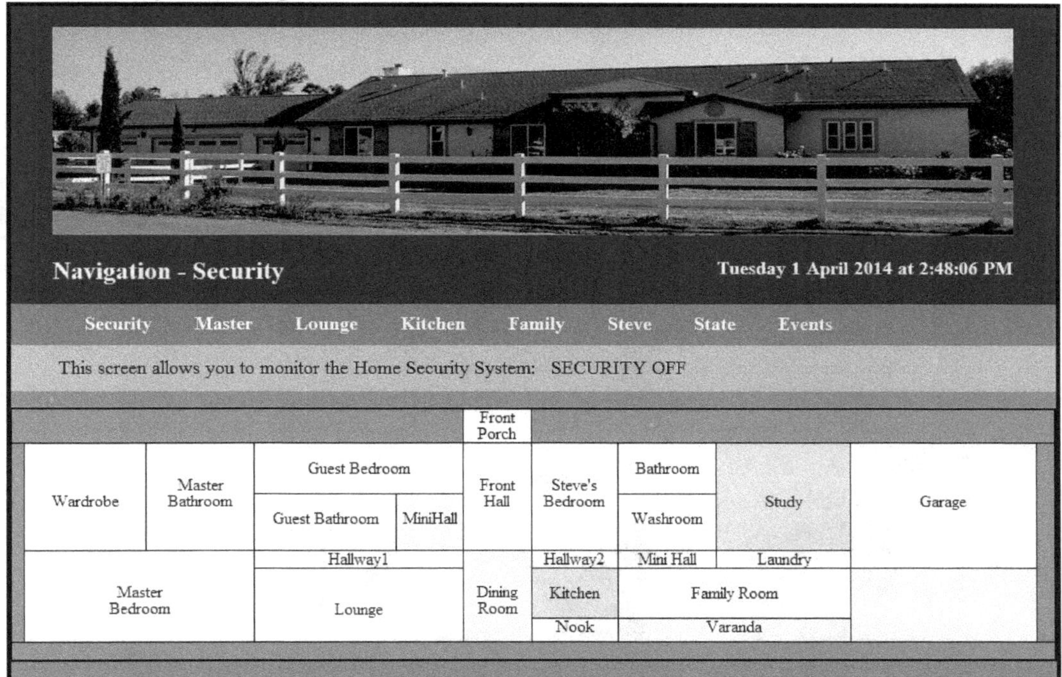

This screen permits the operator to navigate their way to the other screens.

The text description identifies the current status of the security system.

The rest of the screen provides a plan layout of the home and provides identification of the various family members (in the above screen there is someone in the kitchen and I am presently in the study). The house perimeter border will be displayed in red if the house security is on otherwise it will be displayed in green. The home sensors are IR (Infra-Red) devices that transmit an RF signal to a base received. This signal identifies a specific code (Home, Unit) and the information is then translated to a colored block on the house plan. During normal operation this information will be used to automatically turn house lights on and off at night, whereas during security mode it will be used to control an alarm.

The Master Bedroom Web Page

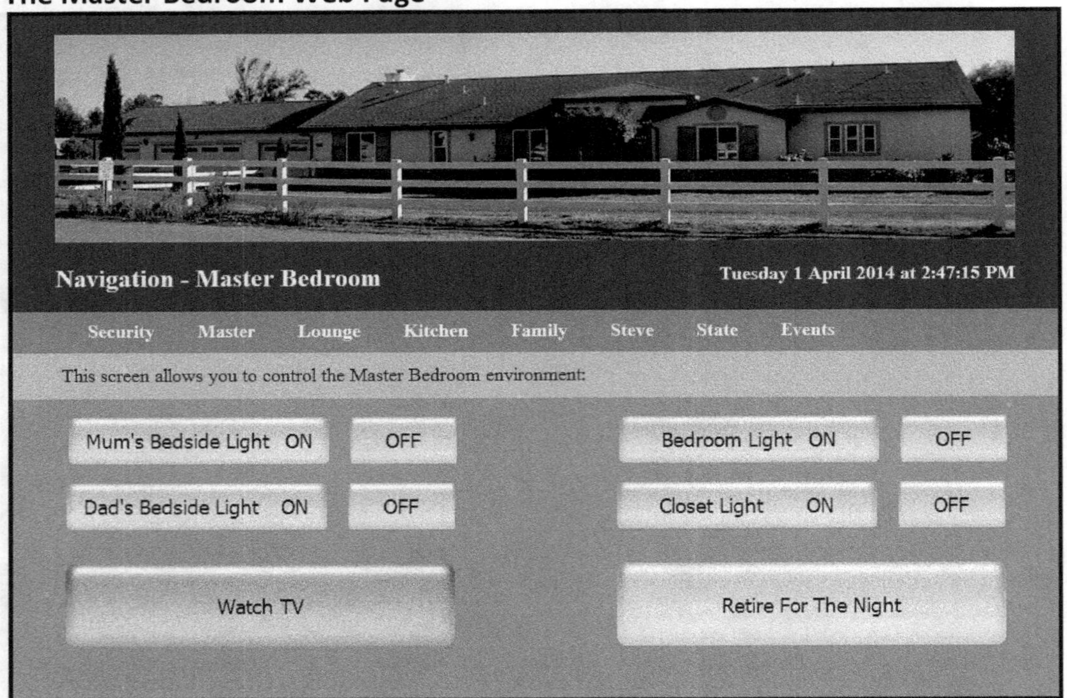

The Master Bedroom screen allows the user to control the lighting environment. Currently four light devices can be switched on or off. These are the two bed side lamps (each can be individually controlled), as can the main bedroom light and the closet light. It should be noted that the X10 controller that is used has the capability of also adjusting the brightness of these lamps. This will be implemented as a future task, however, the current software provides the serial access to the X10 controller. The software 'just' needs to be modified to bring in the light adjustment feature.

The [Watch TV] button, when pressed will switch off the two bedside lamps when it is desired to watch television. The closet light will also be turned off. When watching TV the room lights give the correct viewing ambience so these lamps are turned on. When desiring to turn in for the night, the operator can press the [Retire For The Night] button to switch off the family room, kitchen, lounge and hallway lights.

The Lounge Web Page

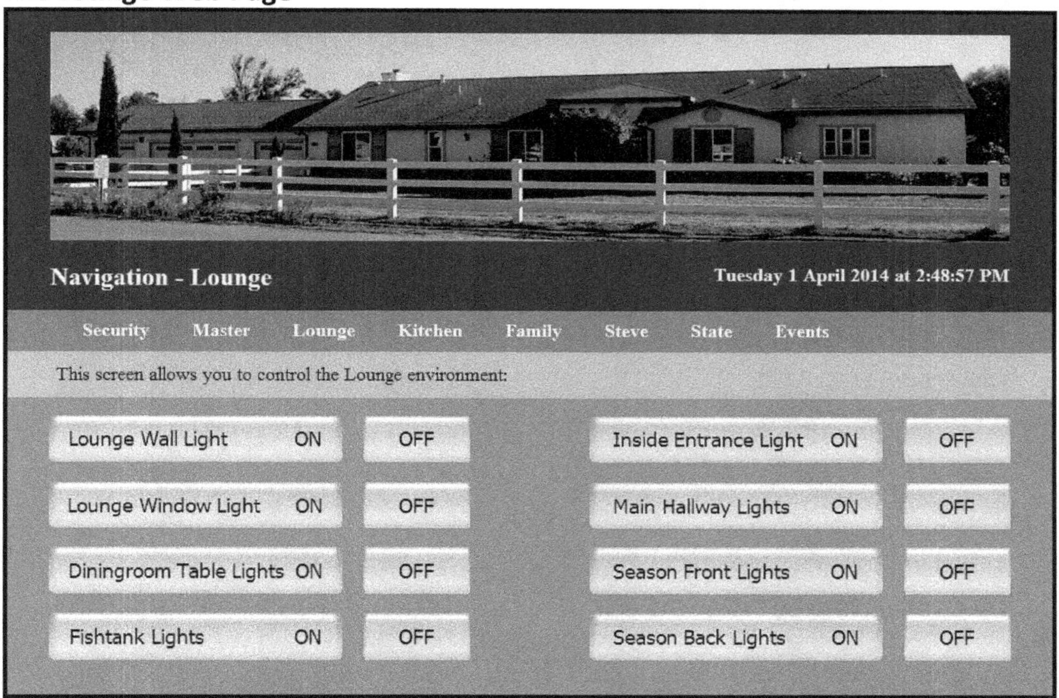

The Lounge screen allows a multitude of different lights to be controlled. The lounge has two lights and each can be individually activated. The dining room table lamps can be turned on or off. The two fish tanks are also in the lounge and the fish tank lights can also be controlled.

The front door inside lights and main hallway lights are accessible as are the outside seasonal lights. The power supplied by these controls terminates in switch boxes located under the eaves of the house. In winter the hanging icicle lights are installed and plugged into these receptacles. These controls then allow the front or the back seasonal lights to be activated. It should also be noted that various timed events are automatically installed when the system is powered up and these include the turning on and off of these seasonal lights (only during December and January, of course). The fish tank lights are also under timed control but the user is free to turn the lights on again after they had been previously turned off by the system (like when my Dad feeds the fish just before going to bed).

The Kitchen Web Page

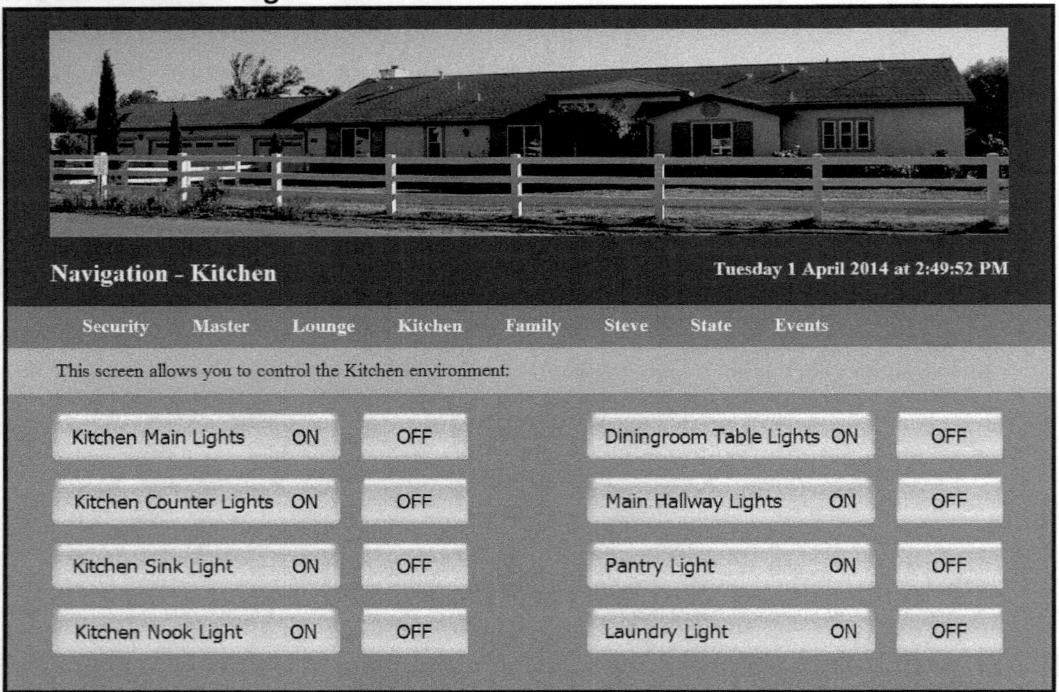

This screen was the impetus for developing this entire package.

In our home, it is often the case that when someone comes into the family room to sit down and watch TV, it is only then when realization hits them that they have left the kitchen light (and other lights) still on. So with much muttering and complaining they would get up to turn off the lights and then return back to their seat. Now there are other home automation software packages out there (and I have used them) but they tend to provide generalized sequence setups and in particular cases there is nothing quite like creating dedicated software for driving the system in a very specific manner. But there is another underlying reason. It simply borders on the sacrilegious for an embedded software engineer to use a software package designed by some other person for an application that they themselves can (and should) develop on their own. Besides, to such persons as us, there is great enjoyment in watching the result of our handiwork as house lights turn on and off as people move through different parts of the home.

The Family Room Web Page

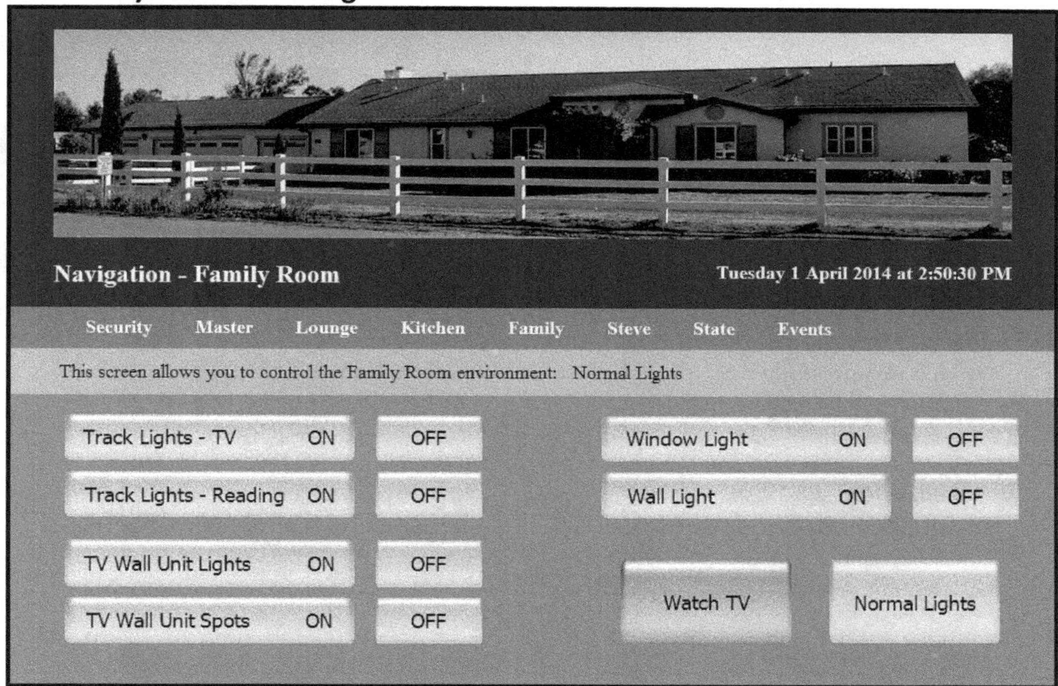

The family room has the television wall unit. In this unit there are some low wattage lights that illuminate various ornaments. These are the general purpose wall unit lights and the wall unit spot lights. There are also ceiling track lights with numerous spots. One set is turned towards the television wall unit whereas another set are turned towards the seats and are used while reading. Both these sets may be individually controlled. Two other lights remain. One is by the window and the other by the wall. The wall light gives some light ambience while viewing the television. The window light, while useful for reading, tends to provide refection off the TV (it doesn't affect my Mum or myself but my Dad gets the full brunt of it). So each evening various lights have to be turned on or off just to setup the lighting conditions (and also turn off the kitchen and hall lights in the process).

Wouldn't it be nice if we had just one button to do this. A button that tuddles (non-tech folk) could use without fear. This is what the [Watch TV] button does; and the [Normal Lights] does the opposite and turns on some lights.

Steve's Bedroom, Bathroom and Study Web Pages

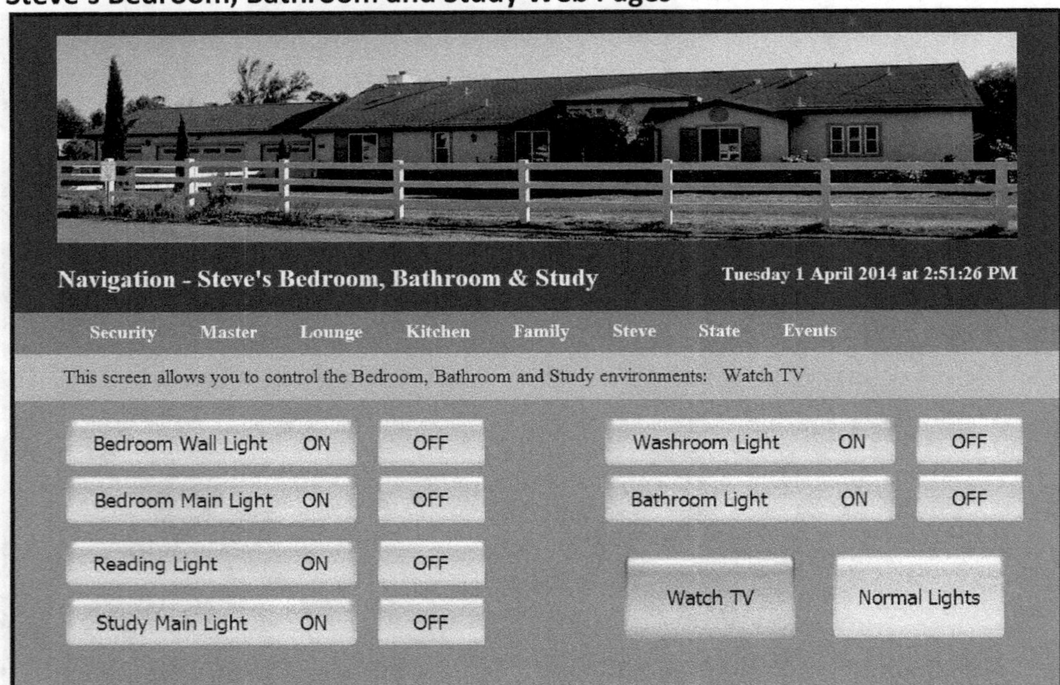

Steve (that's me) has his bedroom, bathroom and study at one end of the house. The bedroom has three main light controls, namely: wall lights, ceiling lights and a reading lamp. These can be individually controlled. The study also has a ceiling light. The washroom has its own light as does the bathroom, hence their own controls.

In the bedroom is a television and there is a need to turn off lights when it is desired to watch. But I may have just come from the study and walked through the washroom and so these lights are on until the predefined times have expired. But I want to turn these lights off right now. So for this we have our own [Watch TV] button. When pressed the study, washroom and bathroom lights are turned off as are the bedroom ceiling lamps, the reading lamp and one of the wall side lamps. The [Normal Lights] button restores the basic bedroom lights to their standard operation. If you have not figured it out yet, embedded software engineers are control-minded individuals.

The Device State Web Pages

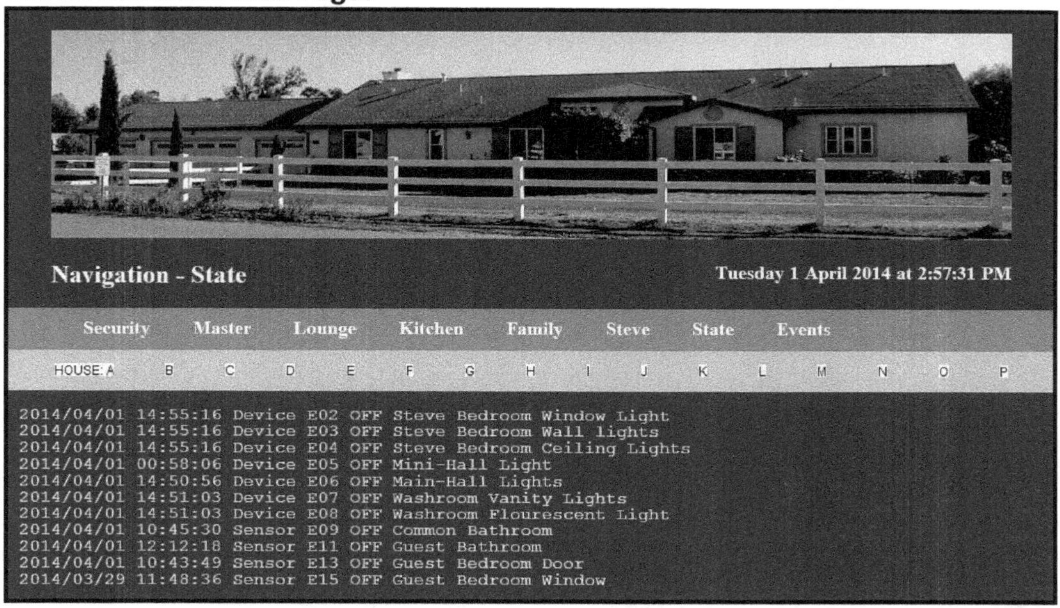

Now every IR sensor in the house transmits an RF coded signal when it detects someone (or something) move in the house. Two minutes (or so) later it transmits another code to say that it has stopped sensing movement. These IR sensors are programmed with various (house, unit) codes in which the house code is usually represented by a letter ('A', 'B', 'C', .. , 'P') and the unit code by a number ('01', '02', '03', .. ,'16'). The code from these sensors is used to indicate if there was movement detected in a specific part of the house. The X10 system also provides devices such as appliance (on/off control) and lamp modules (on/off/brightness control). It would be nice to know when any sensor or device turned on or off. Hence the state screens. These screens, one for each house code ('A' thru 'P'), identify the various sensors and devices and show which ones are in the system along with the last date and time that they turned on or off.

Again, this satisfies the control aspects of our nature.

It is also a very useful screen in determining when to replace sensor batteries (they only last about six months (dependent upon usage).

The Events Log Web Page

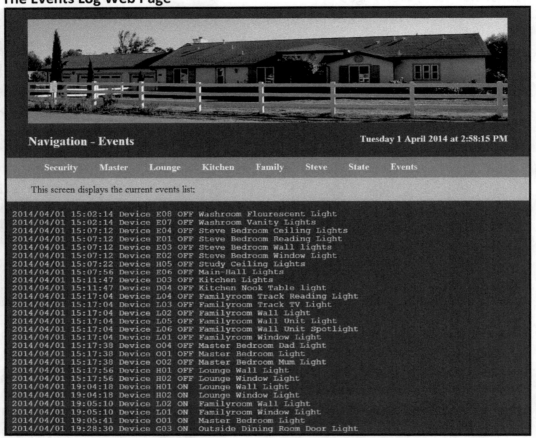

Navigation - Events

Tuesday 1 April 2014 at 2:58:15 PM

Security Master Lounge Kitchen Family Steve State Events

This screen displays the current events list:

```
2014/04/01 15:02:14 Device E08 OFF Washroom Flourescent Light
2014/04/01 15:02:14 Device E07 OFF Washroom Vanity Lights
2014/04/01 15:07:12 Device E04 OFF Steve Bedroom Ceiling Lights
2014/04/01 15:07:12 Device E01 OFF Steve Bedroom Reading Light
2014/04/01 15:07:12 Device E03 OFF Steve Bedroom Wall lights
2014/04/01 15:07:12 Device E02 OFF Steve Bedroom Window Light
2014/04/01 15:07:22 Device H05 OFF Study Ceiling Lights
2014/04/01 15:07:56 Device E06 OFF Main-Hall Lights
2014/04/01 15:11:47 Device D03 OFF Kitchen Lights
2014/04/01 15:11:47 Device D04 OFF Kitchen Nook Table light
2014/04/01 15:17:04 Device L04 OFF Familyroom Track Reading Light
2014/04/01 15:17:04 Device L03 OFF Familyroom Track TV Light
2014/04/01 15:17:04 Device L02 OFF Familyroom Wall Light
2014/04/01 15:17:04 Device L05 OFF Familyroom Wall Unit Light
2014/04/01 15:17:04 Device L06 OFF Familyroom Wall Unit Spotlight
2014/04/01 15:17:04 Device L01 OFF Familyroom Window Light
2014/04/01 15:17:38 Device O04 OFF Master Bedroom Dad Light
2014/04/01 15:17:38 Device O01 OFF Master Bedroom Light
2014/04/01 15:17:38 Device O02 OFF Master Bedroom Mum Light
2014/04/01 15:17:56 Device H01 OFF Lounge Wall Light
2014/04/01 15:17:56 Device H02 OFF Lounge Window Light
2014/04/01 19:04:18 Device H01 ON  Lounge Wall Light
2014/04/01 19:04:18 Device H02 ON  Lounge Window Light
2014/04/01 19:05:10 Device L02 ON  Familyroom Wall Light
2014/04/01 19:05:10 Device L01 ON  Familyroom Window Light
2014/04/01 19:05:41 Device O01 ON  Master Bedroom Light
2014/04/01 19:28:30 Device G03 ON  Outside Dining Room Door Light
```

The Events page is another kind of log in which it provides a look inside the events database. This allows the developer the chance to check when the next timed event is to occur. When the presence of a person is detected moving in a darkened room, an event entry to turn on a specific light might be generated and placed in this table (actually it is a table within a MySQL database). The time when the light should be turned off will also be determined and placed within this same table. By looking through the table entries we can quickly determine if all is well with the system.

The Systems Web Page

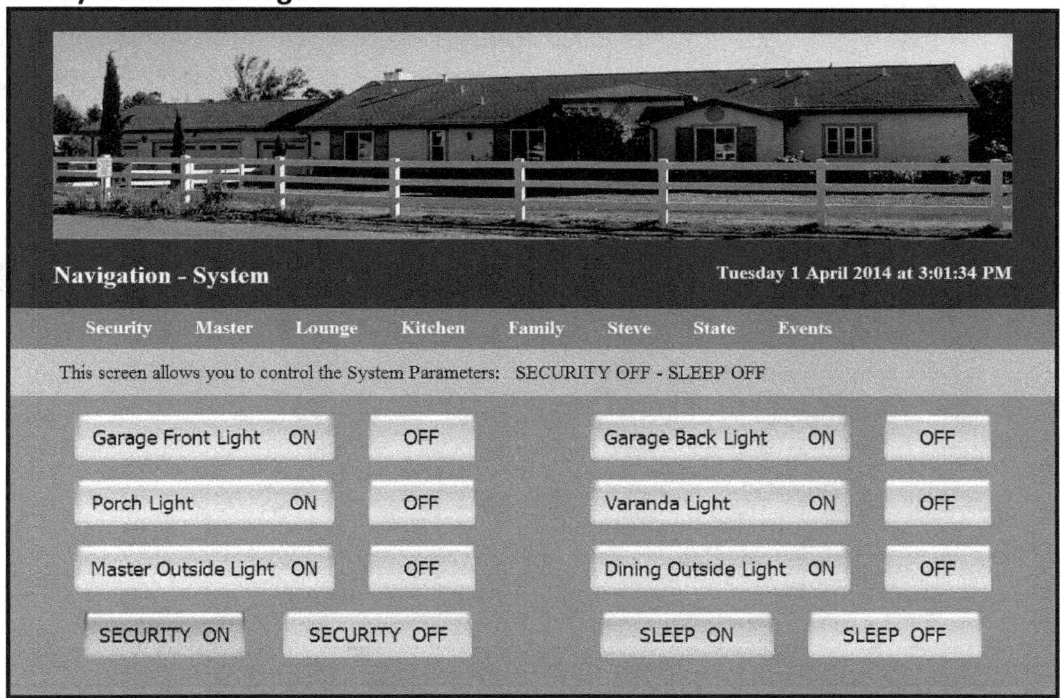

Now this is the screen to which we referred earlier but did not discuss. The reason being is because now all users should have access to this screen. For this is the page that is used to turn the security system on or off. Since there was some screen space I also placed all the outside light controls on this page along with the 'Sleep' control. When the [Sleep On] button is pressed my bedroom goes into sleep mode. The study, washroom, bathroom and my bedroom lights are turned off (after a short delay – long enough for me to hop into bed). The delay ends with the system telling me the time and date using an 'old time' format ('It is quarter past four in the morning on Tuesday the first of April 2014') and then the lights turn off. If I were to get up the lights will remain off (ie. the movement sensor in the room is ignored) until the [Sleep On] button is pressed (or until daybreak is detected).

Pressing the [Security On] button switches the system Security Mode on.

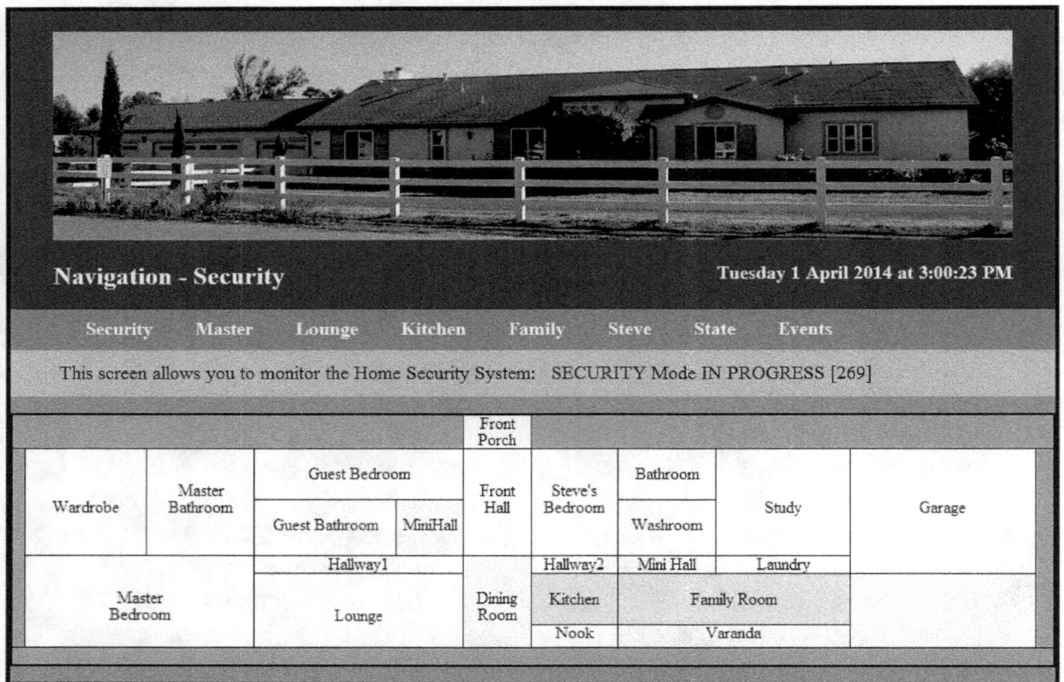

Once the [Security On] button has been pressed, the home owner has five minutes to vacate the premises (of course, this time period can easily be changed).

As the time is decrementing, the Security screen will present an image showing the border of the house plan flashing two colors (blue and red). Once the security timeout has expired the border color will turn to a steady red (see the next screen shot). This simply indicates that the home is now in Secure mode and any detected movement will turn on the alarm and send an email to the home owner (and whoever else). This information can then be accessed remotely via your phone, tablet, remote computer. If the unauthorized intruder walks into the study then a photograph is taken of them and sent off in an email as an attachment. This operation can easily be extended by having multiple cameras setup in various rooms. The code examples in this book clearly illustrate how this is achieved and provide the programmer with the information they need to easily extend this process as per their own requirements.

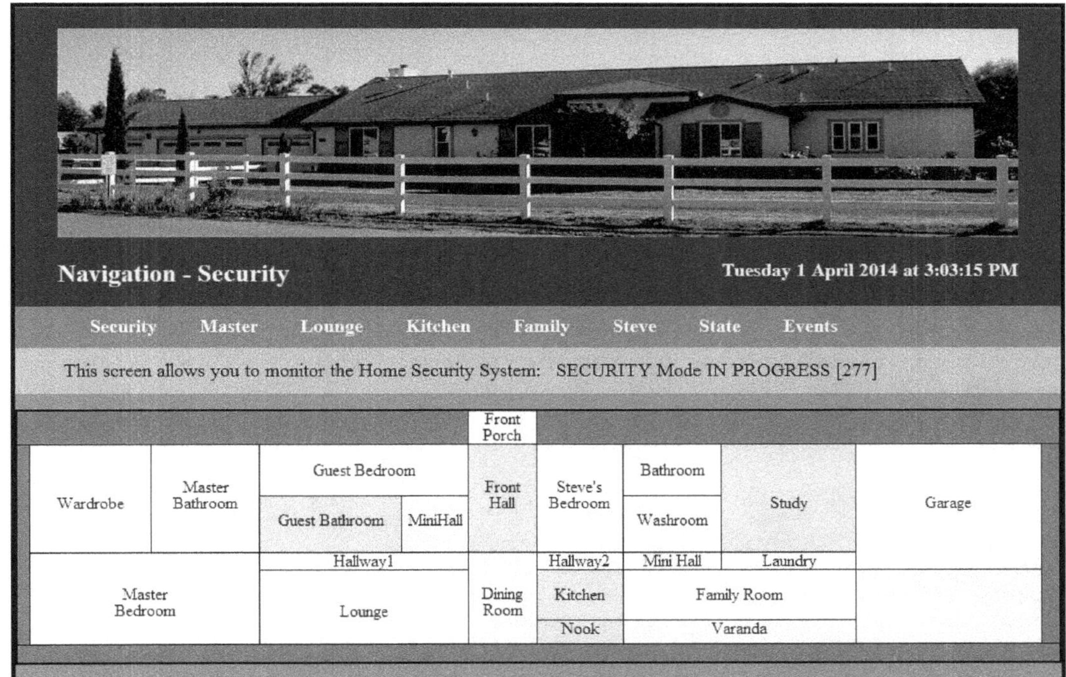

So the sensors that were being used to identify presence for turning lights on and off are now serving a dual role in that of monitoring the security of the home.

As an additional feature, an alternative to detecting an intruder after they have entered the dwelling, the system also sets up an elaborate set of random time sequences for turning various lights on and off to simulate the home environment. This would provide the illusion that the home is still occupied and would make any would-be intruder think twice before entering the building.

Directory: CSS

File: reset.css

The 'reset.css' file is a cascading style sheet and contains styles to reset the browser to a standard format.

```
/* http://meyerweb.com/eric/tools/css/reset/
   v2.0 | 20110126
   License: none (public domain)
*/

html, body, div, span, applet, object, iframe,
h1, h2, h3, h4, h5, h6, p, blockquote, pre,
a, abbr, acronym, address, big, cite, code,
del, dfn, em, img, ins, kbd, q, s, samp,
small, strike, strong, sub, sup, tt, var,
b, u, i, center,
dl, dt, dd, ol, ul, li,
fieldset, form, label, legend,
table, caption, tbody, tfoot, thead, tr, th, td,
article, aside, canvas, details, embed,
figure, figcaption, footer, header, hgroup,
menu, nav, output, ruby, section, summary,
time, mark, audio, video {
    margin: 0;
    padding: 0;
    border: 0;
    font-size: 100%;
    font: inherit;
    vertical-align: baseline;
}
/* HTML5 display-role reset for older browsers */
article, aside, details, figcaption, figure,
footer, header, hgroup, menu, nav, section {
    display: block;
}
body {
    line-height: 1;
}
ol, ul {
    list-style: none;
}
blockquote, q {
    quotes: none;
}
blockquote:before, blockquote:after,
q:before, q:after {
    content: '';
    content: none;
```

```
}
table {
   border-collapse: collapse;
   border-spacing: 0;
}
```

File: styles.css

The 'styles.css' file is an additional cascading style sheet used to reset the browser to a standard format.

```
/*
// File name: styles.css
// Author: Steve McClure
// Book: Designing Embedded Sytems
// Description: This styles file is used by the Home Control /
//    Security application.
*/

/* Full Reset */
* { font-family:Arial, Helvetica, sans-serif;
    font-size:12px;
    color:#000000;
    font-weight:normal;
    font-style:normal;
    margin:0;
    padding:0;
    border:0;
  }

/* Global */

html   {   }

body   { background-color:#eeeeee;       }



h1 {
      font-family:Arial, Helvetica, sans-serif;
      font-size:36px;
      color:#99FF99;
   }

h2 {
      color:yellow;
   }

h3 {
      color:blue;
   }

#top { background-color:#073EF8;
       padding:20px 40px 10px 40px;
}
```

```
#navigation
{
   color:white;
   background-color:#010EA9;
/* font-weight:bold; */
}

#navigation_picture
{
   font-size: large;
   color:white;
   background-color:#010EA9;
   padding:20px 40px 0px 40px;
}


#navigation_heading
{
   color:white;
   font-size:x-large;
   background-color:#010EA9;     /* Dark Blue */
   padding:20px 40px 20px 40px;
   float:left;
}

#navigation_time  /* Works */
{
   color:white;
   font-size: large;
   background-color:#010EA9;
   padding:20px 40px 20px 40px;
   float:right;
}


#navigation_links   /* Works */
{
   color:white;
   background-color:#0780F8;  /* Light Blue */
   clear:both;
   font-size:large;
      padding:10px 10px 30px 50px;  /* Border around navigation buttons
*/
}


#mainNav   /* Works */
{
   color:white;
   background-color:#0780F8;
   clear:both;
   padding:10px 10px 30px 50px;  /* Border around navigation buttons */
```

```
}

#dddmainNav ul li a   { display:inline; text-decoration: none;}

#mainNav ul li a   { text-decoration: none; float:left; padding:0px 20px
10px 20px; display:inline; }

#mainNav  a:link    { color:#ffffff;  }
#mainNav  a:visited { color:#ffffff;  }
#mainNav  a:active  { color:#ffffff;  }
#mainNav  a:hover   { color:#ffffff; background-color:#777777; }
#mainNav  a:focus   { color:#ffffff;  }


#main_stuff
{
   font-size:large;
}

#event_labels
{
   font-size:large;
}


#state_stuff
{
   font-size:x-small;
   font-family:"Courier New", Courier, monospace;
   color:white;
}


#navigation_links ul li a   { text-decoration: none; float:left;
padding:0px 20px 10px 20px; display:inline;}

#navigation_links a:link    { color:#ffffff;  }
#navigation_links a:visited { color:#ffffff;  }
#navigation_links a:active  { color:#ffffff;  }
#navigation_links a:hover   { color:#ffffff; background-color:#777777; }
#navigation_links a:focus   { color:#ffffff;  }


#banner { background-color:#FFCC99;
          padding:30px 60px 50px 60px;
          border-bottom:2px #000000 solid;
}


subbanner {
      color:blue;
```

```
}

#test1
{
   font-size: large;
   color:maroon;
   background-color:#010EA9;
}

#key_background
{
   background-color:#808080;
}

#sensor_background
{
   background-color:#E7E7E7;              /* Light gray */
/* background-color:#F7F7F7; */           /* Almost white */
}


#general_text
{
font-family:"Courier New", Courier, monospace;
   font-size:medium;
   color:white;
   background-color:#010EA9;
}


#event_list
{
font-family:"Courier New", Courier, monospace;
   font-size:medium;
   color:white;
   background-color:#010EA9;
}

#state_list
{
font-family:"Courier New", Courier, monospace;
   font-size:medium;
   color:white;
   background-color:#010EA9;
}

#wrapper {    background-color:#AAAAAA;
   width:980px;
   margin:0px auto;}
```

Directory: Images

This directory contains the house picture and the button images. The user is required to build these images themselves.

Directory: js

The js (Java Script) directory contains the following file:

File: calendar.js

This file is used to provide the calendar data and time that is displayed continuously of the web page.

```
// File name:
//    calendar.js
// Author:
//    Steve McClure
// Book:
//    Designing Embedded Sytems
// Description:
//    This Java Script file is used by the Home Control / Security
//    application to display the system date and time on the Security
//    web page.  It also changes/flashes the border color of the
//    home layout table.

var home_security_state_js = 0;

function startTime()
{
// Get the current time and date
var today=new Date();

// Create a list of day names
var weekday=new Array(7);
weekday[0]="Sunday";
weekday[1]="Monday";
weekday[2]="Tuesday";
weekday[3]="Wednesday";
weekday[4]="Thursday";
weekday[5]="Friday";
weekday[6]="Saturday";

// Create a list of month names
var month_name=new Array(12);
month_name[0] = "January";
month_name[1] = "February";
month_name[2] = "March";
month_name[3] = "April";
month_name[4] = "May";
```

```
month_name[5] = "June";
month_name[6] = "July";
month_name[7] = "August";
month_name[8] = "September";
month_name[9] = "October";
month_name[10]= "November";
month_name[11]= "December";

// Extract the time and date parameters
var hours   = today.getHours();
var minutes = today.getMinutes();
var seconds = today.getSeconds();

var dd=today.getDate();
var mm=today.getMonth();
var yy=today.getFullYear();

// Determine AM or PM indicator
var tt;
if (hours < 12)
   tt = "AM";
else
{
   tt = "PM";
   if (hours > 12)
      hours -= 12;
}

// Add a zero in front of single digit numbers
minutes = check_time(minutes);
seconds = check_time(seconds);

// Build the calendar date, for example: Thursday 28 March 2013 at 2:58
PM
document.getElementById("navigation_time").innerHTML=weekday[today.getDay
()]+" "+dd+" "+month_name[mm]+" "+yy+" at
"+hours+":"+minutes+":"+seconds+" "+tt;

if (home_security_state_js == 0)
{
   document.getElementById("smc1").style.backgroundColor = "#009933";
//"#00FF00";
   document.getElementById("smc2").style.backgroundColor = "#009933";
//"#00FF00";
   document.getElementById("smc3").style.backgroundColor = "#009933";
//"#00FF00";
   document.getElementById("smc4").style.backgroundColor = "#009933";
//"#00FF00";
   document.getElementById("smc5").style.backgroundColor = "#009933";
//"#00FF00";
}
else if (home_security_state_js == 1)
```

```
{
    document.getElementById("smc1").style.backgroundColor = "#6699FF";
//"#0000FF";
    document.getElementById("smc2").style.backgroundColor = "#6699FF";
//"#0000FF";
    document.getElementById("smc3").style.backgroundColor = "#6699FF";
//"#0000FF";
    document.getElementById("smc4").style.backgroundColor = "#6699FF";
//"#0000FF";
    document.getElementById("smc5").style.backgroundColor = "#6699FF";
//"#0000FF";
}
else if (home_security_state_js == 2)
{
    if ((seconds % 2) == 0)
    {
        document.getElementById("smc1").style.backgroundColor = "#6699FF";
//"#0000FF";
        document.getElementById("smc2").style.backgroundColor = "#6699FF";
//"#0000FF";
        document.getElementById("smc3").style.backgroundColor = "#6699FF";
//"#0000FF";
        document.getElementById("smc4").style.backgroundColor = "#6699FF";
//"#0000FF";
        document.getElementById("smc5").style.backgroundColor = "#6699FF";
//"#0000FF";
    }
    else
    {
        document.getElementById("smc1").style.backgroundColor = "#CC3300";
//"#00FF00";
        document.getElementById("smc2").style.backgroundColor = "#CC3300";
//"#00FF00";
        document.getElementById("smc3").style.backgroundColor = "#CC3300";
//"#00FF00";
        document.getElementById("smc4").style.backgroundColor = "#CC3300";
//"#00FF00";
        document.getElementById("smc5").style.backgroundColor = "#CC3300";
//"#00FF00";
    }
}
else if (home_security_state_js == 3)
{
    document.getElementById("smc1").style.backgroundColor = "#FF0000";
    document.getElementById("smc2").style.backgroundColor = "#FF0000";
    document.getElementById("smc3").style.backgroundColor = "#FF0000";
    document.getElementById("smc4").style.backgroundColor = "#FF0000";
    document.getElementById("smc5").style.backgroundColor = "#FF0000";
}

//  Execute the function in another 500ms
var t=setTimeout(function(){startTime()},500);
```

```
}
//==============================================================
// check_time
//
// This function prefixes a '0' before single digit numbers
//==============================================================
function check_time(i)
{
if (i < 10)
    {
        i="0" + i;
    }
return i;
}
```

File: calendar2.js

This file is used to provide the calendar data and time that is displayed continuously on the web page.

```
// File name:
//   calendar2.js
// Author:
//   Steve McClure
// Book:
//   Designing Embedded Sytems
// Description:
//   This Java Script file is used by the Home
//   Control / Security application to display the
//   system date and time on the System, State and
//   Event web pages.

var home_security_state_js = 0;

function startTime()
{
// Get the current time and date
var today=new Date();

// Create a list of day names
var weekday=new Array(7);
weekday[0]="Sunday";
weekday[1]="Monday";
weekday[2]="Tuesday";
weekday[3]="Wednesday";
weekday[4]="Thursday";
weekday[5]="Friday";
weekday[6]="Saturday";

// Create a list of month names
var month_name=new Array(12);
month_name[0] = "January";
month_name[1] = "February";
month_name[2] = "March";
month_name[3] = "April";
month_name[4] = "May";
month_name[5] = "June";
month_name[6] = "July";
month_name[7] = "August";
month_name[8] = "September";
month_name[9] = "October";
month_name[10]= "November";
month_name[11]= "December";
// Extract the time and date parameters
var hour    = today.getHours();
var hours   = today.getHours();
```

```
var minutes = today.getMinutes();
var seconds = today.getSeconds();

var dd=today.getDate();
var mm=today.getMonth();
var yy=today.getFullYear();

// Determine AM or PM indicator
var tt;
if (hours < 12)
   tt = "AM";
else
   {
      tt = "PM";
      if (hours > 12)
         hours -= 12;
   }

// Add a zero in front of single digit numbers
minutes = check_time(minutes);
seconds = check_time(seconds);

// Build the calendar date, for example: Thursday 28 March 2013 at 2:58
PM
document.getElementById("navigation_time").innerHTML=weekday[today.getDay
()]+" "+dd+" "+month_name[mm]+" "+yy+" at
"+hours+":"+minutes+":"+seconds+" "+tt;

var hour  = check_time(hour);
var day   = check_time(dd);
var month = check_time(mm + 1);

// Build the calendar time that will timestamp each entry recorded in the
state able
var calendar_date = yy +"/" + month + "/" + day;
var calendar_time = hour + ":" + minutes + ":" + seconds;
var calendar_full = yy +"/" + month + "/" + day + "%20" + hour + ":" +
minutes + ":" + seconds;

//  Execute the function in another 500ms
var t=setTimeout(function(){startTime()},500);
}
```

```
//=============================================================
// check_time
//
// This function prefixes a '0' before single digit numbers
//=============================================================
function check_time(i)
{
if (i < 10)
  {
    i="0" + i;
  }
return i;
}


//=============================================================
// get_datetime
//
// This function gets the calendar date time and inserts it
// into the html page request.
//=============================================================
function get_datetime()
{
document.getElementById("navigation_time").innerHTML= calendar_time;
}
```

File: master_calendar.js

This file is used to provide the calendar data and time that is displayed continuously on the Master web page.

```
// File name:
//   master_calendar.js
// Author:
//   Steve McClure
// Book:
//   Designing Embedded Sytems
// Description:
//   This Java Script file is used by the Home
//   Control / Security application Master web page.

var home_security_state_js = 0;

function startTime()
{
// Get the current time and date
var today=new Date();

// Create a list of day names
var weekday=new Array(7);
weekday[0]="Sunday";
weekday[1]="Monday";
weekday[2]="Tuesday";
weekday[3]="Wednesday";
weekday[4]="Thursday";
weekday[5]="Friday";
weekday[6]="Saturday";

// Create a list of month names
var month_name=new Array(12);
month_name[0] = "January";
month_name[1] = "February";
month_name[2] = "March";
month_name[3] = "April";
month_name[4] = "May";
month_name[5] = "June";
month_name[6] = "July";
month_name[7] = "August";
month_name[8] = "September";
month_name[9] = "October";
month_name[10]= "November";
month_name[11]= "December";

// Extract the time and date parameters
var hour    = today.getHours();
var hours   = today.getHours();
var minutes = today.getMinutes();
```

```
var seconds = today.getSeconds();

var dd=today.getDate();
var mm=today.getMonth();
var yy=today.getFullYear();

// Determine AM or PM indicator
var tt;
if (hours < 12)
  tt = "AM";
else
{
  tt = "PM";
  if (hours > 12)
    hours -= 12;
}

// Add a zero in front of single digit numbers
minutes = check_time(minutes);
seconds = check_time(seconds);

// Build the calendar date, for example: Thursday 28 March 2013 at 2:58
PM
document.getElementById("navigation_time").innerHTML=weekday[today.getDay
()]+" "+dd+" "+month_name[mm]+" "+yy+" at
"+hours+":"+minutes+":"+seconds+" "+tt;


// Build the calendar time that will timestamp each entry recorded in the
state able
var hour  = check_time(hour);
var day   = check_time(dd);
var month = check_time(mm + 1);

var calendar_date = yy +"/" + month + "/" + day;
var calendar_time = hour + ":" + minutes + ":" + seconds;

var calendar_full = yy +"/" + month + "/" + day + "%20" + hour + ":" +
minutes + ":" + seconds;
```

```
// Reconfigure the buttons to include the full calendar
document.getElementById("smc1a").href =
"master.php?mums_bedside_light_on=1&calendar="  + calendar_full;
document.getElementById("smc1b").href =
"master.php?mums_bedside_light_off=1&calendar=" + calendar_full;
document.getElementById("smc2a").href =
"master.php?dads_bedside_light_on=1&calendar="  + calendar_full;
document.getElementById("smc2b").href =
"master.php?dads_bedside_light_off=1&calendar=" + calendar_full;

document.getElementById("smc3").href  = "master.php?watch_tv=1&calendar="
+ calendar_full;

document.getElementById("smc4a").href =
"master.php?bedroom_light_on=1&calendar="  + calendar_full;
document.getElementById("smc4b").href =
"master.php?bedroom_light_off=1&calendar=" + calendar_full;
document.getElementById("smc5a").href =
"master.php?closet_light_on=1&calendar="   + calendar_full;
document.getElementById("smc5b").href =
"master.php?closet_light_off=1&calendar="  + calendar_full;

document.getElementById("smc6").href  =
"master.php?retire_for_the_night=1&calendar=" + calendar_full;

//  Execute the function in another 500ms
var t=setTimeout(function(){startTime()},500);
}



//==============================================================
// check_time
//
// This function prefixes a '0' before single digit numbers
//==============================================================
function check_time(i)
{
if (i < 10)
  {
    i="0" + i;
  }
return i;
}
```

File: lounge_calendar.js
This file is used to provide the calendar data and time that is displayed continuously on the Lounge web page.

```
// File name:
//    lounge_calendar.js
// Author:
//    Steve McClure
// Book:
//    Designing Embedded Sytems
// Description:
//    This Java Script file is used by the Home
//    Control / Security application Lounge web page.

var home_security_state_js = 0;

function startTime()
{
// Get the current time and date
var today=new Date();

// Create a list of day names
var weekday=new Array(7);
weekday[0]="Sunday";
weekday[1]="Monday";
weekday[2]="Tuesday";
weekday[3]="Wednesday";
weekday[4]="Thursday";
weekday[5]="Friday";
weekday[6]="Saturday";

// Create a list of month names
var month_name=new Array(12);
month_name[0] = "January";
month_name[1] = "February";
month_name[2] = "March";
month_name[3] = "April";
month_name[4] = "May";
month_name[5] = "June";
month_name[6] = "July";
month_name[7] = "August";
month_name[8] = "September";
month_name[9] = "October";
month_name[10]= "November";
month_name[11]= "December";

// Extract the time and date parameters
var hour    = today.getHours();
var hours   = today.getHours();
var minutes = today.getMinutes();
```

```
var seconds = today.getSeconds();

var dd=today.getDate();
var mm=today.getMonth();
var yy=today.getFullYear();

// Determine AM or PM indicator
var tt;
if (hours < 12)
  tt = "AM";
else
{
  tt = "PM";
  if (hours > 12)
    hours -= 12;
}


// Add a zero in front of single digit numbers
minutes = check_time(minutes);
seconds = check_time(seconds);


// Build the calendar date, for example: Thursday 28 March 2013 at 2:58
PM
document.getElementById("navigation_time").innerHTML=weekday[today.getDay
()]+" "+dd+" "+month_name[mm]+" "+yy+" at
"+hours+":"+minutes+":"+seconds+" "+tt;


// Build the calendar time that will timestamp each entry recorded in the
state able
var hour  = check_time(hour);
var day   = check_time(dd);
var month = check_time(mm + 1);

var calendar_date = yy +"/" + month + "/" + day;
var calendar_time = hour + ":" + minutes + ":" + seconds;

var calendar_full = yy +"/" + month + "/" + day + "%20" + hour + ":" +
minutes + ":" + seconds;

// Reconfigure the buttons to include the full calendar
document.getElementById("smc1a").href =
"lounge.php?lounge_wall_light_on=1&calendar="    + calendar_full;
document.getElementById("smc1b").href =
"lounge.php?lounge_wall_light_off=1&calendar="   + calendar_full;
document.getElementById("smc2a").href =
"lounge.php?lounge_window_light_on=1&calendar="  + calendar_full;
document.getElementById("smc2b").href =
"lounge.php?lounge_window_light_off=1&calendar=" + calendar_full;
```

```
document.getElementById("smc3a").href =
"lounge.php?diningroom_table_lights_on=1&calendar="  + calendar_full;
document.getElementById("smc3b").href =
"lounge.php?diningroom_table_lights_off=1&calendar=" + calendar_full;
document.getElementById("smc4a").href =
"lounge.php?fishtank_lights_on=1&calendar="          + calendar_full;
document.getElementById("smc4b").href =
"lounge.php?fishtank_lights_off=1&calendar="         + calendar_full;

document.getElementById("smc5a").href =
"lounge.php?inside_entrance_light_on=1&calendar="  + calendar_full;
document.getElementById("smc5b").href =
"lounge.php?inside_entrance_light_off=1&calendar=" + calendar_full;
document.getElementById("smc6a").href =
"lounge.php?main_hallway_lights_on=1&calendar="    + calendar_full;
document.getElementById("smc6b").href =
"lounge.php?main_hallway_lights_off=1&calendar="   + calendar_full;

document.getElementById("smc7a").href =
"lounge.php?season_front_lights_on=1&calendar="  + calendar_full;
document.getElementById("smc7b").href =
"lounge.php?season_front_lights_off=1&calendar=" + calendar_full;
document.getElementById("smc8a").href =
"lounge.php?season_back_lights_on=1&calendar="   + calendar_full;
document.getElementById("smc8b").href =
"lounge.php?season_back_lights_off=1&calendar="  + calendar_full;


//  Execute the function in another 500ms
var t=setTimeout(function(){startTime()},500);
}



//================================================================
// check_time
//
// This function prefixes a '0' before single digit numbers
//================================================================
function check_time(i)
{
if (i < 10)
  {
    i="0" + i;
  }
return i;
}
```

File: kitchen_calendar.js

This file is used to provide the calendar data and time that is displayed continuously on the Kitchen web page.

```
// File name:
//   kitchen_calendar.js
// Author:
//   Steve McClure
// Book:
//   Designing Embedded Sytems
// Description:
//   This Java Script file is used by the Home
//   Control / Security application Kitchen web page.

var home_security_state_js = 0;

function startTime()
{
// Get the current time and date
var today=new Date();

// Create a list of day names
var weekday=new Array(7);
weekday[0]="Sunday";
weekday[1]="Monday";
weekday[2]="Tuesday";
weekday[3]="Wednesday";
weekday[4]="Thursday";
weekday[5]="Friday";
weekday[6]="Saturday";

// Create a list of month names
var month_name=new Array(12);
month_name[0] = "January";
month_name[1] = "February";
month_name[2] = "March";
month_name[3] = "April";
month_name[4] = "May";
month_name[5] = "June";
month_name[6] = "July";
month_name[7] = "August";
month_name[8] = "September";
month_name[9] = "October";
month_name[10]= "November";
month_name[11]= "December";
// Extract the time and date parameters
var hour    = today.getHours();
var hours   = today.getHours();
var minutes = today.getMinutes();
var seconds = today.getSeconds();
```

```
var dd=today.getDate();
var mm=today.getMonth();
var yy=today.getFullYear();

// Determine AM or PM indicator
var tt;
if (hours < 12)
  tt = "AM";
else
{
  tt = "PM";
  if (hours > 12)
    hours -= 12;
}


// Add a zero in front of single digit numbers
minutes = check_time(minutes);
seconds = check_time(seconds);

// Build the calendar date, for example: Thursday 28 March 2013 at 2:58
PM
document.getElementById("navigation_time").innerHTML=weekday[today.getDay
()]+" "+dd+" "+month_name[mm]+" "+yy+" at
"+hours+":"+minutes+":"+seconds+" "+tt;


// Build the calendar time that will timestamp each entry recorded in the
state able
var hour  = check_time(hour);
var day   = check_time(dd);
var month = check_time(mm + 1);

var calendar_date = yy +"/" + month + "/" + day;
var calendar_time = hour + ":" + minutes + ":" + seconds;

var calendar_full = yy +"/" + month + "/" + day + "%20" + hour + ":" +
minutes + ":" + seconds;


// Reconfigure the buttons to include the full calendar
document.getElementById("smc1a").href="kitchen.php?kitchen_main_lights_on
=1&calendar="      + calendar_full;
document.getElementById("smc1b").href="kitchen.php?kitchen_main_lights_of
f=1&calendar="     + calendar_full;
document.getElementById("smc2a").href="kitchen.php?kitchen_counter_lights
_on=1&calendar="   + calendar_full;
document.getElementById("smc2b").href="kitchen.php?kitchen_counter_lights
_off=1&calendar=" + calendar_full;
```

```
document.getElementById("smc3a").href="kitchen.php?kitchen_sink_light_on=
1&calendar="  + calendar_full;
document.getElementById("smc3b").href="kitchen.php?kitchen_sink_light_off
=1&calendar=" + calendar_full;
document.getElementById("smc4a").href="kitchen.php?kitchen_nook_light_on=
1&calendar="  + calendar_full;
document.getElementById("smc4b").href="kitchen.php?kitchen_nook_light_off
=1&calendar=" + calendar_full;

document.getElementById("smc5a").href="kitchen.php?diningroom_table_light
s_on=1&calendar="  + calendar_full;
document.getElementById("smc5b").href="kitchen.php?diningroom_table_light
s_off=1&calendar=" + calendar_full;
document.getElementById("smc6a").href="kitchen.php?main_hallway_lights_on
=1&calendar="      + calendar_full;
document.getElementById("smc6b").href="kitchen.php?main_hallway_lights_of
f=1&calendar="     + calendar_full;

document.getElementById("smc7a").href="kitchen.php?pantry_light_on=1&cale
ndar="   + calendar_full;
document.getElementById("smc7b").href="kitchen.php?pantry_light_off=1&cal
endar="  + calendar_full;
document.getElementById("smc8a").href="kitchen.php?laundry_light_on=1&cal
endar="  + calendar_full;
document.getElementById("smc8b").href="kitchen.php?laundry_light_off=1&ca
lendar=" + calendar_full;

//  Execute the function in another 500ms
var t=setTimeout(function(){startTime()},500);
}



//============================================================
// check_time
//
// This function prefixes a '0' before single digit numbers
//============================================================
function check_time(i)
{
if (i < 10)
  {
    i="0" + i;
  }
return i;
}
```

File: family_calendar.js

This file is used to provide the calendar data and time that is displayed continuously on the Family web page.

```
// File name:
//   family_calendar.js
// Author:
//   Steve McClure
// Book:
//   Designing Embedded Sytems
// Description:
//   This Java Script file is used by the Home
//   Control / Security application Family web page.

var home_security_state_js = 0;

function startTime()
{
// Get the current time and date
var today=new Date();

// Create a list of day names
var weekday=new Array(7);
weekday[0]="Sunday";
weekday[1]="Monday";
weekday[2]="Tuesday";
weekday[3]="Wednesday";
weekday[4]="Thursday";
weekday[5]="Friday";
weekday[6]="Saturday";

// Create a list of month names
var month_name=new Array(12);
month_name[0] = "January";
month_name[1] = "February";
month_name[2] = "March";
month_name[3] = "April";
month_name[4] = "May";
month_name[5] = "June";
month_name[6] = "July";
month_name[7] = "August";
month_name[8] = "September";
month_name[9] = "October";
month_name[10]= "November";
month_name[11]= "December";
// Extract the time and date parameters
var hour    = today.getHours();
var hours   = today.getHours();
var minutes = today.getMinutes();
var seconds = today.getSeconds();
```

```
var dd=today.getDate();
var mm=today.getMonth();
var yy=today.getFullYear();

// Determine AM or PM indicator
var tt;
if (hours < 12)
  tt = "AM";
else
{
  tt = "PM";
  if (hours > 12)
    hours -= 12;
}


// Add a zero in front of single digit numbers
minutes = check_time(minutes);
seconds = check_time(seconds);

// Build the calendar date, for example: Thursday 28 March 2013 at 2:58
PM
document.getElementById("navigation_time").innerHTML=weekday[today.getDay
()]+" "+dd+" "+month_name[mm]+" "+yy+" at
"+hours+":"+minutes+":"+seconds+" "+tt;


// Build the calendar time that will timestamp each entry recorded in the
state able
var hour  = check_time(hour);
var day   = check_time(dd);
var month = check_time(mm + 1);

var calendar_date = yy +"/" + month + "/" + day;
var calendar_time = hour + ":" + minutes + ":" + seconds;

var calendar_full = yy +"/" + month + "/" + day + "%20" + hour + ":" +
minutes + ":" + seconds;


// Reconfigure the buttons to include the full calendar
document.getElementById("smc1a").href="family.php?track_lights_tv_on=1&ca
lendar="       + calendar_full;
document.getElementById("smc1b").href="family.php?track_lights_tv_off=1&c
alendar="      + calendar_full;
document.getElementById("smc2a").href="family.php?track_lights_reading_on
=1&calendar="  + calendar_full;
document.getElementById("smc2b").href="family.php?track_lights_reading_of
f=1&calendar=" + calendar_full;
```

```
document.getElementById("smc3a").href="family.php?tv_wall_unit_lights_on=
1&calendar="  + calendar_full;
document.getElementById("smc3b").href="family.php?tv_wall_unit_lights_off
=1&calendar=" + calendar_full;
document.getElementById("smc4a").href="family.php?tv_wall_unit_spots_on=1
&calendar="   + calendar_full;
document.getElementById("smc4b").href="family.php?tv_wall_unit_spots_off=
1&calendar="  + calendar_full;

document.getElementById("smc5a").href="family.php?window_light_on=1&calen
dar="  + calendar_full;
document.getElementById("smc5b").href="family.php?window_light_off=1&cale
ndar=" + calendar_full;
document.getElementById("smc6a").href="family.php?wall_light_on=1&calenda
r="    + calendar_full;
document.getElementById("smc6b").href="family.php?wall_light_off=1&calend
ar="   + calendar_full;

document.getElementById("smc7").href="family.php?watch_tv=1&calendar="
+ calendar_full;
document.getElementById("smc8").href="family.php?normal_lights=1&calendar
=" + calendar_full;

// Execute the function in another 500ms
var t=setTimeout(function(){startTime()},500);
}


//=============================================================
// check_time
//
// This function prefixes a '0' before single digit numbers
//=============================================================
function check_time(i)
{
if (i < 10)
  {
    i="0" + i;
  }
return i;
}
```

File: steve_calendar.js

This file is used to provide the calendar data and time that is displayed continuously on the Steve web page.

```
// File name:
//    steve_calendar.js
// Author:
//    Steve McClure
// Book:
//    Designing Embedded Sytems
// Description:
//    This Java Script file is used by the Home
//    Control / Security application Steve web page.

var home_security_state_js = 0;

function startTime()
{
// Get the current time and date
var today=new Date();

// Create a list of day names
var weekday=new Array(7);
weekday[0]="Sunday";
weekday[1]="Monday";
weekday[2]="Tuesday";
weekday[3]="Wednesday";
weekday[4]="Thursday";
weekday[5]="Friday";
weekday[6]="Saturday";

// Create a list of month names
var month_name=new Array(12);
month_name[0]  = "January";
month_name[1]  = "February";
month_name[2]  = "March";
month_name[3]  = "April";
month_name[4]  = "May";
month_name[5]  = "June";
month_name[6]  = "July";
month_name[7]  = "August";
month_name[8]  = "September";
month_name[9]  = "October";
month_name[10]= "November";
month_name[11]= "December";

// Extract the time and date parameters
var hour    = today.getHours();
var hours   = today.getHours();
var minutes = today.getMinutes();
```

```
var seconds = today.getSeconds();

var dd=today.getDate();
var mm=today.getMonth();
var yy=today.getFullYear();

// Determine AM or PM indicator
var tt;
if (hours < 12)
  tt = "AM";
else
{
  tt = "PM";
  if (hours > 12)
    hours -= 12;
}


// Add a zero in front of single digit numbers
minutes = check_time(minutes);
seconds = check_time(seconds);

// Build the calendar date, for example: Thursday 28 March 2013 at 2:58
PM
document.getElementById("navigation_time").innerHTML=weekday[today.getDay
()]+" "+dd+" "+month_name[mm]+" "+yy+" at
"+hours+":"+minutes+":"+seconds+" "+tt;


// Build the calendar time that will timestamp each entry recorded in the
state able
var hour  = check_time(hour);
var day   = check_time(dd);
var month = check_time(mm + 1);

var calendar_date = yy +"/" + month + "/" + day;
var calendar_time = hour + ":" + minutes + ":" + seconds;

var calendar_full = yy +"/" + month + "/" + day + "%20" + hour + ":" +
minutes + ":" + seconds;


// Reconfigure the buttons to include the full calendar
document.getElementById("smc1a").href="steve.php?bedroom_wall_light_on=1&
calendar="  + calendar_full;
document.getElementById("smc1b").href="steve.php?bedroom_wall_light_off=1
&calendar=" + calendar_full;
document.getElementById("smc2a").href="steve.php?bedroom_main_light_on=1&
calendar="  + calendar_full;
document.getElementById("smc2b").href="steve.php?bedroom_main_light_off=1
&calendar=" + calendar_full;
```

```
document.getElementById("smc3a").href="steve.php?reading_light_on=1&calen
dar="     + calendar_full;
document.getElementById("smc3b").href="steve.php?reading_light_off=1&cale
ndar="    + calendar_full;
document.getElementById("smc4a").href="steve.php?study_main_light_on=1&ca
lendar="  + calendar_full;
document.getElementById("smc4b").href="steve.php?study_main_light_off=1&c
alendar=" + calendar_full;

document.getElementById("smc5a").href="steve.php?washroom_light_on=1&cale
ndar="  + calendar_full;
document.getElementById("smc5b").href="steve.php?washroom_light_off=1&cal
endar=" + calendar_full;
document.getElementById("smc6a").href="steve.php?bathroom_light_on=1&cale
ndar="  + calendar_full;
document.getElementById("smc6b").href="steve.php?bathroom_light_off=1&cal
endar=" + calendar_full;

document.getElementById("smc7").href="steve.php?watch_tv=1&calendar="
+ calendar_full;
document.getElementById("smc8").href="steve.php?normal_lights=1&calendar=
" + calendar_full;

//  Execute the function in another 500ms
var t=setTimeout(function(){startTime()},500);
}




//=============================================================
// check_time
//
// This function prefixes a '0' before single digit numbers
//=============================================================
function check_time(i)
{
if (i < 10)
  {
    i="0" + i;
  }
return i;
}
```

Directory: php

This directory contains a number of html web pages that each contain php constructs. PHP (Hypertext Preprocessor) instructions are a server-side scripting language that permits the web server to dynamically build/process the web page.

The php directory contains the following PHP files:

1. security.php
2. master.php
3. lounge.php
4. kitchen.php
5. family.php
6. steve.php
7. state.php
8. events.php
9. system.php

<u>Please Note</u>: For obvious reasons the button image '.gif' files and the house .jpg file has not been provided in this book (would you really want to type in all the data bytes pertaining to an image file?). Please use Microsoft Expression 4 (or some other web building package) in order to build your web application buttons.

File: security.php

```
<!DOCTYPE HTML>
<html>
<head>
<meta http-equiv="refresh" content="4">
<title>HC-Security</title>

<!--
File name:
   security.php
Author:
   Steve McClure
Book:
   Designing Embedded Sytems
Description:
   This file is used by the Home Control / Security
   application to build the Security Web page.
-->


<link href="../css/reset.css" rel="stylesheet" type="text/css"
media="screen">
<link href="../css/styles.css" rel="stylesheet" type="text/css"
media="screen">

<script type="text/javascript" src="../js/calendar.js"> </script>

<style type="text/css">
.auto-style1 {
   color: #FFFFFF;
}
</style>


<style>
table,th,td
{
border:1px solid black
}
</style>

<style>
table,th,td
{
padding:500
}
.auto-style2 {
   border-style: solid;
   border-width: 2px;
}
```

```
.auto-style3 {
    text-align: center;
}
.auto-style4 {
    font-size: small;
}
.auto-style5 {
    font-size: large;
}

</style>



</head>

<body onload=" startTime()">
<div style="width:980px; margin: 0 auto; overflow: hidden;">
<div id="wrapper">
  <div id="navigation">
    <div id="navigation_picture">
      <img src="../images/HouseFront1.jpg" height="200" width="900" />
    </div>

    <div id="navigation_heading">
      <p><span class="auto-style1">Navigation</span> <span class="auto-
style1">- Security</span></p>
    </div>

    <div id="navigation_time">
      <p>Date and Time</p>
    </div>

   <div id="navigation_links">
       <ul>
            <li><a href="security.php">Security</a></li>
            <li><a href="master.php">Master</a></li>
            <li><a href="lounge.php">Lounge</a></li>
            <li><a href="kitchen">Kitchen</a></li>

            <li><a href="family.php">Family</a></li>
            <li><a href="steve.php">Steve</a></li>
            <li><a href="state.php">State</a></li>
            <li><a href="events.php">Events</a></li>
       </ul>
   </div>
  </div>


    <?php

    // Connect to the MySQL Database Environment
```

```
    //==========================================
     $con = mysql_connect("192.168.1.176","steve","william");    // This
works on Archimedes
     if (!$con)
     {
       die('Could not connect as: ' . mysql_error());
       echo "<br />";
     }



   // Access the 'system_control' database
   //====================================
     mysql_select_db("system_control", $con);


   // Insert data into the 'house_state' table
   //====================================

   if ($_POST["home_button"] == 1)
   {
      mysql_query ("UPDATE house_state SET security = 0, security_delay
= 0");        // Zero or NULL is 'Home' Mode
    }


   if ($_POST["security_button"] == 1)
    {
       $result = mysql_query("SELECT * FROM house_state");

       $row = mysql_fetch_array($result);

      // Enter SECURITY mode ONLY if we are currently in HOME mode
       if ($row['security'] == 0)
      {
        mysql_query ("UPDATE house_state SET security = 1,
security_delay = 0");  // Zero or NULL is 'Home' Mode
      }
    }



    $presence_detected = 1;
    $no_one_detected   = 0;

   $steve_bedroom_sensor_house_code     = 1;
   $steve_bedroom_sensor_unit_code      = 2;
   $mini_hallway_sensor_house_code      = 1;
   $mini_hallway_sensor_unit_code       = 5;
   $study_sensor_house_code             = 1;
   $study_sensor_unit_code              = 7;
```

```
$master_bedroom_sensor_house_code       = 1;
$master_bedroom_sensor_unit_code        = 9;
$family_room_sensor_house_code          = 1;
$family_room_sensor_unit_code           = 11;
$inside_front_door_sensor_house_code = 1;
$inside_front_door_sensor_unit_code  = 13;

$main_hallway_sensor_house_code         = 2;
$main_hallway_sensor_unit_code          = 5;
$lounge_hallway_sensor_house_code       = 2;
$lounge_hallway_sensor_unit_code        = 7;
$master_hallway_sensor_house_code       = 2;
$master_hallway_sensor_unit_code        = 9;

$pantry_sensor_house_code               = 3;
$pantry_sensor_unit_code                = 1;
$kitchen_sensor_house_code              = 3;
$kitchen_sensor_unit_code               = 3;
$kitchen_nook_sensor_house_code         = 3;
$kitchen_nook_sensor_unit_code          = 11;
$master_closet_sensor_house_code        = 3;
$master_closet_sensor_unit_code         = 13;
$garage_fridge_sensor_house_code        = 3;
$garage_fridge_sensor_unit_code         = 15;

$laundry_sensor_house_code              = 4;
$laundry_sensor_unit_code               = 11;
$common_washroom_sensor_house_code      = 4;
$common_washroom_sensor_unit_code       = 13;
$front_porch_sensor_house_code          = 4;
$front_porch_sensor_unit_code           = 15;

$common_bathroom_sensor_house_code      = 5;
$common_bathroom_sensor_unit_code       = 9;
$guest_bathroom_sensor_house_code       = 5;
$guest_bathroom_sensor_unit_code        = 11;
$guest_bedroom_sensor_house_code        = 5;
$guest_bedroom_sensor_unit_code         = 13;

$master_bathroom_sensor_house_code      = 8;
$master_bathroom_sensor_unit_code       = 9;


$result = mysql_query("SELECT * FROM house_code_states");

while($row = mysql_fetch_array($result))
   {

      if ($row['description'] == "No Description")
        continue;

      // A1 - Steve's Room
```

```
if (($row['house'] == $steve_bedroom_sensor_house_code) &&
    ($row['unit']  == $steve_bedroom_sensor_unit_code))
{
    if ($row['state'] == $no_one_detected)
        $steve_color = "#FFFFFF";  // Off
    elseif ($row['state'] == $presence_detected)
        $steve_color = "#FFCC66";  // On
    else
        $steve_color = "#FFFFFF";  // ---
}

// A5 - Mini Hall
if (($row['house'] == $mini_hallway_sensor_house_code) &&
    ($row['unit']  == $mini_hallway_sensor_unit_code))
{
    if ($row['state'] == $no_one_detected)
        $mini_hall_color = "#FFFFFF";  // Off
    elseif ($row['state'] == $presence_detected)
        $mini_hall_color = "#FFCC66";  // On
    else
        $mini_hall_color = "#FFFFFF";  // ---
}

// A7 - Lab
if (($row['house'] == $study_sensor_house_code) &&
    ($row['unit']  == $study_sensor_unit_code))
{
    if ($row['state'] == $no_one_detected)
        $lab_color = "#FFFFFF";  // Off
    elseif ($row['state'] == $presence_detected)
        $lab_color = "#FFCC66";  // On
    else
        $lab_color = "#FFFFFF";  // ---
}

// A9 - Master Bedroom
if (($row['house'] == $master_bedroom_sensor_house_code) &&
    ($row['unit']  == $master_bedroom_sensor_unit_code))
{
    if ($row['state'] == $no_one_detected)
        $master_bedroom_color = "#FFFFFF";  // Off
    elseif ($row['state'] == $presence_detected)
        $master_bedroom_color = "#FFCC66";  // On
    else
        $master_bedroom_color = "#FFFFFF";  // ---
}

// A11 - Family Room
if (($row['house'] == $family_room_sensor_house_code) &&
    ($row['unit']  == $family_room_sensor_unit_code))
{
    if ($row['state'] == $no_one_detected)
```

```
        $family_color = "#FFFFFF";  // Off
    elseif ($row['state'] == $presence_detected)
        $family_color = "#FFCC66";  // On
    else
        $family_color = "#FFFFFF";  // ---
}


// A13 - Front Hall
if (($row['house'] == $inside_front_door_sensor_house_code) &&
     ($row['unit']  == $inside_front_door_sensor_unit_code))
{
    if ($row['state'] == $no_one_detected)
        $front_hall_color = "#FFFFFF";  // Off
    elseif ($row['state'] == $presence_detected)
        $front_hall_color = "#FFCC66";  // On
    else
        $front_hall_color = "#FFFFFF";  // ---
}


// B5 - Main Hallway 'Hallway2'
if (($row['house'] == $main_hallway_sensor_house_code) &&
     ($row['unit']  == $main_hallway_sensor_unit_code))
{
    if ($row['state'] == $no_one_detected)
        $hallway2_color = "#FFFFFF";  // Off
    elseif ($row['state'] == $presence_detected)
        $hallway2_color = "#FFCC66";  // On
    else
        $hallway2_color = "#FFFFFF";  // ---
}

// B7 - Lounge Hallway 'Lounge'
if (($row['house'] == $lounge_hallway_sensor_house_code) &&
     ($row['unit']  == $lounge_hallway_sensor_unit_code))
{
    if ($row['state'] == $no_one_detected)
        $lounge_color = "#FFFFFF";  // Off
    elseif ($row['state'] == $presence_detected)
        $lounge_color = "#FFCC66";  // On
    else
        $lounge_color = "#FFFFFF";  // ---
}

// B9 - Master Hallway 'Hallway1'
if (($row['house'] == $master_hallway_sensor_house_code) &&
     ($row['unit']  == $master_hallway_sensor_unit_code))
{
    if ($row['state'] == $no_one_detected)
        $hallway1_color = "#FFFFFF";  // Off
    elseif ($row['state'] == $presence_detected)
```

```
        $hallway1_color = "#FFCC66";  // On
    else
        $hallway1_color = "#FFFFFF";  // ---
}

// C3 - Kitchen
if (($row['house'] == $kitchen_sensor_house_code) &&
     ($row['unit']  == $kitchen_sensor_unit_code))
{
    if ($row['state'] == $no_one_detected)
        $kitchen_color = "#FFFFFF";  // Off
    elseif ($row['state'] == $presence_detected)
        $kitchen_color = "#FFCC66";  // On
    else
        $kitchen_color = "#FFFFFF";  // ---
}

// C11 - Nook
if (($row['house'] == $kitchen_nook_sensor_house_code) &&
     ($row['unit']  == $kitchen_nook_sensor_unit_code))
{
    if ($row['state'] == $no_one_detected)
        $nook_color = "#FFFFFF";  // Off
    elseif ($row['state'] == $presence_detected)
        $nook_color = "#FFCC66";  // On
    else
        $nook_color = "#FFFFFF";  // ---
}

// C13 - Master Closet
if (($row['house'] == $master_closet_sensor_house_code) &&
     ($row['unit']  == $master_closet_sensor_unit_code))
{
    if ($row['state'] == $no_one_detected)
        $master_closet_color = "#FFFFFF";  // Off
    elseif ($row['state'] == $presence_detected)
        $master_closet_color = "#FFCC66";  // On
    else
        $master_closet_color = "#FFFFFF";  // ---
}

// C15 - Garage Fridge
if (($row['house'] == $garage_fridge_sensor_house_code) &&
     ($row['unit']  == $garage_fridge_sensor_unit_code))
{
    if ($row['state'] == $no_one_detected)
        $garage_fridge_color = "#FFFFFF";  // Off
    elseif ($row['state'] == $presence_detected)
        $garage_fridge_color = "#FFCC66";  // On
    else
        $garage_fridge_color = "#FFFFFF";  // ---
}
```

```
// D11 - Laundry
if (($row['house'] == $laundry_sensor_house_code) &&
    ($row['unit']  == $laundry_sensor_unit_code))
{
    if ($row['state'] == $no_one_detected)
       $laundry_color = "#FFFFFF";  // Off
    elseif ($row['state'] == $presence_detected)
       $laundry_color = "#FFCC66";  // On
    else
       $laundry_color = "#FFFFFF";  // ---
}

// D13 - Common Washroom
if (($row['house'] == $common_washroom_sensor_house_code) &&
    ($row['unit']  == $common_washroom_sensor_unit_code))
{
    if ($row['state'] == $no_one_detected)
       $common_washroom_color = "#FFFFFF";  // Off
    elseif ($row['state'] == $presence_detected)
       $common_washroom_color = "#FFCC66";  // On
    else
       $common_washroom_color = "#FFFFFF";  // ---
}

// D15 - Outside Front Porch
if (($row['house'] == $front_porch_sensor_house_code) &&
    ($row['unit']  == $front_porch_sensor_unit_code))
{
    if ($row['state'] == $no_one_detected)
       $front_porch_color = "#FFFFFF"; // Off
    elseif ($row['state'] == $presence_detected)
       $front_porch_color = "#FFCC66";  // On
    else
       $front_porch_color = "#FFFFFF";  // ---
}

// E9 - Common Bathroom
if (($row['house'] == $common_bathroom_sensor_house_code) &&
    ($row['unit']  == $common_bathroom_sensor_unit_code))
{
    if ($row['state'] == $no_one_detected)
       $common_bathroom_color = "#FFFFFF";  // Off
    elseif ($row['state'] == $presence_detected)
       $common_bathroom_color = "#FFCC66";  // On
    else
       $common_bathroom_color = "#FFFFFF";  // ---
}

// E11 - Guest Bathroom
if (($row['house'] == $guest_bathroom_sensor_house_code) &&
    ($row['unit']  == $guest_bathroom_sensor_unit_code))
```

```
        {
            if ($row['state'] == $no_one_detected)
                $guest_bathroom_color = "#FFFFFF";  // Off
            elseif ($row['state'] == $presence_detected)
                $guest_bathroom_color = "#FFCC66";  // On
            else
                $guest_bathroom_color = "#FFFFFF";  // ---
        }

        // E13 - Guest Bedroom Door
        if (($row['house'] == $guest_bedroom_sensor_house_code) &&
             ($row['unit']  == $guest_bedroom_sensor_unit_code))
        {
            if ($row['state'] == $no_one_detected)
                $guest_bedroom_color = "#FFFFFF";  // Off
            elseif ($row['state'] == $presence_detected)
                $guest_bedroom_color = "#FFCC66";  // On
            else
                $guest_bedroom_color = "#FFFFFF";  // ---
        }

        // H9 - Master Bathroom
        if (($row['house'] == $master_bathroom_sensor_house_code) &&
             ($row['unit']  == $master_bathroom_sensor_unit_code))
        {
            if ($row['state'] == $no_one_detected)
                $master_bathroom_color = "#FFFFFF";  // Off
            elseif ($row['state'] == $presence_detected)
                $master_bathroom_color = "#FFCC66";  // On
            else
                $master_bathroom_color = "#FFFFFF";  // ---
        }

    }

  ?>

<div id="main_stuff">
    <?php
   $result = mysql_query("SELECT * FROM house_state");

   $row = mysql_fetch_array($result);

   if ($row['security'] == 0)
   {
     ?><p class="auto-style4"> </p><?php
     ?><p class="auto-
style5">         This screen
allows you to monitor the Home Security System:   SECURITY
OFF</p><?php
     ?><p class="auto-style4"> </p><?php
     $home_security_state = 0;
```

```
        $home_security_color = "#009933";    // "#00FF00";
      }

      elseif ($row['security'] == 1)
      {
        ?><p class="auto-style4"> </p><?php
        ?><p class="auto-
style5">         This screen
allows you to monitor the Home Security System:   SECURITY
Mode INITIATED...</p><?php
        ?><p class="auto-style4"> </p><?php
        $home_security_state = 1;
        $home_security_color = "#6699FF";
      }

      elseif ($row['security'] == 2)
      {
        ?><p class="auto-style4"> </p><?php
        echo "         This
screen allows you to monitor the Home Security
System:   ";
        if ($row['security_delay'] > 0)
        {
          echo "SECURITY Mode IN PROGRESS [";
          echo ($row['security_delay']);
           echo "]";
        }
        else
        {
           echo "SECURITY Mode IN PROGRESS...";
        }
        ?><p class="auto-style4"> </p><?php
        $home_security_state = 2;
        $home_security_color = "#CC3300";
      }


      elseif ($row['security'] == 3)
      {
        ?><p class="auto-style4"> </p><?php
        echo "         This
screen allows you to monitor the Home Security
System:   SECURITY ACTIVE";
        ?><p class="auto-style4"> </p><?php
        $home_security_state = 3;
        $home_security_color = "#CC3300";
      }

     // Close the 'home_control' database
     //====================================
      mysql_close($con);
```

```
    ?>
  </div>

  <script>
  home_security_state_js = <?php echo $home_security_state ?>;
  </script>


<div id="key_background">
<p> </p>
</div>
<div id="sensor_background">

<table align="center" cellpadding="10" cellspacing="5" class="auto-
style2" style="width: 100%">
    <tr>
<!--       <td id="smc1" colspan="5" style="background-color: <?php echo
$home_security_color; ?>">   </td>
-->
        <td id="smc1" colspan="5" style="background-color: <?php echo
$home_security_color; ?>">   </td>

<!--        <td id="smc1" colspan="5" style="background-color: <?php echo
$home_security_color; ?>">   </td>
-->
       <td class="auto-style3" style="width: 71px; background-color:
<?php echo $front_porch_color; ?>">Front Porch</td>
       <td id="smc2" colspan="5" style="background-color: <?php echo
$home_security_color; ?>">   </td>
    </tr>
    <tr>
       <td id="smc3" rowspan="5" style="width: 14px; background-color:
<?php echo $home_security_color; ?>">
        </td>
       <td class="auto-style3" rowspan="2" style="width: 131px;
background-color: <?php echo $master_closet_color; ?>"><br><br>
       <br>Wardrobe</td>
       <td class="auto-style3" rowspan="2" style="width: 114px;
background-color: <?php echo $master_bathroom_color;
?>"><br><br>Master<br>
       Bathroom</td>
       <td class="auto-style3" colspan="2" style="background-color: <?php
echo $guest_bedroom_color; ?>"><br>Guest Bedroom<br><br></td>
       <td class="auto-style3" rowspan="2" style="width: 71px;
background-color: <?php echo $front_hall_color; ?>"><br><br>Front<br>
       Hall<br></td>
       <td class="auto-style3" rowspan="2" style="width: 89px;
background-color: <?php echo $steve_color; ?>"><br><br>Steve's<br>
       Bedroom</td>
       <td class="auto-style3" style="width: 100px; background-color:
<?php echo $common_bathroom_color; ?>"><br>Bathroom</td>
```

```
        <td class="auto-style3" rowspan="2" style="width: 151px;
background-color: <?php echo $lab_color; ?>">
        <br><br><br>Study</td>
        <td class="auto-style3" rowspan="3" style="width: 220px;
background-color: <?php echo $garage_fridge_color;
?>"><br><br><br>Garage</td>
        <td id="smc4" rowspan="5" style="width: 20px; background-color:
<?php echo $home_security_color; ?>">
         </td>
    </tr>
    <tr>
        <td class="auto-style3" style="width: 158px; height: 54px;
background-color: <?php echo $guest_bathroom_color; ?>"><br>Guest
Bathroom<br><br>
        </td>
        <td class="auto-style3" style="width: 66px; height:
54px;"><br>MiniHall</td>
        <td class="auto-style3" style="width: 100px; height: 54px;
background-color: <?php echo $common_washroom_color;
?>"><br>Washroom</td>
    </tr>
    <tr>
        <td colspan="2" rowspan="3" class="auto-style3" style="background-
color: <?php echo $master_bedroom_color;
?>"><br><br>Master<br>Bedroom</td>
        <td class="auto-style3" colspan="2" style="background-color: <?php
echo $hallway1_color; ?>">Hallway1</td>
        <td class="auto-style3" rowspan="3" style="width:
71px"><br><br>Dining<br>Room</td>
        <td class="auto-style3" style="width: 89px;  background-color:
<?php echo $hallway2_color;  ?>">Hallway2</td>
        <td class="auto-style3" style="width: 100px; background-color:
<?php echo $mini_hall_color; ?>">Mini Hall</td>
        <td class="auto-style3" style="width: 151px; background-color:
<?php echo $laundry_color;  ?>">Laundry</td>
    </tr>
    <tr>
        <td colspan="2" class="auto-style3" rowspan="2" style="background-
color: <?php echo $lounge_color; ?>"><br><br>Lounge</td>
        <td class="auto-style3" style="width: 89px; background-color:
<?php echo $kitchen_color; ?>"><br>Kitchen<br><br></td>
        <td class="auto-style3" colspan="2" ; style="background-color:
<?php echo $family_color; ?>"><br>Family Room</td>
        <td rowspan="2" style="width: 22px"> </td>
    </tr>
    <tr>
        <td class="auto-style3" style="height: 22px; width: 89px;
background-color: <?php echo $nook_color; ?>">Nook</td>
        <td class="auto-style3" colspan="2" style="height:
22px">Varanda</td>
    </tr>
    <tr>
```

```
        <td id="smc5" colspan="11" style="background-color: <?php echo
$home_security_color; ?>">
         </td>
    </tr>
</table>
</div>
<div id="key_background">
<p> </p>
</div>
</div>
</div>
</body>
</html>
```

File: master.php

```
<!DOCTYPE HTML>
<html>
<head>
<title>HC-Master</title>

<!--
File name:
   master.php
Author:
   Steve McClure
Book:
   Designing Embedded Sytems
Description:
   This file is used by the Home Control / Security application
   to build the Master Web page.
-->

<link href="../css/reset.css" rel="stylesheet" type="text/css"
media="screen">
<link href="../css/styles.css" rel="stylesheet" type="text/css"
media="screen">

<script type="text/javascript" src="../js/master_calendar.js"> </script>

<style type="text/css">
.auto-style1 {
   color: #FFFFFF;
}
.auto-style2 {
   text-align: center;
}
.auto-style3 {
   font-size: large;
}
.auto-style4 {
   font-size: small;
}
</style>
</head>

<body onload=" startTime()">

<div style="width:980px; margin: 0 auto; overflow: hidden;">
<div id="wrapper">
  <div id="navigation">
    <div id="navigation_picture">
      <img src="../images/HouseFront1.jpg" height="200" width="900" />
    </div>
```

```
    <div id="navigation_heading">
      <p><span class="auto-style1">Navigation</span> <span class="auto-style1">- Master Bedroom</span></p>
    </div>
    <div id="navigation_time">
      <p>Date and Time</p>
    </div>

   <div id="navigation_links">
      <ul>
          <li><a href="security.php">Security</a></li>
          <li><a href="master.php">Master</a></li>
          <li><a href="lounge.php">Lounge</a></li>
          <li><a href="kitchen">Kitchen</a></li>
          <li><a href="family.php">Family</a></li>
          <li><a href="steve.php">Steve</a></li>
          <li><a href="state.php">State</a></li>
          <li><a href="events.php">Events</a></li>
      </ul>
   </div>
  </div>

  <div id="main_stuff">
    <p class="auto-style4"> </p>
    <p><strong>         This screen allows you to control the Master Bedroom environment:</strong></p>
      <p class="auto-style4"> </p>
  </div>
</div>

    <?php

    // Connect to the MySQL Database Environment
    //============================================
     $con = mysql_connect("192.168.1.176","steve","william");    // This works on Archimedes

     if (!$con)
     {
       die('Could not connect as: ' . mysql_error());
       echo "<br />";
     }

   // Access the 'system_control' database
   //====================================
     mysql_select_db("system_control", $con);


   // Insert data into the 'house_state' table
   //====================================

   if ($_GET["watch_tv"] == 1)
```

```
    {
       mysql_query ("UPDATE house_state SET master_watch_tv = 1");
     }

    if ($_GET["retire_for_the_night"] == 1)
     {
       mysql_query ("UPDATE house_state SET go_to_bed = 1");
     }


    // Insert data into the 'house_code_events' table
    //================================================

    // Mum's Bedside Light ON
    if ($_GET["mums_bedside_light_on"] == 1)
    {
      mysql_query ("INSERT INTO house_code_events (house, unit, type,
state, timeout, timestamp) VALUES (15, 2, 1, 1, 777,
'".$_GET["calendar"]."')");
     }

    // Mum's Bedside Light OFF
    if ($_GET["mums_bedside_light_off"] == 1)
    {
      mysql_query ("INSERT INTO house_code_events (house, unit, type,
state, timeout, timestamp) VALUES (15, 2, 1, 0, 777,
'".$_GET["calendar"]."')");
     }


    // Dad's Bedside Light ON
    if ($_GET["dads_bedside_light_on"] == 1)
    {
      mysql_query ("INSERT INTO house_code_events (house, unit, type,
state, timeout, timestamp) VALUES (15, 4, 1, 1, 777,
'".$_GET["calendar"]."')");
     }

    // Dad's Bedside Light OFF
    if ($_GET["dads_bedside_light_off"] == 1)
    {
      mysql_query ("INSERT INTO house_code_events (house, unit, type,
state, timeout, timestamp) VALUES (15, 4, 1, 0, 777,
'".$_GET["calendar"]."')");
     }


    // Bedroom Light ON
    if ($_GET["bedroom_light_on"] == 1)
    {
```

```
      mysql_query ("INSERT INTO house_code_events (house, unit, type,
state, timeout, timestamp) VALUES (15, 1, 1, 1, 777,
'".$_GET["calendar"]."')");
     }

   // Bedroom Light OFF
   if ($_GET["bedroom_light_off"] == 1)
   {
      mysql_query ("INSERT INTO house_code_events (house, unit, type,
state, timeout, timestamp) VALUES (15, 1, 1, 0, 777,
'".$_GET["calendar"]."')");
     }


   // Closet Light ON
   if ($_GET["closet_light_on"] == 1)
   {
      mysql_query ("INSERT INTO house_code_events (house, unit, type,
state, timeout, timestamp) VALUES (15, 3, 1, 1, 777,
'".$_GET["calendar"]."')");
     }

   // Closet Light OFF
   if ($_GET["closet_light_off"] == 1)
   {
      mysql_query ("INSERT INTO house_code_events (house, unit, type,
state, timeout, timestamp) VALUES (15, 3, 1, 0, 777,
'".$_GET["calendar"]."')");
     }


   // Close the 'home_control' database
   //====================================
    mysql_close($con);
    ?>

<div id="key_background">
    <form action="family.php" method="post">
       <div class="auto-style2">
           <span class="auto-style3">  </span><br class="auto-
style3"> <a id="smc1a"
href="master.php?mums_bedside_light_on=1"><img id="img42" alt="Mum's
Bedside Light   ON" fp-style="fp-btn: Embossed Rectangle 6; fp-font-size:
14; fp-img-hover: 0; fp-img-press: 0; fp-preload: 0; fp-transparent: 1;
fp-proportional: 0" fp-title="Mum's Bedside Light   ON" height="45"
src="../images/buttonD1.gif" style="border: 0"
width="244"></a>    
           <a id="smc1b" href="master.php?mums_bedside_light_off=1">
   <img id="img43" alt="OFF" fp-style="fp-btn: Embossed Rectangle 6; fp-
font-size: 14; fp-img-hover: 0; fp-img-press: 0; fp-preload: 0; fp-
transparent: 1; fp-proportional: 0" fp-title="OFF" height="45"
src="../images/buttonD3.gif" style="border: 0"
```

```
width="100"></a>         &nb
sp;           &nbs
p;            
;   
            <a id="smc4a" href="master.php?bedroom_light_on=1">
    <img id="img44" alt="Bedroom Light   ON" fp-style="fp-btn: Embossed
Rectangle 6; fp-font-size: 14; fp-font-color-hover: #FF0000; fp-font-
color-press: #0000FF; fp-img-hover: 0; fp-img-press: 0; fp-preload: 0;
fp-transparent: 1; fp-proportional: 0" fp-title="Bedroom Light   ON"
height="45" src="../images/buttonD6.gif" style="border: 0"
width="244"></a>    
            <a id="smc4b" href="master.php?bedroom_light_off=1">
    <img id="img45" alt="OFF" fp-style="fp-btn: Embossed Rectangle 6; fp-
font-size: 14; fp-font-color-hover: #FF0000; fp-font-color-press:
#0000FF; fp-img-hover: 0; fp-img-press: 0; fp-preload: 0; fp-transparent:
1; fp-proportional: 0" fp-title="OFF" height="45"
src="../images/buttonD8.gif" style="border: 0" width="100"></a><br><br>
            <a id="smc2a" href="master.php?dads_bedside_light_on=1">
    <img id="img46" alt="Dad's Bedside Light    ON" fp-style="fp-btn:
Embossed Rectangle 6; fp-font-size: 14; fp-img-hover: 0; fp-img-press: 0;
fp-preload: 0; fp-transparent: 1; fp-proportional: 0" fp-title="Dad's
Bedside Light    ON" height="45" src="../images/buttonD2.gif"
style="border: 0" width="244"></a>    
            <a id="smc2b" href="master.php?dads_bedside_light_off=1">
    <img id="img52" alt="OFF" fp-style="fp-btn: Embossed Rectangle 6; fp-
font-size: 14; fp-img-hover: 0; fp-img-press: 0; fp-preload: 0; fp-
transparent: 1; fp-proportional: 0" fp-title="OFF" height="45"
src="../images/buttonD4.gif" style="border: 0"
width="100"></a>         &nb
sp;           &nbs
p;            
;   
            <a id="smc5a" href="master.php?closet_light_on=1">
    <img id="img48" alt="Closet Light       ON" fp-style="fp-btn:
Embossed Rectangle 6; fp-font-size: 14; fp-font-color-hover: #FF0000; fp-
img-hover: 0; fp-img-press: 0; fp-preload: 0; fp-transparent: 1; fp-
proportional: 0" fp-title="Closet Light       ON" height="45"
src="../images/buttonD7.gif" style="border: 0"
width="244"></a>    
            <a id="smc5b" href="master.php?closet_light_off=1">
    <img id="img49" alt="OFF" fp-style="fp-btn: Embossed Rectangle 6; fp-
font-size: 14; fp-font-color-hover: #FF0000; fp-img-hover: 0; fp-img-
press: 0; fp-preload: 0; fp-transparent: 1; fp-proportional: 0" fp-
title="OFF" height="45" src="../images/buttonD9.gif" style="border: 0"
width="100"></a><br><br><br>
            <a id="smc3" href="master.php?watch_tv=1">
    <img id="img50" alt="Watch TV" fp-style="fp-btn: Embossed Rectangle
9; fp-font-size: 14; fp-img-hover: 0; fp-img-press: 0; fp-preload: 0; fp-
transparent: 1; fp-proportional: 0" fp-title="Watch TV" height="80"
src="../images/buttonD5.gif" style="border: 0"
width="365"></a>         &nb
sp;           &nbs
```

```
p;             
;   
          <a id="smc6" href="master.php?retire_for_the_night=1">
   <img id="img51" alt="Retire For The Night" fp-style="fp-btn: Embossed
Rectangle 4; fp-font-size: 14; fp-img-hover: 0; fp-img-press: 0; fp-
preload: 0; fp-transparent: 1; fp-proportional: 0" fp-title="Retire For
The Night" height="80" src="../images/buttonDA.gif" style="border: 0"
width="365"></a><br><br>
   </div>
   <p> </p>
   <p> </p>

</form>
</div>
</div>
</body>
</html>
```

File: lounge.php

```
<!DOCTYPE HTML>
<html>
<head>
<title>HC-Lounge</title>

<!--
File name:
   lounge.php
Author:
   Steve McClure
Book:
   Designing Embedded Sytems
Description:
   This file is used by the Home Control / Security application
   to build the Lounge Web page.
 -->

<link href="../css/reset.css" rel="stylesheet" type="text/css"
media="screen">
<link href="../css/styles.css" rel="stylesheet" type="text/css"
media="screen">

<script type="text/javascript" src="../js/lounge_calendar.js">
</script>

<style type="text/css">
.auto-style1 {
   color: #FFFFFF;
}
.auto-style2 {
   text-align: center;
}
.auto-style3 {
   font-size: large;
}
.auto-style4 {
   font-size: small;
}
</style>

</head>

<body onload=" startTime()">
<div style="width:980px; margin: 0 auto; overflow: hidden;">
<div id="wrapper">

  <div id="navigation">
    <div id="navigation_picture">
      <img src="../images/HouseFront1.jpg" height="200" width="900" />
```

```
    </div>

    <div id="navigation_heading">
      <p><span class="auto-style1">Navigation</span> <span class="auto-
style1">- Lounge</span></p>
    </div>

    <div id="navigation_time">
      <p>Date and Time</p>
    </div>

   <div id="navigation_links">
      <ul>
          <li><a href="security.php">Security</a></li>
          <li><a href="master.php">Master</a></li>
          <li><a href="lounge.php">Lounge</a></li>
          <li><a href="kitchen">Kitchen</a></li>
          <li><a href="family.php">Family</a></li>
          <li><a href="steve.php">Steve</a></li>
          <li><a href="state.php">State</a></li>
          <li><a href="events.php">Events</a></li>
      </ul>
   </div>
  </div>

  <div id="main_stuff">
    <p class="auto-style4"> </p>
    <p><strong>         This
screen allows you to control the Lounge environment:</strong></p>
      <p class="auto-style4"> </p>
  </div>
</div>


    <?php

    // Connect to the MySQL Database Environment
    //=======================================
     $con = mysql_connect("192.168.1.176","steve","william");    // This
works on Archimedes

     if (!$con)
     {
       die('Could not connect as: ' . mysql_error());
       echo "<br />";
     }

   // Access the 'system_control' database
   //==================================
     mysql_select_db("system_control", $con);
```

```
    // Insert data into the 'house_state' table
    //===================================

    if ($_GET["watch_tv"] == 1)
    {
       mysql_query ("UPDATE house_state SET watch_tv = 1");
     }


    if ($_GET["go_to_bed"] == 1)
     {
       mysql_query ("UPDATE house_state SET go_to_bed = 1");
     }


    // Insert data into the 'house_code_events' table
    //===============================================

    // Lounge Wall Light ON
    if ($_GET["lounge_wall_light_on"] == 1)
    {
      mysql_query ("INSERT INTO house_code_events (house, unit, type,
state, timeout, timestamp) VALUES (8, 1, 1, 1, 777,
'".$_GET["calendar"]."')");
     }

    // Lounge Wall Light OFF
    if ($_GET["lounge_wall_light_off"] == 1)
    {
      mysql_query ("INSERT INTO house_code_events (house, unit, type,
state, timeout, timestamp) VALUES (8, 1, 1, 0, 777,
'".$_GET["calendar"]."')");
     }


    // Lounge Window Light ON
    if ($_GET["lounge_window_light_on"] == 1)
    {
      mysql_query ("INSERT INTO house_code_events (house, unit, type,
state, timeout, timestamp) VALUES (8, 2, 1, 1, 777,
'".$_GET["calendar"]."')");
     }

    // Lounge Window Light OFF
    if ($_GET["lounge_window_light_off"] == 1)
    {
      mysql_query ("INSERT INTO house_code_events (house, unit, type,
state, timeout, timestamp) VALUES (8, 2, 1, 0, 777,
'".$_GET["calendar"]."')");
     }
```

```
    // Diningroom Table Lights ON
    if ($_GET["diningroom_table_lights_on"] == 1)
    {
       mysql_query ("INSERT INTO house_code_events (house, unit, type,
state, timeout, timestamp) VALUES (8, 3, 1, 1, 777,
'".$_GET["calendar"]."')");
     }

    // Diningroom Table Lights OFF
    if ($_GET["diningroom_table_lights_off"] == 1)
    {
       mysql_query ("INSERT INTO house_code_events (house, unit, type,
state, timeout, timestamp) VALUES (8, 3, 1, 0, 777,
'".$_GET["calendar"]."')");
     }


    // Fishtank Lights ON
    if ($_GET["fishtank_lights_on"] == 1)
    {
       mysql_query ("INSERT INTO house_code_events (house, unit, type,
state, timeout, timestamp) VALUES (8, 4, 1, 1, 777,
'".$_GET["calendar"]."')");
     }

    // Fishtank Lights OFF
    if ($_GET["fishtank_lights_off"] == 1)
    {
       mysql_query ("INSERT INTO house_code_events (house, unit, type,
state, timeout, timestamp) VALUES (8, 4, 1, 0, 777,
'".$_GET["calendar"]."')");
     }


    // Inside Entrance Light ON
    if ($_GET["inside_entrance_light_on"] == 1)
    {
       mysql_query ("INSERT INTO house_code_events (house, unit, type,
state, timeout, timestamp) VALUES (7, 7, 1, 1, 777,
'".$_GET["calendar"]."')");
     }

    // Inside Entrance Light OFF
    if ($_GET["inside_entrance_light_off"] == 1)
    {
       mysql_query ("INSERT INTO house_code_events (house, unit, type,
state, timeout, timestamp) VALUES (7, 7, 1, 0, 777,
'".$_GET["calendar"]."')");
     }


    // Main Hallway Light ON
```

```
    if ($_GET["main_hallway_lights_on"] == 1)
    {
       mysql_query ("INSERT INTO house_code_events (house, unit, type,
state, timeout, timestamp) VALUES (5, 6, 1, 1, 777,
'".$_GET["calendar"]."')");
     }

    // Main Hallway Light OFF
    if ($_GET["main_hallway_lights_off"] == 1)
    {
       mysql_query ("INSERT INTO house_code_events (house, unit, type,
state, timeout, timestamp) VALUES (5, 6, 1, 0, 777,
'".$_GET["calendar"]."')");
     }


    // Season Front Lights ON
    if ($_GET["season_front_lights_on"] == 1)
    {
       mysql_query ("INSERT INTO house_code_events (house, unit, type,
state, timeout, timestamp) VALUES (16, 2, 1, 1, 777,
'".$_GET["calendar"]."')");
     }

    // Season Front Lights OFF
    if ($_GET["season_front_lights_off"] == 1)
    {
       mysql_query ("INSERT INTO house_code_events (house, unit, type,
state, timeout, timestamp) VALUES (16, 2, 1, 0, 777,
'".$_GET["calendar"]."')");
     }


    // Season Back Lights ON
    if ($_GET["season_back_lights_on"] == 1)
    {
       mysql_query ("INSERT INTO house_code_events (house, unit, type,
state, timeout, timestamp) VALUES (16, 3, 1, 1, 777,
'".$_GET["calendar"]."')");
     }

    // Season Back Lights OFF
    if ($_GET["season_back_lights_off"] == 1)
    {
       mysql_query ("INSERT INTO house_code_events (house, unit, type,
state, timeout, timestamp) VALUES (16, 3, 1, 0, 777,
'".$_GET["calendar"]."')");
     }


    // Close the 'home_control' database
    //==================================
```

```
    mysql_close($con);
    ?>
<div id="key_background">
<form action="family.php" method="post">
   <div class="auto-style2">
      <span class="auto-style3">  </span><br class="auto-style3">
      <a id="smc1a" href="lounge.php?lounge_wall_light_on=1">
      <img id="img22" alt="Lounge Wall Light             ON" fp-style="fp-
btn: Embossed Rectangle 6; fp-font-size: 14; fp-img-hover: 0; fp-img-
press: 0; fp-preload: 0; fp-transparent: 1; fp-proportional: 0" fp-
title="Lounge Wall Light             ON" height="45"
src="../images/buttonF0.gif" style="border: 0"
width="275"></a>    
      <a id="smc1b" href="lounge.php?lounge_wall_light_off=1">
      <img id="img23" alt="OFF" fp-style="fp-btn: Embossed Rectangle 6;
fp-font-size: 14; fp-img-hover: 0; fp-img-press: 0; fp-preload: 0; fp-
transparent: 1; fp-proportional: 0" fp-title="OFF" height="45"
src="../images/buttonF4.gif" style="border: 0"
width="100"></a>         &nb
sp;           &nbs
p;     
      <a id="smc5a" href="lounge.php?inside_entrance_light_on=1">
      <img id="img24" alt="Inside Entrance Light     ON" fp-style="fp-
btn: Embossed Rectangle 6; fp-font-size: 14; fp-img-hover: 0; fp-img-
press: 0; fp-preload: 0; fp-transparent: 1; fp-proportional: 0" fp-
title="Inside Entrance Light     ON" height="45"
src="../images/buttonF9.gif" style="border: 0"
width="275"></a>    
      <a id="smc5b" href="lounge.php?inside_entrance_light_off=1">
      <img id="img25" alt="OFF" fp-style="fp-btn: Embossed Rectangle 6;
fp-font-size: 14; fp-img-hover: 0; fp-img-press: 0; fp-preload: 0; fp-
transparent: 1; fp-proportional: 0" fp-title="OFF" height="45"
src="../images/buttonFD.gif" style="border: 0" width="100"></a><br>
      <br><a id="smc2a" href="lounge.php?lounge_window_light_on=1">
      <img id="img26" alt="Lounge Window Light      ON" fp-style="fp-
btn: Embossed Rectangle 6; fp-font-size: 14; fp-img-hover: 0; fp-img-
press: 0; fp-preload: 0; fp-transparent: 1; fp-proportional: 0" fp-
title="Lounge Window Light      ON" height="45"
src="../images/buttonF1.gif" style="border: 0"
width="275"></a>    
      <a id="smc2b" href="lounge.php?lounge_window_light_off=1">
      <img id="img27" alt="OFF" fp-style="fp-btn: Embossed Rectangle 6;
fp-font-size: 14; fp-img-hover: 0; fp-img-press: 0; fp-preload: 0; fp-
transparent: 1; fp-proportional: 0" fp-title="OFF" height="45"
src="../images/buttonF5.gif" style="border: 0"
width="100"></a>         &nb
sp;           &nbs
p;     
      <a id="smc6a" href="lounge.php?main_hallway_lights_on=1">
      <img id="img28" alt="Main Hallway Lights      ON" fp-style="fp-
btn: Embossed Rectangle 6; fp-font-size: 14; fp-img-hover: 0; fp-img-
press: 0; fp-preload: 0; fp-transparent: 1; fp-proportional: 0" fp-
```

```
title="Main Hallway Lights       ON" height="45"
src="../images/buttonFA.gif" style="border: 0"
width="275"></a>    
      <a id="smc6b" href="lounge.php?main_hallway_lights_off=1">
      <img id="img29" alt="OFF" fp-style="fp-btn: Embossed Rectangle 6;
fp-font-size: 14; fp-img-hover: 0; fp-img-press: 0; fp-preload: 0; fp-
transparent: 1; fp-proportional: 0" fp-title="OFF" height="45"
src="../images/buttonFE.gif" style="border: 0" width="100"></a><br>
      <br><a id="smc3a" href="lounge.php?diningroom_table_lights_on=1">
      <img id="img30" alt="Diningroom Table Lights  ON" fp-style="fp-
btn: Embossed Rectangle 6; fp-font-size: 14; fp-img-hover: 0; fp-img-
press: 0; fp-preload: 0; fp-transparent: 1; fp-proportional: 0" fp-
title="Diningroom Table Lights  ON" height="45"
src="../images/buttonF2.gif" style="border: 0"
width="275"></a>    
      <a id="smc3b" href="lounge.php?diningroom_table_lights_off=1">
      <img id="img31" alt="OFF" fp-style="fp-btn: Embossed Rectangle 6;
fp-font-size: 14; fp-img-hover: 0; fp-img-press: 0; fp-preload: 0; fp-
transparent: 1; fp-proportional: 0" fp-title="OFF" height="45"
src="../images/buttonF6.gif" style="border: 0"
width="100"></a>         &nb
sp;           &nbs
p;     
      <a id="smc7a" href="lounge.php?season_front_lights_on=1">
      <img id="img32" alt="Season Front Lights       ON" fp-style="fp-
btn: Embossed Rectangle 6; fp-font-size: 14; fp-img-hover: 0; fp-img-
press: 0; fp-preload: 0; fp-transparent: 1; fp-proportional: 0" fp-
title="Season Front Lights       ON" height="45"
src="../images/buttonFB.gif" style="border: 0"
width="275"></a>    
      <a id="smc7b" href="lounge.php?season_front_lights_off=1">
      <img id="img33" alt="OFF" fp-style="fp-btn: Embossed Rectangle 6;
fp-font-size: 14; fp-img-hover: 0; fp-img-press: 0; fp-preload: 0; fp-
transparent: 1; fp-proportional: 0" fp-title="OFF" height="45"
src="../images/buttonFF.gif" style="border: 0" width="100"></a><br>
      <br><a id="smc4a" href="lounge.php?fishtank_lights_on=1">
      <img id="img34" alt="Fishtank Lights                   ON" fp-
style="fp-btn: Embossed Rectangle 6; fp-font-size: 14; fp-img-hover: 0;
fp-img-press: 0; fp-preload: 0; fp-transparent: 1; fp-proportional: 0"
fp-title="Fishtank Lights                  ON" height="45"
src="../images/buttonF3.gif" style="border: 0"
width="275"></a>    
      <a id="smc4b" href="lounge.php?fishtank_lights_off=1">
      <img id="img35" alt="OFF" fp-style="fp-btn: Embossed Rectangle 6;
fp-font-size: 14; fp-img-hover: 0; fp-img-press: 0; fp-preload: 0; fp-
transparent: 1; fp-proportional: 0" fp-title="OFF" height="45"
src="../images/buttonF7.gif" style="border: 0"
width="100"></a>         &nb
sp;           &nbs
p;     
      <a id="smc8a" href="lounge.php?season_back_lights_on=1">
```

```
	<img id="img36" alt="Season Back Lights        ON" fp-style="fp-btn: Embossed Rectangle 6; fp-font-size: 14; fp-img-hover: 0; fp-img-press: 0; fp-preload: 0; fp-transparent: 1; fp-proportional: 0" fp-title="Season Back Lights        ON" height="45" src="../images/buttonFC.gif" style="border: 0" width="275"></a>    
	<a id="smc8b" href="lounge.php?season_back_lights_off=1">
	<img id="img37" alt="OFF" fp-style="fp-btn: Embossed Rectangle 6; fp-font-size: 14; fp-img-hover: 0; fp-img-press: 0; fp-preload: 0; fp-transparent: 1; fp-proportional: 0" fp-title="OFF" height="45" src="../images/button100.gif" style="border: 0" width="100"></a></div>
    <p> </p>
    <p> </p>

</form>
</div>
</div>
</body>
</html>
```

File: kitchen.php

```
<!DOCTYPE HTML>
<html>
<head>
<title>HC-Kitchen</title>

<!--
File name:
   kitchen.php
Author:
   Steve McClure
Book:
   Designing Embedded Sytems
Description:
   This file is used by the Home Control / Security application
   to build the Kitchen Web page.
 -->

<link href="../css/reset.css" rel="stylesheet" type="text/css"
media="screen">
<link href="../css/styles.css" rel="stylesheet" type="text/css"
media="screen">

<script type="text/javascript" src="../js/kitchen_calendar.js"> </script>

<style type="text/css">
.auto-style1 {
   color: #FFFFFF;
}
.auto-style2 {
   text-align: center;
}
.auto-style3 {
   font-size: small;
}
.auto-style4 {
   font-size: large;
}
</style>

</head>

<body onload=" startTime()">

<div style="width:980px; margin: 0 auto; overflow: hidden;">
<div id="wrapper">
  <div id="navigation">
    <div id="navigation_picture">
      <img src="../images/HouseFront1.jpg" height="200" width="900" />
    </div>
```

```
    <div id="navigation_heading">
      <p><span class="auto-style1">Navigation</span> <span class="auto-
style1">- Kitchen</span></p>
    </div>

    <div id="navigation_time">
      <p>Date and Time</p>
    </div>

   <div id="navigation_links">
       <ul>
           <li><a href="security.php">Security</a></li>
           <li><a href="master.php">Master</a></li>
           <li><a href="lounge.php">Lounge</a></li>
           <li><a href="kitchen">Kitchen</a></li>
           <li><a href="family.php">Family</a></li>
           <li><a href="steve.php">Steve</a></li>
           <li><a href="state.php">State</a></li>
           <li><a href="events.php">Events</a></li>
       </ul>
   </div>
  </div>

  <div id="main_stuff">
    <p class="auto-style3"> </p>
    <p><strong>         This
screen allows you to control the Kitchen environment:</strong></p>
      <p class="auto-style3"> </p>
  </div>
</div>


    <?php

    // Connect to the MySQL Database Environment
    //=========================================
     $con = mysql_connect("192.168.1.176","steve","william");    // This
works on Archimedes

     if (!$con)
     {
       die('Could not connect as: ' . mysql_error());
       echo "<br />";
     }

   // Access the 'system_control' database
   //====================================
     mysql_select_db("system_control", $con);


   // Insert data into the 'house_state' table
```

```
//==================================

if ($_GET["watch_tv"] == 1)
{
   mysql_query ("UPDATE house_state SET watch_tv = 1");
 }


if ($_GET["go_to_bed"] == 1)
 {
   mysql_query ("UPDATE house_state SET go_to_bed = 1");
 }


// Insert data into the 'house_code_events' table
//==============================================

// Kitchen Main Lights ON
if ($_GET["kitchen_main_lights_on"] == 1)
{
   mysql_query ("INSERT INTO house_code_events (house, unit, type,
state, timeout, timestamp) VALUES (4, 3, 1, 1, 777,
'".$_GET["calendar"]."')");
 }

// Kitchen Main Lights OFF
if ($_GET["kitchen_main_lights_off"] == 1)
{
   mysql_query ("INSERT INTO house_code_events (house, unit, type,
state, timeout, timestamp) VALUES (4, 3, 1, 0, 777,
'".$_GET["calendar"]."')");
 }


// Kitchen Counter Lights ON
if ($_GET["kitchen_counter_lights_on"] == 1)
{
   mysql_query ("INSERT INTO house_code_events (house, unit, type,
state, timeout, timestamp) VALUES (4, 5, 1, 1, 777,
'".$_GET["calendar"]."')");
 }

// Kitchen Counter Lights OFF
if ($_GET["kitchen_counter_lights_off"] == 1)
{
   mysql_query ("INSERT INTO house_code_events (house, unit, type,
state, timeout, timestamp) VALUES (4, 5, 1, 0, 777,
'".$_GET["calendar"]."')");
 }


// Kitchen Sink Light ON
```

```
    if ($_GET["kitchen_sink_light_on"] == 1)
    {
       mysql_query ("INSERT INTO house_code_events (house, unit, type,
state, timeout, timestamp) VALUES (4, 6, 1, 1, 777,
'".$_GET["calendar"]."')");
     }

    // Kitchen Sink Light OFF
    if ($_GET["kitchen_sink_light_off"] == 1)
    {
       mysql_query ("INSERT INTO house_code_events (house, unit, type,
state, timeout, timestamp) VALUES (4, 6, 1, 0, 777,
'".$_GET["calendar"]."')");
     }


    // Kitchen Nook Light ON
    if ($_GET["kitchen_nook_light_on"] == 1)
    {
       mysql_query ("INSERT INTO house_code_events (house, unit, type,
state, timeout, timestamp) VALUES (4, 4, 1, 1, 777,
'".$_GET["calendar"]."')");
     }

    // Kitchen Nook Light OFF
    if ($_GET["kitchen_nook_light_off"] == 1)
    {
       mysql_query ("INSERT INTO house_code_events (house, unit, type,
state, timeout, timestamp) VALUES (4, 4, 1, 0, 777,
'".$_GET["calendar"]."')");
     }


    // Diningroom Table Lights ON
    if ($_GET["diningroom_table_lights_on"] == 1)
    {
       mysql_query ("INSERT INTO house_code_events (house, unit, type,
state, timeout, timestamp) VALUES (8, 3, 1, 1, 777,
'".$_GET["calendar"]."')");
     }

    // Diningroom Table Lights OFF
    if ($_GET["diningroom_table_lights_off"] == 1)
    {
       mysql_query ("INSERT INTO house_code_events (house, unit, type,
state, timeout, timestamp) VALUES (8, 3, 1, 0, 777,
'".$_GET["calendar"]."')");
     }


    // Main Hallway Light ON
    if ($_GET["main_hallway_lights_on"] == 1)
```

```
    {
       mysql_query ("INSERT INTO house_code_events (house, unit, type,
state, timeout, timestamp) VALUES (5, 6, 1, 1, 777,
'".$_GET["calendar"]."')");
    }

    // Main Hallway Light OFF
    if ($_GET["main_hallway_lights_off"] == 1)
    {
       mysql_query ("INSERT INTO house_code_events (house, unit, type,
state, timeout, timestamp) VALUES (5, 6, 1, 0, 777,
'".$_GET["calendar"]."')");
    }


    // Pantry Light ON
    if ($_GET["pantry_light_on"] == 1)
    {
       mysql_query ("INSERT INTO house_code_events (house, unit, type,
state, timeout, timestamp) VALUES (7, 8, 1, 1, 777,
'".$_GET["calendar"]."')");
    }

    // Pantry Light OFF
    if ($_GET["pantry_light_off"] == 1)
    {
       mysql_query ("INSERT INTO house_code_events (house, unit, type,
state, timeout, timestamp) VALUES (7, 8, 1, 0, 777,
'".$_GET["calendar"]."')");
    }


    // Laundry Light ON
    if ($_GET["laundry_light_on"] == 1)
    {
       mysql_query ("INSERT INTO house_code_events (house, unit, type,
state, timeout, timestamp) VALUES (7, 10, 1, 1, 777,
'".$_GET["calendar"]."')");
    }

    // Laundry Light OFF
    if ($_GET["laundry_light_off"] == 1)
    {
       mysql_query ("INSERT INTO house_code_events (house, unit, type,
state, timeout, timestamp) VALUES (7, 10, 1, 0, 777,
'".$_GET["calendar"]."')");
    }


    // Close the 'home_control' database
    //==================================
     mysql_close($con);
```

```
    ?>
<div id="key_background">
<form action="family.php" method="post">
   <div class="auto-style2">
      <span class="auto-style4"> </span><br>
      <a id="smc1a" href="kitchen.php?kitchen_main_lights_on=1">
      <img id="img38" alt="Kitchen Main Lights        ON" fp-style="fp-
btn: Embossed Rectangle 6; fp-font-size: 14; fp-img-hover: 0; fp-img-
press: 0; fp-preload: 0; fp-transparent: 1; fp-proportional: 0" fp-
title="Kitchen Main Lights        ON" height="45"
src="../images/buttonA9.gif" style="border: 0"
width="270"></a>    
      <a id="smc1b" href="kitchen.php?kitchen_main_lights_off=1">
      <img id="img39" alt="OFF" fp-style="fp-btn: Embossed Rectangle 6;
fp-font-size: 14; fp-img-hover: 0; fp-img-press: 0; fp-preload: 0; fp-
transparent: 1; fp-proportional: 0" fp-title="OFF" height="45"
src="../images/buttonA13.gif" style="border: 0"
width="100"></a>         &nb
sp;           &nbs
p;     
      <a id="smc5a" href="kitchen.php?diningroom_table_lights_on=1">
      <img id="img40" alt="Diningroom Table Lights  ON" fp-style="fp-
btn: Embossed Rectangle 6; fp-font-size: 14; fp-img-hover: 0; fp-img-
press: 0; fp-preload: 0; fp-transparent: 1; fp-proportional: 0" fp-
title="Diningroom Table Lights  ON" height="45"
src="../images/buttonBC.gif" style="border: 0"
width="270"></a>    
      <a id="smc5b" href="kitchen.php?diningroom_table_lights_off=1">
      <img id="img41" alt="OFF" fp-style="fp-btn: Embossed Rectangle 6;
fp-font-size: 14; fp-img-hover: 0; fp-img-press: 0; fp-preload: 0; fp-
transparent: 1; fp-proportional: 0" fp-title="OFF" height="45"
src="../images/buttonC0.gif" style="border: 0" width="100"></a> <br>
      <span class="auto-style3"> </span><br>
      <a id="smc2a" href="kitchen.php?kitchen_counter_lights_on=1">
      <img id="img42" alt="Kitchen Counter Lights   ON" fp-style="fp-
btn: Embossed Rectangle 6; fp-font-size: 14; fp-img-hover: 0; fp-img-
press: 0; fp-preload: 0; fp-transparent: 1; fp-proportional: 0" fp-
title="Kitchen Counter Lights   ON" height="45"
src="../images/buttonA10.gif" style="border: 0"
width="270"></a>    
      <a id="smc2b" href="kitchen.php?kitchen_counter_lights_off=1">
      <img id="img43" alt="OFF" fp-style="fp-btn: Embossed Rectangle 6;
fp-font-size: 14; fp-img-hover: 0; fp-img-press: 0; fp-preload: 0; fp-
transparent: 1; fp-proportional: 0" fp-title="OFF" height="45"
src="../images/buttonAA.gif" style="border: 0"
width="100"></a>         &nb
sp;           &nbs
p;     
      <a id="smc6a" href="kitchen.php?main_hallway_lights_on=1">
      <img id="img44" alt="Main Hallway Lights        ON" fp-style="fp-
btn: Embossed Rectangle 6; fp-font-size: 14; fp-img-hover: 0; fp-img-
press: 0; fp-preload: 0; fp-transparent: 1; fp-proportional: 0" fp-
```

```
title="Main Hallway Lights        ON" height="45"
src="../images/buttonBD.gif" style="border: 0"
width="270"></a>    
	<a id="smc6b" href="kitchen.php?main_hallway_lights_off=1">
	<img id="img45" alt="OFF" fp-style="fp-btn: Embossed Rectangle 6;
fp-font-size: 14; fp-img-hover: 0; fp-img-press: 0; fp-preload: 0; fp-
transparent: 1; fp-proportional: 0" fp-title="OFF" height="45"
src="../images/buttonC1.gif" style="border: 0" width="100"></a> <br>
	<span class="auto-style3"> </span><br class="auto-style3">
	<a id="smc3a" href="kitchen.php?kitchen_sink_light_on=1">
	<img id="img46" alt="Kitchen Sink Light          ON" fp-style="fp-
btn: Embossed Rectangle 6; fp-font-size: 14; fp-img-hover: 0; fp-img-
press: 0; fp-preload: 0; fp-transparent: 1; fp-proportional: 0" fp-
title="Kitchen Sink Light        ON" height="45"
src="../images/buttonA11.gif" style="border: 0"
width="270"></a>    
	<a id="smc3b" href="kitchen.php?kitchen_sink_light_off=1">
	<img id="img47" alt="OFF" fp-style="fp-btn: Embossed Rectangle 6;
fp-font-size: 14; fp-img-hover: 0; fp-img-press: 0; fp-preload: 0; fp-
transparent: 1; fp-proportional: 0" fp-title="OFF" height="45"
src="../images/buttonAB.gif" style="border: 0"
width="100"></a>       
            &
nbsp;      
	<a id="smc7a" href="kitchen.php?pantry_light_on=1">
	<img id="img48" alt="Pantry Light                    ON" fp-
style="fp-btn: Embossed Rectangle 6; fp-font-size: 14; fp-img-hover: 0;
fp-img-press: 0; fp-preload: 0; fp-transparent: 1; fp-proportional: 0"
fp-title="Pantry Light              ON" height="45"
src="../images/buttonBE.gif" style="border: 0"
width="270"></a>    
	<a id="smc7b" href="kitchen.php?pantry_light_off=1">
	<img id="img49" alt="OFF" fp-style="fp-btn: Embossed Rectangle 6;
fp-font-size: 14; fp-img-hover: 0; fp-img-press: 0; fp-preload: 0; fp-
transparent: 1; fp-proportional: 0" fp-title="OFF" height="45"
src="../images/buttonC2.gif" style="border: 0" width="100"></a> <br>
	<span class="auto-style3"> <br></span>
	<a id="smc4a" href="kitchen.php?kitchen_nook_light_on=1">
	<img id="img50" alt="Kitchen Nook Light       ON" fp-style="fp-
btn: Embossed Rectangle 6; fp-font-size: 14; fp-img-hover: 0; fp-img-
press: 0; fp-preload: 0; fp-transparent: 1; fp-proportional: 0" fp-
title="Kitchen Nook Light      ON" height="45"
src="../images/buttonA12.gif" style="border: 0"
width="270"></a>    
	<a id="smc4b" href="kitchen.php?kitchen_nook_light_off=1">
	<img id="img51" alt="OFF" fp-style="fp-btn: Embossed Rectangle 6;
fp-font-size: 14; fp-img-hover: 0; fp-img-press: 0; fp-preload: 0; fp-
transparent: 1; fp-proportional: 0" fp-title="OFF" height="45"
src="../images/buttonAC.gif" style="border: 0"
width="100"></a>         &nb
sp;           &nbs
p;     
```

```
        <a id="smc8a" href="kitchen.php?laundry_light_on=1">
        <img id="img52" alt="Laundry Light                  ON" fp-
style="fp-btn: Embossed Rectangle 6; fp-font-size: 14; fp-img-hover: 0;
fp-img-press: 0; fp-preload: 0; fp-transparent: 1; fp-proportional: 0"
fp-title="Laundry Light                  ON" height="45"
src="../images/buttonBF.gif" style="border: 0"
width="270"></a>    
        <a id="smc8b" href="kitchen.php?laundry_light_off=1">
        <img id="img53" alt="OFF" fp-style="fp-btn: Embossed Rectangle 6;
fp-font-size: 14; fp-img-hover: 0; fp-img-press: 0; fp-preload: 0; fp-
transparent: 1; fp-proportional: 0" fp-title="OFF" height="45"
src="../images/buttonC3.gif" style="border: 0"
width="100"></a> <br></div>

    <p> </p>
    <p> </p>

</form>
</div>
</div>
</body>
</html>
```

File: family.php

```
<!DOCTYPE HTML>
<html>
<head>
<title>HC-Family</title>

<!--
File name:
   family.php
Author:
   Steve McClure
Book:
   Designing Embedded Sytems
Description:
   This file is used by the Home Control / Security application
   to build the Family Web page.
-->

<link href="../css/reset.css" rel="stylesheet" type="text/css"
media="screen">
<link href="../css/styles.css" rel="stylesheet" type="text/css"
media="screen">

<script type="text/javascript" src="../js/family_calendar.js"> </script>

<style type="text/css">
.auto-style1 {
   color: #FFFFFF;
}
.auto-style2 {
   text-align: center;
}
.auto-style3 {
   vertical-align: middle;
   text-align: center;
}
.auto-style4 {
   vertical-align: middle;
   text-align: center;
   font-size: xx-small;
}
.auto-style5 {
   font-size: xx-small;
}
.auto-style6 {
   font-size: small;
}


</style>
```

```
</head>
<body onload=" startTime()">

<div style="width:980px; margin: 0 auto; overflow: hidden;">
<div id="wrapper">
  <div id="navigation">
    <div id="navigation_picture">
      <img src="../images/HouseFront1.jpg" height="200" width="900" />
    </div>

    <div id="navigation_heading">
      <p><span class="auto-style1">Navigation</span> <span class="auto-
style1">- Family Room</span></p>
    </div>

    <div id="navigation_time">
      <p>Date and Time</p>
    </div>

   <div id="navigation_links">
      <ul>
          <li><a href="security.php">Security</a></li>
          <li><a href="master.php">Master</a></li>
          <li><a href="lounge.php">Lounge</a></li>
          <li><a href="kitchen">Kitchen</a></li>
          <li><a href="family.php">Family</a></li>
          <li><a href="steve.php">Steve</a></li>
          <li><a href="state.php">State</a></li>
          <li><a href="events.php">Events</a></li>
      </ul>
   </div>
  </div>

  <div id="main_stuff">
    <?php

    // Connect to the MySQL Database Environment
    //==========================================
    $con = mysql_connect("192.168.1.176","steve","william");    // This
works on Archimedes

    if (!$con)
    {
       die('Could not connect as: ' . mysql_error());
       echo "<br />";
    }

   // Access the 'system_control' database
   //====================================
   mysql_select_db("system_control", $con);
```

```
    // Insert data into the 'house_code_events' table
    //================================================

     // Track Lights - TV ON
    if ($_GET["track_lights_tv_on"] == 1)
    {
       mysql_query ("INSERT INTO house_code_events (house, unit, type,
state, timeout, timestamp) VALUES (12, 3, 1, 1, 777,
'".$_GET["calendar"]."')");
     }

     // Track Lights - TV OFF
    if ($_GET["track_lights_tv_off"] == 1)
    {
       mysql_query ("INSERT INTO house_code_events (house, unit, type,
state, timeout, timestamp) VALUES (12, 3, 1, 0, 777,
'".$_GET["calendar"]."')");
     }


     // Track Lights - Reading ON
    if ($_GET["track_lights_reading_on"] == 1)
    {
       mysql_query ("INSERT INTO house_code_events (house, unit, type,
state, timeout, timestamp) VALUES (12, 4, 1, 1, 777,
'".$_GET["calendar"]."')");
     }

     // Track Lights - Reading OFF
    if ($_GET["track_lights_reading_off"] == 1)
    {
       mysql_query ("INSERT INTO house_code_events (house, unit, type,
state, timeout, timestamp) VALUES (12, 4, 1, 0, 777,
'".$_GET["calendar"]."')");
     }


     // TV Wall Unit Lights ON
    if ($_GET["tv_wall_unit_lights_on"] == 1)
    {
       mysql_query ("INSERT INTO house_code_events (house, unit, type,
state, timeout, timestamp) VALUES (12, 5, 1, 1, 777,
'".$_GET["calendar"]."')");
     }

     // TV Wall Unit Lights OFF
    if ($_GET["tv_wall_unit_lights_off"] == 1)
    {
       mysql_query ("INSERT INTO house_code_events (house, unit, type,
state, timeout, timestamp) VALUES (12, 5, 1, 0, 777,
'".$_GET["calendar"]."')");
     }
```

```
    // TV Wall Unit Spotlights ON
   if ($_GET["tv_wall_unit_spots_on"] == 1)
   {
      mysql_query ("INSERT INTO house_code_events (house, unit, type,
state, timeout, timestamp) VALUES (12, 6, 1, 1, 777,
'".$_GET["calendar"]."')");
    }

    // TV Wall Unit Spotlights OFF
   if ($_GET["tv_wall_unit_spots_off"] == 1)
   {
      mysql_query ("INSERT INTO house_code_events (house, unit, type,
state, timeout, timestamp) VALUES (12, 6, 1, 0, 777,
'".$_GET["calendar"]."')");
    }



    // Family Window Light ON
   if ($_GET["window_light_on"] == 1)
   {
      mysql_query ("INSERT INTO house_code_events (house, unit, type,
state, timeout, timestamp) VALUES (12, 1, 1, 1, 777,
'".$_GET["calendar"]."')");
    }

    // Family Window Light OFF
   if ($_GET["window_light_off"] == 1)
   {
      mysql_query ("INSERT INTO house_code_events (house, unit, type,
state, timeout, timestamp) VALUES (12, 1, 1, 0, 777,
'".$_GET["calendar"]."')");
    }



    // Family Wall Light ON
   if ($_GET["wall_light_on"] == 1)
   {
      mysql_query ("INSERT INTO house_code_events (house, unit, type,
state, timeout, timestamp) VALUES (12, 2, 1, 1, 777,
'".$_GET["calendar"]."')");
    }

    // Family Wall Light OFF
   if ($_GET["wall_light_off"] == 1)
   {
      mysql_query ("INSERT INTO house_code_events (house, unit, type,
state, timeout, timestamp) VALUES (12, 2, 1, 0, 777,
'".$_GET["calendar"]."')");
    }
```

```
    $HS_NORMAL_MODE         = 0;
    $HS_NORMAL_MODE_TRIGGER = 1;
    $HS_TV_MODE             = 2;
    $HS_TV_MODE_TRIGGER     = 3;


    $result = mysql_query("SELECT * FROM house_state");
    $row = mysql_fetch_array($result);

    // Was the Watch TV button pressed?
    if ($_GET["watch_tv"] == 1)
    {
        // Set TV Mode
        mysql_query ("UPDATE house_state SET family_lights =
$HS_TV_MODE");
        mysql_query ("INSERT INTO house_code_events (house, unit, type,
state, timeout, timestamp) VALUES (12, 5, 1, 1, 1,
'".$_GET["calendar"]."')");  // TV Wall Unit Lights ON
        mysql_query ("INSERT INTO house_code_events (house, unit, type,
state, timeout, timestamp) VALUES (12, 6, 1, 0, 2,
'".$_GET["calendar"]."')");  // TV Wall Unit Spots OFF
        mysql_query ("INSERT INTO house_code_events (house, unit, type,
state, timeout, timestamp) VALUES (12, 2, 1, 1, 3,
'".$_GET["calendar"]."')");  // Set Wall Light ON
        mysql_query ("INSERT INTO house_code_events (house, unit, type,
state, timeout, timestamp) VALUES (12, 1, 1, 0, 4,
'".$_GET["calendar"]."')");  // Set Window Light OFF

        mysql_query ("INSERT INTO house_code_events (house, unit, type,
state, timeout, timestamp) VALUES ( 4, 3, 1, 0, 5,
'".$_GET["calendar"]."')"); // Kitchen light OFF
        mysql_query ("INSERT INTO house_code_events (house, unit, type,
state, timeout, timestamp) VALUES ( 4, 4, 1, 0, 6,
'".$_GET["calendar"]."')");  // Kitchen Nook OFF
        mysql_query ("INSERT INTO house_code_events (house, unit, type,
state, timeout, timestamp) VALUES ( 5, 6, 1, 0, 7,
'".$_GET["calendar"]."')");  // Main Hallway Light OFF

        mysql_query ("INSERT INTO house_code_events (house, unit, type,
state, timeout, timestamp) VALUES (12, 3, 1, 0, 8,
'".$_GET["calendar"]."')");  // Track TV OFF
        mysql_query ("INSERT INTO house_code_events (house, unit, type,
state, timeout, timestamp) VALUES (12, 4, 1, 0, 9,
'".$_GET["calendar"]."')");  // Track Reading OFF
    }

    // Was the Normal Lights button pressed?
    if ($_GET["normal_lights"] == 1)
    {
        // Set Normal Mode
        mysql_query ("UPDATE house_state SET family_lights =
$HS_NORMAL_MODE");
```

```
          mysql_query ("INSERT INTO house_code_events (house, unit, type,
state, timeout, timestamp) VALUES (12, 5, 1, 1, 1,
'".$_GET["calendar"]."')");  // TV Wall Unit Lights ON
          mysql_query ("INSERT INTO house_code_events (house, unit, type,
state, timeout, timestamp) VALUES (12, 6, 1, 1, 2,
'".$_GET["calendar"]."')");  // TV Wall Unit Spots ON
          mysql_query ("INSERT INTO house_code_events (house, unit, type,
state, timeout, timestamp) VALUES (12, 2, 1, 1, 3,
'".$_GET["calendar"]."')");  // Set Wall Light ON
          mysql_query ("INSERT INTO house_code_events (house, unit, type,
state, timeout, timestamp) VALUES (12, 1, 1, 1, 4,
'".$_GET["calendar"]."')");  // Set Window Light OFF
          mysql_query ("INSERT INTO house_code_events (house, unit, type,
state, timeout, timestamp) VALUES (12, 3, 1, 0, 5,
'".$_GET["calendar"]."')");  // Track TV OFF
          mysql_query ("INSERT INTO house_code_events (house, unit, type,
state, timeout, timestamp) VALUES (12, 4, 1, 0, 6,
'".$_GET["calendar"]."')");  // Track Reading OFF
          mysql_query ("INSERT INTO house_code_events (house, unit, type,
state, timeout, timestamp) VALUES ( 4, 3, 1, 0, 7,
'".$_GET["calendar"]."')");  // Kitchen light OFF
       mysql_query ("INSERT INTO house_code_events (house, unit, type,
state, timeout, timestamp) VALUES ( 4, 4, 1, 0, 8,
'".$_GET["calendar"]."')");  // Kitchen Nook OFF
          mysql_query ("INSERT INTO house_code_events (house, unit, type,
state, timeout, timestamp) VALUES ( 5, 6, 1, 0, 9,
'".$_GET["calendar"]."')");  // Main Hallway Light OFF
    }

    $result = mysql_query("SELECT * FROM house_state");

    $row = mysql_fetch_array($result);
      ?>

    <p class="auto-style6">  </p>
     <?php
     echo "         ";
     echo "This screen allows you to control the Family Room
environment:";
     echo "   ";

     if ($row['family_lights'] == $HS_NORMAL_MODE)
     {
       echo "Normal Lights";
      }
     else
     {
       echo "Watch TV";
     }
    ?>

    <p class="auto-style6">  </p>
```

```
    <?php

   // Close the 'home_control' database
   //====================================
     mysql_close($con);

    ?>
  </div>
</div>

<div id="key_background">
<form action="family.php" method="post">
   <span class="auto-style5"> </span><br>
         <table style="width: 967px; height: 30px" align="center">
            <tr>
               <td class="auto-style3" style="width: 482px; height:
55px">
               <a id="smc1a" href="family.php?track_lights_tv_on=1">
               <img id="img44" alt="Track Lights - TV          ON"
fp-style="fp-btn: Embossed Rectangle 6; fp-font-size: 14; fp-img-hover:
0; fp-img-press: 0; fp-preload: 0; fp-transparent: 1; fp-proportional: 0"
fp-title="Track Lights - TV          ON" height="45"
src="../images/button119.gif" style="border: 0"
width="272"></a>    
               <a id="smc1b" href="family.php?track_lights_tv_off=1">
               <img id="img45" alt="OFF" fp-style="fp-btn: Embossed
Rectangle 6; fp-font-size: 14; fp-img-hover: 0; fp-img-press: 0; fp-
preload: 0; fp-transparent: 1; fp-proportional: 0" fp-title="OFF"
height="45" src="../images/button11D.gif" style="border: 0"
width="100"></a>
               </td>
               <td class="auto-style3" style="width: 48px; height:
55px">
                </td>
               <td class="auto-style3" style="height: 55px">
               <a id="smc5a" href="family.php?window_light_on=1">
               <img id="img52" alt="Window Light              ON" fp-
style="fp-btn: Embossed Rectangle 6; fp-font-size: 14; fp-img-hover: 0;
fp-img-press: 0; fp-preload: 0; fp-transparent: 1; fp-proportional: 0"
fp-title="Window Light              ON" height="45"
src="../images/button121.gif" style="border: 0"
width="272"></a>    
               <a id="smc5b" href="family.php?window_light_off=1">
               <img id="img53" alt="OFF" fp-style="fp-btn: Embossed
Rectangle 6; fp-font-size: 14; fp-img-hover: 0; fp-img-press: 0; fp-
preload: 0; fp-transparent: 1; fp-proportional: 0" fp-title="OFF"
height="45" src="../images/button123.gif" style="border: 0"
width="100"></a></td>
               <td class="auto-style2"> </td>
               <td class="auto-style2"> </td>
            </tr>
```

```
            <tr>
               <td class="auto-style3" style="width: 482px; height:
55px">
               <a id="smc2a"
href="family.php?track_lights_reading_on=1">
               <img id="img46" alt="Track Lights - Reading    ON" fp-
style="fp-btn: Embossed Rectangle 6; fp-font-size: 14; fp-img-hover: 0;
fp-img-press: 0; fp-preload: 0; fp-transparent: 1; fp-proportional: 0"
fp-title="Track Lights - Reading    ON" height="45"
src="../images/button11A.gif" style="border: 0"
width="272"></a>    
               <a id="smc2b"
href="family.php?track_lights_reading_off=1">
               <img id="img47" alt="OFF" fp-style="fp-btn: Embossed
Rectangle 6; fp-font-size: 14; fp-img-hover: 0; fp-img-press: 0; fp-
preload: 0; fp-transparent: 1; fp-proportional: 0" fp-title="OFF"
height="45" src="../images/button11E.gif" style="border: 0"
width="100"></a></td>
               <td class="auto-style3" style="width: 48px; height:
55px">
                </td>
               <td class="auto-style3" style="height: 55px">
               <a id="smc6a" href="family.php?wall_light_on=1">
               <img id="img54" alt="Wall Light                    ON"
fp-style="fp-btn: Embossed Rectangle 6; fp-font-size: 14; fp-img-hover:
0; fp-img-press: 0; fp-preload: 0; fp-transparent: 1; fp-proportional: 0"
fp-title="Wall Light                    ON" height="45"
src="../images/button122.gif" style="border: 0"
width="272"></a>    
               <a id="smc6b" href="family.php?wall_light_off=1">
               <img id="img55" alt="OFF" fp-style="fp-btn: Embossed
Rectangle 6; fp-font-size: 14; fp-img-hover: 0; fp-img-press: 0; fp-
preload: 0; fp-transparent: 1; fp-proportional: 0" fp-title="OFF"
height="45" src="../images/button124.gif" style="border: 0"
width="100"></a></td>
            </tr>
            <tr>
               <td class="auto-style4" style="height: 3px; width:
482px;">
               <br></td>
               <td class="auto-style3" style="height: 3px; width:
48px;"></td>
               <td class="auto-style3" style="height: 3px"></td>
            </tr>
            <tr>
               <td class="auto-style3" style="width: 482px; height:
55px">
               <a id="smc3a"
href="family.php?tv_wall_unit_lights_on=1">
               <img id="img50" alt="TV Wall Unit Lights       ON" fp-
style="fp-btn: Embossed Rectangle 6; fp-font-size: 14; fp-img-hover: 0;
fp-img-press: 0; fp-preload: 0; fp-transparent: 1; fp-proportional: 0"
```

```
fp-title="TV Wall Unit Lights         ON" height="45"
src="../images/button11B.gif" style="border: 0"
width="272"></a>    
                    <a id="smc3b"
href="family.php?tv_wall_unit_lights_off=1">
                    <img id="img51" alt="OFF" fp-style="fp-btn: Embossed
Rectangle 6; fp-font-size: 14; fp-img-hover: 0; fp-img-press: 0; fp-
preload: 0; fp-transparent: 1; fp-proportional: 0" fp-title="OFF"
height="45" src="../images/button11F.gif" style="border: 0"
width="100"></a></td>
                    <td class="auto-style3" style="width: 48px; height:
55px">
                     </td>
                    <td class="auto-style3" rowspan="2">
                    <br><a id="smc7" href="family.php?watch_tv=1">
                    <img id="img56" alt="Watch TV" fp-style="fp-btn:
Embossed Rectangle 9; fp-font-size: 14; fp-img-hover: 0; fp-img-press: 0;
fp-preload: 0; fp-transparent: 1; fp-proportional: 0" fp-title="Watch TV"
height="80" src="../images/button125.gif" style="border: 0"
width="160"></a>        
                    <a id="smc8" href="family.php?normal_lights=1">
                    <img id="img57" alt="Normal Lights" fp-style="fp-btn:
Embossed Rectangle 4; fp-font-size: 14; fp-img-hover: 0; fp-img-press: 0;
fp-preload: 0; fp-transparent: 1; fp-proportional: 0" fp-title="Normal
Lights" height="80" src="../images/button126.gif" style="border: 0"
width="160"></a><br></td>
                </tr>
                <tr>
                    <td class="auto-style3" style="width: 482px; height:
55px">
                    <a id="smc4a" href="family.php?tv_wall_unit_spots_on=1">
                    <img id="img48" alt="TV Wall Unit Spots          ON" fp-
style="fp-btn: Embossed Rectangle 6; fp-font-size: 14; fp-img-hover: 0;
fp-img-press: 0; fp-preload: 0; fp-transparent: 1; fp-proportional: 0"
fp-title="TV Wall Unit Spots         ON" height="45"
src="../images/button11C.gif" style="border: 0"
width="272"></a>    
                    <a id="smc4b"
href="family.php?tv_wall_unit_spots_off=1">
                    <img id="img49" alt="OFF" fp-style="fp-btn: Embossed
Rectangle 6; fp-font-size: 14; fp-img-hover: 0; fp-img-press: 0; fp-
preload: 0; fp-transparent: 1; fp-proportional: 0" fp-title="OFF"
height="45" src="../images/button120.gif" style="border: 0"
width="100"></a></td>
                    <td class="auto-style3" style="width: 48px; height:
55px">
                     </td>
                </tr>
            </table>
    <p> </p>
    <p> </p>
```

```
</form>
</div>
</div>
</body>
</html>
```

File: steve.php

```
<!DOCTYPE HTML>
<html>
<head>
<title>HC-Steve</title>

<!--
File name:
   steve.php
Author:
   Steve McClure
Book:
   Designing Embedded Sytems
Description:
   This file is used by the Home Control / Security application
   to build the Steve Web page.
-->

<link href="../css/reset.css" rel="stylesheet" type="text/css"
media="screen">
<link href="../css/styles.css" rel="stylesheet" type="text/css"
media="screen">

<script type="text/javascript" src="../js/steve_calendar.js"></script>

<style type="text/css">
.auto-style1 {
   color:#FFFFFF;
}
.auto-style2 {
   text-align: center;
}
.auto-style3 {
   text-align: center;
   vertical-align: middle;
}
.auto-style4 {
   font-size: large;
}
.auto-style6 {
   font-size: small;
}

</style>
<script type="text/javascript">
<!--
function FP_preloadImgs() {//v1.0
 var d=document,a=arguments; if(!d.FP_imgs) d.FP_imgs=new Array();
 for(var i=0; i<a.length; i++) { d.FP_imgs[i]=new Image;
d.FP_imgs[i].src=a[i]; }
```

```
}
// -->
</script>
</head>
<body
onload="FP_preloadImgs(/*url*/'button22.jpg',/*url*/'button23.jpg',/*url*
/'button58.jpg',/*url*/'button59.jpg'); startTime()">
<div style="width:980px; margin: 0 auto; overflow: hidden;">
<div id="wrapper">

  <div id="navigation">
    <div id="navigation_picture">
      <img src="../images/HouseFront1.jpg" height="200" width="900" />
    </div>

    <div id="navigation_heading">
      <p><span class="auto-style1">Navigation</span> <span class="auto-
style1">- Steve's Bedroom, Bathroom &amp; Study</span></p>
    </div>

    <div id="navigation_time">
      <p>Date and Time</p>
    </div>


    <div id="navigation_links">
      <ul>
        <li><a href="security.php">Security</a></li>
        <li><a href="master.php">Master</a></li>
        <li><a href="lounge.php">Lounge</a></li>
        <li><a href="kitchen">Kitchen</a></li>
        <li><a href="family.php">Family</a></li>
        <li><a href="steve.php">Steve</a></li>
        <li><a href="state.php">State</a></li>
        <li><a href="events.php">Events</a></li>
      </ul>
    </div>
  </div>



  <div id="main_stuff">
    <?php

    // Connect to the MySQL Database Environment
    //==========================================
     $con = mysql_connect("192.168.1.176","steve","william");

     if (!$con)
     {
       die('Could not connect as: ' . mysql_error());
       echo "<br />";
```

```
      }

    // Access the 'system_control' database
    //====================================
      mysql_select_db("system_control", $con);

     // Insert data into the 'house_code_events' table
     //=============================================

     // Bedroom Wall Lights ON
    if ($_GET["bedroom_wall_light_on"] == 1)
    {
      mysql_query ("INSERT INTO house_code_events (house, unit, type,
state, timeout, timestamp) VALUES (5, 2, 1, 1, 777,
'".$_GET["calendar"]."')");        // Window light
      mysql_query ("INSERT INTO house_code_events (house, unit, type,
state, timeout, timestamp) VALUES (5, 3, 1, 1, 777,
'".$_GET["calendar"]."')");     // Wall lights
     }

     // Bedroom Wall Lights OFF
    if ($_GET["bedroom_wall_light_off"] == 1)
    {
      mysql_query ("INSERT INTO house_code_events (house, unit, type,
state, timeout, timestamp) VALUES (5, 2, 1, 0, 777,
'".$_GET["calendar"]."')");        // Window light
      mysql_query ("INSERT INTO house_code_events (house, unit, type,
state, timeout, timestamp) VALUES (5, 3, 1, 0, 777,
'".$_GET["calendar"]."')");     // Wall lights
     }


     // Bedroom Main Lights ON
    if ($_GET["bedroom_main_light_on"] == 1)
    {
      mysql_query ("INSERT INTO house_code_events (house, unit, type,
state, timeout, timestamp) VALUES (5, 4, 1, 1, 777,
'".$_GET["calendar"]."')");
     }

     // Bedroom Main Lights OFF
    if ($_GET["bedroom_main_light_off"] == 1)
    {
      mysql_query ("INSERT INTO house_code_events (house, unit, type,
state, timeout, timestamp) VALUES (5, 4, 1, 0, 777,
'".$_GET["calendar"]."')");
     }


     // Reading Light ON
    if ($_GET["reading_light_on"] == 1)
```

```
    {
      mysql_query ("INSERT INTO house_code_events (house, unit, type,
state, timeout, timestamp) VALUES (5, 1, 1, 1, 777,
'".$_GET["calendar"]."')");
     }

     // Reading Light OFF
    if ($_GET["reading_light_off"] == 1)
    {
      mysql_query ("INSERT INTO house_code_events (house, unit, type,
state, timeout, timestamp) VALUES (5, 1, 1, 0, 777,
'".$_GET["calendar"]."')");
     }


     // Study Main Lights ON
    if ($_GET["study_main_light_on"] == 1)
    {
      mysql_query ("INSERT INTO house_code_events (house, unit, type,
state, timeout, timestamp) VALUES (8, 5, 1, 1, 777,
'".$_GET["calendar"]."')");
     }

     // Study Main Lights OFF
    if ($_GET["study_main_light_off"] == 1)
    {
      mysql_query ("INSERT INTO house_code_events (house, unit, type,
state, timeout, timestamp) VALUES (8, 5, 1, 0, 777,
'".$_GET["calendar"]."')");
     }


     // Washroom Vanity Wall Lights ON
    if ($_GET["washroom_light_on"] == 1)
    {
      mysql_query ("INSERT INTO house_code_events (house, unit, type,
state, timeout, timestamp) VALUES (5, 7, 1, 1, 777,
'".$_GET["calendar"]."')");
     }

     // Washroom Vanity Wall Lights OFF
    if ($_GET["washroom_light_off"] == 1)
    {
      mysql_query ("INSERT INTO house_code_events (house, unit, type,
state, timeout, timestamp) VALUES (5, 7, 1, 0, 777,
'".$_GET["calendar"]."')");        // Vanity lights
      mysql_query ("INSERT INTO house_code_events (house, unit, type,
state, timeout, timestamp) VALUES (5, 8, 1, 0, 777,
'".$_GET["calendar"]."')");        // Flourescent light
     }
```

```
    // Bathroom Light ON
   if ($_GET["bathroom_light_on"] == 1)
   {
      mysql_query ("INSERT INTO house_code_events (house, unit, type,
state, timeout, timestamp) VALUES (8, 8, 1, 1, 777,
'".$_GET["calendar"]."')");
    }

    // Bathroom Light OFF
   if ($_GET["bathroom_light_off"] == 1)
   {
      mysql_query ("INSERT INTO house_code_events (house, unit, type,
state, timeout, timestamp) VALUES (8, 8, 1, 0, 777,
'".$_GET["calendar"]."')");
    }


    $HS_NORMAL_MODE         = 0;
    $HS_NORMAL_MODE_TRIGGER = 1;
    $HS_TV_MODE             = 2;
    $HS_TV_MODE_TRIGGER     = 3;

    $result = mysql_query("SELECT * FROM house_state");
    $row = mysql_fetch_array($result);

    // Is sleep mode off?
    if ($row['sleep'] == 0)
    {
      // Was the Watch TV button pressed?
      if ($_GET["watch_tv"] == 1)
      {
         // Set TV Mode
         mysql_query ("UPDATE house_state SET steve_lights =
$HS_TV_MODE");

         mysql_query ("INSERT INTO house_code_events (house, unit, type,
state, timeout, timestamp) VALUES (5, 3, 1, 1, 0,
'".$_GET["calendar"]."')");       // Bedroom Wall Lights ON
         mysql_query ("INSERT INTO house_code_events (house, unit, type,
state, timeout, timestamp) VALUES (5, 2, 1, 0, 0,
'".$_GET["calendar"]."')");       // Bedroom Window Light OFF

          mysql_query ("INSERT INTO house_code_events (house, unit,
type, state, timeout, timestamp) VALUES (8, 5, 1, 0, 2,
'".$_GET["calendar"]."')");       // Study Main Lights OFF
          mysql_query ("INSERT INTO house_code_events (house, unit,
type, state, timeout, timestamp) VALUES (5, 4, 1, 0, 3,
'".$_GET["calendar"]."')");       // Bedroom Main Lights OFF
          mysql_query ("INSERT INTO house_code_events (house, unit,
type, state, timeout, timestamp) VALUES (5, 3, 1, 1, 4,
'".$_GET["calendar"]."')");       // Bedroom Wall Lights ON
```

```
            mysql_query ("INSERT INTO house_code_events (house, unit,
type, state, timeout, timestamp) VALUES (5, 2, 1, 0, 5,
'".$_GET["calendar"]."')");        // Bedroom Window Light OFF
            mysql_query ("INSERT INTO house_code_events (house, unit,
type, state, timeout, timestamp) VALUES (5, 1, 1, 0, 6,
'".$_GET["calendar"]."')");        // Bedroom Reading Light OFF
            mysql_query ("INSERT INTO house_code_events (house, unit,
type, state, timeout, timestamp) VALUES (5, 8, 1, 0, 7,
'".$_GET["calendar"]."')");        // Washroom Flourescent Light OFF
            mysql_query ("INSERT INTO house_code_events (house, unit,
type, state, timeout, timestamp) VALUES (5, 7, 1, 0, 8,
'".$_GET["calendar"]."')");        // Washroom Lights OFF
            mysql_query ("INSERT INTO house_code_events (house, unit,
type, state, timeout, timestamp) VALUES (8, 8, 1, 0, 9,
'".$_GET["calendar"]."')");        // Bathroom Light OFF
        }

        // Was the Normal Lights button pressed?
        if ($_GET["normal_lights"] == 1)
        {
           // Set Normal Mode
           mysql_query ("UPDATE house_state SET steve_lights =
$HS_NORMAL_MODE");

           mysql_query ("INSERT INTO house_code_events (house, unit, type,
state, timeout, timestamp) VALUES (5, 3, 1, 1, 0,
'".$_GET["calendar"]."')");        // Bedroom Wall Lights ON
           mysql_query ("INSERT INTO house_code_events (house, unit, type,
state, timeout, timestamp) VALUES (5, 2, 1, 1, 0,
'".$_GET["calendar"]."')");        // Bedroom Window Light ON

           mysql_query ("INSERT INTO house_code_events (house, unit, type,
state, timeout, timestamp) VALUES (8, 5, 1, 0, 2,
'".$_GET["calendar"]."')");        // Study Main Lights OFF
           mysql_query ("INSERT INTO house_code_events (house, unit, type,
state, timeout, timestamp) VALUES (5, 4, 1, 0, 3,
'".$_GET["calendar"]."')");        // Bedroom Main Lights OFF
           mysql_query ("INSERT INTO house_code_events (house, unit, type,
state, timeout, timestamp) VALUES (5, 3, 1, 1, 4,
'".$_GET["calendar"]."')");        // Bedroom Wall Lights ON
           mysql_query ("INSERT INTO house_code_events (house, unit, type,
state, timeout, timestamp) VALUES (5, 2, 1, 1, 5,
'".$_GET["calendar"]."')");        // Bedroom Window Light ON
           mysql_query ("INSERT INTO house_code_events (house, unit, type,
state, timeout, timestamp) VALUES (5, 1, 1, 0, 6,
'".$_GET["calendar"]."')");        // Bedroom Reading Light OFF
           mysql_query ("INSERT INTO house_code_events (house, unit, type,
state, timeout, timestamp) VALUES (5, 8, 1, 0, 7,
'".$_GET["calendar"]."')");        // Washroom Flourescent Light OFF
           mysql_query ("INSERT INTO house_code_events (house, unit, type,
state, timeout, timestamp) VALUES (5, 7, 1, 0, 8,
'".$_GET["calendar"]."')");        // Washroom Lights OFF
```

```
            mysql_query ("INSERT INTO house_code_events (house, unit, type,
state, timeout, timestamp) VALUES (8, 8, 1, 0, 9,
'".$_GET["calendar"]."')");        // Bathroom Light OFF
        }
     }

    $result = mysql_query("SELECT * FROM house_state");

    $row = mysql_fetch_array($result);

     ?><p class="auto-style6">  </p><?php
     echo "         ";
     echo "This screen allows you to control the Bedroom, Bathroom and
Study environments:";
     echo "   ";

     if ($row['sleep'] == 0)
     {
        if ($row['steve_lights'] == $HS_NORMAL_MODE)
        {
          echo "Normal Lights";
         }
        else
        {
          echo "Watch TV";
        }
     }
     else
     {
         echo "SLEEP ACTIVE";
     }

     ?><p class="auto-style6">  </p><?php

    // Close the 'home_control' database
    //====================================
     mysql_close($con);

     ?>
    </div>
</div>


<div id="key_background">
<p>       
       
 
<span class="auto-style4"> </span></p>
    <table align="center" cellpadding="5" cellspacing="5" style="width:
970px">
        <tr>
```

```
        <td style="height: 55px; width: 459px;" class="auto-style2">
                    
                <a id="smc1a" href="steve.php?bedroom_wall_light_on=1">
                <img id="img1014" alt="Bedroom Wall Light      ON" fp-
style="fp-btn: Embossed Rectangle 6; fp-font-size: 14; fp-img-hover: 0;
fp-img-press: 0; fp-preload: 0; fp-transparent: 1; fp-proportional: 0"
fp-title="Bedroom Wall Light      ON" height="45"
src="../images/button15A.gif" style="border: 0"
width="272"></a>    
                <a id="smc1b" href="steve.php?bedroom_wall_light_off=1">
                <img id="img1015" alt="OFF" fp-style="fp-btn: Embossed
Rectangle 6; fp-font-size: 14; fp-img-hover: 0; fp-img-press: 0; fp-
preload: 0; fp-transparent: 1; fp-proportional: 0" fp-title="OFF"
height="45" src="../images/button15E.gif" style="border: 0"
width="100"></a></td>
        <td style="height: 21px; width: 59px;"></td>
        <td style="height: 21px" class="auto-style2">
                <a id="smc5a" href="steve.php?washroom_light_on=1">
                <img id="img1016" alt="Washroom Light          ON" fp-
style="fp-btn: Embossed Rectangle 6; fp-font-size: 14; fp-img-hover: 0;
fp-img-press: 0; fp-preload: 0; fp-transparent: 1; fp-proportional: 0"
fp-title="Washroom Light          ON" height="45"
src="../images/button162.gif" style="border: 0"
width="272"></a>    
                <a id="smc5b" href="steve.php?washroom_light_off=1">
                <img id="img1017" alt="OFF" fp-style="fp-btn: Embossed
Rectangle 6; fp-font-size: 14; fp-img-hover: 0; fp-img-press: 0; fp-
preload: 0; fp-transparent: 1; fp-proportional: 0" fp-title="OFF"
height="45" src="../images/button164.gif" style="border: 0"
width="100"></a></td>
      </tr>
      <tr>
        <td class="auto-style2" style="width: 459px; height: 55px">
                    
                <a id="smc2a" href="steve.php?bedroom_main_light_on=1">
                <img id="img1018" alt="Bedroom Main Light     ON" fp-
style="fp-btn: Embossed Rectangle 6; fp-font-size: 14; fp-img-hover: 0;
fp-img-press: 0; fp-preload: 0; fp-transparent: 1; fp-proportional: 0"
fp-title="Bedroom Main Light     ON" height="45"
src="../images/button15B.gif" style="border: 0"
width="272"></a>    
                <a id="smc2b" href="steve.php?bedroom_main_light_off=1">
                <img id="img1019" alt="OFF" fp-style="fp-btn: Embossed
Rectangle 6; fp-font-size: 14; fp-img-hover: 0; fp-img-press: 0; fp-
preload: 0; fp-transparent: 1; fp-proportional: 0" fp-title="OFF"
height="45" src="../images/button15F.gif" style="border: 0"
width="100"></a></td>
        <td style="width: 59px; height: 55px"></td>
        <td class="auto-style2" style="height: 55px">
                <a id="smc6a" href="steve.php?bathroom_light_on=1">
                <img id="img1020" alt="Bathroom Light          ON" fp-
style="fp-btn: Embossed Rectangle 6; fp-font-size: 14; fp-img-hover: 0;
```

```
fp-img-press: 0; fp-preload: 0; fp-transparent: 1; fp-proportional: 0"
fp-title="Bathroom Light           ON" height="45"
src="../images/button163.gif" style="border: 0"
width="272"></a>    
                <a id="smc6b" href="steve.php?bathroom_light_off=1">
                <img id="img1021" alt="OFF" fp-style="fp-btn: Embossed
Rectangle 6; fp-font-size: 14; fp-img-hover: 0; fp-img-press: 0; fp-
preload: 0; fp-transparent: 1; fp-proportional: 0" fp-title="OFF"
height="45" src="../images/button165.gif" style="border: 0"
width="100"></a></td>
        </tr>
        <tr>
            <td class="auto-style2" style="width: 459px; height: 8px">
                </td>
            <td style="width: 59px; height: 8px"></td>
            <td class="auto-style2" style="height: 8px">
                </td>
        </tr>
        <tr>
            <td class="auto-style2" style="width: 459px; height: 55px">
                    
                <a id="smc3a" href="steve.php?reading_light_on=1">
                <img id="img1022" alt="Reading Light            ON"
fp-style="fp-btn: Embossed Rectangle 6; fp-font-size: 14; fp-img-hover:
0; fp-img-press: 0; fp-preload: 0; fp-transparent: 1; fp-proportional: 0"
fp-title="Reading Light           ON" height="45"
src="../images/button15C.gif" style="border: 0"
width="272"></a>    
                <a id="smc3b" href="steve.php?reading_light_off=1">
                <img id="img1023" alt="OFF" fp-style="fp-btn: Embossed
Rectangle 6; fp-font-size: 14; fp-img-hover: 0; fp-img-press: 0; fp-
preload: 0; fp-transparent: 1; fp-proportional: 0" fp-title="OFF"
height="45" src="../images/button160.gif" style="border: 0"
width="100"></a></td>
            <td style="width: 59px"> </td>
            <td class="auto-style3" rowspan="2"><br>
                <a id="smc7" href="steve.php?watch_tv=1">
                <img id="img1026" alt="Watch TV" fp-style="fp-btn:
Embossed Rectangle 9; fp-font-size: 14; fp-img-hover: 0; fp-img-press: 0;
fp-preload: 0; fp-transparent: 1; fp-proportional: 0" fp-title="Watch TV"
height="80" src="../images/button166.gif" style="border: 0"
width="160"></a>        
                <a id="smc8" href="steve.php?normal_lights=1">
                <img id="img1027" alt="Normal Lights" fp-style="fp-btn:
Embossed Rectangle 4; fp-font-size: 14; fp-img-hover: 0; fp-img-press: 0;
fp-preload: 0; fp-transparent: 1; fp-proportional: 0" fp-title="Normal
Lights" height="80" src="../images/button167.gif" style="border: 0"
width="160"></a><br><br></td>
        </tr>
        <tr>
            <td class="auto-style2" style="width: 459px; height: 55px">
                    
```

```
                <a id="smc4a" href="steve.php?study_main_light_on=1">
                <img id="img1024" alt="Study Main Light          ON" fp-
style="fp-btn: Embossed Rectangle 6; fp-font-size: 14; fp-img-hover: 0;
fp-img-press: 0; fp-preload: 0; fp-transparent: 1; fp-proportional: 0"
fp-title="Study Main Light          ON" height="45"
src="../images/button15D.gif" style="border: 0"
width="272"></a>    
                <a id="smc4b" href="steve.php?study_main_light_off=1">
                <img id="img1025" alt="OFF" fp-style="fp-btn: Embossed
Rectangle 6; fp-font-size: 14; fp-img-hover: 0; fp-img-press: 0; fp-
preload: 0; fp-transparent: 1; fp-proportional: 0" fp-title="OFF"
height="45" src="../images/button161.gif" style="border: 0"
width="100"></a></td>
          <td style="width: 59px"> </td>
       </tr>
   </table>
   <p> </p>
   <p> </p>
</div>
</div>
</body>
</html>
```

File: state.php

```
<!DOCTYPE HTML>
<html>
<head>
<title>HC-State</title>

<!--
File name:
   state.php
Author:
   Steve McClure
Book:
   Designing Embedded Sytems
Description:
   This file is used by the Home Control / Security application
   to build the State Web page.
 -->

<link href="../css/reset.css" media="screen" rel="stylesheet"
type="text/css">
<link href="../css/styles.css" media="screen" rel="stylesheet"
type="text/css">

<script type="text/javascript" src="../js/calendar2.js"> </script>

<style type="text/css">
.auto-style1 {
   color: #FFFFFF;
}
.auto-style2 {
   text-align: center;
}
.auto-style3 {
   font-size: small;
}
</style>
</head>

<body onload="startTime()">
<div style="width:980px; margin: 0 auto; overflow: hidden;">
<div id="wrapper" class="auto-style2">
   <div id="navigation">
       <div id="navigation_picture">
          <img alt="images/HouseFront1.jpg" height="200"
src="../images/HouseFront1.jpg" width="900">
       </div>
       <div id="navigation_time">
          <p>Date and Time</p>
       </div>
       <div id="navigation_heading">
```

```
          <p><span class="auto-style1">Navigation</span>
          <span class="auto-style1">- State</span></p>
       </div>

       <div id="navigation_links">
         <ul>
           <li><a href="security.php">Security</a></li>
           <li><a href="master.php">Master</a></li>
           <li><a href="lounge.php">Lounge</a></li>
           <li><a href="kitchen">Kitchen</a></li>
           <li><a href="family.php">Family</a></li>
           <li><a href="steve.php">Steve</a></li>
           <li><a href="state.php">State</a></li>
           <li><a href="events.php">Events</a></li>

         </ul>
       </div>
    </div>

<div id="state_stuff">
<p class="auto-style3">    </p>

<form action="state.php" method="post">

<button name="house_code_selection" value=1>HOUSE:  A</button>
      
<button name="house_code_selection" value=2>B</button>
      
<button name="house_code_selection" value=3>C</button>
      
<button name="house_code_selection" value=4>D</button>
      
<button name="house_code_selection" value=5>E</button>
      
<button name="house_code_selection" value=6>F</button>
      
<button name="house_code_selection" value=7>G</button>
      
<button name="house_code_selection" value=8>H</button>
      
<button name="house_code_selection" value=9>I</button>
      
<button name="house_code_selection" value=10>J</button>
      
<button name="house_code_selection" value=11>K</button>
      
<button name="house_code_selection" value=12>L</button>
      
<button name="house_code_selection" value=13>M</button>
      
<button name="house_code_selection" value=14>N</button>
      
```

```
<button name="house_code_selection" value=15>O</button>
      
<button name="house_code_selection" value=16>P</button>
</form>
<p class="auto-style3"> </p>
</div>

    <div id="general_text">
     <?php

     // Connect to the MySQL Database Environment
     //==============================================
      $con = mysql_connect("192.168.1.176","steve","william");    // This
works on Archimedes

      if (!$con)
      {
        die('Could not connect as: ' . mysql_error());
        echo "<br />";
      }



    // Access the 'system_control' database
    //====================================
      mysql_select_db("system_control", $con);

     ?>

    </div>
</div>

<div id="state_list">
     <?php
      $selection = $_POST["house_code_selection"];

      if ($selection == 0)
        $selection = 1;

      $result = mysql_query("SELECT * FROM house_code_states");

      while($row = mysql_fetch_array($result))
        {
         if ($selection== $row['house'])
         {
           if ($row['description'] == "No Description")
             continue;

           echo "<br />";
           echo " ";

           if ($row['timestamp'] == "No Time")
```

```
        echo "----/--/-- --:--:-- ";
    else
        echo $row['timestamp'] . " ";

    if ($row['type'] == 0)
        echo " Sensor ";
    elseif ($row['type'] == 1)
        echo " Device ";
    else
        echo " ------ ";

    switch ($row['house'])
    {
      case  1: echo "A"; break;
      case  2: echo "B"; break;
      case  3: echo "C"; break;
      case  4: echo "D"; break;
      case  5: echo "E"; break;
      case  6: echo "F"; break;
      case  7: echo "G"; break;
      case  8: echo "H"; break;
      case  9: echo "I"; break;
      case 10: echo "J"; break;
      case 11: echo "K"; break;
      case 12: echo "L"; break;
      case 13: echo "M"; break;
      case 14: echo "N"; break;
      case 15: echo "O"; break;
      case 16: echo "P"; break;
      default: echo "Invalid";
    }

    if ($row['unit'] < 10)
      echo "0" . $row['unit'];
     else
      echo $row['unit'];

    if ($row['state'] == 0)
        echo " OFF ";
    elseif ($row['state'] == 1)
    {
        echo " ON ";
          echo " ";
    }
    else
        echo " --- ";

    echo $row['description'];
  }
}
```

```
        for ($index = 0; $index < 16; $index++)
        {
           echo "<br />";
        }

     // Close the 'home_control' database
     //===================================
      mysql_close($con);

      ?>
</div>
</div>
</body>

</html>
```

File: events.php

```
<!DOCTYPE HTML>
<html>
<head>
<meta http-equiv="refresh" content="60">
<title>HC-Events</title>

<!--
File name:
   events.php
Author:
   Steve McClure
Book:
   Designing Embedded Sytems
Description:
   This file is used by the Home Control / Security application
   to build the Events Web page.  This page is automatically
   refreshed every 60 seconds.
 -->

<link href="../css/reset.css" media="screen" rel="stylesheet"
type="text/css">
<link href="../css/styles.css" media="screen" rel="stylesheet"
type="text/css">

<script type="text/javascript" src="../js/calendar2.js"> </script>

<style type="text/css">
.auto-style1 {
   color: #FFFFFF;
}
.auto-style6 {
   font-size: small;
}

</style>
</head>

<body onload="startTime()">
<div style="width:980px; margin: 0 auto; overflow: hidden;">
<div id="wrapper">
   <div id="navigation">
      <div id="navigation_picture">
         <img alt="images/HouseFront1.jpg" height="200"
src="../images/HouseFront1.jpg" width="900">
      </div>
      <div id="navigation_time">
         <p>Date and Time</p>
      </div>
      <div id="navigation_heading">
```

```
            <p><span class="auto-style1">Navigation</span>
            <span class="auto-style1">- Events</span></p>
        </div>

        <div id="navigation_links">
          <ul>
            <li><a href="security.php">Security</a></li>
            <li><a href="master.php">Master</a></li>
            <li><a href="lounge.php">Lounge</a></li>
            <li><a href="kitchen">Kitchen</a></li>
            <li><a href="family.php">Family</a></li>
            <li><a href="steve.php">Steve</a></li>
            <li><a href="state.php">State</a></li>
            <li><a href="events.php">Events</a></li>
          </ul>
        </div>
    </div>

  <div id="main_stuff">
    <p class="auto-style6"> </p>
    <p><strong>         This
screen displays the current events list:</strong></p>
      <p class="auto-style6"> </p>
  </div>
</div>

<div id="event_list">
    <?php

    // Connect to the MySQL Database Environment
    //=============================================
     $con = mysql_connect("192.168.1.176","steve","william");    // This
works on Archimedes

     if (!$con)
     {
       die('Could not connect as: ' . mysql_error());
       echo "<br />";
     }


   // Access the 'system_control' database
   //====================================
     mysql_select_db("system_control", $con);

    $result = mysql_query("SELECT * FROM house_code_events ORDER BY
timestamp, description ASC");

    while($row = mysql_fetch_array($result))
      {

        echo "<br />";
```

```
  echo " ";
  echo $row['timestamp'];
  echo " ";


  if ($row['type'] == 0)
    echo " Sensor ";
  elseif ($row['type'] == 1)
    echo " Device ";
  else
    echo " ------ ";


  switch ($row['house'])
    {
      case  1: echo "A"; break;
      case  2: echo "B"; break;
      case  3: echo "C"; break;
      case  4: echo "D"; break;
      case  5: echo "E"; break;
      case  6: echo "F"; break;
      case  7: echo "G"; break;
      case  8: echo "H"; break;
      case  9: echo "I"; break;
      case 10: echo "J"; break;
      case 11: echo "K"; break;
      case 12: echo "L"; break;
      case 13: echo "M"; break;
      case 14: echo "N"; break;
      case 15: echo "O"; break;
      case 16: echo "P"; break;
      default: echo "Invalid";
    }

  if ($row['unit'] < 10)
     echo "0" . $row['unit'];
   else
     echo $row['unit'];

  if ($row['state'] == 0)
    echo " OFF ";
  elseif ($row['state'] == 1)
    {
       echo " ON ";
         echo " ";
    }
  else
    echo " --- ";

  echo $row['description'];
}
```

```
        for ($index = 0; $index < 16; $index++)
        {
           echo "<br />";
        }

    // Close the 'home_control' database
    //====================================
      mysql_close($con);

     ?>

</div>
</div>
</body>

</html>
```

File: system.php

```
<!DOCTYPE HTML>
<html>
<head>
<meta http-equiv="refresh" content="60; url=security.php">

<!--
File name:
   system.php
Author:
   Steve McClure
Book:
   Designing Embedded Sytems
Description:
   This file is used by the Home Control / Security application
   to build the System Web page.
 -->

<title>HC-System</title>
<link href="../css/reset.css" rel="stylesheet" type="text/css"
media="screen">
<link href="../css/styles.css" rel="stylesheet" type="text/css"
media="screen">

<script type="text/javascript" src="../js/calendar2.js"> </script>

<style type="text/css">
.auto-style1 {
   color:#FFFFFF;
}
.auto-style2 {
   text-align: center;
}
.auto-style3 {
   font-size: large;
}
.auto-style6 {
   font-size: small;
}
</style>

<script type="text/javascript">
<!--
function FP_preloadImgs() {//v1.0
 var d=document,a=arguments; if(!d.FP_imgs) d.FP_imgs=new Array();
 for(var i=0; i<a.length; i++) { d.FP_imgs[i]=new Image;
d.FP_imgs[i].src=a[i]; }
}
// -->
</script>
```

```
</head>

<body
onload="FP_preloadImgs(/*url*/'button22.jpg',/*url*/'button23.jpg',/*url*
/'button58.jpg',/*url*/'button59.jpg'); startTime()">
<div style="width:980px; margin: 0 auto; overflow: hidden;">
<div id="wrapper">

  <div id="navigation">
    <div id="navigation_picture">
      <img src="../images/HouseFront1.jpg" height="200" width="900" />
    </div>

    <div id="navigation_heading">
      <p><span class="auto-style1">Navigation</span> <span class="auto-
style1">- System</span></p>
    </div>

    <div id="navigation_time">
      <p>Date and Time</p>
    </div>


    <div id="navigation_links">
      <ul>
        <li><a href="security.php">Security</a></li>
        <li><a href="master.php">Master</a></li>
        <li><a href="lounge.php">Lounge</a></li>
        <li><a href="kitchen">Kitchen</a></li>
        <li><a href="family.php">Family</a></li>
        <li><a href="steve.php">Steve</a></li>
        <li><a href="state.php">State</a></li>
        <li><a href="events.php">Events</a></li>
     </ul>
    </div>
  </div>

    <?php

    // Connect to the MySQL Database Environment
    //============================================
     $con = mysql_connect("192.168.1.176","steve","william");

     if (!$con)
     {
       die('Could not connect as: ' . mysql_error());
       echo "<br />";
     }


   // Access the 'system_control' database
   //====================================
```

```
     mysql_select_db("system_control", $con);

    // Insert data into the 'house_state' table
    //==========================================

    if ($_GET["security_off"] == 1)
    {
        mysql_query ("UPDATE house_state SET security = 0, security_delay
= 0");
     }


    if ($_GET["security_on"] == 1)
     {
         $result = mysql_query("SELECT * FROM house_state");

         $row = mysql_fetch_array($result);

        // Enter SECURITY mode ONLY if we are currently in SECURITY OFF
mode
         if ($row['security'] == 0)
        {
          // Force sleep mode off
          mysql_query ("UPDATE house_state SET sleep = 0, sleep_delay = 0,
security = 1, security_delay = 0");
        }
     }



    // Insert data into the 'house_state' table
    //==========================================

    if ($_GET["sleep_off"] == 1)
    {
        mysql_query ("UPDATE house_state SET sleep = 0, sleep_delay = 0");
     }


    if ($_GET["sleep_on"] == 1)
     {
         $result = mysql_query("SELECT * FROM house_state");

         $row = mysql_fetch_array($result);

        // Enter SLEEP mode ONLY if we are currently in SECURITY OFF mode
         if ($row['security'] == 0)
        {
           // Initiate sleep
            mysql_query ("UPDATE house_state SET sleep = 1, sleep_delay =
0");
        }
```

```
    }


   // Insert data into the 'house_code_events' table
   //====================================================

    // If Garage Front Light ON button pressed
   if ($_GET["garage_front_light_on"] == 1)
   {
      mysql_query ("INSERT INTO house_code_events (house, unit, state,
timeout) VALUES (7, 5, 1, 777)");
    }

    // If Garage Front Light OFF button pressed
    if ($_GET["garage_front_light_off"] == 1)
   {
      mysql_query ("INSERT INTO house_code_events (house, unit, state,
timeout) VALUES (7, 5, 0, 777)");
    }


    // If Garage Back Light ON button pressed
   if ($_GET["garage_back_light_on"] == 1)
   {
      mysql_query ("INSERT INTO house_code_events (house, unit, state,
timeout) VALUES (7, 1, 1, 777)");
    }

    // If Garage Back Light OFF button pressed
    if ($_GET["garage_back_light_off"] == 1)
   {
      mysql_query ("INSERT INTO house_code_events (house, unit, state,
timeout) VALUES (7, 1, 0, 777)");
    }


    // If Porch Light ON button pressed
   if ($_GET["porch_light_on"] == 1)
   {
      mysql_query ("INSERT INTO house_code_events (house, unit, state,
timeout) VALUES (7, 6, 1, 777)");
    }

    // If Porch Light OFF button pressed
    if ($_GET["porch_light_off"] == 1)
   {
      mysql_query ("INSERT INTO house_code_events (house, unit, state,
timeout) VALUES (7, 6, 0, 777)");
    }
```

```
    // If Varanda Light ON button pressed
   if ($_GET["varanda_light_on"] == 1)
   {
      mysql_query ("INSERT INTO house_code_events (house, unit, state,
timeout) VALUES (7, 2, 1, 777)");
    }


    // If Varanda Light OFF button pressed
   if ($_GET["varanda_light_off"] == 1)
   {
      mysql_query ("INSERT INTO house_code_events (house, unit, state,
timeout) VALUES (7, 2, 0, 777)");
    }


    // If Master Bedroom Outside Light ON button pressed
   if ($_GET["master_outside_light_on"] == 1)
   {
      mysql_query ("INSERT INTO house_code_events (house, unit, state,
timeout) VALUES (7, 4, 1, 777)");
    }

    // If Master Bedroom Outside Light OFF button pressed
    if ($_GET["master_outside_light_off"] == 1)
   {
      mysql_query ("INSERT INTO house_code_events (house, unit, state,
timeout) VALUES (7, 4, 0, 777)");
    }


    // If Dining Room Outside Light ON button pressed
   if ($_GET["dining_outside_light_on"] == 1)
   {
      mysql_query ("INSERT INTO house_code_events (house, unit, state,
timeout) VALUES (7, 3, 1, 777)");
    }

    // If Dining Room Outside Light OFF button pressed
   if ($_GET["dining_outside_light_off"] == 1)
   {
      mysql_query ("INSERT INTO house_code_events (house, unit, state,
timeout) VALUES (7, 3, 0, 777)");
    }

    ?>


  <div id="main_stuff">
     <?php
    $result = mysql_query("SELECT * FROM house_state");
```

```
$row = mysql_fetch_array($result);

 ?><p class="auto-style6">  </p><?php
echo "         ";
echo "This screen allows you to control the System Parameters:";
echo "   ";

if ($row['security'] == 0)
{
  echo "SECURITY OFF - ";
}
else
{
  echo "SECURITY ACTIVE - ";
}


if ($row['sleep'] == 0)
{
  echo "SLEEP OFF";
 }
else
{
  echo "SLEEP ACTIVE";
}

 ?><p class="auto-style6">  </p><?php

// Close the 'home_control' database
//====================================
 mysql_close($con);

 ?>
</div>
</div>


<div id="key_background">
<!-- Control the buttons -->
   <p>  <span class="auto-style3"> </span></p>
   <p class="auto-style2"> <a
href="system.php?garage_front_light_on=1"><img id="img20" alt="Garage
Front Light      ON" fp-style="fp-btn: Embossed Rectangle 6; fp-font-size:
14; fp-img-hover: 0; fp-img-press: 0; fp-preload: 0; fp-transparent: 1;
fp-proportional: 0" fp-title="Garage Front Light      ON" height="45"
src="../images/button17C.gif" style="border: 0"
width="244"></a>       
   <a href="system.php?garage_front_light_off=1">
   <img id="img21" alt="OFF" fp-style="fp-btn: Embossed Rectangle 6; fp-
font-size: 14; fp-img-hover: 0; fp-img-press: 0; fp-preload: 0; fp-
transparent: 1; fp-proportional: 0" fp-title="OFF" height="45"
```

```
src="../images/button17F.gif" style="border: 0"
width="100"></a>         &nb
sp;           &nbs
p;    
   <a href="system.php?garage_back_light_on=1">
   <img id="img22" alt="Garage Back Light       ON" fp-style="fp-btn:
Embossed Rectangle 6; fp-font-size: 14; fp-img-hover: 0; fp-img-press: 0;
fp-preload: 0; fp-transparent: 1; fp-proportional: 0" fp-title="Garage
Back Light       ON" height="45" src="../images/button184.gif"
style="border: 0"
width="244"></a>       
   <a href="system.php?garage_back_light_off=1">
   <img id="img23" alt="OFF" fp-style="fp-btn: Embossed Rectangle 6; fp-
font-size: 14; fp-img-hover: 0; fp-img-press: 0; fp-preload: 0; fp-
transparent: 1; fp-proportional: 0" fp-title="OFF" height="45"
src="../images/button187.gif" style="border: 0" width="100"></a> 
</p>
   <p> </p>
   <p class="auto-style2"> <a
href="system.php?porch_light_on=1"><img id="img24" alt="Porch Light
ON" fp-style="fp-btn: Embossed Rectangle 6; fp-font-size: 14; fp-img-
hover: 0; fp-img-press: 0; fp-preload: 0; fp-transparent: 1; fp-
proportional: 0" fp-title="Porch Light                    ON" height="45"
src="../images/button17D.gif" style="border: 0"
width="244"></a>       
   <a href="system.php?porch_light_off=1">
   <img id="img25" alt="OFF" fp-style="fp-btn: Embossed Rectangle 6; fp-
font-size: 14; fp-img-hover: 0; fp-img-press: 0; fp-preload: 0; fp-
transparent: 1; fp-proportional: 0" fp-title="OFF" height="45"
src="../images/button180.gif" style="border: 0"
width="100"></a>         &nb
sp;           &nbs
p;    
   <a href="system.php?varanda_light_on=1">
   <img id="img26" alt="Varanda Light            ON" fp-style="fp-btn:
Embossed Rectangle 6; fp-font-size: 14; fp-img-hover: 0; fp-img-press: 0;
fp-preload: 0; fp-transparent: 1; fp-proportional: 0" fp-title="Varanda
Light            ON" height="45" src="../images/button185.gif"
style="border: 0"
width="244"></a>       
   <a href="system.php?varanda_light_off=1">
   <img id="img27" alt="OFF" fp-style="fp-btn: Embossed Rectangle 6; fp-
font-size: 14; fp-img-hover: 0; fp-img-press: 0; fp-preload: 0; fp-
transparent: 1; fp-proportional: 0" fp-title="OFF" height="45"
src="../images/button188.gif" style="border: 0" width="100"></a> 
</p>
   <p> </p>
   <p class="auto-style2"> <a
href="system.php?master_outside_light_on=1"><img id="img28" alt="Master
Outside Light   ON" fp-style="fp-btn: Embossed Rectangle 6; fp-font-size:
14; fp-img-hover: 0; fp-img-press: 0; fp-preload: 0; fp-transparent: 1;
fp-proportional: 0" fp-title="Master Outside Light   ON" height="45"
```

```
src="../images/button17E.gif" style="border: 0"
width="244"></a>       
    <a href="system.php?master_outside_light_off=1">
    <img id="img29" alt="OFF" fp-style="fp-btn: Embossed Rectangle 6; fp-
font-size: 14; fp-img-hover: 0; fp-img-press: 0; fp-preload: 0; fp-
transparent: 1; fp-proportional: 0" fp-title="OFF" height="45"
src="../images/button181.gif" style="border: 0"
width="100"></a>         &nb
sp;           &nbs
p;    
    <a href="system.php?dining_outside_light_on=1">
    <img id="img30" alt="Dining Outside Light    ON" fp-style="fp-btn:
Embossed Rectangle 6; fp-font-size: 14; fp-img-hover: 0; fp-img-press: 0;
fp-preload: 0; fp-transparent: 1; fp-proportional: 0" fp-title="Dining
Outside Light    ON" height="45" src="../images/button186.gif"
style="border: 0"
width="244"></a>       
    <a href="system.php?dining_outside_light_off=1">
    <img id="img31" alt="OFF" fp-style="fp-btn: Embossed Rectangle 6; fp-
font-size: 14; fp-img-hover: 0; fp-img-press: 0; fp-preload: 0; fp-
transparent: 1; fp-proportional: 0" fp-title="OFF" height="45"
src="../images/button189.gif" style="border: 0" width="100"></a> 
</p>
    <p><span class="auto-style3"> </span></p>
    <p class="auto-style2">  <a
href="system.php?security_on=1"><img id="img33" alt="SECURITY  ON" fp-
style="fp-btn: Embossed Rectangle 8; fp-font-size: 14; fp-img-hover: 0;
fp-img-press: 0; fp-preload: 0; fp-transparent: 1; fp-proportional: 0"
fp-title="SECURITY  ON" height="45" src="../images/button182.gif"
style="border: 0"
width="151"></a>        
    <a href="system.php?security_off=1">
    <img id="img32" alt="SECURITY  OFF" fp-style="fp-btn: Embossed
Rectangle 2; fp-font-size: 14; fp-img-hover: 0; fp-img-press: 0; fp-
preload: 0; fp-transparent: 1; fp-proportional: 0" fp-title="SECURITY
OFF" height="45" src="../images/button183.gif" style="border: 0"
width="177"></a>     
            &
nbsp;         
    <a href="system.php?sleep_on=1">
    <img id="img34" alt="SLEEP  ON" fp-style="fp-btn: Embossed Rectangle
1; fp-font-size: 14; fp-img-hover: 0; fp-img-press: 0; fp-preload: 0; fp-
transparent: 1; fp-proportional: 0" fp-title="SLEEP  ON" height="45"
src="../images/button18A.gif" style="border: 0"
width="163"></a>       
    <a href="system.php?sleep_off=1">
    <img id="img35" alt="SLEEP  OFF" fp-style="fp-btn: Embossed Rectangle
4; fp-font-size: 14; fp-img-hover: 0; fp-img-press: 0; fp-preload: 0; fp-
transparent: 1; fp-proportional: 0" fp-title="SLEEP  OFF" height="45"
src="../images/button18B.gif" style="border: 0"
width="163"></a>   </p>
    <p> </p>
```

```
   <p> </p>
</div>
</div>

</body>
</html>
```

File: hc_literals.h

```
//*****************************************************************************
//  Author: Stephen W. McClure
//    Date: March 2014
// Project: Designing Embedded Systems [Book]
//
//*****************************************************************************
// Purpose:
//
// This program provides a home control application.
//
//*****************************************************************************
//
// File Name: hc_literals.c
//
// This file includes all the common literal definitions.
//*****************************************************************************

#ifndef HC_LITERALS
#define HC_LITERALS

// Serial Interface
//#define BAUDRATE B9600
#define  SERIAL_PORT_0     "/dev/ttyS0"
#define  SERIAL_PORT_1     "/dev/ttyS1"
#define  _POSIX_SOURCE     1 /* POSIX compliant source */

#define  BAUDRATE      B4800



// Literal Definitions
#define  Uint8   unsigned char
#define  Uint16  unsigned int

#define  INVALID      0
#define  VALID        1

#define  FAILURE      0
#define  SUCCESS      1

#define  X10_OFF      0
#define  X10_ON       1


// Day Name Literals
#define  SUNDAY       0
#define  MONDAY       1
#define  TUESDAY      2
#define  WEDNESDAY    3
#define  THURSDAY     4
#define  FRIDAY       5
#define  SATURDAY     6
```

```
// Calender Month Literals
#define  JANUARY       1
#define  FEBRUARY      2
#define  MARCH         3
#define  APRIL         4
#define  MAY           5
#define  JUNE          6
#define  JULY          7
#define  AUGUST        8
#define  SEPTEMBER     9
#define  OCTOBER      10
#define  NOVEMBER     11
#define  DECEMBER     12


// Days in year
#define  DAYS_IN_STANDARD_YEAR        365
#define   DAYS_IN_LEAP_YEAR           366


// Sensor/Device Literals
#define  SENSOR        0
#define  DEVICE        1

#define  OFF           0
#define  ON            1


// Main Loop Execution Periodic Sleep
#define  EXECUTION_SLEEP_MS       333   // Execute loop delay in milliseconds


#define  HS_NORMAL_MODE              0
#define  HS_NORMAL_MODE_TRIGGER      1
#define  HS_TV_MODE                  2
#define  HS_TV_MODE_TRIGGER          3

#define  HS_SECURITY                 0
#define  HS_SECURITY_DELAY           1
#define  HS_SLEEP                    2
#define  HS_SLEEP_DELAY              3
#define  HS_FAMILY_LIGHTS            4
#define  HS_STEVE_LIGHTS             5
#define  HS_GO_TO_BED                6
#define  HS_MASTER_WATCH_TV          7

#define  HCE_HOUSE                   0
#define  HCE_UNIT                    1
#define  HCE_TYPE                    2
#define  HCE_STATE                   3
#define  HCE_TIMESTAMP               4
#define  HCE_TIMEOUT                 5
#define  HCE_DESCRIPTION             6
```

```
// Security Mode Literals
#define  SECURITY_MODE_INACTIVE     0
#define  SECURITY_MODE_INITIATED    1
#define  SECURITY_MODE_DELAY        2
#define  SECURITY_MODE_ACTIVE       3


// Sleep Mode Literals
#define  SLEEP_MODE_INACTIVE        0
#define  SLEEP_MODE_INITIATED       1
#define  SLEEP_MODE_DELAY           2
#define  SLEEP_MODE_ACTIVE          3


// Time Offsets
#define  ZERO_PRESENCE_TIMEOUT    ((long int) 0)
#define  MAX_PRESENCE       1800    //  30 minutes (in seconds)

#define  DELAY_EXPIRED         0
#define  ACTIVATE_NOW          0    //    0 seconds
#define  OFFSET_ZERO           0    //    0 seconds

#define  OFFSET_3SEC           3    //    3 seconds
#define  OFFSET_5SEC           5    //    5 seconds
#define  OFFSET_7SEC           7    //    7 seconds
#define  OFFSET_10SEC         10    //   10 seconds
#define  OFFSET_13SEC         13    //   13 seconds
#define  OFFSET_15SEC         15    //   15 seconds
#define  OFFSET_20SEC         20    //   20 seconds
#define  OFFSET_30SEC         30    //   30 seconds
#define  OFFSET_40SEC         40    //   40 seconds
#define  OFFSET_1MIN    ( 1 * 60)   //   60 seconds
#define  OFFSET_1MIN30SEC    (90)   //   90 seconds
#define  OFFSET_2MIN    ( 2 * 60)   //  120 seconds
#define  OFFSET_3MIN    ( 3 * 60)   //  180 seconds
#define  OFFSET_5MIN    ( 5 * 60)   //  300 seconds
#define  OFFSET_10MIN    (10 * 60)  //  600 seconds
#define  OFFSET_13MIN    (13 * 60)  //  780 seconds
#define  OFFSET_15MIN    (15 * 60)  //  900 seconds
#define  OFFSET_20MIN    (20 * 60)  // 1200 seconds
#define  OFFSET_30MIN    (30 * 60)  // 1800 seconds
#define  OFFSET_35MIN    (35 * 60)  // 1800 seconds
#define  OFFSET_40MIN    (40 * 60)  // 2400 seconds
#define  OFFSET_45MIN    (45 * 60)  // 2700 seconds
#define  OFFSET_55MIN    (55 * 60)  // 3000 seconds
#define  OFFSET_59MIN    (59 * 60)  // 3540 seconds
#define  OFFSET_60MIN    (60 * 60)  // 3600 seconds

#define  OFFSET_1HR          ( 1 * 60 * 60)
#define  OFFSET_2HRS         ( 2 * 60 * 60)
#define  OFFSET_3HRS         ( 3 * 60 * 60)
#define  OFFSET_4HRS         ( 4 * 60 * 60)
#define  OFFSET_9HRS         ( 9 * 60 * 60)
#define  OFFSET_12HRS        (12 * 60 * 60)
#define  OFFSET_21HRS        (21 * 60 * 60)
#define  OFFSET_22HRS        (22 * 60 * 60)
#define  OFFSET_23HRS        (23 * 60 * 60)
#define  OFFSET_23HRS_20MIN  ((23 * 60 * 60) + (20 * 60))
```

```
#define  OFFSET_23HRS_40MIN  ((23 * 60 * 60) + (40 * 60))
#define  OFFSET_23HRS_45MIN  ((23 * 60 * 60) + (45 * 60))
#define  OFFSET_23HRS_30MIN  ((23 * 60 * 60) + (30 * 60))
#define  OFFSET_23HRS_58MIN  ((23 * 60 * 60) + (58 * 60))
#define  OFFSET_23HRS_59MIN  ((23 * 60 * 60) + (59 * 60))
#define  OFFSET_24HRS         (24 * 60 * 60)


// EMAIL Definitions
#define  EMAIL_ACTIVE     // Comment definition to disable email feature

#define  MAX_EMAIL_HEADER_SIZE       100
#define  MAX_EMAIL_MESSAGE_SIZE      800

#define  EMAIL_SENDER_ADDRESS        "smc_security@cox.net"
#define  EMAIL_RECEIVER_ADDRESS      "smc_security@cox.net"
#define  EMAIL_CC_ADDRESS     ""

#define  SERVICE_PROVIDER_SMTP       "smtp.cox.net"

// Picture file locations
#define  STUDY_PICTURE_FILE          "/home/orion/Projects/Execs/study.jpg"

// General Definitions
#define  ACTIVE_MODE                 (sleep_mode == FALSE)


#endif
```

File: hc_typedefs.h

```
//************************************************************************
//  Author: Stephen W. McClure
//    Date: March 2014
// Project: Designing Embedded Systems [Book]
//
//************************************************************************
// Purpose:
//
// This program provides a home control application.
//
//************************************************************************
//
// File Name: hc_typedefs.c
//
// This file includes all the common typedef definitions.
//************************************************************************

#ifndef HC_TYPEDEFS
#define HC_TYPEDEFS

typedef struct
{
    Uint16  hour;
    Uint16  minute;
}
TIME_OF_DAY;


typedef struct
{
    char    name[255];
    Uint16  index;
}
    HOUSE_STATE_PARAMETER;


typedef struct
{
    Uint8  house_code;
    Uint8  unit_code;
}
    X10_CODE;


typedef struct
{
    X10_CODE  x10;
    Uint8     type;
    Uint8     state;
    char      description[255];
}
    X10_DEVICE;

#endif
```

File: hc_publics.h

```
//****************************************************************************
//  Author: Stephen W. McClure
//    Date: March 2014
// Project: Designing Embedded Systems [Book]
//
//****************************************************************************
// Purpose:
//
// This program provides a home control application.
//
//
//****************************************************************************
//
// File Name: hc_publics.h
//
// This file includes all the common variable definitions.
//****************************************************************************

#ifndef HC_PUBLICS
#define HC_PUBLICS


// InterruptControl exit flag
static int exit_flag = 0;

// Device reset startup condition
Uint8   device_reset = FALSE;


// MySQL Database Variables
MYSQL  *conn1;
MYSQL  *conn2;


// Global variables
int fd; /* File descriptor for the port */


// Setup serial interface
struct termios new_options;
struct termios old_options;


// House State Table Parameter Names
HOUSE_STATE_PARAMETER  house_state_parameter [ ] =
        { { "security",             0 },
          { "security_delay",       1 },
          { "sleep",                2 },
          { "sleep_delay",          3 },
          { "family_lights",        4 },
          { "steve_lights",         5 },
          { "go_to_bed",            6 },
          { "master_watch_tv",      7 } };
```

```
// Common Devices                                   X10              Sensor/
//                                                  Home, Unit       Device    State
Description
X10_DEVICE  steve_bedroom_sensor          = {{ 1,      2},    SENSOR,   OFF,
"Steve Room"};
X10_DEVICE  garage_z71_sensor             = {{ 1,      3},    SENSOR,   OFF,
"Garage (Z71)"};
X10_DEVICE  mini_hallway_sensor           = {{ 1,      5},    SENSOR,   OFF,
"Mini Hallway"};
X10_DEVICE  study_sensor                  = {{ 1,      7},    SENSOR,   OFF,
"Study"};
X10_DEVICE  master_bedroom_sensor         = {{ 1,      9},    SENSOR,   OFF,
"Master Bedroom"};
X10_DEVICE  familyroom_sensor             = {{ 1,     11},    SENSOR,   OFF,
"Family Room"};
X10_DEVICE  inside_front_door_sensor      = {{ 1,     13},    SENSOR,   OFF,
"Inside Front Door"};
X10_DEVICE  guest_shower_sensor           = {{ 1,     15},    SENSOR,   OFF,
"Guest Shower"};

X10_DEVICE  garage_bike_sensor            = {{ 2,      3},    SENSOR,   OFF,
"Garage (Bike)"};
X10_DEVICE  main_hallway_sensor           = {{ 2,      5},    SENSOR,   OFF,
"Main Hallway"};
X10_DEVICE  lounge_hallway_sensor         = {{ 2,      7},    SENSOR,   OFF,
"Lounge Hallway"};
X10_DEVICE  master_hallway_sensor         = {{ 2,      9},    SENSOR,   OFF,
"Master Hallway"};
X10_DEVICE  pantry_sensor                 = {{ 2,     11},    SENSOR,   OFF,
"Pantry"};
X10_DEVICE  cloakroom_sensor              = {{ 2,     13},    SENSOR,   OFF,
"Cloakroom"};

X10_DEVICE  kitchen_sensor                = {{ 3,      3},    SENSOR,   OFF,
"Kitchen"};
X10_DEVICE  counter_fridge_sensor         = {{ 3,      5},    SENSOR,   OFF,
"Counter Fridge"};
X10_DEVICE  counter_cooktop_left_sensor   = {{ 3,      7},    SENSOR,   OFF,
"Counter Cooktop Left"};
X10_DEVICE  counter_cooktop_right_sensor  = {{ 3,      9},    SENSOR,   OFF,
"Counter Cooktop Right"};
X10_DEVICE  kitchen_nook_sensor           = {{ 3,     11},    SENSOR,   OFF,
"Kitchen Nook"};
X10_DEVICE  master_bedroom_closet_sensor  = {{ 3,     13},    SENSOR,   OFF,
"Master Bedroom Closet"};
X10_DEVICE  garage_fridge_sensor          = {{ 3,     15},    SENSOR,   OFF,
"Garage (Fridge)"};

X10_DEVICE  light_sensor                  = {{ 4,      1},    SENSOR,   OFF,
"Light Detector"};
X10_DEVICE  kitchen_light                 = {{ 4,      3},    DEVICE,   OFF,
"Kitchen Lights"};
X10_DEVICE  kitchen_nook_light            = {{ 4,      4},    DEVICE,   OFF,
"Kitchen Nook Table light"};
X10_DEVICE  kitchen_counter_light         = {{ 4,      5},    DEVICE,   OFF,
"Kitchen Counter Lights"};
X10_DEVICE  kitchen_sink_light            = {{ 4,      6},    DEVICE,   OFF,
"Kitchen Sink Light"};
```

```
X10_DEVICE  garage_light                 = {{ 4,    7},   DEVICE,   OFF,
"Garage Lights"};
X10_DEVICE  guest_bathroom_light         = {{ 4,    8},   DEVICE,   OFF,
"Guest Bathroom Light"};
X10_DEVICE  security_alarm_siren         = {{ 4,    9},   DEVICE,   OFF,
"Security Alarm Siren"};
X10_DEVICE  laundry_sensor               = {{ 4,   11},   SENSOR,   OFF,
"Laundry"};
X10_DEVICE  common_washroom_sensor       = {{ 4,   13},   SENSOR,   OFF,
"Common Washroom"};
X10_DEVICE  front_porch_sensor           = {{ 4,   15},   SENSOR,   OFF,
"Front Porch"};

X10_DEVICE  steve_bedroom_reading_light  = {{ 5,    1},   DEVICE,   OFF,
"Steve Bedroom Reading Light"};
X10_DEVICE  steve_bedroom_window_light   = {{ 5,    2},   DEVICE,   OFF,
"Steve Bedroom Window Light"};
X10_DEVICE  steve_bedroom_wall_light     = {{ 5,    3},   DEVICE,   OFF,
"Steve Bedroom Wall lights"};
X10_DEVICE  steve_bedroom_ceiling_light  = {{ 5,    4},   DEVICE,   OFF,
"Steve Bedroom Ceiling Lights"};
X10_DEVICE  mini_hallway_light           = {{ 5,    5},   DEVICE,   OFF,
"Mini-Hall Light"};
X10_DEVICE  main_hallway_light           = {{ 5,    6},   DEVICE,   OFF,
"Main-Hall Lights"};
X10_DEVICE  common_washroom_light        = {{ 5,    7},   DEVICE,   OFF,
"Washroom Vanity Lights"};
X10_DEVICE  common_washroom_flight       = {{ 5,    8},   DEVICE,   OFF,
"Washroom Flourescent Light"};
X10_DEVICE  common_bathroom_sensor       = {{ 5,    9},   SENSOR,   OFF,
"Common Bathroom"};
X10_DEVICE  guest_bathroom_sensor        = {{ 5,   11},   SENSOR,   OFF,
"Guest Bathroom"};
X10_DEVICE  guest_bedroom_door_sensor    = {{ 5,   13},   SENSOR,   OFF,
"Guest Bedroom Door"};
X10_DEVICE  guest_bedroom_window_sensor  = {{ 5,   15},   SENSOR,   OFF,
"Guest Bedroom Window"};


X10_DEVICE  garage_back_outside_light    = {{ 7,    1},   DEVICE,   OFF,
"Outside Garage Back Door Light"};
X10_DEVICE  familyroom_outside_light     = {{ 7,    2},   DEVICE,   OFF,
"Outside Family Door Light"};
X10_DEVICE  diningroom_outside_light     = {{ 7,    3},   DEVICE,   OFF,
"Outside Dining Room Door Light"};
X10_DEVICE  master_bedroom_outside_light = {{ 7,    4},   DEVICE,   OFF,
"Outside Master Bedroom Door Light"};
X10_DEVICE  garage_front_outside_light   = {{ 7,    5},   DEVICE,   OFF,
"Outside Garage Front Door Lights"};
X10_DEVICE  porch_outside_light          = {{ 7,    6},   DEVICE,   OFF,
"Outside Front Porch Door Light"};
X10_DEVICE  inside_entrance_light        = {{ 7,    7},   DEVICE,   OFF,
"Front Door Inside Entrance Light"};
X10_DEVICE  pantry_light                 = {{ 7,    8},   DEVICE,   OFF,
"Pantry Light"};
X10_DEVICE  laundry_fan                  = {{ 7,    9},   DEVICE,   OFF,
"Laundry Fan"};
```

```
X10_DEVICE  laundry_light                    = {{ 7,    10},   DEVICE,   OFF,
"Laundry Light"};
X10_DEVICE  guest_bathroom_flight            = {{ 7,    11},   DEVICE,   OFF,
"Guest Bathroom Flourescent Light"};
X10_DEVICE  guest_bathroom_fan               = {{ 7,    12},   DEVICE,   OFF,
"Guest Bathroom Fan"};
X10_DEVICE  cloakroom_light                  = {{ 7,    13},   DEVICE,   OFF,
"Cloakroom Light"};

X10_DEVICE  lounge_wall_light                = {{ 8,     1},   DEVICE,   OFF,
"Lounge Wall Light"};
X10_DEVICE  lounge_window_light              = {{ 8,     2},   DEVICE,   OFF,
"Lounge Window Light"};
X10_DEVICE  diningroom_table_light           = {{ 8,     3},   DEVICE,   OFF,
"Dining Room Table Light"};
X10_DEVICE  fishtank_light                   = {{ 8,     4},   DEVICE,   OFF,
"Lounge Fishtank Lights"};
X10_DEVICE  study_ceiling_light              = {{ 8,     5},   DEVICE,   OFF,
"Study Ceiling Lights"};
X10_DEVICE  common_bathroom_light            = {{ 8,     8},   DEVICE,   OFF,
"Common Bathroom Light"};
X10_DEVICE  master_bathroom_sensor           = {{ 8,     9},   SENSOR,   OFF,
"Master Bathroom"};
X10_DEVICE  master_toilet_sensor             = {{ 8,    11},   SENSOR,   OFF,
"Master Toilet"};

X10_DEVICE  barking_doggy                    = {{ 9,     1},   DEVICE,   OFF,
"Barking Doggy"};

X10_DEVICE  guest_main_light                 = {{11,     1},   DEVICE,   OFF,
"Guest Bedroom Main Light"};
X10_DEVICE  guest_bed_light                  = {{11,     2},   DEVICE,   OFF,
"Guest Bedroom Bed Light"};

X10_DEVICE  familyroom_window_light          = {{12,     1},   DEVICE,   OFF,
"Familyroom Window Light"};
X10_DEVICE  familyroom_wall_light            = {{12,     2},   DEVICE,   OFF,
"Familyroom Wall Light"};
X10_DEVICE  familyroom_track_tv_light        = {{12,     3},   DEVICE,   OFF,
"Familyroom Track TV Light"};
X10_DEVICE  familyroom_track_reading_light = {{12,     4},   DEVICE,   OFF,
"Familyroom Track Reading Light"};
X10_DEVICE  familyroom_wall_unit_light       = {{12,     5},   DEVICE,   OFF,
"Familyroom Wall Unit Light"};
X10_DEVICE  familyroom_wall_unit_spotlight = {{12,     6},   DEVICE,   OFF,
"Familyroom Wall Unit Spotlight"};
X10_DEVICE  familyroom_radio                 = {{12,    16},   DEVICE,   OFF,
"Familyroom Radio"};

X10_DEVICE  master_bedroom_light             = {{15,     1},   DEVICE,   OFF,
"Master Bedroom Light"};
X10_DEVICE  master_bedroom_mum_light         = {{15,     2},   DEVICE,   OFF,
"Master Bedroom Mum Light"};
X10_DEVICE  master_bedroom_closet_light      = {{15,     3},   DEVICE,   OFF,
"Master Bedroom Closet Light"};
X10_DEVICE  master_bedroom_dad_light         = {{15,     4},   DEVICE,   OFF,
"Master Bedroom Dad Light"};
```

```
X10_DEVICE  season_front_light              = {{16,     2},   DEVICE,  OFF,
"Season Front Lights"};    // Hanging icicles
X10_DEVICE  season_back_light               = {{16,     3},   DEVICE,  OFF,
"Season Back Lights"};     // Hanging icicles


// Sunrise/Sunset Times
TIME_OF_DAY  sunrise;
TIME_OF_DAY  sunset;


// Common Timeout variables
long int    sunrise_timeout  = 0;
long int    sunset_timeout   = 0;
long int    midday_timeout   = 0;
long int    midnight_timeout = 0;
long int    dusk_timeout     = 0;
long int    dawn_timeout     = 0;


// Time flags
Uint8  daytime  = FALSE;
Uint8  midday   = FALSE;
Uint8  nightime = FALSE;

Uint8  between_dawn_and_dusk  = FALSE;
Uint8  between_dusk_and_dawn  = FALSE;

Uint8  small_hours_of_the_morning = FALSE;


// Reset day/night start flags
Uint8  midnight_start = FALSE;
Uint8  day_start      = FALSE;
Uint8  dawn_start     = FALSE;
Uint8  midday_start   = FALSE;
Uint8  dusk_start     = FALSE;
Uint8  night_start    = FALSE;


// Setup home/security default states
Uint8  security_mode         = FALSE;
Uint8  security_mode_started = FALSE;
Uint8  security_mode_stopped = FALSE;

// Setup active/sleep default states
Uint8  sleep_mode  = FALSE;
Uint8  sleep_mode_pending = FALSE;

Uint8  sleep_mode_start = FALSE;


// Security flags
Uint8   steve_bedroom_sensor_security             = FALSE;
Uint8   common_washroom_sensor_security           = FALSE;
Uint8   common_bathroom_sensor_security           = FALSE;
Uint8   mini_hallway_sensor_security              = FALSE;
Uint8   study_sensor_security                     = FALSE;
```

```
Uint8   familyroom_sensor_security                    = FALSE;
Uint8   inside_front_door_sensor_security             = FALSE;
Uint8   main_hallway_sensor_security                  = FALSE;
Uint8   lounge_hallway_sensor_security                = FALSE;
Uint8   master_hallway_sensor_security                = FALSE;
Uint8   kitchen_sensor_security                       = FALSE;
Uint8   kitchen_nook_sensor_security                  = FALSE;
Uint8   master_bedroom_sensor_security                = FALSE;
Uint8   master_bathroom_sensor_security               = FALSE;
Uint8   master_closet_sensor_security                 = FALSE;
Uint8   garage_sensor_security                        = FALSE;
Uint8   master_bedroom_closet_sensor_security         = FALSE;
Uint8   pantry_sensor_security                        = FALSE;
Uint8   laundry_sensor_security                       = FALSE;
Uint8   guest_bathroom_sensor_security                = FALSE;
Uint8   guest_bedroom_door_sensor_security            = FALSE;

// Security timer
long int    front_porch_sensor_security_timer = DELAY_EXPIRED;


// Detailed time
struct timeval start, end;


// Fast Transition Events
long int  study_event;
long int  common_washroom_event;
long int  common_bathroom_event;
long int  steve_bedroom_event;


// Constants for Sunrise / Sunset time calculations
const   float zenith    = -0.01454;
const   float radians   = (3.141592654 / 180.0);
const   float degrees   = (180.0 / 3.141592654);

#endif
```

File: hc_common.c

```
//****************************************************************************
//  Author: Stephen W. McClure
//    Date: March 2014
// Project: Designing Embedded Systems [Book]
//
//****************************************************************************
// Purpose:
//
// This program provides a home control application.
//
//
//****************************************************************************
//
// File Name: hc_common.h
//
// This file includes all the common functions that are being used by both
// hc_main.c and hc_ti103.c modules.
//****************************************************************************

#ifndef HC_COMMON
#define HC_COMMON



//*****************************************************************************
// Catch Signal Interrupts
//
// This function catches the user termination signal.
// When the main control loop detects exit_flag set to 1 it terminated.
//
//*****************************************************************************

static void catch_signal_interrupts (int signo)
{
    exit_flag = 1;
}
```

```
//****************************************************************************
// Install Signal Interrupt Handler
//
// This function installs the signal interrupt handler.
//
// SIGTERM - Catches Kill
// SIGINT  - Catches ctrl-c          To shut-down in a nice manner...
//****************************************************************************

void install_signal_interrupt_handler (void)
{
    struct sigaction action;

    memset (&action, '\0', sizeof(action));
    action.sa_handler = catch_signal_interrupts;


    if (sigaction(SIGINT, &action, NULL) < 0)
    {
        perror ("sigaction");
        exit(1);
    }

}
```

```
//****************************************************************************
// Julian Day Of Year
//
// The Julian day of the year is the day number for that year.
// This is a number in the range [1..365] (depending upon leay year).
//
// As we know the old rythme...
// Thirty days has September, April, June and November, all the rest have 31
// except February which has 28 days (and 29 on leap years).
// A leap year is defined as a year that is cleanly divisible by
// (cleanly divisible means that no remainder is left behind).
//
// Now this method might not be as 'elegant' as others but I can assure you
// it is very easy to understand and check for its accuracy of operation.
//****************************************************************************

int julian_day_of_year (int day, int month, int year)
{
    int  julian_day_count = 0;

    // Add the days IN the month
    if (month > JANUARY)   julian_day_count += 31;    // Add in days for January
    if (month > FEBRUARY)  julian_day_count +=        // Add in days for February
        ((year % 4) == 0) ? 29 : 28;
    if (month > MARCH)     julian_day_count += 31;    // Add in days for March
    if (month > APRIL)     julian_day_count += 30;    // Add in days for April
    if (month > MAY)       julian_day_count += 31;    // Add in days for May
    if (month > JUNE)      julian_day_count += 30;    // Add in days for June
    if (month > JULY)      julian_day_count += 31;    // Add in days for July
    if (month > AUGUST)    julian_day_count += 31;    // Add in days for August
    if (month > SEPTEMBER) julian_day_count += 30;    // Add in days for September
    if (month > OCTOBER)   julian_day_count += 31;    // Add in days for October
    if (month > NOVEMBER)  julian_day_count += 30;    // Add in days for November

    // Add the remaining days OF the month
    julian_day_count += day;                          // Add in days for current
month

    // Return the Julian day for this year
    return (julian_day_count);
}
```

```
//*****************************************************************************
// Determine Julian Date
//
// The Julian day of the year is the day number for that year.
//
// As we know the old rythme...
// Thirty days has September, April, June and November, all the rest have 31
// except February which has 28 days (and 29 on leap years).
// A leap year is defined as a year that is cleanly divisible by 4
// (cleanly divisible means that no remainder is left behind).
//
// Now this method might not be as 'elegant' as others but I can assure you
// it is very easy to understand and check for its accuracy of operation.
// Since this calculation will be performed infrequently it does not require
// to be very fast and efficient (and inherently difficult to understand)...
//*****************************************************************************

double  determine_julian_date (int day, int month,  int year,
                               int hour, int minute, int second)
{
    int year_index;
    double julian_date = 2451544.0;  // For the date Jan 1st 2000 at time 00:00:00

    // Add in days up till year before this one
    for (year_index = 2000; year_index < year; year_index++)
    {
        // Was this a leap year?
        if ((year_index % 4) == 0)
        {
            // Yes - Add in julian days for a leap year
            julian_date += DAYS_IN_LEAP_YEAR;
        }
        else
        {
            // No - Add in julian days for a standard year
            julian_date += DAYS_IN_STANDARD_YEAR;
        }
    }

    // Add in the days up till the current month
    julian_date += julian_day_of_year (day, month, year);

    // Now add in the offset for the hours, minutes and seconds
    julian_date += ((hour - 12.0) / 24.0) + (minute / 1440.0) + (second /
86400.0);

    // Return the Julian day for this year
    return (julian_date);
}
```

```
//*****************************************************************************
// Determine Sunrise Sunset Times
//
// This function computes the sunrise and sunset times for today at the
// specified location.
//
//*****************************************************************************

double  determine_sunrise_sunset_times (void)
{
    int day, month, year;
    int hour, minute, second;
    int daylight_savings_time_in_effect;
    int n, elevation;
    int set_hour, set_minute, set_second;
    int rise_hour, rise_minute, rise_second;
    double  Jstar;
    double  M, C, lambda, Jtransit;
    double  delta, elevation_adjustment, OmegaZero;
    double set, rise, Jset, Jrise;
    double set2, rise2;
    double latitude, longitude;
    double  Jdate, n_star;
    double  remainder;
    double  julian_date_fraction;

    time_t  td;
    struct tm   *dcp;


#if 0  // Test example
        // Enter your location and elevation
        latitude  = 33.0417111;       // North is positive
        longitude = 116.868082;       // West  is positive
        elevation = 1440;      // Elevation in feet
#endif

        // Enter your location and elevation (from GPS)
        latitude  = 33.02415;         // North is positive
        longitude = 116.8708;         // West  is positive
        elevation = 1426;      // Elevation in feet


    // Get the system time and date (and DST (Daylight Savings Time))
    time(&td);
    dcp = localtime(&td);

    // Determine current day, month, year, etc...
    day    = dcp->tm_mday;
    month  = dcp->tm_mon  + 1;
    year   = dcp->tm_year + 1900;
    hour   = dcp->tm_hour;
    minute = dcp->tm_min;
    second = dcp->tm_sec;
    daylight_savings_time_in_effect = dcp->tm_isdst;


    // Determine the Julian Date
```

```
    Jdate = determine_julian_date (day, month, year, hour, minute, second);

    // Calculate Julian Cycle (2451545.0009 = Saturday 1st Jan 2000 at 12:01:18)
    n_star = Jdate - 2451545.0009 - (longitude / 360.0);
    n = (int)(n_star + 0.5);

    // Approximate solar noon
    Jstar = 2451545.0009 + (longitude / 360.0) + n;

    // Solar mean anomaly
    M = fmod((357.5291 + 0.98560028 * (Jstar - 2451545)), 360.0);

    // Equation of center
    C = (1.9148 * sin(M * radians)) + (0.0200 * sin (2 * M * radians)) + (0.0003 *
sin (3 * M * radians));

    // Ecliptic Longitude
    lambda = fmod ((M + 102.9372 + C + 180), 360.0);

    // Solar transit
    Jtransit = Jstar + (0.0053 * sin (M * radians)) - (0.0069 * sin (2 * lambda *
radians));

    // Declination of the sun
    delta = asin (sin (lambda * radians) * sin(23.45 * radians)) * degrees;

    // Hour angle
    elevation_adjustment = (-1.15 * sqrt(elevation)) / 60.0;

    OmegaZero = acos ((sin ((-0.83 + elevation_adjustment) * radians) - (sin
(latitude * radians) * sin (delta * radians))) / (cos (latitude * radians) * cos
(delta * radians))) * degrees;

    // Calculate Julian date for Sunset
    Jset = 2451545.0009 + ((OmegaZero + longitude) / 360.0) + n + (0.0053 * sin (M
* radians)) - (0.0069 * sin (2 * lambda * radians));

    // Calculate Julian date for Sunrise
    Jrise = Jtransit - (Jset - Jtransit);

    // Convert the Sunrise Julian Date to hours, minutes and seconds
    // First determine the fractional part of the julian date
    julian_date_fraction = Jrise - (int)(Jrise);

    rise_hour   = (julian_date_fraction * 24);
    remainder   = (julian_date_fraction * 24) - rise_hour;
    rise_minute = (remainder * 60);
    remainder   = (remainder * 60) - rise_minute;
    rise_second = (remainder * 60);

    if (julian_date_fraction < 0.5)
        rise_hour += 12;
    else
        rise_hour -= 12;


    // Convert the Sunset Juliam Date to hours, minutes and seconds
    // First determine the fractional part of the julian date
```

```
julian_date_fraction = Jset - (int)(Jset);

set_hour   = (julian_date_fraction * 24);
remainder  = (julian_date_fraction * 24) - set_hour;
set_minute = (remainder * 60);
remainder  = (remainder * 60) - set_minute;
set_second = (remainder * 60);

if (julian_date_fraction < 0.5)
    set_hour += 12;
else
    set_hour -= 12;


// Information regarding the Daylight Savings Rules
// http://www.nist.gov/pml/div688/dst.cfm
//
// Daylight Saving Time in the United States
// begins at 2:00 a.m. on the second Sunday of March and
// ends at 2:00 a.m. on the first Sunday of November
//
// Note that this is taken care of by the Operating System
// so all the user need do is to determine if the DST
// parameter is set and add in another hour.

// Also adjust for longitude
//  rise_hour = fmod ((rise_hour += 16), 24);
//  set_hour  = fmod ((set_hour  += 16), 24);

// Convert UT time into local San Diego, California USA time.
// San Diego, California, USA is 8 hours behind UK time.
// So add on 16 hours and use fmod to take care of 24hrs clock.
// (If it is Daylight Savings Time then add 17 hours.

if (daylight_savings_time_in_effect == 1)
{
    rise_hour = fmod ((rise_hour += 17), 24);  // DST (Add one hour)
    set_hour  = fmod ((set_hour  += 17), 24);  // DST (Add one hour)
}
else
{
    rise_hour = fmod ((rise_hour += 16), 24);  // DST is NOT in effect
    set_hour  = fmod ((set_hour  += 16), 24);  // DST is NOT in effect
}

// Setup final sunrise time
sunrise.hour   = rise_hour;
sunrise.minute = rise_minute + EASTERN_ESCARPMENT_ADJUSTMENT;
sunrise.second = rise_second;

// Did the minutes proceed into the next hour?
if (sunrise.minute > 59)
{
    // Yes - Adjust the minutes and increment the hour
    sunrise.minute -= 60;
    sunrise.hour++;
}
```

```
    // Setup final sunset time
    sunset.hour   = set_hour;
    sunset.minute = set_minute - WESTERN_ESCARPMENT_ADJUSTMENT;
    sunset.second = set_second;

    // Did the minutes step into the previous hour?
    if (sunset.minute < 0)
    {
        // Yes - Adjust the minutes and decrement the hour
        sunset,minute += 60;
        sunset.hour--;
    }


    // Print out computed and expected values
//  printf ("Computed values are: Sunrise = %02d:%02d     and  Sunset =
%02d:%02d\n",
//          sunrise.hour, sunrise.minute, sunset.hour, sunset.minute);

}
```

```
//****************************************************************************
// Determine System Timestamp
//
// This function determines the current system timestamp.
//
//****************************************************************************

void  determine_system_timestamp (char *  timestamp_buffer)
{

    time_t  td;
    struct tm   *dcp;


    // Get system date and time
    time(&td);
    dcp = localtime(&td);

    // Create time stamp
    sprintf (timestamp_buffer, "%04d/%02d/%02d %02d:%02d:%02d",
            dcp->tm_year + 1900,
            dcp->tm_mon + 1,
            dcp->tm_mday,
            dcp->tm_hour,
            dcp->tm_min,
            dcp->tm_sec);

}
```

```
//******************************************************************************
// Print Log
//
// This function prints the timestamped log message.
//
//******************************************************************************

void  print_log (char *  message)
{
    char    timestamp[255];


    // Is a blank line to be printed?
    if (strlen(message) == 0x00)
    {
        // Yes - Print a blank line
        printf ("\n");
        return;
    }


    // Determine current timestamp
    determine_system_timestamp (timestamp);

    // Display timestamped log message
    printf ("%s %s\n", timestamp, message);
}
```

```
//****************************************************************************
// msleep
//
// This function sleeps for the specified number of milliseconds.
//
//****************************************************************************

int msleep (unsigned long   milliseconds)
{
    struct timespec req={0},rem={0};
    time_t seconds;

    seconds = (int)(milliseconds / 1000);
    milliseconds = milliseconds - (seconds * 1000);
    req.tv_sec  = seconds;
    req.tv_nsec = milliseconds * 1000000L;

    // Sleep for nanoseconds
    nanosleep (&req, &rem);
    return 1;
}
```

```
//******************************************************************************
// Get Raw Time
//
// This function gets the elapsed time (in seconds) since start of 1970.
//
//******************************************************************************

ulonglong  get_raw_time (void)
{
    struct tm   *tm_ptr;
    time_t  raw_time;

    raw_time = time ((time_t *) 0x0);
    return (raw_time);

}
```

```
//*******************************************************************************
// Determine Days In Month
//
// This function determines the number of days in the month based on the
// specified date.
//
//*******************************************************************************

Uint16  determine_days_in_month (Uint16 day, Uint16 month, Uint16 year)
{
    Uint8   leap_year;
    Uint8   days_in_month = 0;


    // Determine if this is a leap year
    leap_year = (((year % 4) == 0) && ((year % 100) == 0) && ((year % 400) != 0));

    // Determine days in month
    switch (month)
    {
    case JANUARY   : days_in_month = 31;  break;
    case FEBRUARY  : if (leap_year)
                       days_in_month = 29;
                     else
                       days_in_month = 28;
                     break;
    case MARCH     : days_in_month = 31;  break;
    case APRIL     : days_in_month = 30;  break;
    case MAY       : days_in_month = 31;  break;
    case JUNE      : days_in_month = 30;  break;
    case JULY      : days_in_month = 31;  break;
    case AUGUST    : days_in_month = 31;  break;
    case SEPTEMBER : days_in_month = 30;  break;
    case OCTOBER   : days_in_month = 31;  break;
    case NOVEMBER  : days_in_month = 30;  break;
    case DECEMBER  : days_in_month = 31;  break;
    default:
        print_log ("determine_days_in_month() failed - Invalid month!");
        break;
    }

    // Return days in the month
    return (days_in_month);
}
```

```
//****************************************************************************
// Determine Next Date
//
// This function increments the date by one day.
//
//****************************************************************************

void  determine_next_date (Uint16 *  day, Uint16 *  month, Uint16 *  year)
{
    Uint16  number_days_in_this_month;


    // Determine days in the current month date
    number_days_in_this_month = determine_days_in_month (*day, *month, *year);


    // Determine next date
    *day = *day + 1;

    // Have we exceeded the number of days in this month
    if (*day > number_days_in_this_month)
    {
        // Yes - Reset the day count to 1 and jump to next month
        *day = 1;
        *month = *month + 1;

        // Have we passed december?
        if (*month > DECEMBER)
        {
            // Yes - Reset the month count to January and jump to next year
            *month = JANUARY;
            *year = *year + 1;
        }
    }

}
```

```
//*****************************************************************************
// Determine Standard Time
//
// This function determines the standard time in hours:minutes:seconds
// for the current time (seconds since midnight).
//
//*****************************************************************************

void  determine_standard_time (long int  time_in_seconds, char *  buffer)
{
    Uint16      hours;
    Uint16      minutes;
    Uint16      seconds;
    Uint16      remaining_seconds;
    Uint16      seconds_since_midnight;
    Uint16      day, month, year, hour, minute, second;;
    long int    current_time;
    long int    midnight_offset;


    // Date and time variables
    time_t  td;
    struct tm   *dcp;


    // Get system date and time
    time(&td);
    dcp = localtime(&td);

    // Initialize calandar variables
    day    = dcp->tm_mday;
    month  = dcp->tm_mon + 1;
    year   = dcp->tm_year + 1900;
    hour   = dcp->tm_hour;
    minute = dcp->tm_min;
    second = dcp->tm_sec;


    // Get current time in seconds
    current_time = get_raw_time();

    // Determine current time offset from midnight
    midnight_offset = (hour * 3600) + (minute * 60) + second;

    // Current time for today at first midnight
    midnight_timeout = current_time - midnight_offset;

    // Determine seconds since midnight
    seconds_since_midnight = time_in_seconds - midnight_timeout;

    // Convert to hours:minutes:seconds
    hours = (seconds_since_midnight / 3600);
    remaining_seconds = seconds_since_midnight - (hours * 3600);

    minutes = (remaining_seconds / 60);
    seconds = remaining_seconds - (minutes * 60);
```

```
    // Does the event occur today?
    if (hours < 24)
    {
        // Yes - Use today's date
        sprintf (buffer, "%04d/%02d/%02d %02d:%02d:%02d", year, month, day, hours,
minutes, seconds);
    }
    else
    {
        // Determine tomorrow's date
        hours -= 24;
        determine_next_date (&day, &month, &year);

        sprintf (buffer, "%04d/%02d/%02d %02d:%02d:%02d", year, month, day, hours,
minutes, seconds);
    }

}
```

```
//*****************************************************************************
// Determine Periodic Transition Times
//
// This function determines the raw seconds count for the sunrise/sunset
// for the current day.  It also determines the dawn/dusk and day/night periods.
//
//*****************************************************************************

void  determine_periodic_transition_times (void)
{
    long int    current_time;
    long int    midnight_offset;
    char        time_buffer[255];
    char        message[255];
    Uint16      day, month, year, hour, minute, second;


    // Date and time variables
    time_t  td;
    struct tm   *dcp;


    // Get system date and time
    time(&td);
    dcp = localtime(&td);

    // Print out the current time
    sprintf (time_buffer, "%04d/%02d/%02d %02d:%02d:%02d",
         dcp->tm_year + 1900,
         dcp->tm_mon + 1,
         dcp->tm_mday,
         dcp->tm_hour,
         dcp->tm_min,
         dcp->tm_sec);

    // Initialize calandar variables
    day    = dcp->tm_mday;
    month  = dcp->tm_mon + 1;
    year   = dcp->tm_year + 1900;
    hour   = dcp->tm_hour;
    minute = dcp->tm_min;
    second = dcp->tm_sec;


    // Get current time in seconds
    current_time = get_raw_time();

    // Determine current time offset from midnight
    midnight_offset = (hour * 3600) + (minute * 60) + second;

    // Current time for today at first midnight
    midnight_timeout = current_time - midnight_offset;

    // Current time for midday
    midday_timeout = midnight_timeout + OFFSET_12HRS;

    // Is this the next day?
    // The next day is defined when the next midnight timeout
```

```
// event is calculated to be AFTER (ie. greater than)
// the sunrise timeout event of the previous day.
if (midnight_timeout > sunrise_timeout)
{
    // Yes - Compute sunrise, sunset, dawn and dusk timeout event times
    //       for this specific day of the month.
    determine_sunrise_sunset_times();

    sunrise_timeout =  midnight_timeout +
             (sunrise.hour   * 3600) +
             (sunrise.minute * 60);

    sunset_timeout  =  midnight_timeout +
             (sunset.hour    * 3600) +
             (sunset.minute * 60);

    dawn_timeout = sunrise_timeout + OFFSET_20MIN;   // ie. Just after sunrise
    dusk_timeout = sunset_timeout  - OFFSET_15MIN;   // ie. Just before sunset


    // Print out these event times
    determine_standard_time (sunrise_timeout, time_buffer);

    print_log ("");
    sprintf (message, "Sunrise at %s", time_buffer);
    print_log (message);

    determine_standard_time (dawn_timeout, time_buffer);
    sprintf (message, "   Dawn at %s", time_buffer);
    print_log (message);

    determine_standard_time (dusk_timeout, time_buffer);
    sprintf (message, "   Dusk at %s", time_buffer);
    print_log (message);

    determine_standard_time (sunset_timeout, time_buffer);
    sprintf (message, " Sunset at %s", time_buffer);
    print_log (message);
    print_log ("");

    // Indicate that the midnight event has started.
    // This is used to configure specific event times
    // that are only setup once each day at midnight.
    midnight_start = TRUE;
}



// Is it daytime?
if ((sunrise_timeout < current_time) && (current_time < sunset_timeout))
{
    // Yes - Did the day just start?
    if (daytime == FALSE)
    {
        // Yes - Set flag for processing specific day start events
        day_start = TRUE;
    }
```

```
    // It is day time
    daytime  = TRUE;
    nightime = FALSE;
}
else
{
    // It is night time - Did the night just start?
    if (nightime == FALSE)
    {
        // Yes - Set flag for processing specific night start events
        night_start = TRUE;
    }

    // It is night time
    daytime  = FALSE;
    nightime = TRUE;
}


// Is it after the dawn but before the dusk)?
if ((dawn_timeout < current_time) && (current_time < dusk_timeout))
{
    // Has the dawn just started?
    if (between_dawn_and_dusk == FALSE)
    {
        // Yes - Set flag for processing specific dawn start events
        dawn_start = TRUE;
    }

    // We are in the [Dawn..Dusk] range
    between_dawn_and_dusk = TRUE;
    between_dusk_and_dawn = FALSE;
}
else
{
    // Has the dusk just started?
    if (between_dusk_and_dawn == FALSE)
    {
        // Yes - Set flag for processing specific dawn start events
        dusk_start = TRUE;
    }

    // We are in the [Dusk..Dawn] range
    between_dawn_and_dusk = FALSE;
    between_dusk_and_dawn = TRUE;
}



// Have we passed midday?
if ((midday_timeout <= current_time) && (current_time < sunset_timeout))
{
    // Yes - Did it just start?
    if (midday == FALSE)
    {
        // Yes - Set flag for processing specific midday events
        midday_start = TRUE;
    }
```

```
        midday = TRUE;
    }
    else
    {
        // No - We have not reached midday
        midday = FALSE;
    }

    // Are we in the wee small hours of the morning?
    if ((midnight_timeout <= current_time) && (current_time < sunrise_timeout))
    {
        // Yes we are...
        small_hours_of_the_morning = TRUE;
    }
    else
    {
        // No we are not...
        small_hours_of_the_morning = FALSE;
    }

}
```

```
//**************************************************************************
// Activate Device
//
// This function places a device command into the house_code_events table.
// The retries are to ensure device operation in locations where there is a
// large amount of electrical noise on the mains line (eg. generated by
// CFL lamps).
//
//**************************************************************************

void  activate_device (X10_DEVICE     device,
                       Uint8          device_state,
                       long int       timeout)
{
    Uint8         index;
    Uint8         number_of_tries;
    long int     time_offset = 0;
    char         buffer[255];
    char         time_buffer[255];


    // Are we setting this device?
    if (device_state == ON)
    {
        // Yes - Perform more retries to ensure device is on
        //       Adjust to suit the electrical environment...

        number_of_tries = 1; // Increase for noisy environments;
    }
    else
    {
        // No - Perform more retries to ensure device is off
        //       Adjust to suit the electrical environment...
        number_of_tries = 1; // Increase for noisy environments;
    }


    // Configure device
    device.state = device_state;


    // Issue the device command with retries
    for (index = 0; index < number_of_tries; index++)
    {
        // Determine time in HH:MM:SS format
        determine_standard_time ((timeout + time_offset), time_buffer);

        // Build the event command and enter into the database table
        sprintf (buffer, "INSERT INTO house_code_events VALUES(%d, %d, %d, %d,
'%s', %ld, '%s')",
                 device.x10.house_code,
                 device.x10.unit_code,
                 device.type,
                 device.state,
                 time_buffer,
                 (timeout + time_offset),
                 device.description);
```

```
        //      printf ("%s\n", buffer);
        mysql_query(conn1, buffer);

        // Is the device being switched ON
        if (device_state == ON)
        {
            // Yes - Increment time offset (sequence = 0, 1, 3, 6, 10, 15, etc.)
            //      Insert the commands in close proximity
            //         time_offset += index + 1;
            time_offset += 2;
        }
        else
        {
            // No - Increment time offset (sequence = 0, 7, 14, 21, etc.)
            //      Insert the commands further paced apart to allow other
            //      commands the chance to execute (ie. speeds up process).
            time_offset += 7;
        }
    }
}
```

```
//******************************************************************************
// get_house_state_security
//
// This function access the house_state database table and returns the security
// parameter that lets us know if the SECURITY button has been pressed.
//
//******************************************************************************

int  get_house_state_security (int *  new_house_state_security)
{
    char            message [255];
    int             house_state_security;
    MYSQL_RES      *mysqlResult;
    MYSQL_ROW       mysqlRow;
    MYSQL_FIELD    *mysqlFields;
    my_ulonglong    numRows;
    unsigned int    numFields;


    // Determine if we are engaging security mode (ask for only the security
parameter)
    if (mysql_query(conn1, "SELECT security FROM house_state"))
    {
        // Error detected - Print error message
        sprintf (message, "Error_G0 %u: %s\n", mysql_errno(conn1),
mysql_error(conn1));
        print_log (message);
        return (FAILURE);
    }
    else
    {
        // Determine the number of event entries
        mysqlResult = mysql_store_result (conn1);

        // Are there any entries?
        if (mysqlResult)
        {
            // Yes - Get the number of database table rows and fields
            numRows   = mysql_num_rows (mysqlResult);
            numFields = mysql_num_fields (mysqlResult);

            // Print these out when testing
            // printf ("Number of Rows = %lld,  Number of Fields = %d \n", numRows,
numFields);
        }
        else
        {
            // Print these out when testing
            print_log ("Result set is empty\n");
            return (FAILURE);
        }


        // Get the first row in the table
        mysqlRow = mysql_fetch_row(mysqlResult);

        // Does it exist?
        if (mysqlRow)
```

```
        {
            // Yes - Get the house state security parameter from the MySQL table
            house_state_security = (int) (atoi (mysqlRow[0]));
        }

        // Was a MySQL result pointer returned?
        if (mysqlResult)
        {
            // Yes - Free the pointer
            mysql_free_result(mysqlResult);
            mysqlResult = NULL;
        }
    }

    // Return parameter
    *new_house_state_security = house_state_security;
    return (SUCCESS);
}
```

```
//*****************************************************************************
// get_house_state_sleep
//
// This function access the house_state database table and returns the sleep
// parameter that lets us know if the SLEEP button has been pressed.
//
//*****************************************************************************

int  get_house_state_sleep (int *  new_house_state_sleep)
{
    char              message [255];
    int               house_state_sleep;
    MYSQL_RES        *mysqlResult;
    MYSQL_ROW         mysqlRow;
    MYSQL_FIELD      *mysqlFields;
    my_ulonglong      numRows;
    unsigned int      numFields;


    // Determine if we are engaging sleep mode (ask for only the security
parameter)
    if (mysql_query(conn1, "SELECT sleep FROM house_state"))
    {
        // Error detected - Print error message
        sprintf (message, "Error_G0 %u: %s", mysql_errno(conn1),
mysql_error(conn1));
        print_log (message);
        return (FAILURE);
    }
    else
    {
        // Determine the number of event entries
        mysqlResult = mysql_store_result (conn1);

        // Are there any entries?
        if (mysqlResult)
        {
            // Yes - Get the number of database table rows and fields
            numRows   = mysql_num_rows (mysqlResult);
            numFields = mysql_num_fields (mysqlResult);

            // Print these out when testing
            // printf ("Number of Rows = %lld,  Number of Fields = %d \n", numRows,
numFields);
        }
        else
        {
            // Print these out when testing
            print_log ("Result set is empty");
            return (FAILURE);
        }


        // Get the first row in the table
        mysqlRow = mysql_fetch_row (mysqlResult);

        // Does it exist?
        if (mysqlRow)
```

```
        {
            // Yes - Get the house state sleep parameter from the MySQL table
            house_state_sleep = (int) (atoi (mysqlRow[0]));
        }

        // Was a MySQL result pointer returned?
        if (mysqlResult)
        {
            // Yes - Free the pointer
            mysql_free_result(mysqlResult);
            mysqlResult = NULL;
        }
    }

    // Return parameter
    *new_house_state_sleep = house_state_sleep;
    return (SUCCESS);
}
```

```
//*****************************************************************************
// get_house_state_watch_tv
//
// This function access the house_state database table and returns the watch tv
// parameter that lets us know if the 'Watch TV' button has been pressed.
//
//*****************************************************************************

int  get_house_state_watch_tv (int *  new_house_state_watch_tv)
{
    char             message [255];
    int              house_state_watch_tv;
    MYSQL_RES       *mysqlResult;
    MYSQL_ROW        mysqlRow;
    MYSQL_FIELD     *mysqlFields;
    my_ulonglong     numRows;
    unsigned int     numFields;


    // Determine if the watch tv parameter has been pressed
    if (mysql_query(conn1, "SELECT watch_tv FROM house_state"))
    {
        // Error detected - Print error message
        sprintf (message, "Error_G0 %u: %s", mysql_errno(conn1),
mysql_error(conn1));
        print_log (message);
        return (FAILURE);
    }
    else
    {
        // Determine the number of event entries
        mysqlResult = mysql_store_result (conn1);

        // Are there any entries?
        if (mysqlResult)
        {
            // Yes - Get the number of database table rows and fields
            numRows   = mysql_num_rows (mysqlResult);
            numFields = mysql_num_fields (mysqlResult);

            // Print these out when testing
            // printf ("Number of Rows = %lld,  Number of Fields = %d \n", numRows,
numFields);
        }
        else
        {
            // Print these out when testing
            print_log ("Result set is empty");
            return (FAILURE);
        }


        // Get the first row in the table
        mysqlRow = mysql_fetch_row (mysqlResult);

        // Does it exist?
        if (mysqlRow)
        {
```

```
            // Yes - Get the house state 'watch_tv' parameter from the MySQL table
            house_state_watch_tv = (int) (atoi (mysqlRow[0]));
        }

        // Was a MySQL result pointer returned?
        if (mysqlResult)
        {
            // Yes - Free the pointer
            mysql_free_result(mysqlResult);
            mysqlResult = NULL;
        }
    }

    // Return parameter
    *new_house_state_watch_tv = house_state_watch_tv;
    return (SUCCESS);
}
```

```
//******************************************************************************
// get_house_state_parameter
//
// This function access the house_state database table for a specific parameter.
//
//******************************************************************************

int  get_house_state_parameter (int  hs_index, int *  new_parameter_value)
{
    int               parameter_value;
    MYSQL_RES        *mysqlResult;
    MYSQL_ROW         mysqlRow;
    MYSQL_FIELD      *mysqlFields;
    my_ulonglong      numRows;
    unsigned int      numFields;
    char              buffer[255];
    char              message [255];


    // Determine if the watch tv parameter has been pressed
    sprintf (buffer, "SELECT %s FROM house_state",
house_state_parameter[hs_index].name);

    if (mysql_query(conn1, buffer))
    {
        // Error detected - Print error message
        sprintf (message, "Error_GA0 %u: %s", mysql_errno(conn1),
mysql_error(conn1));
        print_log (message);
        return (FAILURE);
    }
    else
    {
        // Determine the number of event entries
        mysqlResult = mysql_store_result (conn1);

        // Are there any entries?
        if (mysqlResult)
        {
            // Yes - Get the number of database table rows and fields
            numRows   = mysql_num_rows (mysqlResult);
            numFields = mysql_num_fields (mysqlResult);

            // Print these out when testing
            // printf ("Number of Rows = %lld,  Number of Fields = %d \n", numRows,
numFields);
        }
        else
        {
            // Print these out when testing
            print_log ("Result set is empty");
            return (FAILURE);
        }


        // Get the first row in the table
        mysqlRow = mysql_fetch_row (mysqlResult);
```

```
        // Does it exist?
        if (mysqlRow)
        {
            // Yes - Get the parameter value from the MySQL table
            parameter_value = (int) (atoi (mysqlRow[0]));                    // We
have only requested one parameter
            // printf ("Parameter = %d\n", parameter_value);
        }

        // Was a MySQL result pointer returned?
        if (mysqlResult)
        {
            // Yes - Free the pointer
            mysql_free_result(mysqlResult);
            mysqlResult = NULL;
        }
    }

    //  Return the parameter value);
    *new_parameter_value = parameter_value;
    return (SUCCESS);
}
```

```
//*****************************************************************************
// get_house_state_go_to_bed
//
// This function access the house_state database table and returns the go to bed
// parameter that lets us know if the 'Go To Bed' button has been pressed.
//
//*****************************************************************************

int  get_house_state_go_to_bed (int *  new_house_state_go_to_bed)
{
    int              house_state_go_to_bed;
    MYSQL_RES       *mysqlResult;
    MYSQL_ROW        mysqlRow;
    MYSQL_FIELD     *mysqlFields;
    my_ulonglong     numRows;
    unsigned int     numFields;
    char             message [255];


    // Determine if the 'go_to_bed' parameter has been pressed
    if (mysql_query(conn1, "SELECT go_to_bed FROM house_state"))
    {
        // Error detected - Print error message
        sprintf (message, "Error_G0 %u: %s", mysql_errno(conn1),
mysql_error(conn1));
        print_log (message);
        return (FAILURE);
    }
    else
    {
        // Determine the number of event entries
        mysqlResult = mysql_store_result (conn1);

        // Are there any entries?
        if (mysqlResult)
        {
            // Yes - Get the number of database table rows and fields
            numRows   = mysql_num_rows (mysqlResult);
            numFields = mysql_num_fields (mysqlResult);

            // Print these out when testing
            // printf ("Number of Rows = %lld,  Number of Fields = %d \n", numRows,
numFields);
        }
        else
        {
            // Print these out when testing
            print_log ("Result set is empty");
            return (FAILURE);
        }


        // Get the first row in the table
        mysqlRow = mysql_fetch_row (mysqlResult);

        // Does it exist?
        if (mysqlRow)
        {
```

```
            // Yes - Get the house state 'go_to_bed' parameter from the MySQL table
            house_state_go_to_bed = (int) (atoi (mysqlRow[0]));
        }

        // Was a MySQL result pointer returned?
        if (mysqlResult)
        {
            // Yes - Free the pointer
            mysql_free_result(mysqlResult);
            mysqlResult = NULL;
        }
    }

    // Return parameter
    *new_house_state_go_to_bed = house_state_go_to_bed;
    return (SUCCESS);
}



//*******************************************************************************
// Delete House Code Events
//
// This function deletes all the house code events for a specific device.
// This includes both ON and OFF events.
//
//*******************************************************************************

void  delete_house_code_events (X10_DEVICE  device)
{
    char    buffer[255];


    sprintf (buffer, "DELETE FROM house_code_events WHERE house=%d AND unit=%d",
            device.x10.house_code,
            device.x10.unit_code);

    //  printf ("%s \n", buffer);
    mysql_query(conn1, buffer);
}
```

```
//*****************************************************************************
// Delete House Code OFF Events
//
// This function deletes all the house code OFF events for a specific device.
//
//*****************************************************************************

void  delete_house_code_off_events (X10_DEVICE  device)
{
    char    buffer[255];


    sprintf (buffer, "DELETE FROM house_code_events WHERE house=%d AND unit=%d AND
state=0",
             device.x10.house_code,
             device.x10.unit_code);

    //  printf ("%s \n", buffer);
    mysql_query(conn1, buffer);
}




//*****************************************************************************
// Delete House Code ON Events
//
// This function deletes all the house code ON events for a specific device.
//
//*****************************************************************************

void  delete_house_code_on_events (X10_DEVICE  device)
{
    char    buffer[255];


    sprintf (buffer, "DELETE FROM house_code_events WHERE house=%d AND unit=%d AND
state=1",
             device.x10.house_code,
             device.x10.unit_code);

    //  printf ("%s \n", buffer);
    mysql_query(conn1, buffer);
}
```

```
//********************************************************************************
// Delete House Code OFF Events Before Dusk
//
// This function deletes all the house code OFF events for a specific device
// with a specific timeout value.
//
//********************************************************************************

void  delete_house_code_off_events_at_timeout (X10_DEVICE  device, long int
turn_off_time)
{
    char    buffer[255];


    sprintf (buffer, "DELETE FROM house_code_events WHERE house=%d AND unit=%d AND
state=0 AND timeout=%ld",
              device.x10.house_code,
              device.x10.unit_code,
              turn_off_time);

    // printf ("%s \n", buffer);
    mysql_query(conn1, buffer);
}




//********************************************************************************
// Delete House Code OFF Events Before Dusk
//
// This function deletes all the house code OFF events for a specific device
// prior to dusk.
//
//********************************************************************************

void  delete_house_code_off_events_before_dusk (X10_DEVICE  device)
{
    char    buffer[255];


    sprintf (buffer, "DELETE FROM house_code_events WHERE house=%d AND unit=%d AND
state=0 AND timeout<%ld",
              device.x10.house_code,
              device.x10.unit_code,
              dusk_timeout);

    // printf ("%s \n", buffer);
    mysql_query(conn1, buffer);
}
```

```
//*****************************************************************************
// Delete House Code Events After Dusk
//
// This function deletes all the house code events for a specific device
// after dusk.
//
//*****************************************************************************

void  delete_house_code_events_after_dusk (X10_DEVICE  device)
{
    char    buffer[255];


    sprintf (buffer, "DELETE FROM house_code_events WHERE house=%d AND unit=%d AND
timeout>%ld",
            device.x10.house_code,
            device.x10.unit_code,
            dusk_timeout);

    //  printf ("%s \n", buffer);
    mysql_query(conn1, buffer);
}




//*****************************************************************************
// Delete House Code Events After Sunset
//
// This function deletes all the house code events for a specific device
// after sunset.
//
//*****************************************************************************

void  delete_house_code_events_after_sunset (X10_DEVICE  device)
{
    char    buffer[255];


    sprintf (buffer, "DELETE FROM house_code_events WHERE house=%d AND unit=%d AND
timeout>%ld",
            device.x10.house_code,
            device.x10.unit_code,
            sunset_timeout);

    //  printf ("%s \n", buffer);
    mysql_query(conn1, buffer);
}
```

```
//*****************************************************************************
// Delete All House Code Events
//
// This function deletes all the house code events from the table.
//
//*****************************************************************************

void  delete_all_house_code_events (void)
{
    Uint8   house_code;
    Uint8   unit_code;
    char    buffer[255];


    // Delete all house code events
    print_log ("*** Delete ALL house code events...");

    // Delete all the events for each house code
    for (house_code = 1; house_code < 17; house_code++)
    {
        sprintf (buffer, "DELETE FROM house_code_events WHERE house=%d",
house_code);
        mysql_query(conn1, buffer);
    }

}



//*****************************************************************************
// Turn Alarm Siren On
//
// This function places required alarm siren on event into the
// house_code_events table.
//
//*****************************************************************************

void  turn_alarm_siren_on (void)
{
    long int    current_time;
    long int    turn_off_time;


    // Get current system time
    current_time = get_raw_time();

    turn_off_time = current_time + OFFSET_5MIN;

    // Delete any existing alarm siren events
    delete_house_code_events (security_alarm_siren);

    // Turn alarm siren ON
    activate_device (security_alarm_siren, ON, current_time);

    // Turn alarm siren OFF after delay
    activate_device (security_alarm_siren, OFF, turn_off_time);
}
```

```
//*****************************************************************************
// Turn Alarm Siren Off
//
// This function places required alarm siren off event into the
// house_code_events table.
//
//*****************************************************************************

void  turn_alarm_siren_off (void)
{
    long int    current_time;


    // Get current system time
    current_time = get_raw_time();

    // Delete any existing alarm siren events
    delete_house_code_events (security_alarm_siren);

    // Turn alarm siren OFF
    activate_device (security_alarm_siren, OFF, current_time);
}




//*****************************************************************************
// Kick The Dog
//
// This function gets the dog to start barking.
//
//*****************************************************************************

void  kick_the_dog (void)
{
    long int    current_time;


    // Get current system time
    current_time = get_raw_time();

    // Delete any existing alarm siren events
    delete_house_code_events (barking_doggy);

    // Turn alarm siren ON
    activate_device (barking_doggy, ON, current_time);

}
```

```
//******************************************************************************
// Tell The Dog To Be Quiet
//
// This function forces the dog to stop barking.
//
//******************************************************************************

void  tell_the_dog_to_be_quiet (void)
{
    long int    current_time;


    // Get current system time
    current_time = get_raw_time();

    // Delete any existing alarm siren events
    delete_house_code_events (barking_doggy);

    // Turn alarm siren OFF
    activate_device (barking_doggy, OFF, current_time);
}
```

```
//*****************************************************************************
// Send Security Email
//
// This function builds and then sends the security email message.
// If we do not limit the buffer sizes then we run the risk of memory
// corruption and the generation of a system page fault.
//
//*****************************************************************************

void  send_security_email (char * header, char * message)
{

    char    buffer[1024];


#ifdef EMAIL_ACTIVE

    // Is the header too big?
    if (strlen(header) > MAX_EMAIL_HEADER_SIZE)
    {
        // Yes - limit the header size
        header[MAX_EMAIL_HEADER_SIZE] = 0x00;
    }


    // Is the message too big?
    if (strlen(message) > MAX_EMAIL_MESSAGE_SIZE)
    {
        // Yes - limit the message size
        message[MAX_EMAIL_MESSAGE_SIZE] = 0x00;
    }


    // Build email command
    sprintf (buffer, "sendemail -f %s -t %s -cc %s -s %s -u \"%s\" -m \"%s\" ",
             EMAIL_SENDER_ADDRESS,
             EMAIL_RECEIVER_ADDRESS,
             EMAIL_CC_ADDRESS,
             SERVICE_PROVIDER_SMTP,
             header,
             message);

    // Send email
    system (buffer);

#endif
}
```

```
//****************************************************************************
// Send Security Email
//
// This function builds and then sends the security email message.
// If we do not limit the buffer sizes then we run the risk of memory
// corruption and the generation of a system page fault.
//
//****************************************************************************

void  send_security_email_with_attachment (char * header, char * message, char *
attachment)
{

    char    buffer[1024];


#ifdef EMAIL_ACTIVE

    // Is the header too big?
    if (strlen(header) > MAX_EMAIL_HEADER_SIZE)
    {
        // Yes - limit the header size
        header[MAX_EMAIL_HEADER_SIZE] = 0x00;
    }


    // Is the message too big?
    if (strlen(message) > MAX_EMAIL_MESSAGE_SIZE)
    {
        // Yes - limit the message size
        message[MAX_EMAIL_MESSAGE_SIZE] = 0x00;
    }


    // Build email command
    sprintf (buffer, "sendemail -f %s -t %s -cc %s -s %s -u \"%s\" -m \"%s\" -a
\"%s\"",
            EMAIL_SENDER_ADDRESS,
            EMAIL_RECEIVER_ADDRESS,
            EMAIL_CC_ADDRESS,
            SERVICE_PROVIDER_SMTP,
            header,
            message,
            attachment);

    // Send email
    system (buffer);

#endif
}
```

```
//****************************************************************************
// Determine Current Day Name
//
// This function determines the current day name.
//
//****************************************************************************

void  determine_current_day_name (char *  day_name)
{
    // Date and time variables
    time_t  td;
    struct tm   *dcp;
    Uint16  day_of_week;


    // Get system date and time
    time(&td);
    dcp = localtime(&td);

    // Initialize calandar variables
    day_of_week = dcp->tm_wday;

    // Determine day of week name
    switch (day_of_week)
    {
        case  SUNDAY:    strcpy (day_name, "Sunday");       break;
        case  MONDAY:    strcpy (day_name, "Monday");       break;
        case  TUESDAY:   strcpy (day_name, "Tuesday");      break;
        case  WEDNESDAY: strcpy (day_name, "Wednesday");    break;
        case  THURSDAY:  strcpy (day_name, "Thursday");     break;
        case  FRIDAY:    strcpy (day_name, "Friday");       break;
        case  SATURDAY:  strcpy (day_name, "Saturday");     break;
    }

}
```

```
//****************************************************************************
// Determine Current Month
//
// This function determines the current month.
//
//****************************************************************************

void  determine_current_month (Uint16 *  month_index)
{
    // Date and time variables
    time_t  td;
    struct tm   *dcp;
    Uint16  day, month, year, hour, minute, second;


    // Get system date and time
    time(&td);
    dcp = localtime(&td);

    // Initialize calandar variables
    day    = dcp->tm_mday;
    month  = dcp->tm_mon + 1;
    year   = dcp->tm_year + 1900;
    hour   = dcp->tm_hour;
    minute = dcp->tm_min;
    second = dcp->tm_sec;

    // Return the current month
    *month_index = month;
}
```

```
//******************************************************************************
// Determine Current Month Name
//
// This function determines the current month name.
//
//******************************************************************************

void  determine_current_month_name (char *  month_name)
{
    // Date and time variables
    Uint16  month_index;


    determine_current_month (&month_index);

    switch (month_index)
    {
        case  JANUARY:   strcpy (month_name, "January");     break;
        case  FEBRUARY:  strcpy (month_name, "February");    break;
        case  MARCH:     strcpy (month_name, "March");       break;
        case  APRIL:     strcpy (month_name, "April");       break;
        case  MAY:       strcpy (month_name, "May");         break;
        case  JUNE:      strcpy (month_name, "June");        break;
        case  JULY:      strcpy (month_name, "July");        break;
        case  AUGUST:    strcpy (month_name, "August");      break;
        case  SEPTEMBER: strcpy (month_name, "September");   break;
        case  OCTOBER:   strcpy (month_name, "October");     break;
        case  NOVEMBER:  strcpy (month_name, "November");    break;
        case  DECEMBER:  strcpy (month_name, "December");    break;
        default:                                             .
            strcpy (month_name, "");
            break;
    }

}
```

```
//****************************************************************************
// Speak
//
// This function builds and speak command for the passed text message.
// The festival utility is used to generate the speech sounds.
//
// Basic command to say 'good morning': echo "Good morning."  | festival --tts
//
//****************************************************************************

void  speak (char * message)
{

    char    buffer[1024];

    // Build the speech command
    sprintf (buffer, "echo \"%s\" | festival --tts", message);

    // Speak the words
    system (buffer);

}
```

```
//******************************************************************************
// Speak Time And Date
//
// This function determines the current time and date and then speaks it out.
//
// The format is as shown in the following example:
// It is 26 minutes past 2 in the afternoon, on Saturday the 29th of March 2014
//
//******************************************************************************

void  speak_time_and_date (void)
{

    time_t  td;
    struct tm   *dcp;
    Uint16  day, month, year, hour, minute, second;

    char    message[255]          = "Not defined";
    char    old_time[255]         = "Not defined";
    char    day_name[24]          = "Not defined";
    char    month_name[24]        = "Not defined";
    char    part_of_day[48]       = "Not defined";
    char    day_number_suffix[16] = "Not defined";


    // Get system date and time
    time(&td);
    dcp = localtime(&td);

    // Initialize calandar variables
    day    = dcp->tm_mday;
    month  = dcp->tm_mon + 1;
    year   = dcp->tm_year + 1900;
    hour   = dcp->tm_hour;
    minute = dcp->tm_min;
    second = dcp->tm_sec;


    // Determine the part of day
    if (hour < 12)
    {
        // It is morning - which part?
        if (hour < 4)
        {
            // It is the wee hours of the morning
            strcpy (part_of_day, "in the early hours of the morning");
        }
        else
        {
            // It is later on in the morning
            strcpy (part_of_day, "in the morning");
        }
    }
    else
    {
        // Is it the afternoon [24 hour clock]?
        if (hour < 18)
        {
```

```
        // Yes - It is the afternoon
        strcpy (part_of_day, "in the afternoon");
    }
    // Is this the evening?
    else if (hour < 20)
    {
        // Yes - It is the evening
        strcpy (part_of_day, "in the evening");
    }
    else
    {
        // Yes - It is the evening
        strcpy (part_of_day, "at night");
    }
}


// Determine the day index
switch (day)
{
    case 1:
    case 21:
    case 31:    strcpy (day_number_suffix, "st");
                break;

    case 2:
    case 22:    strcpy (day_number_suffix, "nd");
                break;

    case 3:
    case 23:    strcpy (day_number_suffix, "rd");
                break;

    default :   strcpy (day_number_suffix, "th");
                break;
}



// Determine the 'old time' description
if ((hour == 0) && (minute == 0))
{
    sprintf (old_time, "midnight");
    strcpy (part_of_day, "");              // Erase part of day description
}
else if ((hour == 12) && (minute == 0))
{
    sprintf (old_time, "midday");
    strcpy (part_of_day, "");              // Erase part of day description
}
else
{
    // Is this the midnight hour?
    if (hour == 0)
    {
        // Yes - make it now 12 "am"
        hour = 12;
    }
```

```
        if (minute == 0)
            sprintf (old_time, "%d o'clock", (hour <= 12) ? hour : (hour - 12));
        else if (minute == 15)
            sprintf (old_time, "quarter past %d", (hour <= 12) ? hour : (hour -
12));
        else if (minute == 30)
            sprintf (old_time, "half past %d", (hour <= 12) ? hour : (hour - 12));
        else if (minute == 45)
            sprintf (old_time, "quarter to %d", (hour <= 12) ? hour : (hour - 12));
        else if (minute < 2)
            sprintf (old_time, "one minute after %d", (hour <= 12) ? hour : (hour -
12));
        else if (minute < 30)
            sprintf (old_time, "%d minutes after %d", minute, (hour <= 12) ? hour :
(hour - 12));
        else if (minute < 59)
            sprintf (old_time, "%d minutes before %d", (60 - minute), (++hour <=
12) ? hour : (hour - 12));
        else
            sprintf (old_time, "one minute to %d", (++hour <= 12) ? hour : (hour -
12));
    }

    // Determine the day and month names
    determine_current_day_name (day_name);
    determine_current_month_name (month_name);

    // Say the time and date.  It should have the following format...
    // It is 26 minutes past 2 in the afternoon, on Saturday the 29th of March
2014
    sprintf (message, "It is %s %s on %s the %d%s of %s %d %d",
            old_time,
            part_of_day,
            day_name,
            day,
            day_number_suffix,
            month_name,
            (year / 100) * 100,
            year % 100);

    print_log (message);

    speak(message);

}
```

```
//*****************************************************************************
// Snap Picture
//
// This function builds and then executes the security email message.
// If we do not limit the buffer sizes then we run the risk of memory
// corruption and the generation of a system page fault.
//
// Different command line examples:
// fswebcam -save /home/orion/Projects/Execs/steve.jpg
// fswebcam -save /home/orion/Projects/Execs/steve.jpg -r 960x720 -s
brightness=150
// fswebcam -save /home/orion/Projects/Execs/steve.jpg -r 1920x1080 -s
brightness=150
//*****************************************************************************
void  snap_picture (char * file_name)
{

    char    buffer[1024];


    // Build command
    sprintf (buffer, "fswebcam -r 1920x1080 -s brightness=150 -save \"%s\"",
file_name);

    // Execute the command
    system (buffer);

}
```

```
//***************************************************************************
// Reset Security Detection Flags
//
// This function resets all the security flags.
//
//***************************************************************************

void  reset_security_detection_flags (void)
{

    // Reset all security detection flags
    steve_bedroom_sensor_security             = FALSE;
    common_washroom_sensor_security           = FALSE;
    common_bathroom_sensor_security           = FALSE;
    mini_hallway_sensor_security              = FALSE;
    study_sensor_security                     = FALSE;
    familyroom_sensor_security                = FALSE;
    inside_front_door_sensor_security         = FALSE;
    main_hallway_sensor_security              = FALSE;
    lounge_hallway_sensor_security            = FALSE;
    master_hallway_sensor_security            = FALSE;
    kitchen_sensor_security                   = FALSE;
    kitchen_nook_sensor_security              = FALSE;
    master_bedroom_sensor_security            = FALSE;
    master_bathroom_sensor_security           = FALSE;
    master_closet_sensor_security             = FALSE;
    garage_sensor_security                    = FALSE;
    master_bedroom_closet_sensor_security     = FALSE;
    pantry_sensor_security                    = FALSE;
    laundry_sensor_security                   = FALSE;
    guest_bathroom_sensor_security            = FALSE;
    guest_bedroom_door_sensor_security        = FALSE;
}




//***************************************************************************
// Limit Turn Off Time To Just After Dusk
//
// This function ensures that if the lamp turn off time is at or past the dusk
// time then it will be adjusted to just after the dusk timeout period.
// This will then permit the IR sensor some time in triggering and by
// such extending the turn off time without switching off the light.
//
//***************************************************************************

void  limit_turn_off_time_to_just_after_dusk (long int *  time)
{

    if (*time > dusk_timeout)
    {
        // Force turn off time to just after dusk
        *time = dusk_timeout + OFFSET_1MIN30SEC;
    }
}
```

```
//*******************************************************************************
// Get High Resolution Timer
//
// This function obtains a system timer count with milliseconds resolution.
//
//*******************************************************************************

long int  get_high_resolution_timer (void)
{
    long int    milliseconds;
    struct      timeval timer;


    // Get the current timer count
    gettimeofday(&timer, NULL);

    // Convert it into milliseconds
    milliseconds = (timer.tv_sec * 1000) + (timer.tv_usec / 1000.0) + 0.5;

    return (milliseconds);

}


#endif
```

File: hc_main.c

```
//****************************************************************************
//  Author: Stephen W. McClure
//    Date: March 2014
// Project: Designing Embedded Systems [Book]
//
//****************************************************************************
// Purpose:
//
// This program is part of the X10 Home Control Project.
//
// InfraRed RF Sensors are used to detect the presence of a person in a
// specific room or area of the home.  When a presence is detected, the
// InfraRed Sensor transmits an RF code.  Each InfraRed Sensor my be
// programmed with its own user assigned RF code.  This code consists of a
// House / Unit set of values.  For example [A,1] for house code 'A' and
// unit code '1'.
//
// A device called the WF800 RF32A Receiver is used to pick up the InfraRed
// RF transmissions and provide them to the Linux Computer system as an RS232
// serial transmission over a serial port.  Each of these serial
// transmissions are decoded and the contained house / unit codes extracted
// and stored in a MySQL Database.
//
// These sensors are easily purchased from Home Control supply stores.
//
// When this program is started, the MySQL databases will be created if they
// do not currently exist. Device codes and descriptions are also placed into
// the databases tables.
//
//****************************************************************************
//
// File Name: hc_main.c
//
// Build command
// gcc hc_main.c -o hc_main `mysql_config --cflags --libs`
//
// Execution Command
// ./hc_main > hc_main.log &
//
//
// But first don't forget to sign in as SU and give the appropriate serial
// ports the access right permissions (eg.: chmod a+rw /dev/ttyS1) and to
// also use the static ip address: 192.168.1.176 (set by using wired network
// connection icon in the bottom right of the Mint 13 GUI)
//
// For example:
// $ su
// Password: enter super user password
// # chmod a+rw  /dev/ttyS0
// # chmod a+rw  /dev/ttyS1
// # exit
//
// chmod a+r  /dev/ttyS0  Set ttyS0 for Input Only  [ORION-ITX TOP    Port]
// chmod a+rw /dev/ttyS1  Set ttyS1 for I/O         [ORION-ITX BOTTOM Port]
//
```

```
// ttyS0  -  Top Port    = RF X10 Commands
// ttyS1  -  Bottom Port = TI-103
//
// Or make the user 'orion' part of the "dialout" group
// which will give it RW permission to the ttys0 and ttys1 serial ports
// by issuing the following instruction: sudo adduser orion dialout
// (will need to provide the su password).
//
// When using autostart a delay is required at the start of this program's
// execution in order to allow the MySQL system to be initialized prior to it
// being accessed.
//****************************************************************************


// Include Files
#include <sys/types.h>
#include <sys/stat.h>
#include <fcntl.h>
#include <termios.h>
#include <stdio.h>
#include <my_global.h>
#include <mysql.h>
#include <sys/time.h>
#include <unistd.h>
#include <signal.h>
#include <string.h>
#include <time.h>


// Include local header Files
#include "hc_literals.h"
#include "hc_typedefs.h"
#include "hc_publics.h"

// Include local modules
#include "hc_common.c"


// X10 Validity
Uint8  x10_rf_code = INVALID;


// Bytes received from W800RF32A:
Uint8  byte_1;
Uint8  byte_2;
Uint8  byte_3;
Uint8  byte_4;

// Translation into House and Unit Codes:
Uint8  house_code;
Uint8  unit_code;
Uint8  command;
Uint8  x10_rf_code;
```

```
//*****************************************************************************
// Initialize Serial Port for WF800
//
// This function opens the serial port for reading the WF800 32A RF
// X10 Control Codes from the InfraRed Sensors.
//
//*****************************************************************************

void  initialize_serial_port_for_wf800 (void)
{

    // Open the Serial Port [TOP PORT ON ORION-ITX, Read Only]
    fd = open(SERIAL_PORT_0, O_RDWR | O_NOCTTY );

    // Error detected in opening port?
    if (fd < 0)
    {
        // Yes - Display error message
        perror(SERIAL_PORT_1);
        exit(-1);    // Exit application with Error
    }


    // Save current serial port settings
    tcgetattr(fd, &old_options);

    // Setup the Serial Port Configuration
    new_options.c_cflag = BAUDRATE | CRTSCTS | CS8 | CLOCAL | CREAD;
    new_options.c_iflag = IGNPAR;
    new_options.c_oflag = 0;


    // Set input mode (non-canonical, no echo,...)
    new_options.c_lflag = 0;

    // Wait until either 4 characters have been received;
    // OR the time interval between characters exceeds 100ms
    new_options.c_cc[VTIME] = 10;     /* inter-character timer used */
    new_options.c_cc[VMIN]  = 4;      /* blocking read until 4 chars received */

    // Flush the input buffer
    tcflush(fd, TCIFLUSH);

    // Configure the Serial Port
    tcsetattr(fd, TCSANOW, &new_options);

}
```

```
//*****************************************************************************
// Process Events That Occur At Midnight                        UNIQUE TO HC_MAIN
//
// This function handles events that occur at midnight.
//
//*****************************************************************************

void  process_events_that_occur_at_midnight (void)
{

    // Has midnight just started?
    if (midnight_start == TRUE)
    {
        // Place all midnight start events here...
        // ========================================
        reset_security_detection_flags();

        // Reset event flag
        midnight_start = FALSE;
    }

}




//*****************************************************************************
// Process Events That Occur At Sunrise                         UNIQUE TO HC_MAIN
//
// This function handles events that occur as night transitions into day.
//
//*****************************************************************************

void  process_events_that_occur_at_sunrise (void)
{

    // Has the day just started?
    if (day_start == TRUE)
    {
        // Place all day start events here...
        // ==================================


        // Reset event flag
        day_start = FALSE;
    }

}
```

```
//****************************************************************************
// Process Events That Occur At Sunset                         UNIQUE TO HC_MAIN
//
// This function handles events that occur as day transitions into night.
//
//****************************************************************************

void  process_events_that_occur_at_sunset (void)
{

    // Has the night just started?
    if (night_start == TRUE)
    {
        // Place all night start events here...
        // ====================================


        // Reset event flag
        night_start = FALSE;
    }

}
```

```
//*****************************************************************************
// Initialize House Code States Table
//
// This function places default data into the MySQL 'house_code_state' table.
// This sets all table entries to 'No Time' and 'No Description'.
//
// Translation from W800RF32A to House/Unit Codes:
//
// Provides the following:
// =======================
//
// house_code  in range [1..16]
// unit_code   in range [1..16]
// command     in range [X10_OFF, X10_ON]
// x10_rf_code in range [INVALID, VALID]
//
//*****************************************************************************

#define NO_PRESENCE 0
#define NO_TIMEOUT  0
#define NO_TYPE  0

void  initialize_house_code_states_table (void)
{
    char    buffer [255];
    char    message [255];


    for (house_code = 1; house_code <= 16; house_code++)
    {
        for (unit_code = 1; unit_code <= 16; unit_code++)
        {
            sprintf (buffer, "INSERT INTO house_code_states VALUES(%d, %d, 2, 2,
'No Time', %d, %d, 'No Description')",
                    house_code, unit_code, NO_TIMEOUT, NO_PRESENCE);

            if (mysql_query(conn2, buffer))
            {
                sprintf (message, "Error_Init %u: %s\n", mysql_errno(conn2),
mysql_error(conn2));
                print_log (message);
            }
        }
    }

}
```

```
//*******************************************************************************
// Update House Code States
//
// This function updates the house code states description for a specific device.
//
//*******************************************************************************

void  update_house_code_states (X10_DEVICE  device)
{
    char    buffer[255];


    sprintf (buffer, "UPDATE house_code_states SET description='%s', type=%d WHERE
house=%d AND unit=%d",
            device.description,
            device.type,
            device.x10.house_code,
            device.x10.unit_code);

    //  printf ("%s \n", buffer);
    mysql_query(conn2, buffer);
}
```

```
//*****************************************************************************
// Initialize States Table Descriptions
//
// This function places description data into the MySQL 'house_code_state_table'
// for specific House and Unit codes.
//
//*****************************************************************************
void  initialize_states_table_descriptions (void)
{
    // Add in State Descriptions

    // General Descriptions
    update_house_code_states (light_sensor);

    // Porch Descriptions
    update_house_code_states (front_porch_sensor);
    update_house_code_states (porch_outside_light);

    // Inside Front Door Descriptions
    update_house_code_states (inside_front_door_sensor);

    update_house_code_states (inside_entrance_light);

    // Hallway Descriptions
    update_house_code_states (main_hallway_sensor);
    update_house_code_states (mini_hallway_sensor);
    update_house_code_states (lounge_hallway_sensor);
    update_house_code_states (master_hallway_sensor);
    update_house_code_states (mini_hallway_light);
    update_house_code_states (main_hallway_light);

    // Laundry Descriptions
    update_house_code_states (laundry_sensor);
    update_house_code_states (laundry_fan);
    update_house_code_states (laundry_light);

    // Pantry Descriptions
    update_house_code_states (pantry_sensor);
    update_house_code_states (pantry_light);

    // Kitchen Descriptions
    update_house_code_states (kitchen_sensor);
    update_house_code_states (counter_fridge_sensor);
    update_house_code_states (counter_cooktop_left_sensor);
    update_house_code_states (counter_cooktop_right_sensor);
    update_house_code_states (kitchen_nook_sensor);
    update_house_code_states (kitchen_light);
    update_house_code_states (kitchen_nook_light);
    update_house_code_states (kitchen_counter_light);
    update_house_code_states (kitchen_sink_light);

    // Lounge Area Descriptions
    update_house_code_states (lounge_wall_light);
    update_house_code_states (lounge_window_light);
    update_house_code_states (fishtank_light);
```

```
// Dining Room Descriptions
update_house_code_states (diningroom_outside_light);
update_house_code_states (diningroom_table_light);

// Family Room Descriptions
update_house_code_states (familyroom_sensor);
update_house_code_states (familyroom_window_light);
update_house_code_states (familyroom_wall_light);
update_house_code_states (familyroom_track_tv_light);
update_house_code_states (familyroom_track_reading_light);
update_house_code_states (familyroom_radio);
update_house_code_states (familyroom_outside_light);

// Cloakroom Descriptions
update_house_code_states (cloakroom_sensor);
update_house_code_states (cloakroom_light);

// Guest Bathroom Descriptions
update_house_code_states (guest_shower_sensor);
update_house_code_states (guest_bathroom_sensor);
update_house_code_states (guest_bathroom_light);
update_house_code_states (guest_bathroom_flight);

update_house_code_states (guest_bathroom_fan);

// Guest Bedroom Descriptions
update_house_code_states (guest_bedroom_door_sensor);
update_house_code_states (guest_bedroom_window_sensor);
update_house_code_states (guest_main_light);
update_house_code_states (guest_bed_light);

// Steve's Room Descriptions
update_house_code_states (steve_bedroom_sensor);
update_house_code_states (steve_bedroom_wall_light);
update_house_code_states (steve_bedroom_window_light);
update_house_code_states (steve_bedroom_ceiling_light);

// Study Descriptions
update_house_code_states (study_sensor);
update_house_code_states (study_ceiling_light);

// Common Washroom Descriptions
update_house_code_states (common_washroom_sensor);
update_house_code_states (common_washroom_light);
update_house_code_states (common_washroom_flight);


// Common Bathroom Descriptions
update_house_code_states (common_bathroom_sensor);
update_house_code_states (common_bathroom_light);

// Master Bedroom Descriptions
update_house_code_states (master_bedroom_sensor);
update_house_code_states (master_bedroom_dad_light);
update_house_code_states (master_bedroom_mum_light);

update_house_code_states (master_bedroom_outside_light);
update_house_code_states (master_bedroom_closet_sensor);
```

```
    update_house_code_states (master_bedroom_closet_light);
    update_house_code_states (master_bathroom_sensor);
    update_house_code_states (master_toilet_sensor);

    // Garage Descriptions
    update_house_code_states (garage_z71_sensor);
    update_house_code_states (garage_bike_sensor);
    update_house_code_states (garage_fridge_sensor);
    update_house_code_states (garage_light);
    update_house_code_states (garage_front_outside_light);
    update_house_code_states (garage_back_outside_light);

    // Season Icicle Descriptions
    update_house_code_states (season_front_light);
    update_house_code_states (season_back_light);

    // Security Descriptions
    update_house_code_states (security_alarm_siren);
    update_house_code_states (barking_doggy);

}
```

```
//****************************************************************************
// Initialize System Control Database
//
// This funtion attempts to connect to the MySQL System running on the Linux
// machine.  If connection is established then a connection attempt is made to
// the system control database.  If the database does not exist then it is
// created.
//
// The MySQL database name is "system_control".
//
// This database contains the following three tables:
//
// 1. house_state (Home Mode or Security Mode)
// 2. house_code_events (acive inputs to be processed)
// 3. house_code_states (current house code states)
//
// If any error is detected, an error message is displayed and
// the program exits.
//****************************************************************************

void  initialize_system_control_database (void)
{
    char    message [255];


    // Access the MySQL system
    // =======================
    conn1 = mysql_init(NULL);

    if (conn1 == NULL)
    {
        // Cannot access the MySQL system - Error Exit
        sprintf (message, "Error_A %u: %s", mysql_errno(conn1),
mysql_error(conn1));
        print_log (message);
        exit(1);
    }


    // MySQL Active - Connect to MySQL Environment, "system_control" database
    // ======================================================================
    if (mysql_real_connect (conn1,
                            "192.168.1.176",
                            "steve",
                            "william",
                            "system_control",
                            0,
                            NULL,
                            0) == NULL)
    {
        // Can't connect to database - Perhaps database does not exist...
        sprintf (message, "Error_B %u: %s", mysql_errno(conn1),
mysql_error(conn1));
        print_log (message);
        print_log ("Creating 'system_control' database...");


        // If cannot connect to database then just log in to MySQL
```

```
        if (mysql_real_connect (conn1,
                              "192.168.1.176",
                              "steve",
                              "william",
                              NULL,
                              0,
                              NULL,
                              0) == NULL)
        {
            // Cannot log in - Error Exit
            sprintf (message, "Error_C %u: %s", mysql_errno(conn1),
mysql_error(conn1));
            print_log (message);
            exit(1);
        }

        // All is well, logged into MySQL
        print_log ("Logged into MySQL database system...");


        // Create the 'system_control' Data Base
        // ======================================
        if (mysql_query(conn1, "create database system_control"))
        {
            // Cannot create database - Error Exit
            sprintf (message, "Error_D %u: %s", mysql_errno(conn1),
mysql_error(conn1));
            print_log (message);
            exit(1);
        }

        // 'system_control' database successfully created
        print_log ("Created 'system_control' database...");


        // Now connect to the 'system_control' database
        // =============================================
        conn2 = mysql_init(NULL);

        if (mysql_real_connect (conn2,
                              "192.168.1.176",
                              "steve",
                              "william",
                              "system_control",
                              0,
                              NULL,
                              0) == NULL)
        {
            // Cannot connect to the database - Error Exit
            sprintf (message, "Error_E %u: %s", mysql_errno(conn2),
mysql_error(conn2));
            print_log (message);
            exit(1);
        }

        print_log ("Logged into MySQL 'system_control' database...");
```

```
        // Create table 'house_state'
        // ===========================
        if (mysql_query(conn2, "CREATE TABLE house_state (security int,
security_delay int, sleep int, sleep_delay int, family_lights int, steve_lights
int, go_to_bed int, master_watch_tv int)"))
        {
            // Cannot create table - Error Exit
            sprintf (message, "Error_F %u: %s", mysql_errno(conn2),
mysql_error(conn2));
            print_log (message);
            exit(1);
        }
        else
        {
            print_log ("Created table 'system_control:house_state'...");

            // Initialize 'house_state' table if it has just been created.
            // Security not active (ie. home mode), sleep is inactive
            if (mysql_query(conn2, "INSERT INTO house_state
VALUES(0,0,0,0,0,0,0,0)"))
            {
                // Cannot initialize house state to 'HOME Mode' - Error Exit
                sprintf (message, "Error_G %u: %s", mysql_errno(conn2),
mysql_error(conn2));
                print_log (message);
                exit(1);
            }
            else
                print_log ("Initialized table 'system_control:house_state'...");
        }


        // Create table 'house_code_events'
        // =================================
        if (mysql_query(conn2, "CREATE TABLE house_code_events (house int, unit
int, type int, state int, timestamp VARCHAR(20), timeout int, description
VARCHAR(50))"))
        {
            // Cannot create table - Error Exit
            sprintf (message, "Error_H %u: %s", mysql_errno(conn2),
mysql_error(conn2));
            print_log (message);
            exit(1);
        }
        else
            print_log ("Created table 'system_control:house_code_events'...");


        // Create table 'house_code_states'
        // =================================
        if (mysql_query(conn2, "CREATE TABLE house_code_states (house int, unit
int, type int, state int, timestamp VARCHAR(20), timeout int, presence int,
description VARCHAR(50))"))
        {
            // Cannot create table - Error Exit
            sprintf (message, "Error_I %u: %s", mysql_errno(conn2),
mysql_error(conn2));
```

```
            print_log (message);
            exit(1);
        }
        else
        {
            print_log ("Created table 'system_control:house_code_states'...");

            initialize_house_code_states_table();
            initialize_states_table_descriptions();
            print_log ("Initialized.. 'system_control:house_code_states'...");
        }

        // Now use conn1 to access database
        conn1 = conn2;
    }
    else
    {
        //  system_control database already exists!!!
        print_log ("system_control database already exists!!!");
    }

}
```

```
//******************************************************************************
// Convert RF Codes
//
// Convert RF Received Codes to House and Unit Codes
//
//******************************************************************************

void  convert_rf_codes (Uint8  house, Uint8  unit,  Uint8  offset)
{

    // Determine House Code - Convert to Range [1..16]
    house_code = house + 1;

    // Determine Unit ON/OFF Codes - Range [1..16]
    switch (unit)
    {
    // Unit Code '1' or '9'
    case 0x00: unit_code = 0x01 + offset; command = X10_ON;   return;
    case 0x20: unit_code = 0x01 + offset; command = X10_OFF;  return;

    // Unit Code '2' or '10'
    case 0x10: unit_code = 0x02 + offset; command = X10_ON;   return;
    case 0x30: unit_code = 0x02 + offset; command = X10_OFF;  return;

    // Unit Code '3' or '11'
    case 0x08: unit_code = 0x03 + offset; command = X10_ON;   return;
    case 0x28: unit_code = 0x03 + offset; command = X10_OFF;  return;

    // Unit Code '4' or '12'
    case 0x18: unit_code = 0x04 + offset; command = X10_ON;   return;
    case 0x38: unit_code = 0x04 + offset; command = X10_OFF;  return;

    // Unit Code '5' or '13'
    case 0x40: unit_code = 0x05 + offset; command = X10_ON;   return;
    case 0x60: unit_code = 0x05 + offset; command = X10_OFF;  return;

    // Unit Code '6' or '14'
    case 0x50: unit_code = 0x06 + offset; command = X10_ON;   return;
    case 0x70: unit_code = 0x06 + offset; command = X10_OFF;  return;

    // Unit Code '7' or '15'
    case 0x48: unit_code = 0x07 + offset; command = X10_ON;   return;
    case 0x68: unit_code = 0x07 + offset; command = X10_OFF;  return;

    // Unit Code '8' or '16'
    case 0x58: unit_code = 0x08 + offset; command = X10_ON;   return;
    case 0x78: unit_code = 0x08 + offset; command = X10_OFF;  return;

    // Error condition - Ignore message
    //      default:
    }

    // X10 RF Code Validity
    x10_rf_code = INVALID;

}
```

```
//*****************************************************************************
// x10_convert_rf_codes
//
// This fucnction converts the X10 RF Codes to House and Unit codes.
//
//*****************************************************************************

void  x10_convert_rf_codes (Uint8  byte_1, Uint8  byte_3)
{
    // X10 RF Code - Assume initially valid
    x10_rf_code = VALID;

    switch (byte_1)
    {
    // House Code 'A'
    case 0x60: convert_rf_codes (0x00, byte_3, 0x00); return;  // House A, Unit,
Offset
    case 0x64: convert_rf_codes (0x00, byte_3, 0x08); return;

    // House Code 'B'
    case 0x70: convert_rf_codes (0x01, byte_3, 0x00); return;  // House B, Unit,
Offset
    case 0x74: convert_rf_codes (0x01, byte_3, 0x08); return;

    // House Code 'C'
    case 0x40: convert_rf_codes (0x02, byte_3, 0x00); return;  // House C, Unit,
Offset
    case 0x44: convert_rf_codes (0x02, byte_3, 0x08); return;

    // House Code 'D'
    case 0x50: convert_rf_codes (0x03, byte_3, 0x00); return;  // House D, Unit,
Offset
    case 0x54: convert_rf_codes (0x03, byte_3, 0x08); return;

    // House Code 'E'
    case 0x80: convert_rf_codes (0x04, byte_3, 0x00); return;  // House E, Unit,
Offset
    case 0x84: convert_rf_codes (0x04, byte_3, 0x08); return;

    // House Code 'F'
    case 0x90: convert_rf_codes (0x05, byte_3, 0x00); return;  // House F, Unit,
Offset
    case 0x94: convert_rf_codes (0x05, byte_3, 0x08); return;

    // House Code 'G'
    case 0xA0: convert_rf_codes (0x06, byte_3, 0x00); return;  // House G, Unit,
Offset
    case 0xA4: convert_rf_codes (0x06, byte_3, 0x08); return;

    // House Code 'H'
    case 0xB0: convert_rf_codes (0x07, byte_3, 0x00); return;  // House H, Unit,
Offset
    case 0xB4: convert_rf_codes (0x07, byte_3, 0x08); return;

    // House Code 'I'
    case 0xE0: convert_rf_codes (0x08, byte_3, 0x00); return;  // House I, Unit,
Offset
    case 0xE4: convert_rf_codes (0x08, byte_3, 0x08); return;
```

```
    // House Code 'J'
    case 0xF0: convert_rf_codes (0x09, byte_3, 0x00); return;  // House J, Unit,
Offset
    case 0xF4: convert_rf_codes (0x09, byte_3, 0x08); return;

    // House Code 'K'
    case 0xC0: convert_rf_codes (0x0A, byte_3, 0x00); return;  // House K, Unit,
Offset
    case 0xC4: convert_rf_codes (0x0A, byte_3, 0x08); return;

    // House Code 'L'
    case 0xD0: convert_rf_codes (0x0B, byte_3, 0x00); return;  // House L, Unit,
Offset
    case 0xD4: convert_rf_codes (0x0B, byte_3, 0x08); return;

    // House Code 'M'
    case 0x00: convert_rf_codes (0x0C, byte_3, 0x00); return;  // House M, Unit,
Offset
    case 0x04: convert_rf_codes (0x0C, byte_3, 0x08); return;

    // House Code 'N'
    case 0x10: convert_rf_codes (0x0D, byte_3, 0x00); return;  // House N, Unit,
Offset
    case 0x14: convert_rf_codes (0x0D, byte_3, 0x08); return;

    // House Code 'O'
    case 0x20: convert_rf_codes (0x0E, byte_3, 0x00); return;  // House O, Unit,
Offset
    case 0x24: convert_rf_codes (0x0E, byte_3, 0x08); return;

    // House Code 'P'
    case 0x30: convert_rf_codes (0x0F, byte_3, 0x00); return;  // House P, Unit,
Offset
    case 0x34: convert_rf_codes (0x0F, byte_3, 0x08); return;

    // Error condition - Ignore message
    //      default:

    }

    // X10 RF Code - No code found - Code Invalid
    x10_rf_code = INVALID;

}
```

```
//*****************************************************************************
// Device Code Set
//
// This function returns TRUE if the house and unit codes equals those of the
// X10 device parameter.
//
//*****************************************************************************

Uint8  device_code_set (X10_DEVICE  device)
{

    // Is this device code set?
    return ((device.x10.house_code == house_code) &&
            (device.x10.unit_code  == unit_code));
}
```

```
//*****************************************************************************
// Process Intruder Check
//
// This function determines if there was any activity within the home and if
// any such presence was detected then the alarm siren will be activated.
// A single email message (per location) is also broadcast.
//
//*****************************************************************************

void  process_intruder_check (void)
{
    char        message[255];
    char        time_buffer[255];
    long int    current_time;


    // Compute current timestamp
    determine_system_timestamp (time_buffer);

    // Get current time in seconds
    current_time = get_raw_time();

    // Intruder at front door?
    if (device_code_set (front_porch_sensor))
    {
        // Yes - Has the timer expired?
        if (front_porch_sensor_security_timer == DELAY_EXPIRED)
        {
            // Yes - Send security alert email
            front_porch_sensor_security_timer = current_time + OFFSET_5MIN;
            sprintf (message, "%s - Someone is at the Front Door", time_buffer);
            send_security_email ("*** SECURITY ALERT ***", message);

            print_log ("A person is at the front door.");
            speak     ("A person is at the front door.");
        }
    }

    // Has the security timer expired
    if (current_time >= front_porch_sensor_security_timer)
    {
        // Yes - Reset the timer
        front_porch_sensor_security_timer = DELAY_EXPIRED;
    }


    // Intruder in Study?
    if (device_code_set (study_sensor) && (!study_sensor_security))
    {
        // Yes - Turn alarm siren on and send security alert email
        turn_alarm_siren_on();
        study_sensor_security = TRUE;

        print_log ("A person is in the study.");
        speak     ("A person is in the study.");

        snap_picture (STUDY_PICTURE_FILE);
        sprintf (message, "%s - Intruder in Study", time_buffer);
```

```
        send_security_email_with_attachment ("*** SECURITY ALERT ***", message,
STUDY_PICTURE_FILE);

        speak ("Your picture has been taken and sent to thee authorities.");  //
Spelling the as 'thee' sounds better
    }

    // Intruder in Steve's Bedroom?
    if (device_code_set (steve_bedroom_sensor) &&
(!steve_bedroom_sensor_security))
    {
        // Yes - Turn alarm siren on and send security alert email
        turn_alarm_siren_on();
        steve_bedroom_sensor_security = TRUE;

        print_log ("A person is in steve's bedroom.");
        speak     ("A person is in steve's bedroom.");

        sprintf (message, "%s - Intruder in Steve's Bedroom", time_buffer);
        send_security_email ("*** SECURITY ALERT ***", message);
    }

    // Intruder in Common Washroom?
    if (device_code_set (common_washroom_sensor) &&
(!common_washroom_sensor_security))
    {
        // Yes - Turn alarm siren on and send security alert email
        turn_alarm_siren_on();
        common_washroom_sensor_security = TRUE;

        print_log ("A person is in the common washroom.");
        speak     ("A person is in the common washroom.");

        sprintf (message, "%s - Intruder in Common Washroom", time_buffer);
        send_security_email ("*** SECURITY ALERT ***", message);
    }

    // Intruder in Common Bathroom?
    if (device_code_set (common_bathroom_sensor) &&
(!common_bathroom_sensor_security))
    {
        // Yes - Turn alarm siren on and send security alert email
        turn_alarm_siren_on();
        common_bathroom_sensor_security = TRUE;

        print_log ("A person is in the common bathroom.");
        speak     ("A person is in the common bathroom.");

        sprintf (message, "%s - Intruder in Common Bathroom", time_buffer);
        send_security_email ("*** SECURITY ALERT ***", message);
    }

    // Intruder in Mini-Hallway?
    if (device_code_set (mini_hallway_sensor) && (!mini_hallway_sensor_security))
    {
        // Yes - Turn alarm siren on and send security alert email
        turn_alarm_siren_on();
        mini_hallway_sensor_security = TRUE;
```

```
        print_log ("A person is in the mini hall way");
        speak     ("A person is in the mini hall way");

        sprintf (message, "%s - Intruder in Mini-Hallway", time_buffer);
        send_security_email ("*** SECURITY ALERT ***", message);
    }

    // Intruder in Familyroom?
    if (device_code_set (familyroom_sensor) && (!familyroom_sensor_security))
    {
        // Yes - Turn alarm siren on and send security alert email
        turn_alarm_siren_on();
        familyroom_sensor_security = TRUE;

        print_log ("A person is in the family room.");
        speak     ("A person is in the family room.");

        sprintf (message, "%s - Intruder in Familyroom", time_buffer);
        send_security_email ("*** SECURITY ALERT ***", message);
    }

    // Intruder at Inside Front Door?
    if (device_code_set (inside_front_door_sensor) &&
(!inside_front_door_sensor_security))
    {
        // Yes - Turn alarm siren on and send security alert email
        turn_alarm_siren_on();
        inside_front_door_sensor_security = TRUE;

        print_log ("A person is at the inside front door.");
        speak     ("A person is at the inside front door.");

        sprintf (message, "%s - Intruder at Inside Front Door", time_buffer);
        send_security_email ("*** SECURITY ALERT ***", message);
    }

    // Intruder in Main Hallway?
    if (device_code_set (main_hallway_sensor) && (!main_hallway_sensor_security))
    {
        // Yes - Turn alarm siren on and send security alert email
        turn_alarm_siren_on();
        main_hallway_sensor_security = TRUE;

        print_log ("A person is in the main hall way.");
        speak     ("A person is in the main hall way.");

        sprintf (message, "%s - Intruder in Main Hallway", time_buffer);
        send_security_email ("*** SECURITY ALERT ***", message);
    }

    // Intruder in Lounge Hallway?
    if (device_code_set (lounge_hallway_sensor) &&
(!lounge_hallway_sensor_security))
    {
        // Yes - Turn alarm siren on and send security alert email
        turn_alarm_siren_on();
        lounge_hallway_sensor_security = TRUE;
```

```
        print_log ("A person is in the lounge hall way.");
        speak     ("A person is in the lounge hall way.");

        sprintf (message, "%s - Intruder in Lounge Hallway", time_buffer);
        send_security_email ("*** SECURITY ALERT ***", message);
    }

    // Intruder in Master Hallway?
    if (device_code_set (master_hallway_sensor) &&
(!master_hallway_sensor_security))
    {
        // Yes - Turn alarm siren on and send security alert email
        turn_alarm_siren_on();
        master_hallway_sensor_security = TRUE;

        print_log ("A person is in the master hall way.");
        speak     ("A person is in the master hall way.");

        sprintf (message, "%s - Intruder in Master Hallway", time_buffer);
        send_security_email ("*** SECURITY ALERT ***", message);
    }

    // Intruder in Kitchen?
    if ((device_code_set (kitchen_sensor)                    ||
            device_code_set (counter_fridge_sensor)          ||
            device_code_set (counter_cooktop_left_sensor)    ||
            device_code_set (counter_cooktop_right_sensor)) &&
(!kitchen_sensor_security))
    {
        // Yes - Turn alarm siren on and send security alert email
        turn_alarm_siren_on();
        kitchen_sensor_security = TRUE;

        print_log ("A person is in the kitchen.");
        speak     ("A person is in the kitchen.");

        sprintf (message, "%s - Intruder in Kitchen", time_buffer);
        send_security_email ("*** SECURITY ALERT ***", message);
    }

    // Intruder in Kitchen Nook?
    if (device_code_set (kitchen_nook_sensor) && (!kitchen_nook_sensor_security))
    {
        // Yes - Turn alarm siren on and send security alert email
        turn_alarm_siren_on();
        kitchen_nook_sensor_security = TRUE;

        print_log ("A person is in the kitchen nook.");
        speak     ("A person is in the kitchen nook.");

        sprintf (message, "%s - Intruder in Kitchen Nook", time_buffer);
        send_security_email ("*** SECURITY ALERT ***", message);
    }


    // Intruder in Master Bedroom?
    if (device_code_set (master_bedroom_sensor) &&
(!master_bedroom_sensor_security))
```

```
    {
        // Yes - Turn alarm siren on and send security alert email
        turn_alarm_siren_on();
        master_bedroom_sensor_security = TRUE;

        print_log ("A person is in the master bedroom.");
        speak     ("A person is in the master bedroom.");

        sprintf (message, "%s - Intruder in Master Bedroom", time_buffer);
        send_security_email ("*** SECURITY ALERT ***", message);
    }

    // Intruder in Master Bathroom?
    if (device_code_set (master_bathroom_sensor) &&
(!master_bathroom_sensor_security))
    {
        // Yes - Turn alarm siren on and send security alert email
        turn_alarm_siren_on();
        master_bathroom_sensor_security = TRUE;

        print_log ("A person is in the master bathroom.");
        speak     ("A person is in the master bathroom.");

        sprintf (message, "%s - Intruder in Master Bathroom", time_buffer);
        send_security_email ("*** SECURITY ALERT ***", message);
    }

    // Intruder in Master Closet?
    if (device_code_set (master_bedroom_closet_sensor) &&
(!master_bedroom_closet_sensor_security))
    {
        // Yes - Turn alarm siren on and send security alert email
        turn_alarm_siren_on();
        master_bedroom_closet_sensor_security = TRUE;

        print_log ("A person is in the master closet.");
        speak     ("A person is in the master closet.");

        sprintf (message, "%s - Intruder in Master Bedroom Closet", time_buffer);
        send_security_email ("*** SECURITY ALERT ***", message);
    }

    // Intruder in Garage?
    if ((device_code_set (garage_fridge_sensor) ||
         device_code_set (garage_bike_sensor)    ||
         device_code_set (garage_z71_sensor))    && (!garage_sensor_security))
    {
        // Yes - Turn alarm siren on and send security alert email
        turn_alarm_siren_on();
        garage_sensor_security = TRUE;

        print_log ("A person is in the garage.");
        speak     ("A person is in the garage.");

        sprintf (message, "%s - Intruder in Garage", time_buffer);
        send_security_email ("*** SECURITY ALERT ***", message);
    }
```

```
    // Intruder in Pantry?
    if (device_code_set (pantry_sensor) && (!pantry_sensor_security))
    {
        // Yes - Turn alarm siren on and send security alert email
        turn_alarm_siren_on();
        pantry_sensor_security = TRUE;

        print_log ("A person is in the pantry.");
        speak     ("A person is in the pantry.");

        sprintf (message, "%s - Intruder in Pantry", time_buffer);
        send_security_email ("*** SECURITY ALERT ***", message);
    }

    // Intruder in Laundry?
    if (device_code_set (laundry_sensor) && (!laundry_sensor_security))
    {
        // Yes - Turn alarm siren on and send security alert email
        turn_alarm_siren_on();
        laundry_sensor_security = TRUE;

        print_log ("A person is in the laundry.");
        speak     ("A person is in the laundry.");

        sprintf (message, "%s - Intruder in Laundry", time_buffer);
        send_security_email ("*** SECURITY ALERT ***", message);
    }

    // Intruder in Guest Bathroom?
    if (device_code_set (guest_bathroom_sensor) &&
(!guest_bathroom_sensor_security))
    {
        // Yes - Turn alarm siren on and send security alert email
        turn_alarm_siren_on();
        guest_bathroom_sensor_security = TRUE;

        print_log ("A person is in the guest bathroom.");
        speak     ("A person is in the guest bathroom.");

        sprintf (message, "%s - Intruder in Guest Bathroom", time_buffer);
        send_security_email ("*** SECURITY ALERT ***", message);
    }

    // Intruder in Guest Bedroom?
    if (device_code_set (guest_bedroom_door_sensor) &&
(!guest_bedroom_door_sensor_security))
    {
        // Yes - Turn alarm siren on and send security alert email
        turn_alarm_siren_on();
        guest_bedroom_door_sensor_security = TRUE;

        print_log ("A person is in the guest bedroom.");
        speak     ("A person is in the guest bedroom.");

        sprintf (message, "%s - Intruder in Guest Bedroom", time_buffer);
        send_security_email ("*** SECURITY ALERT ***", message);
    }
}
```

```
//*******************************************************************************
// Process Laundry Light
//
// This function places required laundry light on/off events into the
// house_code_events table.
//
//*******************************************************************************

void  process_laundry_light (void)
{
    long int    turn_off_time;
    long int    current_time;


    // Laundry Sensor activated?
    if (device_code_set (laundry_sensor))
    {
        // Yes - Get current system time
        current_time = get_raw_time();


        // Yes - Delete any existing laundry light OFF events
        delete_house_code_events (laundry_light);

        // Determine light timeout
        turn_off_time = current_time + OFFSET_1MIN;

        // Turn laundry light ON now
        activate_device (laundry_light, ON,  current_time);

        // Turn laundry light OFF after delay
        activate_device (laundry_light, OFF, turn_off_time);
        activate_device (laundry_light, OFF, turn_off_time + OFFSET_10SEC);
        activate_device (laundry_light, OFF, turn_off_time + OFFSET_20SEC);
    }
}
```

```
//******************************************************************************
// Process Pantry Light
//
// This function places required pantry light on/off events into the
// house_code_events table.
//
//******************************************************************************

void  process_pantry_light (void)
{
    long int    turn_off_time;
    long int    current_time;


    // Pantry Sensor activated?
    if (device_code_set (pantry_sensor))
    {
        // Get current system time
        current_time = get_raw_time();


        // Yes - Delete any existing pantry light device OFF events
        delete_house_code_events (pantry_light);

        // Determine light timeout
        turn_off_time = current_time + OFFSET_1MIN;

        // Turn pantry light ON now
        activate_device (pantry_light,  ON, current_time);

        // Turn pantry light OFF after delay
        activate_device (pantry_light, OFF, turn_off_time);
        activate_device (pantry_light, OFF, turn_off_time + OFFSET_10SEC);
        activate_device (pantry_light, OFF, turn_off_time + OFFSET_20SEC);
    }
}
```

```
//******************************************************************************
// Process Front Porch Light
//
// This function places required front porch light on/off events into the
// house_code_events table.
//
//******************************************************************************

void  process_front_porch_light (void)
{
    long int   inside_entrance_turn_on_time;
    long int   inside_entrance_turn_off_time;
    long int   porch_turn_on_time;
    long int   porch_turn_off_time;
    long int   current_time;


    // Is it night time?
    if (nightime)
    {
        // Yes - Was the porch sensor activated?
        if (device_code_set (front_porch_sensor))
        {
            // Yes - Inform those at home
            speak ("Someone is at the front door.");

            // Delete any existing events
            delete_house_code_events (porch_outside_light);
            delete_house_code_events (inside_entrance_light);

            // Get current system time
            current_time = get_raw_time();

            // Determine light times
            inside_entrance_turn_on_time = current_time +
                    OFFSET_10SEC +
                    (rand() % OFFSET_7SEC);

            porch_turn_on_time = inside_entrance_turn_on_time +
                    OFFSET_3SEC                   +
                    (rand() % OFFSET_10SEC);

            inside_entrance_turn_off_time = porch_turn_on_time +
                    OFFSET_1MIN        +
                    (rand() % OFFSET_2MIN);

            porch_turn_off_time = porch_turn_on_time +
                    OFFSET_5MIN        +
                    (rand() % OFFSET_10MIN);


            // Turn lights ON
            activate_device (inside_entrance_light, ON,
inside_entrance_turn_on_time);
            activate_device (porch_outside_light,   ON, porch_turn_on_time);

            // Turn lights OFF
```

```
            activate_device (inside_entrance_light, OFF,
inside_entrance_turn_off_time);
            activate_device (porch_outside_light,   OFF, porch_turn_off_time);
        }
    }
}
```

```
//******************************************************************************
// Process Barking Doggy
//
// This function places required barking doggy on events into the
// house_code_events table.
//
// Note: The 'barking doggy' is an X10 device which when triggered will produce
//       approximately 25 seconds of digital barking over an amplified speaker.
//******************************************************************************

void  process_barking_doggy (void)
{
    long int    watchdog_trigger_time;
    long int    current_time;
    static int retrigger_time = 0;


    // Is the house in SECURITY Mode
    if (security_mode)
    {
        // Yes - Was the porch sensor activated?
        if (device_code_set (front_porch_sensor))
        {
            // Yes - Kick the doggy
            // Get current system time
            current_time = get_raw_time();

            // Is it time to let the dog bark once more?
            if (current_time > retrigger_time)
            {
                // Yes - Reconfigure retrigger time
                retrigger_time = current_time + OFFSET_40SEC + (rand() %
OFFSET_30SEC);

                // Determine when to start barking
                watchdog_trigger_time = current_time + OFFSET_5SEC + (rand() %
OFFSET_10SEC);

                // Activate the watchdog
                activate_device (barking_doggy, ON, watchdog_trigger_time);
            }
        }
    }
}
```

```
//***************************************************************************
// Process Main Hallway Light                                ONLY AT NIGHTTIME
//
// This function places required hallway lights on/off events into the
// house_code_events table.
//
//***************************************************************************
void  process_main_hallway_light  (void)
{
    char        buffer[255];
    long int    turn_off_time;
    long int    current_time;


    // Is it between dusk and dawn?
    if (between_dusk_and_dawn)
    {
        // Yes - Is the house active mode engaged
        if (!sleep_mode) //(ACTIVE_MODE)
        {
            // Yes - Were the main hallway sensor activated?
            if (device_code_set (main_hallway_sensor)         ||
                device_code_set (lounge_hallway_sensor)       ||
                device_code_set (master_hallway_sensor))
            {
                // Yes - Delete any existing main hallway light device OFF events
                delete_house_code_events (main_hallway_light);


                // Get current system time
                current_time = get_raw_time();

                // Determine light timeout
                turn_off_time = current_time + OFFSET_1MIN;

                // Turn main hallway light ON now
                activate_device (main_hallway_light,  ON, current_time);

                // Turn main hallway light OFF after delay
                activate_device (main_hallway_light, OFF, turn_off_time);
            }
        }
    }
    else
    {
        // No - It is daytime - Was some movement detected in the hallway?
        if (device_code_set (main_hallway_sensor)             ||
            device_code_set (lounge_hallway_sensor)           ||
            device_code_set (master_hallway_sensor))
        {
            // Yes - We may have the condition in which the lights were manually
turned on.
            //       The system will automatically turn them off after a short
delay.

            // Delete any existing device OFF events
            delete_house_code_off_events_before_dusk (main_hallway_light);
```

```
            // Get current system time
            current_time = get_raw_time();

            // Determine light timeout
            turn_off_time = current_time + OFFSET_10MIN;

            // Ensure lights turned off just after dusk do not affect any existing
timers
            limit_turn_off_time_to_just_after_dusk (&turn_off_time);

            delete_house_code_off_events_at_timeout (main_hallway_light,
turn_off_time);

            // Turn light OFF after delay
            activate_device (main_hallway_light, OFF, turn_off_time);
        }
    }
}
```

```
//******************************************************************************
// Process Lounge Light                               EXTENDS LIGHTS UNTIL DAWN
//
// This function places required lounge light on/off events into the
// house_code_events table if there is movement in the hallways AFTER the sleep
// mode has been engaged.  The lounge light is used instead of the hallway
// lights since it is of a lower intensity.
//
//******************************************************************************

void  process_lounge_light (void)
{
    char        buffer[255];
    long int    turn_off_time;
    long int    current_time;


    // Get current system time
    current_time = get_raw_time();

    // Is it between dusk and dawn?
    if (between_dusk_and_dawn)
    {
        // Yes - Is the house sleep mode engaged
        if (sleep_mode)
        {
            // Yes - Were the main hallway sensors activated?
            if (device_code_set (main_hallway_sensor)        ||
                device_code_set (lounge_hallway_sensor)      ||
                device_code_set (master_hallway_sensor))
            {
                // Yes - Delete any existing lounge light events
                delete_house_code_events (lounge_wall_light);
                delete_house_code_events (lounge_window_light);

                // Determine turn off time
                turn_off_time = current_time + OFFSET_1MIN;

                // Turn only the lounge window light ON now
                activate_device (lounge_window_light,  ON, current_time);

                // Turn lounge lights OFF after delay
                activate_device (lounge_wall_light,   OFF, turn_off_time);
                activate_device (lounge_window_light, OFF, turn_off_time);
            }
        }
        else
        {
            // No - We are in active mode
            // Was the lounge hallway sensor activated?
            if (device_code_set (lounge_hallway_sensor))
            {
                // Yes - The lights are expected to still be on,
                //       so extend the lights turn off time until dawn.

                // Delete existing OFF events
                delete_house_code_off_events (lounge_wall_light);
                delete_house_code_off_events (lounge_window_light);
```

```
                // Is the time currently between midnight and sunrise?
                if (current_time < dawn_timeout)
                {
                    // Yes - Set the turn off time for dawn today
                    turn_off_time = dawn_timeout;
                }
                else
                {
                    // No - We are between dusk and midnight.
                    //      So set the turn off time for dawn tomorrow.
                    turn_off_time = dawn_timeout + OFFSET_24HRS;
                }


                // Turn lounge lights OFF after delay
                activate_device (lounge_wall_light,   OFF, turn_off_time);
                activate_device (lounge_window_light, OFF, turn_off_time);
            }
        }
    }
    else
    {
        // No - It is daytime - Was some movement detected in the lounge hallway?
        if (device_code_set (lounge_hallway_sensor))
        {
            // Yes - We may have the condition in which the lights were manually
turned on.
            //       The system will automatically turn them off after a short
delay.

            // Delete any existing device OFF events
            delete_house_code_off_events_before_dusk (lounge_wall_light);
            delete_house_code_off_events_before_dusk (lounge_window_light);

            // Get current system time
            current_time = get_raw_time();

            // Determine light timeout
            turn_off_time = current_time + OFFSET_20MIN;

            // Ensure lights turned off just after dusk do not affect any existing
timers
            limit_turn_off_time_to_just_after_dusk (&turn_off_time);

            delete_house_code_off_events_at_timeout (lounge_wall_light,
turn_off_time);
            delete_house_code_off_events_at_timeout (lounge_window_light,
turn_off_time);

            // Turn light OFF after delay
            activate_device (lounge_wall_light,   OFF, turn_off_time);
            activate_device (lounge_window_light, OFF, turn_off_time);
        }
    }
}
```

```
//****************************************************************************
// Process Familyroom Light                            EXTENDS LIGHTS UNTIL DAWN
//
// This function places required familyroom window light on/off events into the
// house_code_events table. If movement is detected then the lights turn off
// time is extended until dawn.
//
//****************************************************************************

void  process_familyroom_light (void)
{
    char       buffer[255];
    long int   turn_off_time;
    long int   current_time;


    // Get current system time
    current_time = get_raw_time();

    // Is it between dusk and dawn?
    if (between_dusk_and_dawn)
    {
        // Yes - Was the familyroom sensor activated?
        if (device_code_set (familyroom_sensor))
        {
            // Yes - The lights are expected to still be on,
            //       so extend the lights turn off time until dawn.

            // Delete existing OFF events
            delete_house_code_off_events (familyroom_wall_light);
            delete_house_code_off_events (familyroom_window_light);
            delete_house_code_off_events (familyroom_track_tv_light);
            delete_house_code_off_events (familyroom_track_reading_light);
            delete_house_code_off_events (familyroom_wall_unit_light);
            delete_house_code_off_events (familyroom_wall_unit_spotlight);

            // Setup the OFF time for dawn
            // Is the time currently between midnight and sunrise?
            if (current_time < dawn_timeout)
            {
                // Yes - Set the turn off time for dawn today
                turn_off_time = dawn_timeout;
            }
            else
            {
                // No - We are between dusk and midnight.
                //       So set the turn off time for dawn tomorrow.
                turn_off_time = dawn_timeout + OFFSET_24HRS;
            }

            // Turn familyroom lights OFF after delay
            activate_device (familyroom_wall_light,           OFF, turn_off_time);
            activate_device (familyroom_window_light,         OFF, turn_off_time);
            activate_device (familyroom_track_tv_light,       OFF, turn_off_time);
            activate_device (familyroom_track_reading_light,  OFF, turn_off_time);
            activate_device (familyroom_wall_unit_light,      OFF, turn_off_time);
            activate_device (familyroom_wall_unit_spotlight,  OFF, turn_off_time);
        }
```

```
    }
    else
    {
        // No - It is daytime - Was some movement detected in the family room?
        if (device_code_set (familyroom_sensor))
        {
            // Yes - We may have the condition in which the lights were manually
turned on.
            //        The system will automatically turn them off after a short
delay.

            // Delete any existing device OFF events
            delete_house_code_off_events_before_dusk (familyroom_wall_light);
            delete_house_code_off_events_before_dusk (familyroom_window_light);
            delete_house_code_off_events_before_dusk (familyroom_track_tv_light);
            delete_house_code_off_events_before_dusk
(familyroom_track_reading_light);
            delete_house_code_off_events_before_dusk (familyroom_wall_unit_light);
            delete_house_code_off_events_before_dusk
(familyroom_wall_unit_spotlight);

            // Get current system time
            current_time = get_raw_time();

            // Determine light timeout
            turn_off_time = current_time + OFFSET_20MIN;

            // Ensure lights turned off just after dusk do not affect any existing
timers
            limit_turn_off_time_to_just_after_dusk (&turn_off_time);

            delete_house_code_off_events_at_timeout (familyroom_wall_light,
turn_off_time);
            delete_house_code_off_events_at_timeout (familyroom_window_light,
turn_off_time);
            delete_house_code_off_events_at_timeout (familyroom_track_tv_light,
turn_off_time);
            delete_house_code_off_events_at_timeout
(familyroom_track_reading_light, turn_off_time);
            delete_house_code_off_events_at_timeout (familyroom_wall_unit_light,
turn_off_time);
            delete_house_code_off_events_at_timeout
(familyroom_wall_unit_spotlight, turn_off_time);


            // Turn light OFF after delay
            activate_device (familyroom_wall_light,           OFF, turn_off_time);
            activate_device (familyroom_window_light,         OFF, turn_off_time);
            activate_device (familyroom_track_tv_light,       OFF, turn_off_time);
            activate_device (familyroom_track_reading_light, OFF, turn_off_time);
            activate_device (familyroom_wall_unit_light,      OFF, turn_off_time);
            activate_device (familyroom_wall_unit_spotlight, OFF, turn_off_time);
        }
    }
}
```

```
//****************************************************************************
// Process Master Bedroom Light                          EXTENDS LIGHTS UNTIL DAWN
//
// This function places required master bedroom light on/off events into the
// house_code_events table.  If movement is detected then the lights turn off
// time is extended until dawn.  In addition, the first time movement is
// detected, the bed side lamps for Mom and Dad will be turned on.
//
//****************************************************************************

void  process_master_bedroom_light (void)
{
    char        buffer[255];
    long int    turn_off_time;
    long int    current_time;
    static int repeated_night_access = TRUE; // Prevent lights turning on at night
if system restarted.
                                             // Mum and Dad will appreciate
this...

    // Get current system time
    current_time = get_raw_time();

    // Is it between dusk and dawn?
    if (between_dusk_and_dawn)
    {
        // Yes - Was the master bedroom, bathroom or closet sensors activated?
        if ((device_code_set (master_bedroom_sensor))        ||
            (device_code_set (master_bathroom_sensor))       ||
            (device_code_set (master_bedroom_closet_sensor)))
        {
            // Yes - Extend the bedroom lights turn off time until dawn
            //       First delete existing events
            delete_house_code_events (master_bedroom_light);
            delete_house_code_events (master_bedroom_dad_light);
            delete_house_code_events (master_bedroom_mum_light);

            // Setup the OFF time for dawn
            // Is the time currently between midnight and dawn?
            if (current_time < dawn_timeout)
            {
                // Yes - Set the turn off time for dawn today
                turn_off_time = dawn_timeout;
            }
            else
            {
                // No - We are between dusk and midnight.
                //       So set the turn off time for dawn tomorrow.
                turn_off_time = dawn_timeout + OFFSET_24HRS;
            }

            // Turn all the master bedroom lights OFF after delay
            activate_device (master_bedroom_light,     OFF, turn_off_time);
            activate_device (master_bedroom_dad_light, OFF, turn_off_time);
            activate_device (master_bedroom_mum_light, OFF, turn_off_time);

            // Have we been in the Master Bedroom previously this night?
            if (repeated_night_access)
```

```
            {
                // Yes - Don't do anything
                return;
            }

            // No - Remember we have been in the master bedroom
            repeated_night_access = TRUE;

            // Turn all the master bedroom lights ON
            activate_device (master_bedroom_light,      ON, current_time);
            activate_device (master_bedroom_dad_light,  ON, current_time);
            activate_device (master_bedroom_mum_light,  ON, current_time);
        }
    }
    else
    {
        // No - It is daytime - Was some movement detected in the master bedroom?
        if ((device_code_set (master_bedroom_sensor))        ||
            (device_code_set (master_bathroom_sensor))       ||
            (device_code_set (master_bedroom_closet_sensor)))
        {
            // Yes - We may have the condition in which the lights were manually
turned on.
            //       The system will automatically turn them off after a short
delay.

            // Delete any existing device OFF events
            delete_house_code_off_events_before_dusk (master_bedroom_light);
            delete_house_code_off_events_before_dusk (master_bedroom_dad_light);
            delete_house_code_off_events_before_dusk (master_bedroom_mum_light);

            // Get current system time
            current_time = get_raw_time();

            // Determine light timeout
            turn_off_time = current_time + OFFSET_20MIN;

            // Ensure lights turned off just after dusk do not affect any existing
timers
            limit_turn_off_time_to_just_after_dusk (&turn_off_time);

            delete_house_code_off_events_at_timeout (master_bedroom_light,
turn_off_time);
            delete_house_code_off_events_at_timeout (master_bedroom_dad_light,
turn_off_time);
            delete_house_code_off_events_at_timeout (master_bedroom_mum_light,
turn_off_time);

            // Turn light OFF after delay
            activate_device (master_bedroom_light,     OFF, turn_off_time);
            activate_device (master_bedroom_dad_light, OFF, turn_off_time);
            activate_device (master_bedroom_mum_light, OFF, turn_off_time);
        }

        // Reset access
        repeated_night_access = FALSE;
    }
}
```

```
//****************************************************************************
// Process Master Bedroom Closet Light
//
// This function places required master bedroom closet light on/off events into
// the house_code_events table.
//
//****************************************************************************

void  process_master_bedroom_closet_light (void)
{
    long int   turn_off_time;
    long int   current_time;


    // Master closet Sensor activated?
    if (device_code_set (master_bedroom_closet_sensor))
    {
        // Get current system time
        current_time = get_raw_time();


        // Yes - Delete any existing master closet light device OFF events
        delete_house_code_events (master_bedroom_closet_light);

        // Determine light timeout
        turn_off_time = current_time + OFFSET_5MIN;

        // Turn master closet light ON now
        activate_device (master_bedroom_closet_light,  ON, current_time);

        // Turn master closet light OFF after delay
        activate_device (master_bedroom_closet_light, OFF, turn_off_time);
    }
}
```

```
//******************************************************************************
// Process Inside Entrance Light
//
// This function places required inside entrance lights on/off events into the
// house_code_events table.
//
//******************************************************************************

void  process_inside_entrance_light (void)
{
    char        buffer[255];
    long int    turn_off_time;
    long int    current_time;


    // Is it between dusk and dawn?
    if (between_dusk_and_dawn)
    {
        // Yes - Have we gone to sleep?
        if (sleep_mode)
        {
            // Yes - Do nothing
            return;
        }

        // Was the inside entrance sensor activated?
        if (device_code_set (inside_front_door_sensor))
        {
            // Yes - Delete any existing pantry light device events
            delete_house_code_events (inside_entrance_light);


            // Get current system time
            current_time = get_raw_time();

            // Determine light timeout
            turn_off_time = current_time + OFFSET_1MIN;

            // Turn inside entrance light ON now
            activate_device (inside_entrance_light,  ON, current_time);

            // Turn inside entrance light OFF after delay
            activate_device (inside_entrance_light, OFF, turn_off_time);
        }
    }
    else
    {
        // No - It is daytime - Was some movement detected in the inside entrance?
        if (device_code_set (inside_front_door_sensor))
        {
            // Yes - We may have the condition in which the lights were manually
turned on.
            //       The system will automatically turn them off after a short
delay.

            // Delete any existing device OFF events
            delete_house_code_off_events_before_dusk (inside_entrance_light);
```

```
            // Get current system time
            current_time = get_raw_time();

            // Determine light timeout
            turn_off_time = current_time + OFFSET_5MIN;

            // Ensure lights turned off just after dusk do not affect any existing
timers
            limit_turn_off_time_to_just_after_dusk (&turn_off_time);

            delete_house_code_off_events_at_timeout (inside_entrance_light,
turn_off_time);

            // Turn light OFF after delay
            activate_device (inside_entrance_light, OFF, turn_off_time);
        }
    }
}
```

```
//*****************************************************************************
// Process Kitchen Light
//
// This function places required kitchen lights on/off events into the
// house_code_events table.
//
//*****************************************************************************

void  process_kitchen_light (void)
{
    char        buffer[255];
    long int    turn_off_time;
    long int    current_time;


    // Is it between dusk and dawn?
    if (between_dusk_and_dawn)
    {
        // Yes - Were any Kitchen Nook / Kitchen sensors activated?
        if (device_code_set (kitchen_nook_sensor)           ||
            device_code_set (kitchen_sensor)                ||
            device_code_set (counter_fridge_sensor)         ||
            device_code_set (counter_cooktop_left_sensor)   ||
            device_code_set (counter_cooktop_right_sensor))
        {
            // Yes - Delete any existing kitchen light device OFF events
            delete_house_code_events (kitchen_light);


            // Get current system time
            current_time = get_raw_time();

            // Determine light timeout
            turn_off_time = current_time + OFFSET_10MIN;

            // Turn kitchen light ON now
            activate_device (kitchen_light,  ON, current_time);

            // Turn kitchen light OFF after delay
            activate_device (kitchen_light, OFF, turn_off_time);
        }
    }
    else
    {
        // No - It is daytime - Was some movement detected in the kitchen?
        if (device_code_set (kitchen_nook_sensor)           ||
            device_code_set (kitchen_sensor)                ||
            device_code_set (counter_fridge_sensor)         ||
            device_code_set (counter_cooktop_left_sensor)   ||
            device_code_set (counter_cooktop_right_sensor))
        {
            // Yes - We may have the condition in which the lights were manually
turned on.
            //       The system will automatically turn them off after a short
delay.

            // Delete any existing device OFF events
            delete_house_code_off_events_before_dusk (kitchen_light);
```

```
            delete_house_code_off_events_before_dusk (kitchen_nook_light);

            // Get current system time
            current_time = get_raw_time();

            // Determine light timeout
            turn_off_time = current_time + OFFSET_15MIN;

            // Ensure lights turned off just after dusk do not affect any existing
timers
            limit_turn_off_time_to_just_after_dusk (&turn_off_time);

            delete_house_code_off_events_at_timeout (kitchen_light,
turn_off_time);
            delete_house_code_off_events_at_timeout (kitchen_nook_light,
turn_off_time);

            // Turn light OFF after delay
            activate_device (kitchen_light,      OFF, turn_off_time);
            activate_device (kitchen_nook_light, OFF, turn_off_time);
        }
    }
}
```

```
//******************************************************************************
// Process Kitchen Nook Light
//
// This function places required kitchen nook light on/off events into the
// house_code_events table.
//
//******************************************************************************

void  process_kitchen_nook_light (void)
{
    char        buffer[255];
    long int    turn_off_time;
    long int    current_time;


    // Is it between dusk and dawn?
    if (between_dusk_and_dawn)
    {
        // Yes - Was the kitchen nook sensor activated?
        if (device_code_set (kitchen_nook_sensor))
        {
            // Yes - Delete any existing kitchen nook light device events
            delete_house_code_events (kitchen_nook_light);


            // Get current system time
            current_time = get_raw_time();

            // Determine light timeout
            turn_off_time = current_time + OFFSET_10MIN;

            // Turn kitchen nook light ON now
            activate_device (kitchen_nook_light,  ON, current_time);

            // Turn kitchen nook light OFF after delay
            activate_device (kitchen_nook_light, OFF, turn_off_time);
        }
    }
    else
    {
        // No - It is daytime - Was some movement detected in the kitchen nook?
        if (device_code_set (kitchen_nook_sensor))
        {
            // Yes - We may have the condition in which the lights were manually
turned on.
            //       The system will automatically turn them off after a short
delay.

            // Delete any existing device OFF events
            delete_house_code_off_events_before_dusk (kitchen_light);
            delete_house_code_off_events_before_dusk (kitchen_nook_light);

            // Get current system time
            current_time = get_raw_time();

            // Determine light timeout
            turn_off_time = current_time + OFFSET_15MIN;
```

```
            // Ensure lights turned off just after dusk do not affect any existing
timers
            limit_turn_off_time_to_just_after_dusk (&turn_off_time);

            delete_house_code_off_events_at_timeout (kitchen_light,
turn_off_time);
            delete_house_code_off_events_at_timeout (kitchen_nook_light,
turn_off_time);

            // Turn light OFF after delay
            activate_device (kitchen_light,      OFF, turn_off_time);
            activate_device (kitchen_nook_light, OFF, turn_off_time);
        }
    }
}
```

```
//*****************************************************************************
// Process Common Bathroom Light
//
// This function places required common bathroom light on/off events into the
// house_code_events table.
//
//*****************************************************************************

void  process_common_bathroom_light (void)
{
    char        buffer[255];
    long int    turn_off_time;
    long int    current_time;


    // Is it between dusk and dawn?
    if (between_dusk_and_dawn)
    {
        // Yes - Was the common bathroom sensor activated?
        if (device_code_set (common_bathroom_sensor))
        {
            // Yes - Get current system time
            current_time = get_raw_time();

            // Get high resolution timer
            common_bathroom_event = get_high_resolution_timer();

            // Delete any existing common bathroom device OFF events
            delete_house_code_events (common_bathroom_light);

            // Determine light timeout
            turn_off_time = current_time + OFFSET_3MIN;

            // Turn common bathroom light ON now
            activate_device (common_bathroom_light,  ON, current_time);

            // Turn common bathroom light OFF after delay
            activate_device (common_bathroom_light, OFF, turn_off_time);
        }
    }
    else
    {
        // No - It is daytime - Was some movement detected in the common bathroom?
        if (device_code_set (common_bathroom_sensor))
        {
            // Yes - We may have the condition in which the lights were manually
turned on.
            //        The system will automatically turn them off after a short
delay.

            // Delete any existing device OFF events
            delete_house_code_off_events_before_dusk (common_bathroom_light);

            // Get current system time
            current_time = get_raw_time();

            // Determine light timeout
            turn_off_time = current_time + OFFSET_5MIN;
```

```
            // Ensure lights turned off just after dusk do not affect any existing
timers
            limit_turn_off_time_to_just_after_dusk (&turn_off_time);

            delete_house_code_off_events_at_timeout (common_bathroom_light,
turn_off_time);

            // Turn light OFF after delay
            activate_device (common_bathroom_light, OFF, turn_off_time);
        }
    }
}
```

```
//*****************************************************************************
// Process Common Washroom Light
//
// This function places required common washroom light on/off events into the
// house_code_events table.
//
//*****************************************************************************

void  process_common_washroom_light (void)
{
    char        buffer[255];
    long int    turn_off_time;
    long int    current_time;


    // Is it between dusk and dawn?
    if (between_dusk_and_dawn)
    {
        // Yes - Was the common washroom sensor activated?
        if (device_code_set (common_washroom_sensor))
        {
            // Yes - Get current system time
            current_time = get_raw_time();

            // Get high resolution timer
            common_washroom_event = get_high_resolution_timer();

            // Delete any existing common washroom device OFF events
            delete_house_code_events (common_washroom_light);
            delete_house_code_events (common_washroom_flight);
            delete_house_code_events (common_bathroom_light);

            // Determine light timeout
            turn_off_time = current_time + OFFSET_3MIN;

            // Turn common washroom light ON
            activate_device (common_washroom_light,  ON, current_time);

            // Since we are in the washroom, turn off the common bathroom light
            activate_device (common_bathroom_light,  OFF, current_time+10);

            // Turn common washroom light OFF after delay
            activate_device (common_washroom_light,  OFF, turn_off_time);
            activate_device (common_washroom_flight, OFF, turn_off_time);
        }
    }
    else
    {
        // No - It is daytime - Was some movement detected in the common washroom?
        if (device_code_set (common_washroom_sensor))
        {
            // Yes - We may have the condition in which the lights were manually
turned on.
            //       The system will automatically turn them off after a short
delay.

            // Delete any existing device OFF events
            delete_house_code_off_events_before_dusk (common_washroom_light);
```

```
            delete_house_code_off_events_before_dusk (common_washroom_flight);

            // Get current system time
            current_time = get_raw_time();

            // Determine light timeout
            turn_off_time = current_time + OFFSET_5MIN;

            // Ensure lights turned off just after dusk do not affect any existing
timers
            limit_turn_off_time_to_just_after_dusk (&turn_off_time);

            delete_house_code_off_events_at_timeout (common_washroom_light,
turn_off_time);
            delete_house_code_off_events_at_timeout (common_washroom_flight,
turn_off_time);

            // Turn light OFF after delay
            activate_device (common_washroom_light,  OFF, turn_off_time);
            activate_device (common_washroom_flight, OFF, turn_off_time);
        }
    }
}
```

```
//**************************************************************************
// Process Steve Bedroom Wall Light
//
// This function places required Steve bedroom wall light on/off events into the
// house_code_events table.
//
//**************************************************************************

void  process_steve_bedroom_wall_light (void)
{
    int         parameter;
    char        buffer[255];
    long int    turn_off_time;
    long int    current_time;


    // Have we turned in for the night?
    if (sleep_mode)
    {
        // Yes - Do not activate any wall lights in Steve's bedroom
        return;
    }


    // Is it between dusk and dawn?
    if (between_dusk_and_dawn)
    {
        // Yes - Was Steve's bedroom sensor activated?
        if (device_code_set (steve_bedroom_sensor))
        {
            // Yes - Get current system time
            current_time = get_raw_time();

            // Get high resolution timer
            steve_bedroom_event = get_high_resolution_timer();

            // Get Steve's lights control parameter
            if (get_house_state_parameter (HS_STEVE_LIGHTS, &parameter) == SUCCESS)
            {
                // Are we watching TV?
                if (parameter == HS_TV_MODE)
                {
                    // Yes - Do not switch on Steve's room lights
                    return;
                }
            }

            // Delete any existing Steve's bedroom light device events
            delete_house_code_events (steve_bedroom_ceiling_light);
            delete_house_code_events (steve_bedroom_window_light);
            delete_house_code_events (steve_bedroom_wall_light);
            delete_house_code_events (steve_bedroom_reading_light);

            // Get current system time
            current_time = get_raw_time();

            // Determine light timeout
            turn_off_time = current_time + OFFSET_10MIN;
```

```
            // Turn Steve's bedroom light ON now
            activate_device (steve_bedroom_wall_light,   ON, current_time);
            activate_device (steve_bedroom_window_light, ON, current_time);

            // Turn Steve's bedroom light OFF after delay
            activate_device (steve_bedroom_ceiling_light, OFF, turn_off_time);
            activate_device (steve_bedroom_wall_light,    OFF, turn_off_time);
            activate_device (steve_bedroom_window_light,  OFF, turn_off_time);
            activate_device (steve_bedroom_reading_light, OFF, turn_off_time);
        }
    }
    else
    {
        // No - It is daytime - Was some movement detected in the common bathroom?
        if (device_code_set (steve_bedroom_sensor))
        {
            // Yes - We may have the condition in which the lights were manually
turned on.
            //      The system will automatically turn them off after a short
delay.

            // Delete any existing device OFF events
            delete_house_code_off_events_before_dusk (steve_bedroom_ceiling_light);
            delete_house_code_off_events_before_dusk (steve_bedroom_window_light);
            delete_house_code_off_events_before_dusk (steve_bedroom_wall_light);
            delete_house_code_off_events_before_dusk (steve_bedroom_reading_light);

            // Get current system time
            current_time = get_raw_time();

            // Determine light timeout
            turn_off_time = current_time + OFFSET_10MIN;

            // Ensure lights turned off just after dusk do not affect any existing
timers
            limit_turn_off_time_to_just_after_dusk (&turn_off_time);

            delete_house_code_off_events_at_timeout (steve_bedroom_ceiling_light,
turn_off_time);
            delete_house_code_off_events_at_timeout (steve_bedroom_wall_light,
turn_off_time);
            delete_house_code_off_events_at_timeout (steve_bedroom_window_light,
turn_off_time);
            delete_house_code_off_events_at_timeout (steve_bedroom_reading_light,
turn_off_time);

            // Turn light OFF after delay
            activate_device (steve_bedroom_ceiling_light, OFF, turn_off_time);
            activate_device (steve_bedroom_wall_light,    OFF, turn_off_time);
            activate_device (steve_bedroom_window_light,  OFF, turn_off_time);
            activate_device (steve_bedroom_reading_light, OFF, turn_off_time);
        }
    }
}
```

```
//******************************************************************************
// Process Study Ceiling Light
//
// This function places required study ceiling light on/off events into the
// house_code_events table.
//
//******************************************************************************

void  process_study_ceiling_light (void)
{
    char              buffer[255];
    long int          turn_off_time;
    long int          current_time;



    // Is it between dusk and dawn?
    if (between_dusk_and_dawn)
    {
        // Yes - Was the study sensor activated?
        if (device_code_set (study_sensor))
        {
            // Yes - Get current system time
            current_time = get_raw_time();

            // Get high resolution timer
            study_event = get_high_resolution_timer();

            // Delete any existing study ceiling light device OFF events
            delete_house_code_events (study_ceiling_light);

            // Determine light timeout
            turn_off_time = current_time + OFFSET_15MIN;

            // Turn Study ceiling light ON now
            activate_device (study_ceiling_light,  ON, current_time);

            // Turn Study ceiling light OFF after delay
            activate_device (study_ceiling_light, OFF, turn_off_time);
        }
    }
    else
    {
        // No - It is daytime - Was some movement detected in the common bathroom?
        if (device_code_set (study_sensor))
        {
            // Yes - We may have the condition in which the lights were manually
turned on.
            //       The system will automatically turn them off after a short
delay.

            // Delete any existing device OFF events
            delete_house_code_off_events_before_dusk (study_ceiling_light);

            // Get current system time
            current_time = get_raw_time();

            // Determine light timeout
```

```
            turn_off_time = current_time + OFFSET_10MIN;

            // Ensure lights turned off just after dusk do not affect any existing
timers
            limit_turn_off_time_to_just_after_dusk (&turn_off_time);

            delete_house_code_off_events_at_timeout (study_ceiling_light,
turn_off_time);

            // Turn light OFF after delay
            activate_device (study_ceiling_light, OFF, turn_off_time);
        }
    }
}
```

```
//****************************************************************************
// Fast Transition
//
// This function determines if the first event occurred prior to the second
// event.  Remember that these event counts are in milliseconds.
//
//****************************************************************************

Uint8  fast_transition (long int  event1,  long int  event2)
{

    // Did the two events take place within fifteen seconds of each other?
    if (abs(event1 - event2) < 15000)
    {
        // Yes - Determine the order of the events
        return (event1 < event2);
    }
    else
    {
        // No - Ignore the transition
        return (FALSE);
    }

}
```

```
//****************************************************************************
// Determine Fast Transition Events
//
// This function attempts to switch lights off determined upon the user's
// movement from one room to another.
//
//****************************************************************************

void  determine_fast_transition_events (void)
{
    long int    current_time;
    long int    turn_off_time;
    char        message[255];

    static Uint8   study_to_steve_bedroom    = FALSE;
    static Uint8   steve_bedroom_to_study    = FALSE;
    static Uint8   study_to_common_bathroom = FALSE;
    static Uint8   steve_bedroom_to_common_bathroom = FALSE;
    static Uint8   common_bathroom_to_study_or_steve_bedroom = FALSE;


    // Yes - Get current system time
    current_time = get_raw_time();

    // Determine light timeout
    turn_off_time = current_time + OFFSET_30SEC;


    // Person leaving study and entering Steve's bedroom
    if (fast_transition (study_event, common_washroom_event) &&
        fast_transition (common_washroom_event, steve_bedroom_event))
    {
        if (!study_to_steve_bedroom)
        {
            // Print log message
            print_log ("Fast Transition: Study -> Steve's Bedroom");

            // Delete any existing device ON/OFF events
            delete_house_code_events (study_ceiling_light);
            delete_house_code_events (common_washroom_light);
            delete_house_code_events (common_washroom_flight);

            // Turn lights OFF after delay
            activate_device (study_ceiling_light,    OFF, turn_off_time);
            activate_device (common_washroom_light,  OFF, turn_off_time+3);
            activate_device (common_washroom_flight, OFF, turn_off_time+3);

            // Prevent repeated operation
            study_to_steve_bedroom = TRUE;
        }
    }
    else
    {
        study_to_steve_bedroom = FALSE;
    }


    // Person leaving Steve's bedroom and entering Study
```

```
if (fast_transition (steve_bedroom_event, common_washroom_event) &&
    fast_transition (common_washroom_event, study_event))
{
    if (!steve_bedroom_to_study)
    {
        // Print log message
        print_log ("Fast Transition: Steve's Bedroom -> Study");

        // Delete any existing device ON/OFF events
        delete_house_code_events (steve_bedroom_ceiling_light);
        delete_house_code_events (steve_bedroom_window_light);
        delete_house_code_events (steve_bedroom_wall_light);
        delete_house_code_events (steve_bedroom_reading_light);
        delete_house_code_events (common_washroom_flight);
        delete_house_code_events (common_washroom_light);
        delete_house_code_events (common_bathroom_light);

        // Turn lights OFF after delay
        activate_device (steve_bedroom_ceiling_light, OFF, turn_off_time);
        activate_device (steve_bedroom_window_light,  OFF, turn_off_time);
        activate_device (steve_bedroom_wall_light,    OFF, turn_off_time);
        activate_device (steve_bedroom_reading_light, OFF, turn_off_time);
        activate_device (common_washroom_flight,      OFF, turn_off_time+3);
        activate_device (common_washroom_light,       OFF, turn_off_time+3);
        activate_device (common_bathroom_light,       OFF, turn_off_time+3);

        // Prevent repeated operation
        steve_bedroom_to_study = TRUE;
    }
}
else
{
    steve_bedroom_to_study = FALSE;
}


// Person leaving Steve's bedroom to enter the Common Bathroom
if (fast_transition (steve_bedroom_event, common_washroom_event) &&
    fast_transition (common_washroom_event, common_bathroom_event))
{
    if (!steve_bedroom_to_common_bathroom)
    {
        // Print log message
        print_log ("Fast Transition: Steve's Bedroom -> Common Bathroom");

        // Delete any existing device ON/OFF events
        delete_house_code_events (steve_bedroom_ceiling_light);
        delete_house_code_events (steve_bedroom_window_light);
        delete_house_code_events (steve_bedroom_wall_light);
        delete_house_code_events (steve_bedroom_reading_light);
        delete_house_code_events (common_washroom_light);
        delete_house_code_events (common_washroom_flight);

        // Turn lights OFF after delay
        activate_device (steve_bedroom_ceiling_light, OFF, turn_off_time);
        activate_device (steve_bedroom_window_light,  OFF, turn_off_time);
        activate_device (steve_bedroom_wall_light,    OFF, turn_off_time);
        activate_device (steve_bedroom_reading_light, OFF, turn_off_time);
```

```
            activate_device (common_washroom_light,       OFF, turn_off_time+3);
            activate_device (common_washroom_flight,      OFF, turn_off_time+3);

            // Prevent repeated operation
            steve_bedroom_to_common_bathroom = TRUE;
        }
    }
    else
    {
        steve_bedroom_to_common_bathroom = FALSE;
    }


    // Person leaving Study to enter the Common Bathroom
    if (fast_transition (study_event, common_washroom_event) &&
        fast_transition (common_washroom_event, common_bathroom_event))
    {
        if (!study_to_common_bathroom)
        {
            // Print log message
            print_log ("Fast Transition: Study -> Common Bathroom");

            // Delete any existing device ON/OFF events
            delete_house_code_events (study_ceiling_light);
            delete_house_code_events (common_washroom_light);
            delete_house_code_events (common_washroom_flight);

            // Turn lights OFF after delay
            activate_device (study_ceiling_light,    OFF, turn_off_time);
            activate_device (common_washroom_light,  OFF, turn_off_time+3);
            activate_device (common_washroom_flight, OFF, turn_off_time+3);

            // Prevent repeated operation
            study_to_common_bathroom = TRUE;
        }
    }
    else
    {
        study_to_common_bathroom = FALSE;
    }


    // Person leaving Common Bathroom to enter Study or Steve's Bedroom
    if (fast_transition (common_bathroom_event, common_washroom_event) &&
        (fast_transition (common_washroom_event, study_event) ||
        fast_transition (common_washroom_event, steve_bedroom_event)))
    {
        if (!common_bathroom_to_study_or_steve_bedroom)
        {
            // Print log message
            print_log ("Fast Transition: Common Bathroom -> Study or Steve's
Bedroom");

            // Delete any existing device ON/OFF events
            delete_house_code_events (common_bathroom_light);
            delete_house_code_events (common_washroom_light);
            delete_house_code_events (common_washroom_flight);
```

```
            // Turn lights OFF after delay
            activate_device (common_bathroom_light,  OFF, turn_off_time);
            activate_device (common_washroom_light,  OFF, turn_off_time+3);
            activate_device (common_washroom_flight, OFF, turn_off_time+3);

            // Prevent repeated operation
            common_bathroom_to_study_or_steve_bedroom = TRUE;
        }
    }
    else
    {
        common_bathroom_to_study_or_steve_bedroom = FALSE;
    }

}
```

```
//*****************************************************************************
// Process ON Events
//
// This function places required events into the house_code_events table
//
//*****************************************************************************

void  process_on_events (void)
{
    int  house_state_security;
    int  house_state_sleep;


    // Determine home security state
    if (get_house_state_security (&house_state_security) == SUCCESS)
    {
        // Has the house security mode been engaged?
        if (house_state_security == SECURITY_MODE_ACTIVE)
        {
            // Yes - Security mode status engaged
            security_mode = TRUE;
        }
        else
        {
            // No - Home mode status engaged
            security_mode = FALSE;

            // Reset the security detection flags
            reset_security_detection_flags();
        }
    }


    // Determine sleep state
    if (get_house_state_sleep (&house_state_sleep) == SUCCESS)
    {
        // Has the house active mode been engaged?
        if (house_state_sleep == SLEEP_MODE_INACTIVE)
        {
            // Yes - Active mode status engaged
            sleep_mode = FALSE;
        }

        // Has the house sleep mode been activated?
        else if (house_state_sleep == SLEEP_MODE_INITIATED)
        {
            // Yes - Sleep mode status pending

        }
        else if (house_state_sleep == SLEEP_MODE_DELAY)
        {
            // Yes - Sleep mode status pending

        }
        else if (house_state_sleep == SLEEP_MODE_ACTIVE)
        {
            // Sleep mode status fully engaged
            sleep_mode  = TRUE;
```

```
        }
    }


    // Is the HOME SECURITY mode engaged?
    if (security_mode)
    {
        // Yes - Keep a watchfull eye on things...
        process_front_porch_light();
        process_barking_doggy();

        // Check to see if there is an intruder
        process_intruder_check();
    }
    else
    {
        // No - Home Security is deactivated
        // Let the user control the house lights
        process_laundry_light();
        process_pantry_light();
        process_main_hallway_light();
        process_front_porch_light();
        process_inside_entrance_light();
        process_kitchen_light();
        process_kitchen_nook_light();
        process_steve_bedroom_wall_light();
        process_common_bathroom_light();
        process_common_washroom_light();
        process_study_ceiling_light();
        process_familyroom_light();
        process_lounge_light();
        process_master_bedroom_light();
        process_master_bedroom_closet_light();

        // Determine if fast transition occured which might
        // allow the system to turn off lights quicker.
        determine_fast_transition_events();
    }

}
```

```
//*****************************************************************************
// Process WF800 State Changes
//
// This function reads data from the serial port attached to the WF800 device.
// The received data provides X10 house and unit codes of the infra-red sensor
// device that detected someone's presence.
//
//*****************************************************************************

void  process_wf800_state_changes (void)
{
    int         hu_state;
    int         num_bytes_read;
    char        buffer[255];
    char        input_buffer[255];
    char        time_buffer[255];
    char        message [255];
    long int    current_time;

    static int          last_hu_state   = 0;
    static int          last_house_code = 0;
    static int          last_unit_code  = 0;
    static long int     last_time = 0;



    // Blocking read characters from the Serial Port.
    // Wait until 4 chars read or a 100ms inter-character timeout occurs.
    // This does NOT wait for 100ms if no characters are received!!!
    num_bytes_read = read(fd, input_buffer, 255);


    // Convert First and Third RF Message Bytes into House / Unit Codes
    x10_convert_rf_codes (input_buffer[0], input_buffer[2]);

    // Was a valid RF code received?
    if (x10_rf_code == VALID)
    {
        // Get current system time
        current_time = get_raw_time();

        // Indicate if ON or OFF operation
        if (command == X10_ON)
        {
            hu_state = 1;
        }
        else
        {
            hu_state = 0;
        }

        // Was this a repeat message?
        if ((hu_state  == last_hu_state)      &&
                (house_code == last_house_code)       &&
                (unit_code  == last_unit_code))
        {
            // Yes - Was it within the last 5 seconds?
            if ((current_time - last_time) < 5)
```

```
            {
                // Yes - Ignore this command
                return;
            }
        }
        else
        {
            // No - This is a new message
            //      Remember this message parameters
            last_hu_state   = hu_state;
            last_house_code = house_code;
            last_unit_code  = unit_code;
        }


        // Remember last time the same message was processed
        last_time = current_time;

        // Compute current timestamp
        determine_system_timestamp (time_buffer);



        // House Code States DATABASE
        // ==========================
        // Create the MySQL command to update the 'house_code_states' table
        // with an entry for the RF house/unit code data received

        if (hu_state == 1)
        {
            // Configure state ON
            sprintf (buffer,
                    "UPDATE house_code_states SET state=%d, timestamp='%s',
timeout=%ld, presence=%ld WHERE house=%d AND unit=%d",
                    hu_state,
                    time_buffer,
                    current_time + OFFSET_2MIN,
                    ZERO_PRESENCE_TIMEOUT,
                    //                    current_time +
presence_timeout[house_code][unit_code],
                    house_code,
                    unit_code);

            // Yes - Display House and Unit Codes
            // printf ("House = %c, Unit = %d, ON\n", (0x40 + house_code),
unit_code);

            // We now have received a valid X10 Infra-Red code
            // Process the command for this event time
            process_on_events();
        }
        else
        {
            // Configure state OFF
            sprintf (buffer,
                    "UPDATE house_code_states SET state=%d, timestamp='%s'  WHERE
house=%d AND unit=%d",
                    hu_state,
```

```
                    time_buffer,
                    house_code,
                    unit_code);

            // Yes - Display House and Unit Codes
            // printf ("House = %c, Unit = %d, OFF\n", (0x40 + house_code),
unit_code);
        }

        // Display the MySQL Command on the terminal (or log file)
        // printf ("%s\n", buffer);

        // Issue the update command to the MySQL Database
        if (mysql_query(conn1, buffer))
        {
            // Error Detected - Print error message but still continue...
            sprintf (message, "Error_E1 %u: %s", mysql_errno(conn1),
mysql_error(conn1));
            print_log (message);
        }
    }
    else
    {
        // An invalid RF Code was received
        // printf ("Invalid House and Unit Codes!!!\n");
    }
}
```

```
//***************************************************************************
// main()
//
// The RF control codes are converted from their
// internal representation into standard X10 House/Unit codes.
//
// These codes are subsequently placed into the MySQL database.
//
//***************************************************************************

main()
{
    char    message[255];
    char    time_buffer[255];


    // Identify program
    print_log ("");
    print_log ("Program 'hc_main' Started...\n");

    // Install the termination interrupt handler
    install_signal_interrupt_handler();

    // Sleep a few seconds [May require more if initializing all the databases!!!]
    // This allows the Mysql system to startup
    msleep (5000);      // Five seconds

    // Compute current timestamp
    determine_system_timestamp (time_buffer);

    // Send email stating Security Mode Activation
    sprintf (message, "%s - Home Control Program Started [HC_MAIN]...",
time_buffer);
//  send_security_email ("*** SECURITY INFO ***", message);

    // Verify System Startup snap picture and email operation
    print_log ("Program 'hc_main' has taken a test picture...\n");
    snap_picture (STUDY_PICTURE_FILE);
    msleep (1000);

    snap_picture (STUDY_PICTURE_FILE);
    sprintf (message, "%s - System Startup [HC_MAIN] - Study Test Image",
time_buffer);
//  send_security_email_with_attachment ("*** SECURITY INFO ***", message,
STUDY_PICTURE_FILE);
    speak ("A test picture has been taken.");

    // Initialize serial port for WF800 RF32A Receiver
    initialize_serial_port_for_wf800();

    // Initialize the 'system_control' database
    initialize_system_control_database();

    // Prepare to start the main loop
    print_log ("*");
    print_log ("* Initialization completed *");
    print_log ("*");
```

```
    // Do Forever
    while (!exit_flag)
    {
        // Determine Day/Night Transition Times
        determine_periodic_transition_times();

        // Process events that occur at start of solar periods
        process_events_that_occur_at_midnight();
        process_events_that_occur_at_sunrise();
        process_events_that_occur_at_sunset();

        // Process any IR-RF X-10 state changes (Blocking)
        process_wf800_state_changes();
    }


    // Program is being terminated...
    // Restore the Serial Port to its previous configuration
    tcsetattr(fd, TCSANOW, &old_options);

    // Program terminated
    speak ("The program has been terminated.");
    print_log ("");
    print_log ("Program 'hc_main' has been terminated.");
}
```

File: hc_ti103.c

```
//***************************************************************************
//  Author: Stephen W. McClure
//    Date: March 2014
// Project: Designing Embedded Systems [Book]
//
//***************************************************************************
// Purpose:
//
// This program interfaces with the TI103 X-10 Line Interface Unit.
//
// The TI103 Interface is a device that can transmit and receive X10 commands
// over the household 110VAC mains wiring.  The TI103 program interface is
// controlled by sending commands over the computer system RS232 Serial Port.
//
// Commands may be sent to this unit and status replies received.
// Currently the TI103 is configured only for transmitted commands.
//
//***************************************************************************
//
// File Name: hc_ti103.c
//
// Build command
// gcc hc_ti103.c -o hc_ti103 `mysql_config --cflags --libs`
//
// Execution Command
// ./hc_ti103 > hc_ti103.log &
//
//
// But first don't forget to sign in as SU and give the appropriate serial
// ports the access right permissions (eg.: chmod a+rw /dev/ttyS1) and to
// also use the static ip address: 192.168.1.176 (set by using wired network
// connection icon in the bottom right of the Mint 13 GUI)
//
// For example:
// $ su
// Password: enter super user password
// # chmod a+rw  /dev/ttyS0
// # chmod a+rw  /dev/ttyS1
// # exit
//
// chmod a+r  /dev/ttyS0  Set ttyS0 for Input Only  [ORION-ITX TOP    Port]
// chmod a+rw /dev/ttyS1  Set ttyS1 for I/O         [ORION-ITX BOTTOM Port]
//
// ttyS0  -  Top Port    = RF X10 Commands
// ttyS1  -  Bottom Port = TI-103
//
// Or make the user 'orion' part of the "dialout" group
// which will give it RW permission to the ttys0 and ttys1 serial ports
// by issuing the following instruction: sudo adduser orion dialout
// (will need to provide the su password).
//
// When using autostart a delay is required at the start of this program's
// execution in order to allow the MySQL system to be initialized prior to it
// being accessed.
//***************************************************************************
```

```
// Include System Files
#include <sys/types.h>
#include <sys/stat.h>
#include <fcntl.h>
#include <unistd.h>
#include <stdio.h>
#include <stdlib.h>
#include <my_global.h>
#include <mysql.h>
#include <sys/time.h>
#include <string.h>
#include <termios.h>
#include <signal.h>
#include <time.h>

// Include local header Files
#include "hc_literals.h"
#include "hc_typedefs.h"
#include "hc_publics.h"

// Include local modules
#include "hc_common.c"
```

```
//*****************************************************************************
// initialize_serial_port_for_ti103_control
//
// Initialize the serial port for X-10 TI103 control.
//
//*****************************************************************************

void  initialize_serial_port_for_ti103_control (void)
{

    // Open Com1 for Read/Write Operations
    fd = open(SERIAL_PORT_1, O_RDWR | O_NOCTTY | O_NDELAY);

    // Was the serial port opened successfully?
    if (fd == -1)
    {
        // No - Display error message and exit
        perror("open_port: Unable to open /dev/ttyS1");
        exit(1);
    }
    else
    {
        // Yes -
        fcntl(fd, F_SETFL, FNDELAY);    // Return immediately
    //  fcntl(fd, F_SETFL, 0);          // Block if no characters are available
    }


    // Save the current options for the port...
    tcgetattr(fd, &old_options);

    // Get the current options for the port...
    tcgetattr(fd, &new_options);

    // Set the baud rates to 9600...
    cfsetispeed(&new_options, B9600);
    cfsetospeed(&new_options, B9600);

    // Enable the receiver and set local mode...
    new_options.c_cflag |= (CLOCAL | CREAD);

    // Set No Parity, 8-N-1
    new_options.c_cflag &= ~PARENB;
    new_options.c_cflag &= ~CSTOPB;
    new_options.c_cflag &= ~CSIZE;
    new_options.c_cflag |= CS8;

    // Set the new options for the port...
    tcsetattr(fd, TCSANOW, &new_options);
}
```

```
//***************************************************************************
// Setup Outside Light OFF Events
//
// This function performs the following operations:
//
// 1. Remove all existing light events from event database table
// 2. Create new light events
// 3. Lights activate at sunset + delta
//
// Note: Included retries in case of electrical noise affecting lamp turn off.
//***************************************************************************

void  setup_outside_light_OFF_events (void)
{
    long int    timeout1, timeout2, timeout3;
    long int    timeout4, timeout5, timeout6;
    long int    override_off_timeout;
    long int    current_time;


    // Log operation
    print_log ("Processed Outside Light OFF events");

    // Get current time in seconds
    current_time = get_raw_time();


    // Setup Sunrise lamp off events
    timeout1 = sunrise_timeout + OFFSET_30MIN + (rand() % OFFSET_30MIN);
    timeout2 = sunrise_timeout + OFFSET_30MIN + (rand() % OFFSET_30MIN);
    timeout3 = sunrise_timeout + OFFSET_30MIN + (rand() % OFFSET_30MIN);
    timeout4 = sunrise_timeout + OFFSET_30MIN + (rand() % OFFSET_30MIN);
    timeout5 = sunrise_timeout + OFFSET_30MIN + (rand() % OFFSET_30MIN);
    timeout6 = sunrise_timeout + OFFSET_30MIN + (rand() % OFFSET_30MIN);


    // Program the lamp OFF events (Only if it is between midnight and dusk)
    if (current_time <= dusk_timeout)
    {
        // Delete existing outside light events
        delete_house_code_off_events (garage_back_outside_light);
        delete_house_code_off_events (familyroom_outside_light);
        delete_house_code_off_events (diningroom_outside_light);
        delete_house_code_off_events (master_bedroom_outside_light);
        delete_house_code_off_events (garage_front_outside_light);
        delete_house_code_off_events (porch_outside_light);


        activate_device (garage_back_outside_light,     OFF, timeout1);
        activate_device (garage_back_outside_light,     OFF, timeout1+OFFSET_5MIN);
        activate_device (garage_back_outside_light,     OFF,
timeout1+OFFSET_10MIN);

        activate_device (familyroom_outside_light,      OFF, timeout2);
        activate_device (familyroom_outside_light,      OFF, timeout2+OFFSET_5MIN);
        activate_device (familyroom_outside_light,      OFF,
timeout2+OFFSET_10MIN);
```

```
        activate_device (diningroom_outside_light,     OFF, timeout3);
        activate_device (diningroom_outside_light,     OFF, timeout3+OFFSET_5MIN);
        activate_device (diningroom_outside_light,     OFF,
timeout3+OFFSET_10MIN);

        activate_device (master_bedroom_outside_light, OFF, timeout4);
        activate_device (master_bedroom_outside_light, OFF, timeout4+OFFSET_5MIN);
        activate_device (master_bedroom_outside_light, OFF,
timeout4+OFFSET_10MIN);

        activate_device (garage_front_outside_light,   OFF, timeout5);
        activate_device (garage_front_outside_light,   OFF, timeout5+OFFSET_5MIN);
        activate_device (garage_front_outside_light,   OFF,
timeout5+OFFSET_10MIN);

        activate_device (porch_outside_light,          OFF, timeout6);
        activate_device (porch_outside_light,          OFF, timeout6+OFFSET_5MIN);
        activate_device (porch_outside_light,          OFF,
timeout6+OFFSET_10MIN);
    }

}
```

```
//****************************************************************************
// Setup Outside Light ON Events
//
// This function performs the following operations:
//
// 1. Remove all existing light events from event database table
// 2. Create new light events
// 3. Lights activate at sunset + delta
//
// Note: Included retries in case of electrical noise affecting lamp turn on.
//****************************************************************************

void  setup_outside_light_ON_events (void)
{
    long int    timeout1, timeout2, timeout3;
    long int    timeout4, timeout5, timeout6;
    long int    override_off_timeout;
    long int    current_time;


    // Log operation
    print_log ("Processed Outside Light ON events");

    // Get current time in seconds
    current_time = get_raw_time();

    // Setup Sunset lamp on events
    timeout1 = sunset_timeout + OFFSET_10MIN + (rand() % OFFSET_15MIN);
    timeout2 = sunset_timeout + OFFSET_10MIN + (rand() % OFFSET_15MIN);
    timeout3 = sunset_timeout + OFFSET_10MIN + (rand() % OFFSET_15MIN);
    timeout4 = sunset_timeout + OFFSET_10MIN + (rand() % OFFSET_15MIN);
    timeout5 = sunset_timeout + OFFSET_10MIN + (rand() % OFFSET_15MIN);
    timeout6 = sunset_timeout + OFFSET_10MIN + (rand() % OFFSET_15MIN);


    // Delete existing outside light ON events
    delete_house_code_on_events (garage_back_outside_light);
    delete_house_code_on_events (familyroom_outside_light);
    delete_house_code_on_events (diningroom_outside_light);
    delete_house_code_on_events (garage_front_outside_light);


    // Program the lamp ON events
    activate_device (garage_back_outside_light,    ON, timeout1);
    activate_device (familyroom_outside_light,     ON, timeout2);
    activate_device (diningroom_outside_light,     ON, timeout3);
    activate_device (garage_front_outside_light,   ON, timeout4);

    activate_device (garage_back_outside_light,    ON, timeout1+OFFSET_5MIN);
    activate_device (familyroom_outside_light,     ON, timeout2+OFFSET_5MIN);
    activate_device (diningroom_outside_light,     ON, timeout3+OFFSET_5MIN);
    activate_device (garage_front_outside_light,   ON, timeout4+OFFSET_5MIN);

    activate_device (garage_back_outside_light,    ON, timeout1+OFFSET_10MIN);
    activate_device (familyroom_outside_light,     ON, timeout2+OFFSET_10MIN);
    activate_device (diningroom_outside_light,     ON, timeout3+OFFSET_10MIN);
    activate_device (garage_front_outside_light,   ON, timeout4+OFFSET_10MIN);
```

```
    // Master bedroom outside light override OFF [between 10pm and 10:30pm]
    // Dad does not like the light shining in through the bedroom window
    override_off_timeout = midnight_timeout + OFFSET_22HRS + (rand() %
OFFSET_30MIN);

    // Only install ON/OFF events if master bedroom outside lamp is not about to
be turned off
    if (current_time < (override_off_timeout - OFFSET_2MIN))
    {
        delete_house_code_events (master_bedroom_outside_light);

        activate_device (master_bedroom_outside_light, ON, timeout5);
        activate_device (master_bedroom_outside_light, ON, timeout5+OFFSET_5MIN);
        activate_device (master_bedroom_outside_light, ON, timeout5+OFFSET_10MIN);

        activate_device (master_bedroom_outside_light, OFF, override_off_timeout);
        activate_device (master_bedroom_outside_light, OFF,
override_off_timeout+OFFSET_5MIN);
        activate_device (master_bedroom_outside_light, OFF,
override_off_timeout+OFFSET_10MIN);
    }
    else
    {
        // Otherwise just switch the lamp off
        delete_house_code_off_events (master_bedroom_outside_light);

        activate_device (master_bedroom_outside_light, OFF, current_time);
        activate_device (master_bedroom_outside_light, OFF,
current_time+OFFSET_5MIN);
        activate_device (master_bedroom_outside_light, OFF,
current_time+OFFSET_10MIN);
    }


    // Front porch outside light override OFF [between 9pm and 9:40pm]
    override_off_timeout = midnight_timeout + OFFSET_21HRS + (rand() %
OFFSET_40MIN);

    // Only install ON/OFF events if porch lamp is not about to be turned off
    if (current_time < (override_off_timeout - OFFSET_2MIN))
    {
        delete_house_code_events (porch_outside_light);

        activate_device (porch_outside_light,  ON, timeout6);
        activate_device (porch_outside_light,  ON, timeout6+OFFSET_5MIN);
        activate_device (porch_outside_light,  ON, timeout6+OFFSET_10MIN);

        activate_device (porch_outside_light, OFF, override_off_timeout);
        activate_device (porch_outside_light, OFF,
override_off_timeout+OFFSET_5MIN);
        activate_device (porch_outside_light, OFF,
override_off_timeout+OFFSET_10MIN);
    }
    else
    {
        // Otherwise just switch the lamp off
        delete_house_code_off_events (porch_outside_light);
```

```
        activate_device (porch_outside_light, OFF, current_time);
        activate_device (porch_outside_light, OFF, current_time+OFFSET_5MIN);
        activate_device (porch_outside_light, OFF, current_time+OFFSET_10MIN);
    }

}
```

```
//*****************************************************************************
// Setup Seasonal Light Events  (Hanging Icicles)
//
// This function performs the following operations:
//
// 1. Remove all existing light events from event database table
// 2. Create new light events
// 3. Lights activate at sunset + delta offset
//
//*****************************************************************************

void  setup_seasonal_light_events (void)
{
    long int   front_turn_on_time, front_turn_off_time;
    long int   back_turn_on_time,  back_turn_off_time;
    long int   current_time;
    Uint16     month;


    // Get current month
    determine_current_month (&month);

    // Does the month fall in [DECEMBER..JANUARY] range?
    if ((month != JANUARY) && (month != DECEMBER))
    {
        // No - Delete any existing icicle time events
        print_log ("Processed Non-Seasonal Light events");

        delete_house_code_events (season_front_light);
        delete_house_code_events (season_back_light);

        // Ensure icicle Lights are turned OFF
        activate_device (season_front_light, OFF, current_time);
        activate_device (season_back_light,  OFF, current_time);
        return;
    }


    // Log operation
    print_log ("Processed Seasonal Light events");

    // Get current time in seconds
    current_time = get_raw_time();

    // We are in month range [DECEMBER..JANUARY]
    // Setup front icicle turn on/off timeout events
    front_turn_on_time  = sunset_timeout     + OFFSET_10MIN + (rand() %
OFFSET_15MIN);  // On  [10min..25min] after sunset
    front_turn_off_time = front_turn_on_time + OFFSET_3HRS  + (rand() %
OFFSET_15MIN);  // Off [3HRS..3HRS15min] later

    // Is current time before the 'turn off' time?
    if (current_time < (front_turn_off_time - OFFSET_2MIN))
    {
        // Yes - Delete existing front seasonal light events
        delete_house_code_events (season_front_light);

        // Install seasonal lights turn on/off events
```

```
        activate_device (season_front_light, ON,  front_turn_on_time);
        activate_device (season_front_light, OFF, front_turn_off_time);
    }

    // We are in month range [DECEMBER..JANUARY]
    // Setup back icicle turn on/off timeout events
    back_turn_on_time   = sunset_timeout    + OFFSET_10MIN + (rand() %
OFFSET_15MIN);  // On  [10min..25min] after sunset
    back_turn_off_time  = back_turn_on_time + OFFSET_3HRS  + (rand() %
OFFSET_15MIN);  // Off [3HRS..3HRS15min] later

    // Is current time before the 'turn off' time?
    if (current_time < (back_turn_off_time  - OFFSET_2MIN))
    {
        // Yes - Delete existing back seasonal light events
        delete_house_code_events (season_back_light);

        // Install seasonal lights turn on/off events
        activate_device (season_back_light,  ON,  back_turn_on_time);
        activate_device (season_back_light,  OFF, back_turn_off_time);
    }

}
```

```
//**************************************************************************
// Setup Fishtank Light Events
//
// This function performs the following operations:
//
// 1. Remove all existing fishtank light events from event database table
// 2. Create new light events
//
// Note: The command is repeated a number of times since the fishtank
//       lights use flourescent tubes which are inherently noisy and sometimes
//       cause the X10 controlling switch to turn on and immediately turn off.
//**************************************************************************

void  setup_fishtank_light_events (void)
{
    long int   turn_on_time;
    long int   turn_off_time;
    long int   current_time;


    // Log operation
    print_log ("Processed Fishtank light events");

    // Get current time in seconds
    current_time = get_raw_time();

    // Setup Fishtank Light turn on/off timeout events
    turn_on_time  = midnight_timeout + OFFSET_9HRS;    //  9am
    turn_off_time = midnight_timeout + OFFSET_23HRS;   // 11pm


    // Is current time before the 'turn off' time?
    if (current_time < (turn_off_time - OFFSET_2MIN))
    {
        // Delete existing fishtank light events
        delete_house_code_events (fishtank_light);

        // Install the Fishtank Lights turn on events
        activate_device (fishtank_light, ON,  turn_on_time);
        activate_device (fishtank_light, ON,  turn_on_time+OFFSET_15SEC);
        activate_device (fishtank_light, ON,  turn_on_time+OFFSET_30SEC);

        // Install the Fishtank Lights turn off events
        activate_device (fishtank_light, OFF, turn_off_time);
        activate_device (fishtank_light, OFF, turn_off_time+OFFSET_15SEC);
        activate_device (fishtank_light, OFF, turn_off_time+OFFSET_30SEC);
    }

}
```

```
//*****************************************************************************
// Setup Family Room Light Events
//
// This function performs the following operations during HOME mode:
//
// 1. Remove all existing family room light events from event database table
// 2. Create new light events
// 3. The general case has the family room lights being turned off at night,
//    however, if movement is detected during that time the turn off time
//    is extended to dawn the following day as a convenience to the user for
//    they just might be staying up all night and we don't want the lights
//    turning off prematurely.
//
//*****************************************************************************

void  setup_family_room_light_events (void)
{
    long int   turn_on_time;
    long int   turn_off_time;
    long int   current_time;


    // Log operation
    print_log ("Processed Family Room lights events");

    // Get current time in seconds
    current_time = get_raw_time();

    // Setup family room light turn on/off timeout events
    turn_on_time  = dusk_timeout + OFFSET_2MIN + (rand() % OFFSET_2MIN);
// Dusk-ish
    turn_off_time = midnight_timeout + OFFSET_23HRS + (rand() % OFFSET_20MIN);
// 11pm..11:20pm


    // Is current time before the 'turn off' time?
    if (current_time < (turn_off_time - OFFSET_2MIN))
    {
        // Delete existing family room light events
        delete_house_code_events_after_sunset (familyroom_window_light);
        delete_house_code_events_after_sunset (familyroom_wall_light);

        // Family room light turn on events
        activate_device (familyroom_wall_light,   ON, turn_on_time);
        activate_device (familyroom_window_light, ON, turn_on_time);

        // Family room light turn off events
        activate_device (familyroom_wall_light,   OFF, turn_off_time);
        activate_device (familyroom_window_light, OFF, turn_off_time);
    }

}
```

```
//****************************************************************************
// Setup Master Bedroom Light Events
//
// This function performs the following operations during HOME mode:
//
// 1. Remove all existing master bedroom light events from event database table
// 2. Create new light events
//
//****************************************************************************

void  setup_master_bedroom_light_events (void)
{
    long int   turn_on_time;
    long int   turn_off_time;
    long int   current_time;


    // Log operation
    print_log ("Processed Master Bedroom light events");

    // Get current time in seconds
    current_time = get_raw_time();

    // Setup master bedroom Light turn on/off timeout events
    turn_on_time  = dusk_timeout + OFFSET_2MIN + (rand() % OFFSET_3MIN);
// Dusk-ish;
    turn_off_time = midnight_timeout + OFFSET_23HRS_40MIN + (rand() %
OFFSET_20MIN);   // 11:40pm..11:59pm

    // Is current time before the 'turn off' time?
    if (current_time < (turn_off_time - OFFSET_2MIN))
    {
        // Delete existing master bedroom light events
        delete_house_code_events_after_sunset (master_bedroom_light);
        delete_house_code_events_after_sunset (master_bedroom_dad_light);
        delete_house_code_events_after_sunset (master_bedroom_mum_light);

        // Master bedroom Lights turn on events
        activate_device (master_bedroom_light,  ON, turn_on_time);

        // Master bedroom Lights turn off events
        activate_device (master_bedroom_light,        OFF, turn_off_time);
        activate_device (master_bedroom_dad_light,    OFF, turn_off_time);
        activate_device (master_bedroom_mum_light,    OFF, turn_off_time);
        activate_device (master_bedroom_closet_light, OFF, turn_off_time);
    }

}
```

```
//****************************************************************************
// Setup Lounge Light Events
//
// This function performs the following operations during HOME mode:
//
// 1. Remove all existing lounge light events from event database table
// 2. Create new light events
//
//****************************************************************************

void  setup_lounge_light_events (void)
{
    long int   turn_on_time;
    long int   turn_off_time;
    long int   current_time;


    // Log report
    print_log ("Processed Lounge Light events()");

    // Get current time in seconds
    current_time = get_raw_time();

    // Setup lounge light turn on/off timeout events
    turn_on_time  = dusk_timeout + OFFSET_2MIN + (rand() % OFFSET_3MIN);
// Dusk-ish
    turn_off_time = midnight_timeout + OFFSET_23HRS_20MIN + (rand() %
OFFSET_20MIN);    // 11:20pm..11:39pm

    // Is current time before the 'turn off' time?
    if (current_time < (turn_off_time - OFFSET_2MIN))
    {
        // Delete existing lounge light events
        delete_house_code_events_after_sunset (lounge_wall_light);
        delete_house_code_events_after_sunset (lounge_window_light);

        // Lounge light turn on events
        activate_device (lounge_wall_light,   ON,  turn_on_time);
        activate_device (lounge_window_light, ON,  turn_on_time);

        // Lounge light turn off events
        activate_device (lounge_wall_light,   OFF, turn_off_time);
        activate_device (lounge_window_light, OFF, turn_off_time);
    }
}
```

```
//***************************************************************************
// SECURITY Setup Master Bedroom Light Events
//
// This function performs the following operations during SECURITY mode:
//
// 1. Remove all existing master bedroom light events from event database table
// 2. Create new light events
//
//***************************************************************************

void  SECURITY_setup_master_bedroom_light_events (void)
{
    long int   turn_on_time;
    long int   turn_off_time;
    long int   current_time;
    char        time_on  [255];
    char        time_off [255];
    char        message [255];


    // Log file
    print_log ("\n");
    print_log ("SECURITY - Setup Master Bedroom Light Events");

    // Get current time in seconds
    current_time = get_raw_time();

    // Setup master bedroom Light turn on/off timeout events
    turn_on_time  = sunset_timeout   + OFFSET_10MIN + (rand() % OFFSET_60MIN);  //
After Sunset
    turn_off_time = midnight_timeout + OFFSET_23HRS + (rand() % OFFSET_59MIN);  //
11pm..11:59pm

    // Is current time past the 'turn off' time?
    if (current_time > (turn_off_time - OFFSET_5MIN))
    {
        // Yes - Do not install these events
        print_log ("SECURITY - Events ignored since activation time already
expired...");
        return;
    }

    // Delete existing master bedroom light events
    delete_house_code_events_after_sunset (master_bedroom_light);
    delete_house_code_events_after_sunset (master_bedroom_mum_light);
    delete_house_code_events_after_sunset (master_bedroom_dad_light);
    delete_house_code_events_after_sunset (master_bedroom_closet_light);

    // Master bedroom Lights turn on events
    activate_device (master_bedroom_light, ON, turn_on_time);

    // Master bedroom Lights turn off events
    activate_device (master_bedroom_light,        OFF, turn_off_time);
    activate_device (master_bedroom_mum_light,    OFF, turn_off_time);
    activate_device (master_bedroom_dad_light,    OFF, turn_off_time);
    activate_device (master_bedroom_closet_light, OFF, turn_off_time);

    // Display security times
```

```
    determine_standard_time (turn_on_time,  time_on);
    determine_standard_time (turn_off_time, time_off);
    sprintf (message, "SECURITY - [ON=%s,  OFF=%s]", time_on, time_off);
    print_log (message);

}
```

```
//****************************************************************************
// SECURITY Setup Lounge Light Events
//
// This function performs the following operations during SECURITY mode:
//
// 1. Remove all existing lounge light events from event database table
// 2. Create new light events
*/****************************************************************************

void  SECURITY_setup_lounge_light_events (void)
{
    long int   turn_on_time;
    long int   turn_off_time;
    long int   current_time;
    char        time_on  [255];
    char        time_off [255];
    char        message [255];

    // Log file
    print_log ("");
    print_log ("SECURITY - Setup Lounge Light Events");

    // Get current time in seconds
    current_time = get_raw_time();

    // Setup lounge light turn on/off timeout events
    turn_on_time  = sunset_timeout   + OFFSET_10MIN + (rand() % OFFSET_20MIN);  //
Sunset..+30min
    turn_off_time = midnight_timeout + OFFSET_22HRS + (rand() % OFFSET_59MIN);  //
10pm..10:59pm

    // Is current time past the 'turn off' time?
    if (current_time > (turn_off_time - OFFSET_5MIN))
    {
        // Yes - Do not install these events
        print_log ("SECURITY - Events ignored since activation time already
expired...");
        return;
    }

    // Delete existing lounge light events
    delete_house_code_events_after_sunset (lounge_wall_light);
    delete_house_code_events_after_sunset (lounge_window_light);

    // Lounge light turn on events
    activate_device (lounge_wall_light,   ON,  turn_on_time);
    activate_device (lounge_window_light, ON,  turn_on_time);

    // Lounge light turn off events
    activate_device (lounge_wall_light,   OFF, turn_off_time);
    activate_device (lounge_window_light, OFF, turn_off_time);

    // Display security times
    determine_standard_time (turn_on_time,  time_on);
    determine_standard_time (turn_off_time, time_off);
    sprintf (message, "SECURITY - [ON=%s,  OFF=%s]", time_on, time_off);
    print_log (message);
}
```

```
//*****************************************************************************
// SECURITY Setup Family Room Light Events
//
// This function performs the following operations during SECURITY mode:
//
// 1. Remove all existing family room light events from event database table
// 2. Create new light events
//
//*****************************************************************************

void  SECURITY_setup_family_room_light_events (void)
{
    long int   turn_on_time;
    long int   turn_off_time;
    long int   current_time;
    char        time_on  [255];
    char        time_off [255];
    char        message [255];


    // Log file
    print_log ("");
    print_log ("SECURITY - Setup Family Room Light Events");

    // Get current time in seconds
    current_time = get_raw_time();

    // Setup family room light turn on/off timeout events
    turn_on_time  = sunset_timeout + OFFSET_2MIN + (rand() % OFFSET_5MIN);       //
Sunset-ish;
    turn_off_time = midnight_timeout + OFFSET_23HRS + (rand() % OFFSET_55MIN);  //
11pm..11:55pm

    // Is current time past the 'turn off' time?
    if (current_time > (turn_off_time - OFFSET_5MIN))
    {
        // Yes - Do not install these events
        print_log ("SECURITY - Events ignored since activation time already
expired...");
        return;
    }

    // Delete existing family room light events
    delete_house_code_events_after_sunset (familyroom_window_light);
    delete_house_code_events_after_sunset (familyroom_wall_light);

    // Family room light turn on events
    activate_device (familyroom_wall_light,   ON, turn_on_time);
    activate_device (familyroom_window_light, ON, turn_on_time);

    // Family room light turn off events
    activate_device (familyroom_wall_light,          OFF, turn_off_time);
    activate_device (familyroom_window_light,        OFF, turn_off_time);
    activate_device (familyroom_track_tv_light,      OFF, turn_off_time);
    activate_device (familyroom_track_reading_light, OFF, turn_off_time);
    activate_device (familyroom_wall_unit_light,     OFF, turn_off_time);
    activate_device (familyroom_wall_unit_spotlight, OFF, turn_off_time);
```

```
    // Display security times
    determine_standard_time (turn_on_time,  time_on);
    determine_standard_time (turn_off_time, time_off);
    sprintf (message, "SECURITY - [ON=%s,  OFF=%s]", time_on, time_off);
    print_log (message);
}
```

```
//******************************************************************************
// SECURITY Setup Guest Bedroom Light Events
//
// This function performs the following operations during SECURITY mode:
//
// 1. Remove all existing guest room light events from event database table
// 2. Create new light events
//
//******************************************************************************

void  SECURITY_setup_guest_bedroom_light_events (void)
{
    Uint8       index;
    Uint8       event_count;
    Uint8       existing_light_events_deleted = FALSE;
    long int    max_on_time;
    long int    turn_on_time;
    long int    turn_off_time;
    long int    current_time;
    char        time_on  [255];
    char        time_off [255];
    char        message [255];


    // Determine number of random events
    event_count = (rand() % 3) + 1;       // Range [1..3]

    // Log file
    print_log ("");
    sprintf (message, "SECURITY - Setup Guest Bedroom [%d events]", event_count);
    print_log (message);

    // Get current time in seconds
    current_time = get_raw_time();

    // Determine maximum on time based upon the number of events for the evening
    max_on_time = OFFSET_3HRS / event_count;

    // Initialize first turn on time
    turn_on_time  = sunset_timeout + OFFSET_2MIN + (rand() % OFFSET_30MIN);

    // Setup random time events
    for (index = 0; index < event_count; index++)
    {
        // Determine the turn off time
        turn_off_time = turn_on_time + (max_on_time - OFFSET_45MIN) + (rand() %
OFFSET_35MIN);

        // Is current time past the 'turn off' time?
        if (current_time > (turn_off_time - OFFSET_5MIN))
        {
            // Yes - Do not install these events
            sprintf (message, "SECURITY - Event %d ignored since activation time
already expired...", (index + 1));
            print_log (message);
            continue;
        }
```

```
        // Have we deleted the existing events?
        if (!existing_light_events_deleted)
        {
            // No - Go ahead and delete these events
            existing_light_events_deleted = TRUE;

            // Delete existing guest bedroom light events
            delete_house_code_events_after_sunset (guest_main_light);
        }

        // Does the last event finish before 11:58pm?
        if (turn_off_time > (midnight_timeout + OFFSET_23HRS_58MIN))
        {
            // No - Force last even to finish at 11:58pm
            turn_off_time = midnight_timeout + OFFSET_23HRS_58MIN - (rand() %
OFFSET_10MIN);
        }

        // Program the guest light on/off events
        activate_device (guest_main_light,  ON, turn_on_time);
        activate_device (guest_main_light, OFF, turn_off_time);

        // Display security times
        determine_standard_time (turn_on_time,  time_on);
        determine_standard_time (turn_off_time, time_off);
        sprintf (message, "SECURITY#%d - [ON=%s,  OFF=%s]", index+1, time_on,
time_off);
        print_log (message);

        // Determine next turn on time
        turn_on_time  = turn_off_time + OFFSET_15MIN + (rand() % OFFSET_15MIN);

        // Does the last event start before 11:30pm?
        if (turn_on_time > (midnight_timeout + OFFSET_23HRS_30MIN))
        {
            // No - Cancel any additional events
            break;
        }
    }

}
```

```
//***************************************************************************
// SECURITY Setup Steve Bedroom Light Events
//
// This function performs the following operations during SECURITY mode:
//
// 1. Remove all existing room light events from event database table
// 2. Create new light events
//
//***************************************************************************

void  SECURITY_setup_steve_bedroom_light_events (void)
{
    Uint8       index;
    Uint8       event_count;
    Uint8       existing_light_events_deleted = FALSE;
    long int    max_on_time;
    long int    turn_on_time;
    long int    turn_off_time;
    long int    current_time;
    char        time_on  [255];
    char        time_off [255];
    char        message [255];


    // Determine number of random events
    event_count = (rand() % 3) + 2;       // Range [2..4]

    // Log file
    print_log ("");
    sprintf (message, "SECURITY - Setup Steve's Bedroom [%d events]",
event_count);
    print_log (message);

    // Get current time in seconds
    current_time = get_raw_time();


    // Determine maximum on time based upon the number of events for the evening
    max_on_time = OFFSET_4HRS / event_count;

    // Initialize first turn on time
    turn_on_time  = sunset_timeout + OFFSET_2MIN + (rand() % OFFSET_30MIN);

    // Setup random time events
    for (index = 0; index < event_count; index++)
    {
        // Determine the turn off time
        turn_off_time = turn_on_time + (max_on_time - OFFSET_45MIN) + (rand() %
OFFSET_35MIN);

        // Does the last event finish before 11:58pm?
        if (turn_off_time > (midnight_timeout + OFFSET_23HRS_58MIN))
        {
            // No - Force last even to finish at 11:58pm
            turn_off_time = midnight_timeout + OFFSET_23HRS_58MIN - (rand() %
OFFSET_10MIN);
        }
```

```
        // Is current time past the 'turn off' time?
        if (current_time > (turn_off_time - OFFSET_5MIN))
        {
            // Yes - Do not install these events
            sprintf (message, "SECURITY - Event %d ignored since activation time
already expired...", (index + 1));
            print_log (message);
            continue;
        }

        // Have we deleted the existing events?
        if (!existing_light_events_deleted)
        {
            // No - Go ahead and delete these events
            existing_light_events_deleted = TRUE;

            // Delete existing Steve's bedroom light events
            delete_house_code_events_after_sunset (steve_bedroom_ceiling_light);
            delete_house_code_events_after_sunset (steve_bedroom_wall_light);
            delete_house_code_events_after_sunset (steve_bedroom_window_light);
            delete_house_code_events_after_sunset (steve_bedroom_reading_light);
        }


        // Program Steve's bedroom light on/off events
        activate_device (steve_bedroom_window_light,  ON, turn_on_time);
        activate_device (steve_bedroom_window_light, OFF, turn_off_time);

        // Display security times
        determine_standard_time (turn_on_time,  time_on);
        determine_standard_time (turn_off_time, time_off);
        sprintf (message, "SECURITY#%d - [ON=%s,  OFF=%s]", index+1, time_on,
time_off);
        print_log (message);

        // Determine next turn on time
        turn_on_time  = turn_off_time + OFFSET_15MIN + (rand() % OFFSET_15MIN);

        // Does the last event start before 11:30pm?
        if (turn_on_time > (midnight_timeout + OFFSET_23HRS_30MIN))
        {
            // No - Cancel any additional events
            break;
        }
    }

}
```

```
//*****************************************************************************
// SECURITY Setup Common Bathroom Light Events
//
// This function performs the following operations during SECURITY mode:
//
// 1. Remove all existing room light events from event database table
// 2. Create new light events
//
//*****************************************************************************

void  SECURITY_setup_common_bathroom_light_events (void)
{
    Uint8       index;
    Uint8       event_count;
    Uint8       existing_light_events_deleted = FALSE;
    long int    max_on_time;
    long int    turn_on_time;
    long int    turn_off_time;
    long int    current_time;
    char        time_on  [255];
    char        time_off [255];
    char        message [255];


    // Determine number of random evening events
    event_count = (rand() % 3) + 3;        // Range [3..5]

    // Log file
    print_log ("");
    sprintf (message, "SECURITY - Setup Common Bathroom Room [%d evening events]",
event_count);
    print_log (message);

    // Get current time in seconds
    current_time = get_raw_time();

    // Initialize first turn on time
    turn_on_time  = sunset_timeout + OFFSET_2MIN + (rand() % OFFSET_30MIN);

    // Setup random time events
    for (index = 0; index < event_count; index++)
    {
        // Determine the turn off time
        turn_off_time = turn_on_time + (OFFSET_3MIN + (rand() % OFFSET_15MIN));

        // Does the last event finish after 11:58pm?
        if (turn_off_time > (midnight_timeout + OFFSET_23HRS_58MIN))
        {
            // Yes - Force last event to finish at 11:58pm
            turn_off_time = midnight_timeout + OFFSET_23HRS_58MIN - (rand() %
OFFSET_10MIN);
        }

        // Is current time past the 'turn off' time?
        if (current_time > (turn_off_time - OFFSET_5MIN))
        {
            // Yes - Do not install these events
```

```
            sprintf (message, "SECURITY - Event %d ignored since activation time
already expired...", (index + 1));
            print_log (message);
            continue;
        }

        // Have we deleted the existing events?
        if (!existing_light_events_deleted)
        {
            // No - Go ahead and delete these events
            existing_light_events_deleted = TRUE;

            // Delete existing common bathroom light events
            delete_house_code_events_after_sunset (common_bathroom_light);
        }


        // Program light on/off events
        activate_device (common_bathroom_light,  ON, turn_on_time);
        activate_device (common_bathroom_light, OFF, turn_off_time);

        // Display security times
        determine_standard_time (turn_on_time,  time_on);
        determine_standard_time (turn_off_time, time_off);
        sprintf (message, "SECURITY#%d - [ON=%s,  OFF=%s]", index+1, time_on,
time_off);
        print_log (message);

        // Determine next turn on time
        turn_on_time  = turn_off_time + OFFSET_35MIN + (rand() % OFFSET_20MIN);

        // Does the last event start after 11:30pm?
        if (turn_on_time > (midnight_timeout + OFFSET_23HRS_30MIN))
        {
            // Yes - Cancel any additional events
            break;
        }
    }



    // Determine number of random early hour events (after midnight but before the
dawn)
    event_count = (rand() % 3) + 1;        // Range [1..3]

    // Log file
    print_log ("");
    sprintf (message, "SECURITY - Setup Common Bathroom Room [%d early hour
events]", event_count);
    print_log (message);

    // Initialize first turn on time
    turn_on_time  = midnight_timeout + OFFSET_1HR + (rand() % OFFSET_1HR);

    // Setup random time events
    for (index = 0; index < event_count; index++)
    {
        // Determine the turn off time
```

```
        turn_off_time = turn_on_time + (OFFSET_1MIN + (rand() % OFFSET_3MIN));

        // Does the last event finish less than 30 minutes before dawn?
        if (turn_off_time > (dawn_timeout - OFFSET_30MIN))
        {
            // Yes - Force last event to finish 30 minutes before dawn
            turn_off_time = dawn_timeout - OFFSET_30MIN - (rand() % OFFSET_20MIN);
        }

        // Is current time past the 'turn off' time?
        if (current_time > (turn_off_time - OFFSET_5MIN))
        {
            // Yes - Do not install these events
            sprintf (message, "SECURITY - Event %d ignored since activation time
already expired...", (index + 1));
            print_log (message);
            continue;
        }

        // Have we deleted the existing events?
        if (!existing_light_events_deleted)
        {
            // No - Go ahead and delete these events
            existing_light_events_deleted = TRUE;

            // Delete existing common bathroom light events
            delete_house_code_events (common_bathroom_light);
        }

        // Program light on/off events
        activate_device (common_bathroom_light,  ON, turn_on_time);
        activate_device (common_bathroom_light, OFF, turn_off_time);

        // Display security times
        determine_standard_time (turn_on_time, time_on);
        determine_standard_time (turn_off_time, time_off);
        sprintf (message, "SECURITY#%d - [ON=%s,  OFF=%s]", index+1, time_on,
time_off);
        print_log (message);

        // Determine next turn on time
        turn_on_time  = turn_off_time + OFFSET_45MIN + (rand() % OFFSET_45MIN);

        // Does the last event start less than 1 hour before dawn?
        if (turn_on_time > (dawn_timeout - OFFSET_1HR))
        {
            // Yes - Cancel any additional events
            break;
        }
    }

}
```

```
//*****************************************************************************
// SECURITY Setup Study Light Events
//
// This function performs the following operations during SECURITY mode:
//
// 1. Remove all existing room light events from event database table
// 2. Create new light events
//
//*****************************************************************************

void  SECURITY_setup_study_light_events (void)
{
    Uint8       index;
    Uint8       event_count;
    Uint8       existing_light_events_deleted = FALSE;
    long int    max_on_time;
    long int    turn_on_time;
    long int    turn_off_time;
    long int    current_time;
    char        time_on  [255];
    char        time_off [255];
    char        message [255];


    // Determine number of random events
    event_count = (rand() % 4) + 1;        // Range [1..4]

    // Log file
    print_log ("");

    sprintf (message, "SECURITY - Setup Study [%d events]", event_count);
    print_log (message);

    // Get current time in seconds
    current_time = get_raw_time();

    // Determine maximum on time based upon the number of events for the evening
    max_on_time = OFFSET_4HRS / event_count;


    // Initialize first turn on time
    turn_on_time  = sunset_timeout + OFFSET_2MIN + (rand() % OFFSET_30MIN);

    // Setup random time events
    for (index = 0; index < event_count; index++)
    {
        // Determine the turn off time
        turn_off_time = turn_on_time + (max_on_time - OFFSET_45MIN) + (rand() %
OFFSET_35MIN);

        // Does the last event finish before 11:58pm?
        if (turn_off_time > (midnight_timeout + OFFSET_23HRS_58MIN))
        {
            // No - Force last even to finish at 11:58pm
            turn_off_time = midnight_timeout + (OFFSET_23HRS_58MIN - (rand() %
OFFSET_10MIN));
        }
```

```
        // Is current time past the 'turn off' time?
        if (current_time > (turn_off_time - OFFSET_5MIN))
        {
            // Yes - Do not install these events
            sprintf (message, "SECURITY - Event %d ignored since activation time
already expired...", (index + 1));
            print_log (message);
            continue;
        }

        // Have we deleted the existing events?
        if (!existing_light_events_deleted)
        {
            // No - Go ahead and delete these events
            existing_light_events_deleted = TRUE;

            // Delete existing study light events
            delete_house_code_events_after_sunset (study_ceiling_light);
        }


        // Program light on/off events
        activate_device (study_ceiling_light,  ON, turn_on_time);
        activate_device (study_ceiling_light, OFF, turn_off_time);

        // Display security times
        determine_standard_time (turn_on_time,  time_on);
        determine_standard_time (turn_off_time, time_off);
        sprintf (message, "SECURITY#%d - [ON=%s,  OFF=%s]", index+1, time_on,
time_off);
        print_log (message);

        // Determine next turn on time
        turn_on_time  = turn_off_time + OFFSET_15MIN + (rand() % OFFSET_15MIN);

        // Does the last event start before 11:30pm?
        if (turn_on_time > (midnight_timeout + OFFSET_23HRS_30MIN))
        {
            // No - Cancel any additional events
            break;
        }
    }

}
```

```
//****************************************************************************
// SECURITY Setup Kitchen Light Events
//
// This function performs the following operations during SECURITY mode:
//
// 1. Remove all existing room light events from event database table
// 2. Create new light events
//
//****************************************************************************

void  SECURITY_setup_kitchen_light_events (void)
{
    Uint8       index;
    Uint8       event_count;
    Uint8       existing_light_events_deleted = FALSE;
    long int    max_on_time;
    long int    turn_on_time;
    long int    turn_off_time;
    long int    current_time;
    char        time_on  [255];
    char        time_off [255];
    char        message [255];


    // Determine number of random events
    event_count = (rand() % 4) + 4;       // Range [4..7]

    // Log File
    print_log ("");
    sprintf (message, "SECURITY - Setup Kitchen [%d events]", event_count);
    print_log (message);

    // Get current time in seconds
    current_time = get_raw_time();

    // Determine maximum on time based upon the number of events for the evening
    max_on_time = OFFSET_4HRS / event_count;

    // Initialize first turn on time
    turn_on_time  = sunset_timeout + OFFSET_2MIN + (rand() % OFFSET_30MIN);

    // Setup random time events
    for (index = 0; index < event_count; index++)
    {
        // Determine the turn off time
        turn_off_time = turn_on_time + (max_on_time - OFFSET_20MIN) + (rand() %
OFFSET_15MIN);

        // Does the last event finish before 11:58pm?
        if (turn_off_time > (midnight_timeout + OFFSET_23HRS_58MIN))
        {
            // No - Force last even to finish at 11:58pm
            turn_off_time = midnight_timeout + OFFSET_23HRS_58MIN - (rand() %
OFFSET_10MIN);
        }

        // Is current time past the 'turn off' time?
        if (current_time > (turn_off_time - OFFSET_5MIN))
```

```
        {
            // Yes - Do not install these events
            sprintf (message, "SECURITY - Event %d ignored since activation time
already expired...", (index + 1));
            print_log (message);
            continue;
        }

        // Have we deleted the existing events?
        if (!existing_light_events_deleted)
        {
            // No - Go ahead and delete these events
            existing_light_events_deleted = TRUE;

            // Delete existing kitchen light events
            delete_house_code_events_after_sunset (kitchen_light);
        }


        // Program light on/off events
        activate_device (kitchen_light,  ON, turn_on_time);
        activate_device (kitchen_light, OFF, turn_off_time);

        // Display security times
        determine_standard_time (turn_on_time,  time_on);
        determine_standard_time (turn_off_time, time_off);
        sprintf (message, "SECURITY#%d - [ON=%s,  OFF=%s]", index+1, time_on,
time_off);
        print_log (message);

        // Determine next turn on time
        turn_on_time  = turn_off_time + OFFSET_15MIN + (rand() % OFFSET_15MIN);

        // Does the last event start before 11:30pm?
        if (turn_on_time > (midnight_timeout + OFFSET_23HRS_30MIN))
        {
            // No - Cancel any additional events
            break;
        }
    }

}
```

```
//******************************************************************************
// SECURITY Setup Kitchen Nook Light Events
//
// This function performs the following operations during SECURITY mode:
//
// 1. Remove all existing room light events from event database table
// 2. Create new light events
//
//******************************************************************************

void  SECURITY_setup_kitchen_nook_light_events (void)
{
    Uint8       index;
    Uint8       event_count;
    Uint8       existing_light_events_deleted = FALSE;
    long int    max_on_time;
    long int    turn_on_time;
    long int    turn_off_time;
    long int    current_time;
    char        time_on  [255];
    char        time_off [255];
    char        message [255];


    // Determine number of random events
    event_count = (rand() % 3) + 1;       // Range [1..3]

    // Log File
    print_log ("");
    sprintf (message, "SECURITY - Setup Kitchen Nook [%d events]", event_count);
    print_log (message);

    // Get current time in seconds
    current_time = get_raw_time();

    // Determine maximum on time based upon the number of events for the evening
    max_on_time = OFFSET_45MIN;

    // Initialize first turn on time
    turn_on_time  = sunset_timeout + OFFSET_2MIN + (rand() % OFFSET_30MIN);

    // Setup random time events
    for (index = 0; index < event_count; index++)
    {
        // Determine the turn off time
        turn_off_time = turn_on_time + (max_on_time - OFFSET_20MIN) + (rand() %
OFFSET_20MIN);

        // Does the last event finish before 11:58pm?
        if (turn_off_time > (midnight_timeout + OFFSET_23HRS_58MIN))
        {
            // No - Force last even to finish at 11:58pm
            turn_off_time = midnight_timeout + OFFSET_23HRS_58MIN;
        }

        // Is current time past the 'turn off' time?
        if (current_time > (turn_off_time - OFFSET_5MIN))
        {
```

```
            // Yes - Do not install these events
            sprintf (message, "SECURITY - Event %d ignored since activation time
already expired...", (index + 1));
            print_log (message);
            continue;
        }

        // Have we deleted the existing events?
        if (!existing_light_events_deleted)
        {
            // No - Go ahead and delete these events
            existing_light_events_deleted = TRUE;

            // Delete existing kitchen nook light events
            delete_house_code_events_after_sunset (kitchen_nook_light);
        }


        // Program light on/off events
        activate_device (kitchen_nook_light,  ON, turn_on_time);
        activate_device (kitchen_nook_light, OFF, turn_off_time);

        // Display security times
        determine_standard_time (turn_on_time,  time_on);
        determine_standard_time (turn_off_time, time_off);
        sprintf (message, "SECURITY#%d - [ON=%s,  OFF=%s]", index+1, time_on,
time_off);
        print_log (message);

        // Determine next turn on time
        turn_on_time  = turn_off_time + OFFSET_30MIN + (rand() % OFFSET_15MIN);

        // Does the last event start before 11:30pm?
        if (turn_on_time > (midnight_timeout + OFFSET_23HRS_30MIN))
        {
            // No - Cancel any additional events
            break;
        }
    }

}
```

```
//***************************************************************************
// Access Home Control Database
//
// house_state (Home Mode or Security Mode)
// house_code_inputs (acive inputs to be processed)
// house_code_states (current house code states)
//
//***************************************************************************

void  access_home_control_database (void)
{
    char    message [255];


    // Connect to MySQL system
    conn1 = mysql_init(NULL);

    // Was the connection successfull?
    if (conn1 == NULL)
    {
        // No - Display error message and exit.
        sprintf (message, "Error_A %u: %s", mysql_errno(conn1),
mysql_error(conn1));
        print_log (message);
        exit(1);
    }

    // Successfully connected to the MySQL System.
    // Now connect to the MySQL "system_control" database.
    if (mysql_real_connect(conn1, "192.168.1.176", "steve", "william",
"system_control", 0, NULL, 0) == NULL)
    {
        // Connection not established - Display error message.
        sprintf(message, "Error_B %u: %s", mysql_errno(conn1),
mysql_error(conn1));
        print_log (message);
        print_log("Exiting...");
        exit (1);
    }
    else
    {
        // Now connected to    system_control database.
        print_log ("*** Connected to 'system_control' database.");
    }

}
```

```
//*****************************************************************************
// Hex to ASCII
//
// This function converts a hex digit to an ASCII character.
//
//*****************************************************************************

char  hex_to_ascii (char hex_digit)
{
    // Is the hex digit in the numeric range of [0..9]'?
    if (hex_digit < 10)
    {
        // Yes - Convert the numeric digit into an ASCII character
        return (0x30 + hex_digit);           // Handle '0' .. '9'
    }
    else
    {
        // No - Cater for a hex digit in the numeric range [10..15]
        return (0x41 + (hex_digit - 10));   // Handle 'A' .. 'F'
    }
}
```

```
//****************************************************************************
// TI103 Add Checksum
//
// This function appends the checksum to the message string.
//
//****************************************************************************

void  ti103_add_checksum (char * buffer)
{
    int  index;
    int  msg_size;
    unsigned char checksum;


    // Initialization
    checksum = 0;

    msg_size = strlen (buffer);
    //  printf("msg_size = %d\n", msg_size);


    // Compute checksum
    for (index = 0; index < msg_size; index++)
    {
        checksum += buffer[index];
    }

    // Add checksum to message buffer
    buffer[msg_size++] = hex_to_ascii ((checksum & 0xF0) >> 4);
    buffer[msg_size++] = hex_to_ascii  (checksum & 0x0F);
    buffer[msg_size++] = 0x00;

}
```

```
//*****************************************************************************
// TI103 Build Get Status String
//
// This function builds the 'Get Status' string and appends the checksum.
//
//*****************************************************************************

void  ti103_build_get_status_string (char * buffer)
{

    // Build the Get Status command
    sprintf (buffer, "$>280000");

    // Append the checksum
    ti103_add_checksum (buffer);

    // Finalize with the '#' symbol
    strcat (buffer, "#");

}
```

```
//*****************************************************************************
// TI103 Build Command String
//
// This function builds the TI103 command string and appends the checksum.
//
//*****************************************************************************

void  ti103_build_command_string (char    * buffer,
       int     house_code,
       int     unit_code,
       char  * command)
{
    int  msg_size;


    // Build start of command message
    strcpy (buffer, "$>28001");
    msg_size = strlen (buffer);


    // Bring in the device address
    buffer[msg_size++] = 0x40 + house_code;          // Handle  'A' .. 'P'
    buffer[msg_size++] = 0x30 + (unit_code / 10);    // Handle '01' .. '16'
    buffer[msg_size++] = 0x30 + (unit_code % 10);

    // Add in the device address (one more time)
    buffer[msg_size++] = 0x40 + house_code;          // Handle  'A' .. 'P'
    buffer[msg_size++] = 0x30 + (unit_code / 10);    // Handle '01' .. '16'
    buffer[msg_size++] = 0x30 + (unit_code % 10);

    // Bring in the command
    buffer[msg_size++] = 0x40 + house_code;          // Handle  'A' .. 'P'
    buffer[msg_size++] = 0x00;

    strcat (buffer, command);                        // Add in the command string
    msg_size = strlen (buffer);

    // Bring in the command (one more time)
    buffer[msg_size++] = 0x40 + house_code;          // Handle  'A' .. 'P'
    buffer[msg_size++] = 0x00;

    strcat (buffer, command);                        // Add in the command string
    msg_size = strlen (buffer);


    // Add in the checksum
    ti103_add_checksum (buffer);

    // Finalize with the '#' symbol
    strcat (buffer, "#");
}
```

```
//****************************************************************************
// Process Events
//
// The House Code Events table is used to contain the devices that are to be
// turned ON or OFF.
//
// This function accesses the MySQL database and obtains the device's house
// and unit codes along with its state code.  It then builds an X-10 control
// message and sends it to the device via the TI-103.
//
//****************************************************************************

void  process_events (void)
{
    Uint8            status = FALSE;
    MYSQL_RES       *mysqlResult;
    MYSQL_ROW        mysqlRow;
    MYSQL_FIELD     *mysqlFields;
    my_ulonglong     numRows;
    unsigned int     numFields;
    long int         current_time;
    unsigned long    timeout;

    int     house, unit, state;
    int     num_bytes_written;
    char    buffer[255];
    char    timestamp[255];
    char    message [255];


    // Get current time in seconds
    current_time = get_raw_time();


    // EVENTS DATABASE
    // ===============

    // Determine if there are any event entries in the database
    // These are User Operations requested from the web pages
    sprintf (buffer, "SELECT * FROM house_code_events WHERE timeout<=%ld ORDER BY
timeout",
            (long int)current_time);

    if (mysql_query(conn1, buffer))
    {
        // Error detected - Print error message
        sprintf (message, "Error_G1 %u: %s", mysql_errno(conn1),
mysql_error(conn1));
        print_log (message);
        return;
    }


    // Determine the number of event entries
    mysqlResult = mysql_store_result (conn1);

    // Are there any entries?
    if (mysqlResult)
```

```
    {
        // Yes - Get the number of database table rows and fields
        numRows = mysql_num_rows(mysqlResult);

        numFields = mysql_num_fields (mysqlResult);

        // Print these out when testing
        // printf ("Number of Rows = %lld,  Number of Fields = %d \n", numRows,
numFields);


        // Get the first row in the table
        while (mysqlRow = mysql_fetch_row(mysqlResult))
        {
            // Get the house, unit, etc. parameters from the MySQL table
            house   = (int) (atoi (mysqlRow[HCE_HOUSE]));
            unit    = (int) (atoi (mysqlRow[HCE_UNIT]));
            state   = (int) (atoi (mysqlRow[HCE_STATE]));
            timeout = (int) (atoi (mysqlRow[HCE_TIMEOUT]));

            // Does the timestamp string exist?
            if (mysqlRow[HCE_TIMESTAMP] != NULL)
            {
                // Yes - Use it
                strncpy (timestamp, mysqlRow[HCE_TIMESTAMP], 60);

                // Is the timestamp length valid?
                if (strlen(timestamp) != 19)
                {
                    // No - Use a default time
                    strcpy (timestamp, "----/--/-- --:--:--");
                }
            }
            else
            {
                // No - Use a default time
                strcpy (timestamp, "----/--/-- --:--:--");
            }


            // Build the TI103 Command String
            if (state == 1)
            {
                // Turn the required device identified by (House,Unit) ON
                ti103_build_command_string (buffer, house, unit, "ON");
            }
            else
            {
                // Turn the required device identified by (House, Unit) OFF
                ti103_build_command_string (buffer, house, unit, "OFF");
            }

            // Output this command string to the serial port assigned to the TI103
            num_bytes_written = write(fd, buffer, strlen(buffer));

            if (num_bytes_written != strlen(buffer))
            {
```

```
                sprintf (message, "TI103 CMD ERROR - Bytes written %d/%d",
num_bytes_written, strlen(buffer));
                print_log (message);
            }

            // Display the command information on the terminal screen
            // for user verification.
            // printf ("Command = %s\n", buffer);
            // printf ("Number Bytes Written = %d/%d\n", num_bytes_written,
strlen(buffer));


            // EVENTS DATABASE
            // ===============

            // Now that the specific event has been processed,
            // proceed to build a MySQL command to delete the
            // house/unit code entry for this device from the EVENTS database
            sprintf (buffer, "DELETE FROM house_code_events WHERE house=%d AND
unit=%d AND state=%d AND timeout=%ld",
                    house, unit, state, timeout);

            // Disply this command for user verification
            // printf ("%s\n", buffer);

            // Issue the command to the MySQL database
            if (mysql_query(conn1, buffer))
            {
                // Error - Print error message
                sprintf (message, "Error_E1 %u: %s", mysql_errno(conn1),
mysql_error(conn1));
                print_log (message);
            }


            // Build command to update device info in house_code_states database
table
            // This will identify the current state of the device and also provide
the
            // timestamp as to when the device state was effected.
            sprintf (buffer,
                    "UPDATE house_code_states SET state=%d, timestamp='%s',
timeout=%ld, presence=%ld WHERE house=%d AND unit=%d",
                    state,
                    timestamp,
                    timeout,
                    ZERO_PRESENCE_TIMEOUT,
                    house,
                    unit);

            // Issue the update command to the MySQL Database
            if (mysql_query(conn1, buffer))
            {
                // Error Detected - Print error message but still continue...
                sprintf (message, "Error_E2 %u: %s", mysql_errno(conn1),
mysql_error(conn1));
                print_log (message);
            }
```

```
            // Sleep between successive commands...
            msleep (EXECUTION_SLEEP_MS);
        }


        // Was a MySQL result pointer returned?
        if (mysqlResult)
        {
            // Yes - Free the pointer
            mysql_free_result(mysqlResult);
            mysqlResult = NULL;
        }
    }
}
```

```
//*****************************************************************************
// Determine Initial Security Mode
//
// This function accesses the security parameter in the House_State database.
//
// If the system is powering up and the Security mode is already engaged then
// the Security events are configured.  Otherwise, if the system is in Home
// mode then the Home events are configured.
//
//*****************************************************************************

void  determine_initial_security_mode (void)
{
    int     house_state_security;
    char    time_buffer[255];
    char    message[255];
    char    buffer[255];


    // Get the security mode
    if (get_house_state_security (&house_state_security) == SUCCESS)
    {
        // Is the security mode active?
        if (house_state_security == SECURITY_MODE_ACTIVE)
        {
            // Yes - System is powering up in SECURITY mode
            print_log ("*** System is powering up [SECURITY ON]");

            // Activate SECURITY mode flags
            security_mode         = TRUE;
            security_mode_started = TRUE;
            security_mode_stopped = FALSE;

            // Compute current timestamp
            determine_system_timestamp (time_buffer);

            // Send email stating Security Mode Reactivated
            sprintf (message, "%s - System is powering up [SECURITY ON]",
time_buffer);
            send_security_email ("*** SECURITY INFO ***", message);
            speak ("System startup.  Security mode activated.");
        }
        else
        {
            // No - System is powering up in HOME mode
            //      This is the case even if we had a restart during transition to
SECURITY mode
            print_log ("*** System is powering up [SECURITY OFF]");

            // All transition security modes forced to INACTIVE state
            sprintf (buffer, "UPDATE house_state SET security=%d",
SECURITY_MODE_INACTIVE);
            mysql_query(conn1, buffer);

            // Deactivate SECURITY mode flags
            security_mode         = FALSE;
            security_mode_started = FALSE;
            security_mode_stopped = TRUE;
```

```
            // Compute current timestamp
            determine_system_timestamp (time_buffer);

            // Send email stating Security Mode Reactivated
            sprintf (message, "%s - System is powering up [Security OFF]",
time_buffer);
            send_security_email ("*** SECURITY INFO ***", message);
            speak ("System startup.  Security mode is off.");

            // Test the alarm system
            print_log ("*** Alarm siren test.");
            speak ("Alarm siren test.");
            turn_alarm_siren_on();
            process_events();
            sleep (3);

            // Switch the alarm off
            turn_alarm_siren_off();
            process_events();
            print_log ("*** Alarm siren reset.");
            speak ("Alarm siren reset.");

            // Test the watchdog
            print_log ("*** Watchdog test.");
            speak ("Watchdog test.");
            kick_the_dog();
            process_events();
            sleep (3);

            // Switch the doggy off
            tell_the_dog_to_be_quiet();
            process_events();
            print_log ("*** Watchdog reset.");
            speak ("Watchdog reset.");
        }
    }
}
```

```
//*****************************************************************************
// Monitor Security Mode Transition
//
// This function monitors the MySQL house_state security parameters.
//
// This value can take on the following four different states:
//
// SECURITY_MODE_INACTIVE  = Security mode is deactive.
// SECURITY_MODE_INITIATED = User pressed the SECURITY button on web page.
// SECURITY_MODE_DELAY     = Security delay is counting.
// SECURITY_MODE_ACTIVE    = Delay expired and security mode is now active.
//
// This gives the web page user the facility to initiate the change to security
// mode and provides them with a timed delay during which they can exit the
// building prior to the security mode being fully engaged.
//
//*****************************************************************************

void  monitor_security_mode_transition (void)
{
    int  house_state_security;
    char buffer[255];
    char message[255];
    char time_buffer[255];
    long   int  delay_count;
    long   int  current_time;
    static int  last_current_time = 0;
    static int  security_delay_timeout;


    // Get the house code security parameter
    if (get_house_state_security (&house_state_security) == SUCCESS)
    {
        // Has the web page user pressed the [SECURITY OFF] button?
        if (house_state_security == SECURITY_MODE_INACTIVE)
        {
            // Yes - Was the security mode previously active?
            if (security_mode)
            {
                // Yes - Deactivate security mode and install normal HOME events
                security_mode         = FALSE;
                security_mode_started = FALSE;
                security_mode_stopped = TRUE;

                // Compute current timestamp
                determine_system_timestamp (time_buffer);

                // Send email stating Security Mode Deactivated
                sprintf (message, "%s - SECURITY Mode DEACTIVATED [Operator
action]", time_buffer);
                send_security_email ("*** SECURITY INFO ***", message);
                speak ("Security mode is off.");

                // Switch the alarm off
                turn_alarm_siren_off();
            }
        }
```

```
        // Has the web page user pressed the [SECURITY ON] button?
        else if (house_state_security == SECURITY_MODE_INITIATED)
        {
            // Yes - Initiate the security delay
            sprintf ( buffer, "UPDATE house_state SET security=%d",
SECURITY_MODE_DELAY);
            mysql_query(conn1, buffer);

            // Get current time in seconds
            current_time = get_raw_time();

            // Setup the security delay
            security_delay_timeout = current_time + OFFSET_5MIN;  // Time to exit
the home
            speak ("Security mode has been initiated.");
        }

        // Is the security delay active?
        else if (house_state_security == SECURITY_MODE_DELAY)
        {
            // Yes - Get current time in seconds
            current_time = get_raw_time();

            // Determine the delay count value
            delay_count = security_delay_timeout - current_time;

            // Has the delay count expired?
            if (delay_count < 0)
            {
                // Yes - Force the delay count to zero
                delay_count = DELAY_EXPIRED;
            }

            // Has the second count changed?
            if (last_current_time != current_time)
            {
                // Yes - Remember this current time
                last_current_time = current_time;

                // Update MySQL house_state table security_delay parameter
                // to provide the web page with the decrementing delay count.
                sprintf (buffer,
                        "UPDATE house_state SET security_delay=%ld",
                        delay_count);

                mysql_query(conn1, buffer);
            }

            // Has the security transition delay expired?
            if (delay_count == DELAY_EXPIRED)
            {
                // Yes - SECURITY MODE is now ACTIVE
                //       Reflect this status in the MySQL house_state table
                sprintf (buffer,
                        "UPDATE house_state SET security=%d, security_delay=0",
                        SECURITY_MODE_ACTIVE);

                mysql_query(conn1, buffer);
```

```
                // Activate security mode and install security events
                security_mode          = TRUE;
                security_mode_started = TRUE;
                security_mode_stopped = FALSE;

                // Prepare for security presence detection
                reset_security_detection_flags();

                // Compute current timestamp
                determine_system_timestamp (time_buffer);

                // Send email stating Security Mode Activation
                sprintf (message, "%s - Security Mode Activated [Operator action]",
time_buffer);
                send_security_email ("*** SECURITY INFO ***", message);
                speak ("Security mode is now active.");
            }
        }
    }

}
```

```
//****************************************************************************
// Monitor Sleep Mode Transition
//
// This function monitors the MySQL house_state sleep parameters.
//
// This value can take on the following four different states:
//
// SLEEP_MODE_INACTIVE  = Sleep mode is deactive.
// SLEEP_MODE_INITIATED = User pressed the SLEEP button on web page.
// SLEEP_MODE_DELAY     = Sleep delay is counting.
// SLEEP_MODE_ACTIVE    = Delay expired and sleep mode is now active.
//
// This gives the web page user the facility to initiate the change to sleep
// mode and provides them with a timed delay during which they can get into bed
// prior to the sleep mode being fully engaged.
//
//****************************************************************************

void  monitor_sleep_mode_transition (void)
{
    int  house_state_sleep;
    char buffer[255];
    long   int  delay_count;
    long   int  current_time;
    static int  last_current_time = 0;
    static int  sleep_delay_timeout;


    // Get the house code sleep parameter
    if (get_house_state_sleep (&house_state_sleep) == SUCCESS)
    {
        // Has the web page user pressed the [SLEEP OFF] button?
        if (house_state_sleep == SLEEP_MODE_INACTIVE)
        {
            // Was the sleep mode previously active?
            if (sleep_mode)
            {
                // Yes - Deactivate security mode and install normal user events
                sleep_mode       = FALSE;
                sleep_mode_start  = FALSE;
                //              active_mode_start = TRUE;

                // Yes - Inform the user
//              speak ("Sleep mode cancelled.");
            }
        }

        // Has the web page user pressed the [SLEEP ON] button?
        else if (house_state_sleep == SLEEP_MODE_INITIATED)
        {
            // Yes - Initiate the sleep delay
            speak ("Sleep mode initiated.");
            sprintf ( buffer, "UPDATE house_state SET sleep=%d", SLEEP_MODE_DELAY);
            mysql_query(conn1, buffer);

            // Get current time in seconds
            current_time = get_raw_time();
```

```
            // Setup the sleep delay
            sleep_delay_timeout = current_time + OFFSET_20SEC;  // Twenty seconds
        }

        // Is the sleep delay active?
        else if (house_state_sleep == SLEEP_MODE_DELAY)
        {
            // Yes - Get current time in seconds
            current_time = get_raw_time();

            // Determine the delay count value
            delay_count = sleep_delay_timeout - current_time;

            // Has the delay count expired?
            if (delay_count < 0)
            {
                // Yes - Force the delay count to zero
                delay_count = 0;
            }

            // Has the second count changed?
            if (last_current_time != current_time)
            {
                // Yes - Remember this current time
                last_current_time = current_time;

                // Update MySQL house_state table sleep_delay parameter
                // to provide the web page with the decrementing delay count.
                sprintf (buffer,
                        "UPDATE house_state SET sleep_delay=%ld",
                        delay_count);

                mysql_query(conn1, buffer);
            }

            // Has the sleep transition delay expired?
            if (delay_count == DELAY_EXPIRED)
            {
                // Yes - SLEEP MODE is now ACTIVE
                //       Reflect this status in the MySQL house_state table
                speak_time_and_date();
                speak ("Sleep mode active. Good night Steve.");

                sprintf (buffer,
                        "UPDATE house_state SET sleep=%d, sleep_delay=0",
                        SLEEP_MODE_ACTIVE);

                mysql_query(conn1, buffer);

                // Activate security mode and install security events
                sleep_mode       = TRUE;
                sleep_mode_start = TRUE;
            }
        }
    }
}
```

```
//****************************************************************************
// Setup Events For Retiring To Bedroom
//
// The House State 'go_to_bed' parameter is used to indicate that the user is
// going to the bedroom.  This implies that all the house lounge, family,
// kitchen, etc. lights are to be turned off so that the house can be darkened.
//
//****************************************************************************

void  setup_events_for_retiring_to_bedroom (void)
{
    int house_state_go_to_bed;
    long int    current_time;


    // Get current time in seconds
    current_time = get_raw_time();


    if (get_house_state_go_to_bed (&house_state_go_to_bed) == SUCCESS)
    {
        // Was the 'Go To Bed' button pressed?
        if (house_state_go_to_bed == 1)
        {
            // Set MySQL house_state go_to_bed back to '0'
            mysql_query(conn1, "UPDATE house_state SET go_to_bed=0");


            // Switch on various lamps for going to bed
            // ==========================================
            activate_device (master_bedroom_light,           ON, current_time);
            activate_device (master_bedroom_dad_light,       ON, current_time);
            activate_device (master_bedroom_mum_light,       ON, current_time);


            // Switch off various lamps for going to bed
            // ===========================================
            activate_device (main_hallway_light,            OFF, current_time);
            activate_device (fishtank_light,                OFF, current_time);
            activate_device (lounge_wall_light,             OFF, current_time);
            activate_device (lounge_window_light,           OFF, current_time);
            activate_device (inside_entrance_light,         OFF, current_time);
            activate_device (diningroom_table_light,        OFF, current_time);
            activate_device (kitchen_light,                 OFF, current_time);
            activate_device (kitchen_nook_light,            OFF, current_time);
            activate_device (familyroom_window_light,       OFF, current_time);
            activate_device (familyroom_wall_light,         OFF, current_time);
            activate_device (familyroom_track_tv_light,     OFF, current_time);
            activate_device (familyroom_track_reading_light, OFF, current_time);
            activate_device (familyroom_wall_unit_light,    OFF, current_time);
            activate_device (familyroom_wall_unit_spotlight, OFF, current_time);
            activate_device (familyroom_radio,              OFF, current_time);
            activate_device (pantry_light,                  OFF, current_time);
            activate_device (laundry_light,                 OFF, current_time);
        }
    }

}
```

```
//***************************************************************************
// Setup Events For Master Watching TV
//
// The House State 'go_to_bed' parameter is used to indicate that the user is
// going to the bedroom.  This implies that all the house lounge, family,
// kitchen, etc. lights are to be turned off so that the house can be darkened.
//
//***************************************************************************

void  setup_events_for_master_watching_tv (void)
{
    int          house_state_master_watch_tv;
    long int     current_time;


    // Get current time in seconds
    current_time = get_raw_time();


    if (get_house_state_parameter (HS_MASTER_WATCH_TV,
&house_state_master_watch_tv) == SUCCESS)
    {
        // Was the 'Go To Bed' button pressed?
        if (house_state_master_watch_tv == 1)
        {
            // Set MySQL house_state go_to_bed back to '0'
            mysql_query(conn1, "UPDATE house_state SET master_watch_tv=0");

            // Switch on various lamps for watching TV
            // ==========================================
            activate_device (master_bedroom_light, ON, current_time);

            // Switch off various lamps for going to bed
            // ============================================
            activate_device (master_bedroom_dad_light, OFF, current_time);
            activate_device (master_bedroom_mum_light, OFF, current_time);
        }
    }

}
```

```
//******************************************************************************
// Cancel Locked Device States
//
// Sometimes there are times when an RF sensor OFF command is not received.
// This can occur during simultaneous transmissions from two devices.
// If also affects RF devices that have no OFF command transmission (in this
// home configuration this applies to the front porch sensor).
//
// To overcome this, a timeout number is stored in the house_code_states
// MySQL database table.  This value is the current event time in seconds plus
// 120 seconds.  The function below checks for all devices that are in a set
// state and if the current event time in seconds has exceeded this timeout
// value the sensor state is reset.
//******************************************************************************

void  cancel_locked_device_states (void)
{

    MYSQL_RES       *mysqlResult;
    MYSQL_ROW        mysqlRow;
    MYSQL_FIELD     *mysqlFields;
    my_ulonglong     numRows;
    unsigned int     numFields;

    int         house, unit, state;
    int         num_bytes_written;
    long int    current_time;
    char        buffer[255];
    char        message [255];


    // Get the current time in seconds
    current_time = get_raw_time();


    // STATES DATABASE
    // ===============
    // Determine if there are any event SET entries
    // in the database which have timed out...
    sprintf (buffer, "SELECT * FROM house_code_states WHERE state=1 AND
timeout>=999 AND timeout<%ld",
            (long int)current_time);

    if (mysql_query(conn1, buffer))
    {
        // Error detected - Print error message
        sprintf (message, "Error_G1 %u: %s", mysql_errno(conn1),
mysql_error(conn1));
        print_log (message);
    }
    else
    {
        // Determine the number of event entries
        mysqlResult = mysql_store_result (conn1);

        // Are there any entries?
        if (mysqlResult)
        {
```

```
            // Yes - Get the number of database table rows and fields
            numRows = mysql_num_rows(mysqlResult);

            //          numFields = mysql_field_count (conn1);

            numFields = mysql_num_fields (mysqlResult);
        }


        // Get the first row in the table (if it exists)
        mysqlRow = mysql_fetch_row(mysqlResult);

        while (mysqlRow)
        {
            // Yes - Get the parameters from the MySQL table
            house = (int) (atoi (mysqlRow[0]));
            unit  = (int) (atoi (mysqlRow[1]));

            // Sensor timed out, reset device state to inactive
            sprintf (buffer, "UPDATE house_code_states SET state=0 WHERE house=%d
AND unit=%d", house, unit);

            // Display this command for user verification
            //          printf ("%s\n", buffer);

            // Issue the command to the MySQL database
            if (mysql_query(conn1, buffer))
            {
                // Error - Print error message
                sprintf (message, "Error_E1 %u: %s", mysql_errno(conn1),
mysql_error(conn1));
                print_log (message);
            }


            // Get the next row in the table (if it exists)
            mysqlRow = mysql_fetch_row(mysqlResult);
        }

        // Was a MySQL result pointer returned?
        if (mysqlResult)
        {
            // Yes - Free the pointer
            mysql_free_result(mysqlResult);
            mysqlResult = NULL;
        }
    }
}
```

```
//******************************************************************************
// Switch Off All Controlled Devices
//
// This function switches off every device in the house.
//
//******************************************************************************

void  switch_off_all_controlled_devices (void)
{
    long int   current_time;


    // Set the current time to midnight this morning
    current_time = midnight_timeout;


    // Delete all house code events
    print_log ("*** Switch off ALL controlled devices... ");

    activate_device (study_ceiling_light,            OFF, current_time++);

    activate_device (steve_bedroom_ceiling_light,    OFF, current_time++);

    activate_device (diningroom_table_light,         OFF, current_time++);

    activate_device (steve_bedroom_wall_light,       OFF, current_time++);
    activate_device (steve_bedroom_window_light,     OFF, current_time++);
    activate_device (steve_bedroom_reading_light,    OFF, current_time++);
    activate_device (common_washroom_light,          OFF, current_time++);
    activate_device (common_washroom_flight,         OFF, current_time++);
    activate_device (common_bathroom_light,          OFF, current_time++);

    activate_device (kitchen_light,                  OFF, current_time++);
    activate_device (kitchen_nook_light,             OFF, current_time++);
    activate_device (kitchen_counter_light,          OFF, current_time++);
    activate_device (kitchen_sink_light,             OFF, current_time++);

    activate_device (garage_light,                   OFF, current_time++);

    activate_device (security_alarm_siren,           OFF, current_time++);

    activate_device (pantry_light,                   OFF, current_time++);
    activate_device (laundry_light,                  OFF, current_time++);

    activate_device (mini_hallway_light,             OFF, current_time++);
    activate_device (main_hallway_light,             OFF, current_time++);
    activate_device (inside_entrance_light,          OFF, current_time++);

    if (daytime)
    {
        activate_device (garage_back_outside_light,    OFF, current_time++);
        activate_device (familyroom_outside_light,     OFF, current_time++);
        activate_device (diningroom_outside_light,     OFF, current_time++);
        activate_device (master_bedroom_outside_light, OFF, current_time++);
        activate_device (garage_front_outside_light,   OFF, current_time++);
        activate_device (porch_outside_light,          OFF, current_time++);
    }
```

```
    activate_device (guest_main_light,                  OFF, current_time++);
    activate_device (guest_bed_light,                   OFF, current_time++);
    activate_device (lounge_wall_light,                 OFF, current_time++);
    activate_device (lounge_window_light,               OFF, current_time++);

    activate_device (fishtank_light,                    OFF, current_time++);

    activate_device (familyroom_window_light,           OFF, current_time++);
    activate_device (familyroom_wall_light,             OFF, current_time++);
    activate_device (familyroom_track_tv_light,         OFF, current_time++);
    activate_device (familyroom_track_reading_light,    OFF, current_time++);
    activate_device (familyroom_wall_unit_light,        OFF, current_time++);
    activate_device (familyroom_wall_unit_spotlight,    OFF, current_time++);
    activate_device (familyroom_radio,                  OFF, current_time++);

    activate_device (master_bedroom_light,              OFF, current_time++);
    activate_device (master_bedroom_mum_light,          OFF, current_time++);
    activate_device (master_bedroom_dad_light,          OFF, current_time++);
    activate_device (master_bedroom_closet_light,       OFF, current_time++);

    activate_device (season_front_light,                OFF, current_time++);
    activate_device (season_back_light,                 OFF, current_time++);

}
```

```
//******************************************************************************
// Setup Events For System Startup                              UNIQUE TO HC_TI103
//
// This function creates the initial startup events.
//
//******************************************************************************

void  setup_events_for_system_startup (void)
{
    long int    current_time;


    // Determine the current time conditions
    determine_periodic_transition_times();

    // Get current time in seconds
    current_time = get_raw_time();

    // Determine if we have triggered any start flags
    if (current_time > midnight_timeout) midnight_start     = TRUE;
    if (current_time > sunrise_timeout)        day_start     = TRUE;
    if (current_time > dawn_timeout)   dawn_start            = TRUE;
    if (current_time > midday_timeout)         midday_start  = TRUE;
    if (current_time > dusk_timeout)   dusk_start            = TRUE;
    if (current_time > sunset_timeout)         night_start   = TRUE;

    // Delete all existing events in the database
    delete_all_house_code_events();

    // Is a full device reset in order?
    if (device_reset)
    {
        // Yes - Switch everything off (except the outside lights)
        print_log ("*** Device Reset ***");
        switch_off_all_controlled_devices();
    }

    // Determine if we are coming up in Security or Home mode
    determine_initial_security_mode();

}
```

```
//******************************************************************************
// Setup Events For Midnight                                UNIQUE TO HC_TI103
//
// This function handles events that occur at midnight.
//
//******************************************************************************

void  setup_events_for_midnight (void)
{

    // Has midnight just started?
    if (midnight_start == TRUE)
    {
        // Yes - Process outside light on/off events
        // This is called only once each day at midnight (or at startup)
        print_log ("...Setup events for midnight");

        // Setup common events (which should occur before daybreak)
        setup_outside_light_OFF_events();
        setup_fishtank_light_events();

        // This will setup random activations of the common bathroom lights
        SECURITY_setup_common_bathroom_light_events();

        // Reset event flag
        midnight_start = FALSE;
    }

}
```

```
//****************************************************************************
// Setup Events For Sunrise                                 UNIQUE TO HC_TI103
//
// This function handles events that occur as night transitions into day.
//
//****************************************************************************

void  setup_events_for_sunrise (void)
{

    // Has the day just started?
    if (day_start == TRUE)
    {
        // Place all day start events here...
        // ==================================
        print_log ("...Setup events for sunrise");


        // Reset event flag
        day_start = FALSE;
    }

}
```

```
//******************************************************************************
// Setup Events For Dawn                                      UNIQUE TO HC_TI103
//
// This function handles events that occur at dawn.
// Dawn starts some time AFTER sunrise.
//
//******************************************************************************

void  setup_events_for_dawn (void)
{

    // Has the dawn just started?
    if (dawn_start == TRUE)
    {
        // Place all dawn start events here...
        // ====================================
        print_log ("...Setup events for dawn");

        // Reset SLEEP mode back to ACTIVE,
        // Reset family room and steve's bedroom lights for 'Normal Mode'
        mysql_query(conn1, "UPDATE house_state SET sleep=0, sleep_delay=0,
family_lights=0, steve_lights=0");


        // Reset event flag
        dawn_start = FALSE;
    }

}
```

```
//****************************************************************************
// Setup Events For Midday                                  UNIQUE TO HC_TI103
//
// This function handles events that occur at midday.
//
//****************************************************************************

void  setup_events_for_midday (void)
{

    // Has the midday just started?
    if (midday_start == TRUE)
    {
        // Place all midday start events here...
        // ========================================
        print_log ("...Setup events for midday");

        // Are we operating in SECURITY mode?
        if (security_mode)
        {
            // Yes - Install the SECURITY mode events for today
            //       as per function: setup_events_when_security_activated()
            security_mode_started = TRUE;
        }
        else
        {
            // No  - Install the HOME mode events for today
            //       as per function: setup_events_when_security_deactivated()
            security_mode_stopped = TRUE;
        }


        // Reset event flag
        midday_start = FALSE;
    }

}
```

```
//*****************************************************************************
// Setup Events For Dusk                                   UNIQUE TO HC_TI103
//
// This function handles events that occur at dusk.
// Dusk starts some time BEFORE sunset.
//
//*****************************************************************************

void  setup_events_for_dusk (void)
{


    // Has the dusk just started?
    if (dusk_start == TRUE)
    {
        // Place all dusk start events here...
        // ===================================
        print_log ("...Setup events for dusk");


        // Reset event flag
        dusk_start = FALSE;
    }

}
```

```
//****************************************************************************
// Setup Events For Sunset                                 UNIQUE TO HC_TI103
//
// This function handles events that occur as day transitions into night.
//
//****************************************************************************

void  setup_events_for_sunset (void)
{

    // Has the night just started?
    if (night_start == TRUE)
    {
        // Place all night start events here...
        // ====================================
        print_log ("...Setup events for sunset");

        // Reset event flag
        night_start = FALSE;
    }

}
```

```
//****************************************************************************
// Setup Events For Sleeping                              UNIQUE TO HC_TI103
//
// This function handles events that occur as sleep timeout expires.
//****************************************************************************

void  setup_events_for_sleeping (void)
{
    long int   current_time;

    // Place all sleep events here...
    // ===============================

    // Get current time in seconds
    current_time = get_raw_time();

    // Ensure that the following actions are only performed once
    if (sleep_mode_start == TRUE)
    {
        print_log ("...Setup events for sleeping");

        // Going to sleep, put off all nearby lights
        activate_device (study_ceiling_light,         OFF, current_time);
        activate_device (steve_bedroom_ceiling_light, OFF, current_time+1);
        activate_device (common_bathroom_light,       OFF, current_time+2);
        activate_device (common_washroom_light,       OFF, current_time+3);
        activate_device (steve_bedroom_wall_light,    OFF, current_time+4);
        activate_device (steve_bedroom_window_light,  OFF, current_time+4);
        activate_device (steve_bedroom_reading_light, OFF, current_time+4);
        activate_device (mini_hallway_light,          OFF, current_time+5);
        activate_device (inside_entrance_light,       OFF, current_time+6);
        activate_device (lounge_wall_light,           OFF, current_time+7);

        activate_device (study_ceiling_light,         OFF, current_time+11);
        activate_device (steve_bedroom_ceiling_light, OFF, current_time+12);
        activate_device (common_bathroom_light,       OFF, current_time+13);
        activate_device (common_washroom_light,       OFF, current_time+14);
        activate_device (steve_bedroom_wall_light,    OFF, current_time+15);
        activate_device (steve_bedroom_window_light,  OFF, current_time+15);
        activate_device (steve_bedroom_reading_light, OFF, current_time+15);
        activate_device (mini_hallway_light,          OFF, current_time+16);
        activate_device (inside_entrance_light,       OFF, current_time+17);
        activate_device (lounge_wall_light,           OFF, current_time+18);

        // Reset event flag
        sleep_mode_start = FALSE;
    }
}
```

```
//*****************************************************************************
// Setup Events When Security Activated                        UNIQUE TO HC_TI103
//
// This function handles events that occur when security is activated.
// This occurs when the user presses the SECURITY ON button.
// It is also re-triggered on a daily basis to setup the various security events.
//*****************************************************************************

void  setup_events_when_security_activated (void)
{
    int  house_state_security;


    if (security_mode_started)
    {
        // Log action
        print_log ("");
        print_log ("...Setup events for SECURITY mode...");
        print_log ("");
        print_log ("SECURITY\n");
        print_log ("SECURITY - Configure ON/OFF Events...");
        print_log ("SECURITY - ===========================");
        print_log ("SECURITY");


        // Setup the standard events
        setup_outside_light_ON_events();
        setup_outside_light_OFF_events();
        setup_seasonal_light_events();
        setup_fishtank_light_events();

        // Setup the security mode events
        SECURITY_setup_lounge_light_events();
        SECURITY_setup_family_room_light_events();
        SECURITY_setup_master_bedroom_light_events();
        SECURITY_setup_guest_bedroom_light_events();
        SECURITY_setup_steve_bedroom_light_events();
        SECURITY_setup_common_bathroom_light_events();
        SECURITY_setup_study_light_events();
        SECURITY_setup_kitchen_light_events();
        SECURITY_setup_kitchen_nook_light_events();


        // Reset event flag
        security_mode_started = FALSE;
    }
}
```

```
//******************************************************************************
// Setup Events When Security Deactivated                    UNIQUE TO HC_TI103
//
// This function handles events that occur when security is deactivated.
// This occurs when the user presses the SECURITY OFF button.
// It is also re-triggered on a daily basis to setup the various home events.
//******************************************************************************

void  setup_events_when_security_deactivated (void)
{


    if (security_mode_stopped)
    {
        // Log action
        print_log ("");
        print_log ("...Setup events for SECURITY DEACTIVATED.");
        print_log ("");
        print_log ("SECURITY");
        print_log ("SECURITY - Configure ON/OFF Events...");
        print_log ("SECURITY - ===========================");
        print_log ("SECURITY");

        // Setup the standard events
        setup_outside_light_ON_events();
        setup_outside_light_OFF_events();
        setup_seasonal_light_events();
        setup_fishtank_light_events();

        // Setup the home mode events
        setup_lounge_light_events();
        setup_family_room_light_events();
        setup_master_bedroom_light_events();

        // The following events are initialized but will be
        // replaced when room presence is detected
        SECURITY_setup_study_light_events();
        SECURITY_setup_steve_bedroom_light_events();
        SECURITY_setup_common_bathroom_light_events();


        // Reset event flag
        security_mode_stopped = FALSE;
    }
}
```

```
//******************************************************************************
// main()
//
// This is the main loop.  It first initializes the serial port for TI103
// control then it loops monitoring / processing any X10 control events and
// performing the transition to security mode when required.
//
//******************************************************************************

int main (int argc, char * const argv[], char * const envp[])
{
    char        message[255];
    char        time_buffer[255];
    long int    time_in_seconds;


    // Identify program
    print_log ("");
    print_log ("Program 'hc_ti103' Started...");

//  printf ("%d %s %s\n", argc, argv[0], argv[1]);

    // Determine if device reset is to occur
    if ((argc == 2) && (strcmp(argv[1], "RESET") == 0))
    {
        print_log ("RESET Parameter detected...");
        device_reset = TRUE;
    }

    speak_time_and_date();

    // Install the termination interrupt handler
    install_signal_interrupt_handler();

    // Compute current timestamp
    determine_system_timestamp (time_buffer);

    // Send email stating Security Mode Activation
    sprintf (message, "%s - Home Control Program Started [HC_TI103]...",
time_buffer);
//  send_security_email ("*** SECURITY INFO ***", message);


    // Initialize serial port for x-10 TI103 control
    initialize_serial_port_for_ti103_control();

    // Sleep for a little bit...
    // This allows the Mysql system to startup during AUTOSTART
    // [May require more if 'hc_main()' is initializing all the databases!!!]
    msleep (7000);    // Sleep for  7 seconds (increase if we need to sleep
longer...)

    // Initialize random number generator with time seed
    time_in_seconds = get_raw_time();
    srand ((unsigned int) time_in_seconds);

    // Access/Initialize 'home_control' database
    access_home_control_database();
```

```
    // Setup specific system startup events
    setup_events_for_system_startup();

    // Initialization completed...
    print_log ("*");
    print_log ("* Initialization completed... *");
    print_log ("*");

    // Do Forever
    while (!exit_flag)
    {
        // Process all existing events for this time
        process_events();

        // Determine Day/Night Transition Times
        determine_periodic_transition_times();

        // Setup specific day/night events
        setup_events_for_midnight();
        setup_events_for_sunrise();
        setup_events_for_dawn();
        setup_events_for_midday();
        setup_events_for_dusk();
        setup_events_for_sunset();

        // Setup specific user selected modes
        setup_events_for_retiring_to_bedroom();
        setup_events_for_master_watching_tv();
        setup_events_for_sleeping();

        // Monitor home security
        monitor_security_mode_transition();

        // Control home security events as per the security status
        setup_events_when_security_activated();
        setup_events_when_security_deactivated();

        // Monitor sleep transitions
        monitor_sleep_mode_transition();

        // Cancel any locked states (ie. devices with only set command)
        cancel_locked_device_states();
    }

    // Program is being terminated...
    // Restore the Serial Port to its previous configuration
    tcsetattr(fd, TCSANOW, &old_options);

    // Program terminated
    speak ("The program has been terminated.");
    print_log ("");
    print_log ("Program 'hc_ti103' has been terminated.");

}
```

Project Example (Addendum)

Apache Web Server

The Apache Web server on the Linux machine uses default directory: /var/www

The Home control / Security application is placed in directory: /var/www/HomeControl/

The HomeControl directory was then 'shared' and identified as a 'Windows Network (SMB)' directory with the shared name of 'HomeControl'. (The Linux root password will be required to share this drive. Leave the '[ ] Read Only' box unchecked to permit read/write access by Microsoft Expression Web 4).

When Microsoft Expression Web 4 is used to publish the home control web application it will use the following directories on the Linux system:

/var/www/HomeControl/css
/var/www/HomeControl/download
/var/www/HomeControl/images
/var/www/HomeControl/js
/var/www/HomeControl/php

Microsoft Expression Web 4

The Web design package Microsoft Expression Web 4 should be configured to access the '/var/www/HomeControl/' directory for publishing. This is achieved by first accessing the top menu 'Site' label and then 'Publishing Settings'. Under the 'General' tab enter the directory local to your PC in which the web application is being developed.

For example: c:\Projects\HomeControl\

Then, under the Publishing tab press [Add] and select Connection Type 'File System'.

Next use the [Browse] button to search your network to find the shared Linux network drive 'HomeControl' as identified previously. Once this directory has been selected your web files will be published (ie. transferred) to your Linux system each time you select the 'Publishing' menu item.

Note: The CSS, JavaScript, Images and PHP web directories should be used to contain the home control example files identified in the Handbook + LAMP Project book. The CSS files are placed in the css directory, JS files in the js directory, PHP files in the php directory.

Linux System

Static IP Address

During installation of the LAMP features (the Linux, Apache, MySQL and PHP) a specific IP address was selected. This same IP address must be associated with each of the LAMP features. That implies we do not want the Linux system to use a dynamically allocated IP address since such an address may change. The Linux IP address must be static (ie. fixed to a specific value - the same IP address value that was selected when the LAMP features were installed).

The Linux system (Mint version) displays the Ethernet connection as a symbol consisting of two cables with separated connectors (this symbol is located in the bottom right-hand corner of the Linux monitor screen, just left of the date and time). Place the mouse above the Ethernet connection symbol and right-click. Select 'Edit Connections' and access your IPv4 settings. Set the IP address to be the same address that you entered for the other LAMP features (eg. '192.168.1.176' - be sure that no other devices on your network (other than those associated with LAMP) are using this IP address). The Net Mask can be set to '255.255.255.0' and the Gateway set to '192.168.1.1'. Save these settings and then reboot the Linux system. The Linux system will now be using this static IP address every time your system powers up.

Auto Start

The 'hc_main.c' and 'hc_ti103.c' modules (along with the other header files, etc) may be placed in any suitable development directory. When compiled and you are satisfied that they are functional, the 'hc_main' and 'hc_ti103' executables are then copied across to a separate directory. These two files are to be executed on system startup. This is achieved by first using the mouse to access the Linux Menu (bottom left screen icon). Under 'Applications' select 'Preferences' and in the right-hand column select 'Startup Applications'. Press the [Add] button and then use the [Browse] button to find the appropriate directory where the 'hc_main' executable file is located. Enter a suitable 'Name' for this executable. Press [Add] and the file is now in the startup list. Repeat the process for the 'hc_ti103' executable. The next time the Linux system is started these two home control executables will be automatically started.

Note that if additional development work is performed on the home control system and the system files are executed, you will have multiple copies of the executables executing simultaneously (with surprising effect). To perform any testing the startup executables should first be terminated. This is achieved by once more selecting the Linux 'Menu'. Under 'Applications' select 'System Tools' and in the right-hand column select 'System Monitor'. Using the mouse select your process from the Process Name list and with the right-hand mouse button select 'Kill Process'. Do this for both 'hc_main' and ''hc_ti103'.

Linux applications to be downloaded.
Use the Linux Menu (bottom left screen icon) and select 'Software Manager'. Use the search feature to select and then download the following utilities:

sendemail
festival
fswebcam

Author's Resume

Residency
US Citizen (as of 2001). Born in Glasgow, Scotland, United Kingdom.

University
Bachelor of Science Degree - Computer Science Major
University of the Witwatersrand, South Africa [Multi-Racial]

Experience
I have over 30 years of software system design, development and management experience in real-time computer systems (embedded, PC and mainframe) in both engineering and medical environments. I can read and understand electronic circuit schematic diagrams, I can use software and hardware tools, I interface well with other departments when required to obtain or to provide information, I have excellent engineering writing skills and I fully document my work. I operate efficiently either as an individual or as part of a team and have been involved throughout the entire software lifecycle process from system design right through to coding, testing, production and maintenance phases of projects.

Interpersonal skills
In performing my work I am usually involved directly interfacing with other departments in order to obtain and provide systems information. Many times I receive limited information and when additional knowledge is required, I will seek out the relevant department(s) / person(s). This usually results in my being invited to their design reviews to share my knowledge.

Documentation skills
I have written the following types of documents: customer requirements, system specifications, system architecture, communication protocol interfaces, hardware interfaces (CPLD and FPGA interface register definitions and overall device operation), detailed design and unit / system test documents. I have also managed and mentored other engineers who have implemented code from my design documents. (As a side note, I have self-published ten of my own books which are currently being offered on Amazon and other websites).

Operating Systems

I have utilized ThreadX, VxWorks and pSOS operating systems. When required I have also modified the internal operation of the operating system (ThreadX) to implement specific new features (eg. PowerPC data and instructing caching). I have implemented many embedded systems which did not utilize any operating system (ie. used state machines and interrupt driver ISRs).

Coding skills

I believe in proper coding standards and the code I generate is well laid out, utilizes module and function headers, unambiguous understandable function and variable names, pseudo-code type comments, and results in code that is readable by others. I require little if any guidance when developing code and am often developing code ahead of the hardware platform / FPGA / CPLD, or other required modules becoming available.

I have experience in developing code in C, C++ and assembly languages mostly for embedded processors (eg. PowerPC) and micro-controllers (eg. PIC, Intel, Motorola, Zilog) interfacing with various on-board hardware devices (eg. Flash, EEPROM, CPLDs, FPGAs), using I^2C, SPI or direct register/bit access.

In conclusion

I enjoy being involved in all aspects of project development right from the initial system design concept. Understanding an application's real-world environment and its associated interaction is what makes this line of work most interesting.

Summary of Skills

The following list is a summary of the skills I have gained during my career:

Mainframes: And Minicomputers	Burroughs B6800, B4800 DEC PDP11/73 Data General Nova IV
Microprocessors:	PowerPC (MPC8349EA) IBM PC ARM7
MicroControllers:	Microchip PIC 18F67J50, 18C658, 18F8720, 16F877 Zilog eZ80F91 Acclaim! And Z8 Encore! TI TMS320C6712 SGS Thomson ST20 Motorola 68EN360, 68302 and 68HC05JB4 Intel 8051
Hardware Interfaces:	Flash, I2C, SPI, NAND, LCD, Ethernet TCP/IP, ARINC, CAN, SDcard RS232, USB, HDLC, GPIB (IEEE 488)
Operating Systems:	Microsoft Windows VxWorks (BSP, Device Drivers) ThreadX (BSP, Device Drivers), NetX, FileX PSOS+ (BSP, Device Drivers) Limited UNIX/Linux and QNX experience
Development Project Examples:	Intensive Care Medical Ventilator, Medical "dog tag" with RF interface Ruggedized LCD Display Panel, Satellite Set Top Box Explosives Scanner, Driver's Vision Enhancer (FLIR) Vehicle Computer Power Interface Controller MPEG-2 Transport Encryption Multiplexer Satellite MPEG-2 Transport Scrambler NMR Refrigerated Ship Container Holding Shed Ruggedized Multichannel Audio Communications Recorder Diagnostic Stations for testing Digital Television Encoder Boards Process Control System, Railway Mimic Panel Controller Point Of Sale Business Application

Protocols:	MPEG-2, Open TV ISDN BRI (Basic Rate Interface) Developed USB Device State Machine Developed IRIG-B, IRIG-E Time Code State Machines Developed protocols for RS232, Ethernet Client/Server Interfaces
Software Tools:	PowerPC C/C++ and Assembler, U-Boot Zilog IDE, C Compiler, ZPAK II Ethernet Emulator Microchip MPLAB IDE, ICD2, ICE-2000 and C18 compiler; CCS C Compiler Borland C++ Builder Professional Edition IDE, Pascal, Assembler Eclipse IDE, Texas Instruments Composer Studio IDE Microtec Research C and Assembler Intel PL/M-51, ASM51; IAR C Burroughs TSL, BPL, COBOL, and Symbolic Assembler ClearCase, Visual Source Safe, CMS, PVCS, RCS Software Version Controls IBM Rational ClearQuest to handle Change Requests Microsoft Word, FrontPage, Visio; Data Flow Diagrams, Program Design Language
Hardware Tools:	Various In-Circuit Emulators (BDI3000, MPLAB ICD2 and ICE2000) Altera Quartus II VHDL (Currently learning Mentor Graphics System-Verilog Questa Sim) CanBus CanAnalyzer, Condor ARINC, USB Chief, Various Serial, Logic and Spectrum Analyzers Analog / Digital Oscilloscopes, Multi-Meters and Soldering Stations
Documentation Examples:	System Specifications Functional Specifications System and Development Architecture Specifications High-Level Design Documentation Low-Level Design Documentation Communication Protocol Interface Specifications CPLD and FPGA Hardware System Specifications Unit Test Documentation Verification and Validation Documentation

Author's Library

The following books may be useful to the embedded engineer:

Hardware

The Art of Electronics
Paul Horowitz
Winfield Hill

Practical Electronics Handbook
Fourth Edition
Ian Sinclair

Digital Signal Processing Demystified
James D. Broesch

Practical RF Handbook
Second Edition
Ian Hickman

Electronic Fundamentals
C. Nel

Signals and Systems
Zoher Z. Karu

The 8051
Programming, Interfacing, Applications
Boyet, Katz

Software

Effective C++
Third Edition
Scott Meyers

Design Patterns
Elements of Reusable Object-Oriented Software
Gamma, Helm, Johnson, Vlissides

C
A Reference Manual
Harbison, Steele

C++ from the GROUND UP
Third Edition
Herbert Schildt

Real-Time Design Patterns
Robust Scalable Architecture for Real-Time Systems
Bruce Power Douglass

Software Estimation
Demystifying the Black Art
Steve McConnell

Design Patterns Explained
A New Perspective on Object Oriented Design
Second Edition
Alan Shalloway
James R. Trott

Software (Cont'd)

Code Complete
Second Edition
Steve McConnell

Object-Oriented Analysis and Design
Second Edition
Grady Booch

C++ Neural Networks and Fuzzy Logic
Valluru B. Rao
Hayagriva V. Rao

Understanding the FFT
Second Edition, Revised
Anders E. Zonst

Understanding the FFT
Second Edition, Extensively Revised
Applications
Anders E. Zonst

C Programmer's Guide to Serial Communications
Joe Campbell

Programming in ANSI C
Stephen G. Kochan

Software (Cont'd)

The C Programming Language
Second Edition
Brian W. Kernighan
Dennis M. Ritchie
C Language Algorithms for Digital Signal Processing
Paul M. Embree
Bruce Kimble

Numerical Recipes in C++
The Art of Scientific Computing
Second Edition
Press, Vetterling, Teukolsky, Flannery

Internetworking with TCP/IP
Volumes I, II, III
Douglas E. Comer

Beginning Linux Programming
2nd Edition
Richard Stones
Neil Matthew

Linux Programming
Warren W. Gay

Software (Cont'd)

C for Linux Programming
Erik de Castro Lopo
Peter Aitken
Bradley L. Jones

Borland C++ Builder
The Definitive C++ Builder Problem Solver
John Miano
Tom Cabanski
Harold Howe

The C++ Standard Library
A Tutorial and Reference
Nicolai M. Josuttis

Step by Step
Microsoft Expression Web 4
Chris Leeds

Standards, Guidelines and Examples
on System and Software Requirements Engineering
IEEE Computer Society Press Tutorial
Merlin Dorfman
Richard H. Thayer

Home Control / Security Application (Review)

This book reviews the Software Development and Engineering Principles involved in the Design of Embedded Computer Systems.

A LAMP (Linux Apache MySQL PHP) design for a Web-Based Home Control / Security Application is also provided (source code included).

This book is applicable to both the seasoned Embedded Software Engineer and to the Hobbyist who just wants to learn a little bit about writing code. Information gathered by the author's 30+ years in the field is discussed as he presents what works and what does not work with regard to embedded software engineering. This will help engineers but will also be an aid in assisting those who are tasked with managing embedded engineers.

But what of the novice?

What of the person wanting to gain some understanding in the field of embedded software engineering?

Where do they start?

Do they need a Computer Science or Electrical Engineering degree before they can even begin to learn how to program an embedded system?

All too many books discuss programming from an advanced level.

Well, this book is not like that at all.

The idea is to get anyone that is interested in programming to be up and running in a short period of time. The language of choice today is C or C++. For an easy entrance into the world of programming the C language was chosen for the code examples presented within this book. But what programming application should be tackled? An embedded application is a program that continually executes on a computer system and as it does so, it interacts with its environment.

A home control lighting system would be the ideal application.

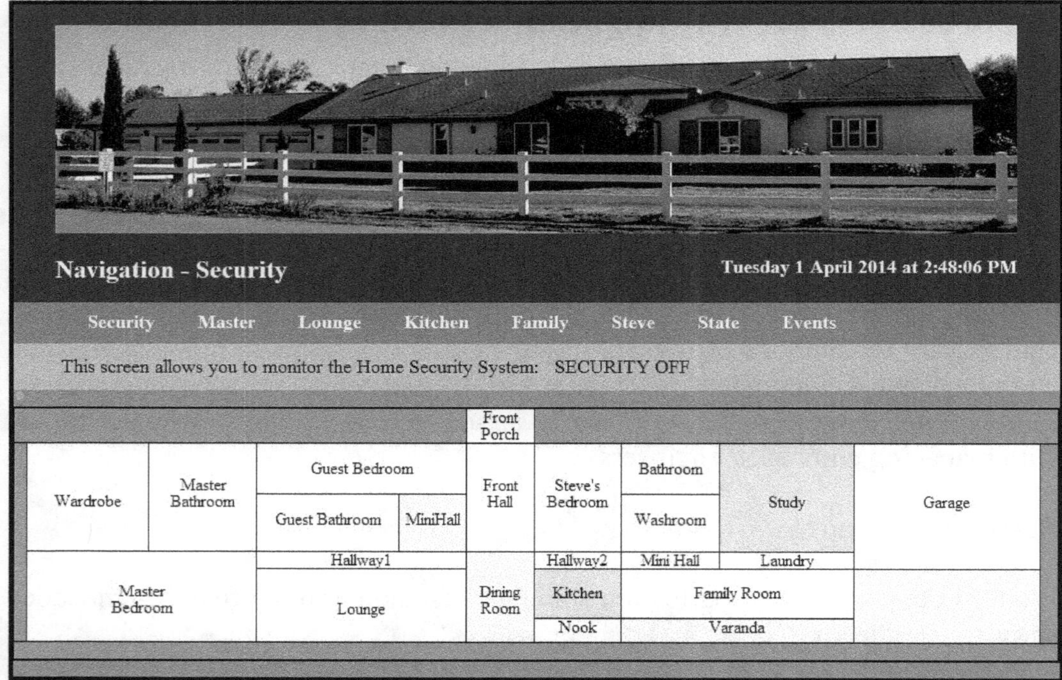

By the time you have finished reading this book you would know how:

- To install LAMP (Linux, Apache (Web Server), MySQL and PHP) on your PC computer
- To backup/restore your Linux hard drive
- To automatically execute your application at system startup
- To apply Java Script to your own Web page
- To apply MySQL to your own Web page
- To apply PHP to your own Web page
- To build a C application that communicates over a serial port.
- To build a C application that use MySQL
- To write a Home Control / Security application
- To have your Home Control / Security application send email messages with webcam picture attachments
- To have your Home Control / Security application speak
- To compute sunrise and sunset times for each day of the year

... more to follow...

Oh! And there's one added bonus. With this system you do not require any monthly monitoring fee. Since your Home Control / Security application simply sends you an email when it detects an intruder, you can immediately go home or call a friend or neighbor to check on the house. No need to fork out $25 or more per month for some 'service' charge.

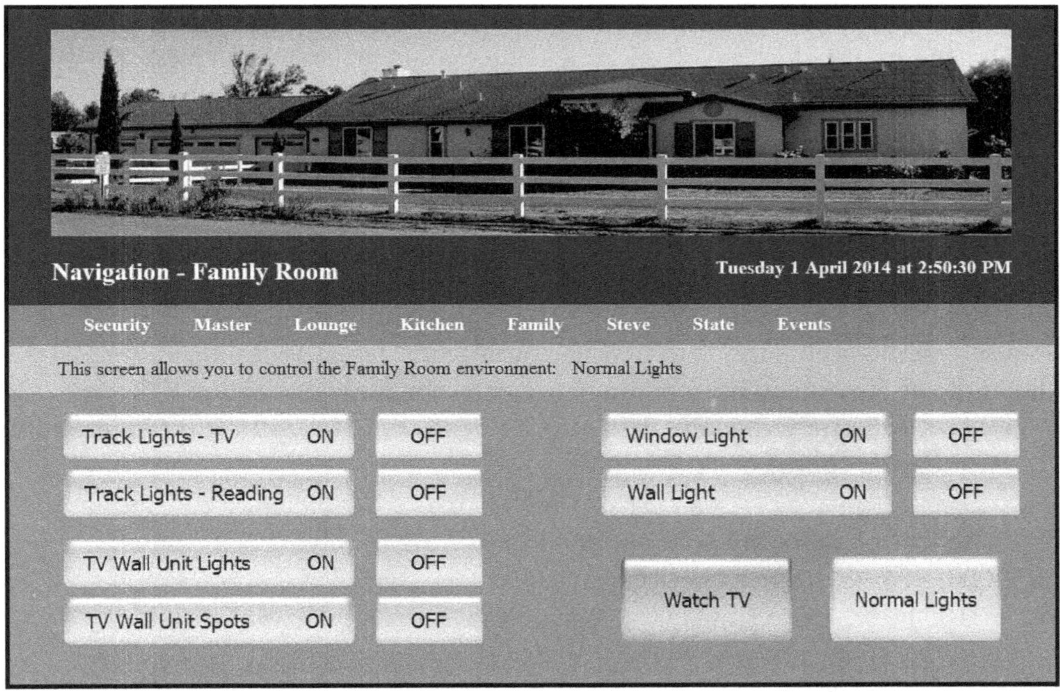

They say that knowledge is power. That may be true, but to sit at home using your iPAD or iPHONE (or some other Tablet, or even a web page on one of your computers) and to bring up your Home Control web page and click on a button to turn on a light or to initiate a sequence of events for evening television viewing, well, that is really neat and this book presents all this information to you in an easy to read form.

This book is also written in such a way that it may be used by both small and large engineering companies. By the time you have completed its reading you will have learned that an embedded project is much more than simply writing software code.

It is an entire documentation process of which code amounts to a small percentage. The reason software generally takes a long time to develop (and costs even more to maintain) is simply because this design process is often overlooked or bypassed. For the documented design is required by all company departments including manufacture and maintenance.

In addition, this book is also applicable to senior management to help aid with understanding the steps involved in developing an embedded product. For if you have an understanding of the work involved you will then comprehend that the term 'aggressive schedule' is but a sure means to project failure.

Authors Web Pages:
www.QuantumBlueTechnology.com
www.StephenWilliamMcclure.com/embedded

Please use this web page to access the buttons zip directory that provides all the .jpg and .gif files of the button images used by the web application. There is also a link on the same web page that may be used to download a zip file of all the directories and source code.

The application software was designed to use the following components:
WF800RF32A RF Receiver (www.wgldesigns.com, www.homeseer.com)
ACT TI103 Interface to transmit X10 signals over household mains wiring
(Obtainable from www.act-remote.com, www.smarthomeusa.com)
MS13A X10 HawkEye Motion Detector (by X10 Active Home)
MS16A ActiveEye Motion Sensor (Outdoor sensor)
X10 Pro Universal Module (Alarm siren plus relay contacts)
X10 On Guard Barking Dog Alarm (SD20a) www.x10.com
X10 Appliance and X10 Lamp Modules

The application software may be modified to suit any interface of your choice.

Additional Useful Web Sites for X10 products:
www.smarthome.com
www.x10.com
www.thehomeautomationstore.com
www.smarthomeusa.com
www.homeseer.com
www.amazon.com

Concepts Presented Within This Book...

This book is written in such a way that it may be used by both small and large engineering companies. By the time you have completed its reading you will have learned that an embedded project is much more than simply writing software code. It is an entire documentation process of which code amounts to a small percentage. The reason software generally takes a long time to develop (and costs even more to maintain) is simply because this design process is often overlooked or bypassed.

The Project Development section of this book provides an instruction manual that identifies the tasks that should be performed by the individual team members. When a company (a group of people with a common goal) allocates time to create a specific product the engineers concerned come from a number of different disciplines. These are namely Systems, Software, Embedded, Firmware and Hardware. In a small company this number can amount to being a few individuals or can even be as low as one. In a large company there can be several such individuals in each group. Be that as it may, the concepts presented in this book still apply to the design, development, testing and building (manufacturing) of the product. It is all a matter of creating the documentation that will finally be used to instruct others as how to manufacture and maintain the product. Source code, no matter how supposedly well documented does not replace proper engineering design/documentation practices.

It is time we developed products in the correct manner.

If you jump to the center of this book you will see what I mean. The graphic at the top of these pages identify the various phases of product development and identify the tasks applicable to each team. This information will assist in ensuring that all the necessary design work is performed. For the engineers involved in creating product it will identify the various stages concerned.

This book is also applicable to senior management to help aid with understanding the steps involved in developing an embedded product. For if you have an understanding of the work involved then you will comprehend that the term 'aggressive schedule' is but a sure means to project failure.

Author Titles

The author is self-published and the following titles are available from Amazon both in e-book and paperback formats.

Technical Books

Designing Embedded Systems - Guidebook

By Steve McClure

This Guidebook reviews the Software Development and Engineering Principles involved in the Design of Embedded Computer Systems. It provides a standard procedure which may be used by the Systems, Software, Embedded, Firmware and Hardware departments. Various design and development documents are produced at specific points in the project and are passed out for review prior to being used by other team members. By having this consistency the entire team now know which design elements will be produced and the need for implementing any reverse-engineering will be eliminated. Product costs for maintenance will be greatly reduced. Manufacturing and Test departments will now have the necessary details with which to complete their work.

ISBN-13: 978-1499117592
ISBN-10: 1499117590

Designing Embedded Systems - Handbook

By Steve McClure

This book expands upon the detail presented in The Guidebook and provides additional detail gleaned by the author during his 30+ years of experience in the field of Embedded Systems Engineering.

ISBN-13: 978-1497592339
ISBN-10: 149759233X

Designing Embedded Systems - LAMP (Linux Apache MySQL PHP)

By Steve McClure

This book expands upon the Handbook and provides an embedded Linux project to implement a Web-based Home Control / Security System (source code listing provided).

ISBN-13: 978-1483916231
ISBN-10: 1483916235

Sci/Fi - Fantasy Novels

Like many in the engineering industry the author has enjoyed both films and books of the Science Fiction and Fantasy genre. After much persuasion he decided to write a novel. This attempt turned out quite successful and encouraging and has expanded itself into the following series of books.

Stryders Odyssey
A fantastic tale of epic proportion
The truth was out there somewhere and it was waiting to be discovered. Travel with Sam and Cody as they jump through Portals to other Worlds, ride Space Ships controlled by Computers with Artificial Intelligence and befriend Strange Creatures that can Shape Shift into anything they or you can imagine. But watch out for 'the Order'. For they have their own plan regarding the dominion of worlds. For readers of all ages.

Stryders Odyssey - 1
New Beginnings
By Steve McClure
ISBN-13: 978-1490442525
ISBN-10: 1490442529

Stryders Odyssey - 2
First Contact
By Steve McClure
ISBN-13: 978-1492855477
ISBN-10: 1492855472

Stryders Odyssey - 3
Shangri Prime
By Steve McClure
ISBN-13: 978-1493695379
ISBN-10: 1493695371

Author Contact E-Mail

steve_mcclure@cox.net

www.ingramcontent.com/pod-product-compliance
Lightning Source LLC
Chambersburg PA
CBHW082107070326
40689CB00052B/3727